REPUBLICAN EMPIRE

American Political Thought
edited by
Wilson Carey McWilliams and Lance Banning

REPUBLICAN EMPIRE

Alexander Hamilton on War and Free Government

Karl-Friedrich Walling

 University Press of Kansas

Published by the University Press of Kansas (Lawrence, Kansas 66049), which was organized by the Kansas Board of Regents and is operated and funded by Emporia State University, Fort Hays State University, Kansas State University, Pittsburg State University, the University of Kansas, and Wichita State University

Library of Congress Cataloging-in-Publication Data

Walling, Karl-Friedrich, 1957–

  Republican empire : Alexander Hamilton on war and free government / Karl-Friedrich Walling.

    p. cm. — (American political thought)

  Based on the author's thesis (Ph.D., University of Chicago, 1992) published under title: The political theory of republican empire.

  Includes bibliographical references and index.

  ISBN 0-7006-0970-9 (alk. paper)

  1. Hamilton, Alexander, 1757–1804—Contributions in political science. 2. Republicanism—United States. 3. War and emergency powers—United States. I. Title. II. Series.

JC176.H27W35 1999

321.8'6—dc21   99-19716

British Library Cataloguing in Publication Data is available.

Printed in the United States of America

10 9 8 7 6 5 4 3 2 1

The paper used in this publication meets the minimum requirements of the American National Standard for Permanence of Paper for Printed Library Materials Z39.48-1984.

For Andrea, who taught me to read

Let us not establish a tyranny.
Energy is a very different thing from violence.
Alexander Hamilton, 1798

Contents

Preface and Acknowledgments

This book began as a doctoral dissertation at the University of Chicago in the late 1980s. At the time, Americans were celebrating two apparently unconnected events: the end of the cold war and the bicentennial of their Constitution. I wish I could say that I had planned the book with the collapse of the Soviet Union and its former allies in mind. Like virtually everyone else, however, I assumed the conflict would go on for decades. I also feared that the struggle would take a great toll on the Western democracies. Would they have the will to prosecute this war effectively? Would the measures that seemed necessary to victory undermine the institutions that had hitherto kept them free? No one could say with certainty at the time. With the end of the cold war, however, we have a right, if not a duty, to ask some important questions that lead from our immediate to a more remote past.

After more than 200 years under essentially the same Constitution, Americans have fought numerous wars, both major and minor, both declared and undeclared, both hot and cold, yet they still remain free. Why? Few nations have been so fortunate. The necessities, accidents, and passions of war contributed mightily to the collapse of free government in ancient Greece and Rome. They were no less important in undermining the efforts of the Germans, Russians, Chinese, Japanese, and many other peoples to secure their liberties in the twentieth century. Why has the United States been the outstanding exception to the well-grounded historical axiom that war is the great destroyer of free governments?

Simple answers are hard to find, but I am inclined to give the principal credit to the American Founders in general and to Alexander Hamilton in particular. My general claim is hardly controversial. Some readers might even regard it as a bit too pious, but the particular thesis cuts against the grain of conventional wisdom. Hamilton's peers often cast him as a militarist, bent on tyranny at home and conquest abroad. Scholars today, who are not immune to the partisanship of those whom they study, often agree. Yet no American statesman of the Founding era wrote more than Hamilton about the great problem of waging war effectively and remaining free at the same time. If we read him with a statesmanlike awareness that liberty may be endangered by too little as well as too much power, we may have to revise our opinion of his controversial role in the Founding era. Turning from history to political theory, we may also learn more about the inevitable tension between the necessities of war and the requirements of free government.

Writing is an inherently lonely activity, but I was not alone as I tried to enter into the mind of Hamilton. Nathan Tarcov and Ralph Lerner first led me to study the Founders seriously. They have since served as models of liberal learning and scholarship at its best for me. Along with them, Stephen Holmes and the late Allan Bloom supervised my dissertation with exemplary care. The Program on Constitutional Government at Harvard University, the Earhart Foundation, and the John M. Olin Foundation provided generous financial support. Over the years, I received invaluable advice from Harvey C. Mansfield Jr., Forrest McDonald, Catherine and Michael Zuckert, David Hendrickson, James Stoner, Matthew J. Frank, Brad Thompson, Peter Schramm, Paul Rahe, Harvey Flaumenhaft, Peter McNamara, Tom West, Robert Scigliano, Stephen and Lorna Knott, Carey McWilliams, Jean Yarbrough, Colleen Sheehan, Lance Banning, John Hittinger, Robert Manzer, John Alvis, Fred Woodward, Barry Nurcombe, Delane Clark, Kevin Lee Taylor, and Mark E. Getzin. Portions of this book have been published by the *Review of Politics* in its series, "The American Faces of Machiavelli" (summer 1995); I am grateful for the permission to integrate them. The Department of Political Science at Colorado College and the Liberty Fund supplied collegial environments for finishing the book. My wife, Lisa, patiently read and reread innumerable drafts. Credit for all that is tolerably well expressed in this book belongs to her. So too does my heart.

1. Hamilton's Place in American Political Thought

On 17 July 1804 the *New York Evening Post* reported the funeral of Gen. Alexander Hamilton. The tribute now seems to be extraordinarily ironic. Insofar as Hamilton's name still lingers in popular memory, it is not because he was a general. Rather, it is because of his broad construction of the Constitution and his labors as the first secretary of the treasury. His contemporaries, however, honored (or despised) him primarily as a military figure, as if the character of the man and his achievement could be understood only by linking the statesman's pen to the soldier's sword. They perhaps understood more about Hamilton than we do today.

At the age of fourteen, Hamilton wrote an equally young friend that he was willing to sacrifice everything, except his character as a gentleman, to rise above the station to which his fortune seemed to condemn him. He concluded his letter by wishing for a war as an honorable way for an adolescent orphan with no money to rise quickly in the world.[1] He soon had his chance. Wealthy patrons helped him attend King's College (now Columbia University) in New York City, but he dropped out shortly before the American Revolution to accept a commission as a captain in the New York Artillery. Although he later became one of the preeminent lawyers of his age, he never finished college. Instead, he served with courage and distinction in the artillery, where he quickly won the notice of Gen. George Washington. The general invited him to join his "family," or staff, as a lieutenant colonel when he was just twenty-two. Thereafter, he was present for most of the principal military engagements of Washington's command. As one of the most valued members of Washington's staff, Hamilton also formed alliances within the army and with Congress. These connections enabled him to play a leading role in early national politics, first in calling for a constitutional convention, then in defending the newly drafted Constitution of 1787, and later as the de facto prime minister of Washington's presidency. Still later, as the French Revolution broke out in Europe and the world went to war again, he became inspector general of the army, with a command in the line. He was made second to Washington, who came back from retirement during the administration of John Adams. Hamilton supervised preparations for an expected war with France. If war were declared, he hoped to take the initiative by seizing New Orleans and perhaps even by liberating Mexico from Spain, which was then dominated by France. His strategic audacity in this era sometimes led his contemporaries to compare him to Napoleon Bonaparte, "that unequaled conqueror," Hamilton remarked ambivalently, "from whom it is painful to detract; in whom one would wish to find virtues worthy of his shining talents."[2]

Generals receive splendid funerals, like those given to Hektor in the *Iliad*. Accordingly, a contingent of artillery, militia, flank companies, the Cincinnati Society (of veteran officers of the American Revolution), and civilian dignitaries from across New York escorted Hamilton's remains to his memorial service. As was customary, his hat and sword lay on the coffin. His gray mount, dressed in mourning, trailed behind, riderless, with the general's boots and spurs reversed in the stirrups. Citizens lined the streets, hoping to take a last look at one of the most dramatic figures in American political history: a "little lion" as soldiers called him in his youth; a "host within himself" as Thomas Jefferson described him in his prime; and finally, the victim of a fatal stomach wound received in a duel of honor with Vice-President Aaron Burr.

In the harbor of New York City, the British ship of war *Boston* and the packet *Lord Charles Spencer* were draped in mourning for the fallen general. So too were the French frigates, *Cybelle* and *Didon*. As the entourage proceeded to its destination, the warships and batteries from the New York Artillery fired regular salutes. Hamilton's friend, Gouverneur Morris, gave the funeral oration. Perhaps Morris's highest encomium was that Washington had dared to "trust the sword of America" to this controversial figure, who was often skeptical about his adopted country's experiment with republican government but who had nonetheless devoted his life to making it succeed. After the oration, the body was carried to the grave and received the usual religious rites. The troops who had entered the churchyard formed an extensive hollow square and ended the solemnities with three volleys over the grave. The *Post* concluded that it had "no observations to add. This scene was enough to melt a monument of marble."[3]

Despite this final tribute, no one has sought to understand Hamilton as he was understood by his friend, Morris, as a soldier-statesman who deserved to be trusted with the sword of his country. To be sure, in the last thirty years or so, the most careful of Hamilton's scholars, Gilbert Lycan, Clinton Rossiter, Gerald Stourzh, Harvey Flaumenhaft, Morton J. Frisch, and Forrest McDonald, have increased our understanding of Hamilton's views on republics, constitutional government, statesmanship, foreign policy, administration, and finance. A few scholars of an earlier generation, such as Edward Meade Earle, made the economic foundations of military power a major theme of their investigations of Hamilton. Broadus Mitchell, Hamilton's military biographer, even remarked that "the statesman who would help devise the Constitution and set the United States Treasury on a prosperous course, began his services in uniform. His political and economic preachments sprang from the lessons of war." Another of Hamilton's biographers, John C. Miller, observed that Hamilton "lived through three great wars in two of which he was an active participant. Whenever he looked abroad, he found wars or rumors of wars. As a result, the conviction was implanted in him that the survival of the United States depended upon its warmaking potential. If this was a harsh and unattractive philosophy, at least it could be said to be based upon the facts of international life as Hamilton knew them."[4] Still, Mitchell never pursued his observation, and Earle himself did not extend his analysis to the political dimensions of Hamilton's thought. Miller stressed the strategic elements more than others, but neither he nor anyone else has attempted a synthesis of the views on war and free government found in the twenty-six volumes of Hamilton's collected papers.

Hamilton's interpreters thus have inadvertently allowed others to misunderstand him in ways that distort his objectives and obscure his unique place in American political thought. The only book-length study to explore war and free government in Hamilton's politics and those of his party is Richard H. Kohn's *Eagle and the Sword: The Federalists and the Origins of the American Military Establishment, 1783–1802.* Kohn explains how an elite group of nation-minded men in the Continental Army and the Continental Congress came to believe that the survival of the Union and American independence depended on a standing army. The Federal Convention of 1787 gave these nationalists what they desired most: the constitutional authority to establish a permanent army. When they later became leading Federalists in the 1790s, they allegedly used every possible war scare to pressure Congress into accepting an expanded army for the sake of preserving and aggrandizing their power.

This is the dark side of Kohn's account of the birth of the American military establishment. In his view, it was the result of "militarism," by which he means a predisposition to settle political disputes, at home and abroad, by "force alone." Not all Federalists were militarists, but Kohn insists that

Hamilton was the leader of an extreme faction of American militarists who rejected "public opinion" in favor of "fear" as the foundation of the new government. Throughout Hamilton's career, Kohn claims,

> he exploited armies for political gain, stimulating a mutiny and using the threat of a coup in 1783, eagerly using force in the 1790s to enforce the law and build up the federal government, and finally using the army as a vehicle to advance his own power and dream of greatness. For all his talent, his brilliance, and his contributions to the birth of the nation, Alexander Hamilton was the personification of American militarism.

Lest we fail to understand the gravity of this charge, Kohn then asserts that the militarist threat posed by Hamilton and his allies was unrivaled in American history until "the Reconstruction years and the era of the Cold War." For Kohn, the Founding era was truly a narrow escape. Only the vigilance of the Jeffersonians and the firmness of Pres. John Adams prevented the new Republic from succumbing to the militarist threat posed by Hamilton. If so, Washington made a serious mistake in trusting the sword of America to Hamilton, the most "dangerous" man of his time.[5]

Like all the Founders, Hamilton certainly had his faults. He was either oblivious of or did not care much about a bill of rights, public education, and the advantages of state and local governments. He did not foresee some of the worst social consequences of the credit economy and manufacturing society he championed for most of his career. As secretary of the treasury, he often meddled in the work of other departments, sometimes acquiring unnecessary enemies as a result. Especially in the presidential election of 1800, his partisanship at times got the better of his judgment, and, some observers say, of his principles. His uncommon candor, combined with his pride and restless energy, also made him indiscreet on more than one occasion. At the end of his career, his vituperative attack on President Adams alienated many of his natural allies. In many respects, his ineptitude as a democratic politician calls into question his greatness as a republican statesman.

No less problematic is the task of deciding where Hamilton fits in the American world, which he belatedly came to think was not made for him. His political thought was far more modern than that of even his most forward-looking contemporaries. Yet his character belonged to an already dying era of eighteenth-century gentlemen, if not to a time even more gloriously anachronistic. If Hamilton's numerous classical pseudonyms are any evidence, he half lived in the age of the noble Greeks and Romans (Pericles, Phocion, Publius) who parade across the stage of Plutarch and other ancient historians. He chose to compete with the greatest Founders and statesmen of antiquity, in their agonistic splendor, because he believed the modern science of politics would supply a more stable and humane form of liberty than had been possible before.

Given both his classical character and his modernizing policies, many of Hamilton's contemporaries did fear him as a militarist, but that does not mean they were right. Perhaps all militarists are hawks, but not all hawks are militarists. If we take Hamilton at his word, the truth appears to be diametrically opposed to Kohn's conclusion. Hamilton's fundamental political objectives were to enable the American Republic to avoid war when possible; to wage it effectively when necessary; and to preserve both political and civil liberty in time of war. Instead of dismissing him as a militarist, citizens and statesmen who fear militarism today would do well to begin by reading Hamilton. Precisely because he thought more than any of his contemporaries about the tension between war and free government, he was most responsible for the unprecedented ability of the United States to combine great power and liberty.

If Hamilton does not fit the militarist mold, where precisely does he fit in American political thought? Because he considered an enormous variety of ideas, there can be no simple answers. He had a synthetic (rather than an eclectic) mind that defies easy classification. We might begin, however, by considering his relation to the variety of opinions about free government that contemporary scholars ascribe to Americans of the Founding era. In a now justly famous article, Isaac Kramnick has summarized at least thirty years of scholarship by identifying four main schools of thought, sometimes called languages or ideologies, that were important throughout Hamilton's career: liberalism, classical republicanism, Protestant work-ethic Christianity, and state building.[6] The liberals stressed limited government for the sake of securing rights, and property rights especially.[7] The classical republicans or civic humanists focused on virtuous dedication to the public good and political participation, or what Hannah Arendt has called *vita activa*, as the fulfillment of human political nature.[8] Those who spoke the language of work-ethic Christianity were also much concerned with virtue but had largely privatized it. Not political activity as such, but independent industry came to be seen as virtue, if not even a means to salvation.[9] The state builders stressed the enduring problems of domestic tranquillity, economic development, and the common defense.[10] Kramnick also identifies, but does not explore in depth, three other ideologies in this era: the languages of jurisprudence, scientific Whiggism, and the moral-sentiment schools of the Scottish Enlightenment.[11]

One might question whether these diverse views constitute different languages. They help explain why the Founders quarreled, but they do not explain their agreements. Perhaps, then, they are best understood as dialects within a common political language. Perhaps the Founders' great quarrels occurred within the broader consensus of the natural rights philosophy that Congress endorsed unanimously in the Declaration of Independence. Yet even if this is true, the diversity of dialects often made it difficult for the Founders to understand each other. It also makes it hard for us to understand them.

Which of these dialects did Hamilton speak? Perhaps the best answer is all of them, with varying degrees of emphasis, proficiency, and enthusiasm, because Hamilton was not an ideologue. As Bernard Bailyn has observed, the ideological approach to American political thought arose from an effort to link intellectual and social history. Until historians began to use the enormous volume of pamphlet literature of the Founding era to construct ideologies, they could not explain how the lofty principles of original political philosophers percolated down to ordinary citizens and politicians.[12] Although Bailyn's approach is useful for taking the average measure of public opinion at a particular time and place, neither Hamilton nor his greatest rivals, Thomas Jefferson, James Madison, and John Adams, were ordinary political minds. They therefore do not fit neatly into the procrustean bed of ideology. As one of the pioneers of the ideological approach, Gordon S. Wood, has observed, "We ought to remember that these boxlike traditions into which the historical participants must be fitted are essentially our inventions, and as such distortions of past reality."[13]

Even Kramnick's diverse ideological boxes sometimes contain more distortion than reality. As Kramnick reveals, those who spoke the liberal language of securing rights, such as James Madison, also hoped that republican elections would promote the leadership of public-spirited elites. Others, like Hamilton, who supported a strong nation-state, simultaneously appealed to the republican principle of popular consent. Was Madison a liberal or a republican? Was Hamilton a state builder or a republican? We cannot say with certainty because Kramnick's categories readily bleed into each other. Hence, rather than write of a "profusion and confusion of political tongues among the founders," we might do better to wonder at the uncommon multilingualism of the most thoughtful among them.[14] With good reason, Kramnick is drawn to such figures as Madison and Hamilton, who seem to be all over the ideological map. The more perceptive the statesman or citizen under investigation, the more likely he was to blend different schools of thought. One might even define the greatest statesmen of this period by their capacity to see the limitations of these different worldviews and to synthesize them. If so, one must wonder whether Gordon Wood is right to suggest that they "must" still be treated as prisoners of ideology. Perhaps instead we should reflect on their uncommon determination and frequent ability to transcend it.[15]

This premise justifies the method of this account of Hamilton's thought. As a group, the Founders were both much more theoretical than American statesmen today and more practical-minded than most political theorists who preceded them. They did not establish their unique claim to fame by developing new theory but by translating existing theory into practice. Nonetheless, this emphasis on the practical often led to theoretical clarity, as was especially true in Hamilton's case. "Most general theories," he observed, "admit of numerous exceptions, and there are few, if any, of the political kind, which do not blend a considerable portion of error with the truths they inculcate." He later suggested that "there is hardly any theoretic hypothesis which carried to a certain extreme, does not become practically false."[16] As a "thinking revolutionary," to use Ralph Lerner's term, Hamilton had no choice but to investigate the practical exceptions and falsehoods contained in principles he generally believed to be true.[17] He was more prudent than most people of his time because he had a better understanding of the uses and abuses of political theory.

Perhaps because of this insight, Hamilton apparently considered writing a theoretical treatise on government that would have used the inductive method of Francis Bacon. Hamilton's introduction (usually unpublished) to The Federalist mentions his desire to promote not merely the new Constitution but also the cause of "truth," and so too does his first essay in that work.[18] Some of the most significant political thinkers in the West, such as Thucydides, Machiavelli, Francis Bacon, Montaigne, Hume, and Tocqueville, were also practicing statesmen who modified existing theories with lessons they had learned from practice. Hence, when Hamilton observes the limits of theory, we ought not to conclude he had no use for it. Indeed, when Hamilton grudgingly encouraged other Federalists to vote for Thomas Jefferson rather than for Aaron Burr for president in 1801, it was because, in his view, Burr had no theory. Is it "a recommendation to have *no theory*? Can that man be a systematic or able statesman who has none?" Hamilton did not think so: "*No general principles* will hardly work much better than erroneous ones." Hamilton was primarily a soldier-statesman, but he also believed he had important ideas to contribute to the theory, as well as to the practice, of modern free government. It is time to discover why.[19]

As a principled, often theoretical, but almost never ideological statesman, Hamilton does not fit well within the pigeonholes of contemporary scholarship, but one must begin somewhere. It may therefore help to employ Kramnick's bevy of languages in order to dispel some prejudices, clear the air, and gain a provisional sense of Hamilton's place in American political thought. Judging by his recurring references to eighteenth-century theorists such as Blackstone, Locke, and Montesquieu, Hamilton was foremost a modern liberal who believed the "natural rights of mankind are written as with a sun beam, in the whole *volume* of human nature, by the divinity itself, and can never be erased or obscured by mortal power."[20] Nonetheless, the dangers of foreign and civil war made him take exception to the common opinion that liberty and power are always adversaries. Those dangers taught him that "vigor of government is essential to the security of liberty," that in fact "their interest can never be separated." Although those dangers led him to call for national strength more consistently than any other Founder, strength itself was a mere means to a liberal end. Kramnick is surely right to conclude that Hamilton was the "premier state-builder in an age of state-builders," but we distort his project significantly if we divorce it from his liberal devotion to natural rights. Hamilton became a state builder because of his liberal principles, not in spite of them.[21]

Hamilton's quarrels with his opponents over the desirability of a stronger national government point to some complex liberal-republican dimensions of his thought, and of theirs as well. As Bernard Bailyn has demonstrated, the radical Whig science of politics that Americans invoked when they first sought to justify their Revolution was fundamentally a politics of suspicion.[22] That suspicious science had both institutional and moral implications. During and after the Revolution, it led to a variety of constitutional experiments to control men in power through such devices as rotation of office and short terms in the state governments. It helped produce the second article of the Articles of Confederation, which limited Congress to the exercise of expressly delegated powers. It also led many Americans to understand jealousy of power (or, more positively, public vigilance) as a necessary check on those who hold power, who are always presumed likely to abuse it. The archsupporter of jealousy as a civic virtue is, of course, Thomas Jefferson. In the *Kentucky Resolutions* of 1798, he defiantly declared that "confidence is everywhere the parent of despotism," that "free government is founded in jealousy, and not in confidence," and that "it is jealousy and not confidence which prescribes limited constitutions, to bind those whom we are obliged to trust with power."[23] As Paul Rahe has suggested, Hamilton's nemesis devoted most of his complicated educational project to encouraging popular jealousy, which he considered far more important than institutional devices for checking power. So long as the people were suspicious of power, he hoped they would be attentive to public affairs. They might therefore anticipate dangers to both their political and their civil rights and act to defend them before they were lost. The sheep would not be devoured by ambitious wolves in power because they would not be sheeplike at all.[24]

Although the politics of suspicion was extremely useful for inspiring a revolution, it also gave birth to political extremism. Hamilton believed it had crippled the military capability of the Confederation during the Revolutionary War. The vigilance that Jefferson and perhaps most other Americans understood as a virtue, Hamilton began to see as a vice that might deny Americans their independence and the liberties it was meant to secure. As he observed, "jealousy" often infects the "noble enthusiasm for liberty" with "a spirit of narrow and illiberal distrust." In turn, that distrust may incapacitate a government in even its most necessary and legitimate purposes, such as the common defense.[25]

Hamilton therefore began to stress the statesmanlike virtue of responsibility as a means to moderate the excesses of political jealousy. Although he sometimes erred in the other extreme, his quarrels with his opponents invite us to transcend the conventions of his time and the ideologies we use to describe it today. Since republican citizens and statesmen have been disputing the meaning of virtue for at least 2,500 years, we ought not to presume that the Founders agreed about its meaning in their time more readily than we do today. Nor should we presume that we know more about virtue than they did; indeed, the opposite might well be true. Investigating Hamilton's quarrel with Jefferson will not settle disputes about this controversial concept, but the dialectic begs us to ask once again the old (and some might say, naive) philosophical questions that gave birth to political science. What is virtue? Is it everywhere and always the same, or does it change according to time and place? Is virtue one thing or many different things? If the latter, which is best and why?

The first reference to responsibility in the *Oxford English Dictionary* is a passage from *Federalist* 63. Its editors may have erred in attributing this essay to Hamilton rather than to Madison, but they also made a significant point. Responsibility emerges as an important moral-political term for perhaps the first time during the Founding era. Its meaning seems to have evolved from the beginning of the Revolution to the framing and ratification of the Constitution. It also seems to have meant different things to people of different persuasions, with the Anti-Federalists often using it in the conventional

Whig sense of accountability and the Federalists using it to mean unswerving dedication to the public good. Together, Hamilton and Madison used "responsibility" twenty-six times in *The Federalist;* they used its cognate, responsible, another ten. Hamilton first employed the term during the Revolutionary War in 1780. He was the first to use it in *The Federalist,* in the twenty-third essay, where he argued that those responsible for the nation's defense had to be granted the powers necessary to serve that end. Both Hamilton and Madison struggled with the tension between a statesman's responsibility to preserve a republic from harm and his responsiveness to constituents, a view of representation often favored by the ever-suspicious Anti-Federalists. The former objective required substantial independence in representatives; the latter, much greater dependence upon constituents. If only because he wrote the most about the presumably most responsible branches, the Senate, the executive, and the judiciary, Hamilton used the term significantly more than Madison. Though perhaps not the first American statesman to make a virtue of responsibility, he was probably the first to make this virtue the standard of his politics.[26]

Jefferson often explained his quarrel with Hamilton in Manichean terms, as the opposition between republican virtue and monarchical ambition. Yet few political quarrels follow the script of a morality play. Their quarrel was not between virtue and vice, or even between virtue and interest (as some scholars suggest today), but between different modern conceptions of political virtue, vigilance and responsibility.[27] These rival modern virtues do not exhaust the many different ways in which the Founders thought about virtue. Yet they do account for the most contentious quarrels between Hamilton and his major opponents over a weak confederation versus a stronger national government; strict versus broad construction of the Constitution; a weak versus a strong executive; the militia versus a permanent army; judicial review versus popular sovereignty; and even agriculture versus commerce. A unique advantage of characterizing this great debate as a quarrel between different virtues is that it enables us to give each side its due. Reconstructing the dialogue between the partisans of these virtues helps us explain why each side believed its motives were just and honorable; it also helps us understand why each was partly right. Not least, the dialectic of these virtues confirms the apparently growing consensus that the "republicanism of the Founding was modern and liberal."[28]

The term "republican" had many meanings for the Founders; as Gerald Stourzh and Clinton Rossiter observe, however, three stand out in Hamilton's case: self-government, the rule of law, and devotion to the public good.[29] Self-government was inherently ambiguous because it implied both popular government and the rule of reason over passion. The theoretical problem was that when either conception of self-government became an end in itself, it tended to undermine the other. The practical problem was that the partisans of vigilance tended to identify themselves with one conception of self-government and the partisans of responsibility with the other. Consequently, each saw the other as a threat to self-government, properly understood. Though Hamilton's lofty, sometimes haughty tone led the vigilant to accuse him of Caesarism, he commonly presented himself as a loyal patrician advocating both restraint and strategic vision for the Republic.[30] By championing responsibility, Hamilton helped make it possible for popular government to approach a kind of rule of reason over passion; he also made it inevitable that he would be understood as an enemy of republicanism, when it is reduced merely to popular government.

Hamilton understood himself as a republican in the three senses identified by Rossiter and Stourzh, but despite his many classical pen names, he was neither a modern democratic nor a classical republican. As a political economist, he was too willing to pursue public benefits through private interests to fit the latter category, especially as scholars use it today. He was also too skeptical to believe that the best cure for the ills of democracy was more democracy. For Hamilton, responsible republican statesmanship required the rule of law but also had to avoid the self-defeating legalism he feared in strict construction of the Constitution. Responsible republican statesmanship had to serve the public good but also had to avoid the moralism Hamilton often ascribed to his opponents. To be both humane and effective, it had to tolerate and make use of the interests and ambitions of ordinary citizens and politicians. However remotely or indirectly, responsible republican statesmanship had to be based on consent, but it also required a way to take the initiative and shape events rather than being shaped by them. Consequently, Hamilton consistently stretched not only republican but also constitutional principles as far as he believed they would admit, and sometimes much further than the vigilant spirit of his people would allow. The stretching testifies to the importance of responsibility in his thought, but the determination to produce this virtue within the framework of the Constitution of 1787 was a vital source of his most innovative contributions to modern republican theory and constitutional government, such as an energetic executive.

What about the other schools of thought Kramnick lists? Are they also relevant for understanding Hamilton? Certainly the author of all the essays on the judiciary in *The Federalist* was more than a little schooled in jurisprudence as a vehicle for building a liberal-republican union (but with far less sympathy for the state governments than common in his time).[31] There is little evidence that Hamilton adhered to the communitarianism that some scholars today associate with the Scottish Enlightenment. Yet his sense of virtue as desirable for its own sake, apart from any immediate or tangible interests we might derive from it, probably owes a great deal to the Scots, and to David Hume especially. Indeed, his dual stress on the pursuit of fame, which makes us useful to ourselves, and on humanity, which makes us useful to others, is virtually incomprehensible without thinking of Hume's quasi-classical correctives of modern liberalism. Together, these Humean virtues helped Hamilton define what it meant to be an eighteenth-century gentleman, which he understood as a combination of gentleness and manliness. Above all, he was indebted to Hume for his defense of modern commercial society in its ability to combine public strength for war with individual security for liberty. For both Hume and Hamilton, this combination constituted one of the chief claims to superiority for modern over ancient free governments. As a liberal-republican, however, Hamilton could never bring himself to endorse Hume's critique of natural rights and the possibility of establishing a social compact by consent. Nonetheless, Hume may have been a source for Hamilton's view of the Constitution as a quasi-independent will to check tyrannical majorities.[32] The vigilant Whig science of politics played a role in Hamilton's justification for resisting England at the beginning of the American Revolution, in his accounts of representation and balanced government in 1787, and especially in his discussions of freedom of speech and the press in 1803. Yet Hume's critique of that science also moved Hamilton to speak heretically in Whig America: executive influence in the legislature and throughout the Union was less a threat than a necessary ingredient in a practically (rather than theoretically) balanced constitution.[33]

Hamilton had moments of deep piety in his early youth, writing at one point a Job-like discussion of the power of God while describing the destruction produced by a hurricane. Near the end of his career, after his eldest son's death in a duel, hope for an afterlife for his son helped him bear his grief. Shortly before his own death, he wrote that Christian scruples against dueling had made him resolve to reserve the first shot in his duel with Burr. Still, between his youth and the last years of his life, religion apparently did not have great significance for him. To be sure, the conviction that rights exist by divine ordinance prior to the establishment of civil society was an important part of his Lockean critique of Hobbes. He also considered piety of some sort necessary to restrain human passions and to promote fidelity in contracts. Hence, he never mocked religion, nor did he display any radical Whig hatred of priestcraft. As the wars of the French Revolution increased in fury, he correctly predicted that the humane Christian doctrine of just war would no longer serve to restrain either modern wars or state terrorism. Partly for this reason, he endorsed a Christian Constitutional Society, which aimed to enlist the aid of religious passion on the side of the Constitution and the Constitution on the side of religious liberty. Yet he generally distrusted political enthusiasts because they resembled religious extremists. He even treated the revolution in France as a paradoxical atheistic sort of religion. For the sake of sobriety, he rarely indulged in millennial thinking and jeremiads.[34]

Hamilton's attitudes toward religion is perhaps best summed up in some youthful, joking, but ultimately serious remarks about the attributes that he sought in a wife. She needed to be young, handsome (he placed special emphasis on a good shape), sensible, well-bred, good-natured, generous, and preferably wealthy. "As to religion," he declared, "a moderate stock will satisfy me. She must believe in God and hate a saint." The same view probably applied in Hamilton's preferences for the American people. They needed enough faith to be humane and civil to each other, but not so much that their political quarrels would be infected with the spirit of religious crusades. Nothing distinguishes Hamilton from Oliver Cromwell (with whom his contemporaries sometimes compared him) more than his hatred of Puritanism, religious and political. Largely because of the humanity he absorbed from Hume, among others, he was less worried that Americans would become decadent or corrupt than that they would become exceedingly self-righteous, as in fact they have on many occasions in their history.

Nonetheless, religious echoes abound in Hamilton's rhetoric. By presenting manufacturing as a positive force for both individual and national independence, for example, Hamilton may have implied that commercial society supported a pull-yourself-up-by-your-bootstraps work-ethic Christianity. By stressing that free government depended on the American "conduct and example" in both The Federalist and his second draft of Washington's Farewell Address, Hamilton simultaneously advised against religious crusades for freedom and reminded the people of the possibility of a modest, yet righteous, world leadership.[35]

Hamilton's quasi-religious sense of America's role in the world deserves special attention because it reveals a dimension of his thought that does not fit within any of the worldviews commonly used to describe his time. Hamilton meant to build not merely a strong state but also a united nation.

These are fundamentally different kinds of tasks requiring radically different kinds of means. Numerous studies have explained the rise of the modern state as the result of developing effective means of employing coercion, raising revenue, and generating capital. These methods enable different countries to maintain authority at home and to vindicate their sovereignty abroad. To this end, Hamilton appealed to the interests of the wealthy and to the ambitions of those who loved power and distinction, the energetic men he relied upon to energize the national government. Yet, even today, no one is quite sure what produces the identity or "we-feeling" that is the essence of nationhood. What makes a people a people? The usual answers are that nationhood is the product of some combination of a common language, territory, religion, ethnicity, history, and so forth. Shared historical memory is perhaps most important. It gives those individuals who associate themselves with one people rather than with another common objects of love, admiration, and even hatred.[36] Nonetheless, we have no formula to capture this identity. Like a marriage, it is unique to the parties who share in it.

To preserve and increase the emotional bonds of American union, Hamilton spoke a significantly different kind of language from that of a mere state builder. He frequently appealed to his people's sense of themselves as a quasi-chosen people. By making such appeals, Hamilton and many others of his age half-consciously stumbled toward a union quite different from a classical republic and one more modern even than a Lockean civil society.[37] The modern liberal-democratic nation-state is not an ancient polis, but it is much more than a contract among individuals to avoid suffering harm. It is not merely a way to preserve life and acquire property; it is also the reflection of a people's determination to live a certain way of life, based on respect for individual rights, the rule of law, and consent as the appropriate means to settle political disputes. Rather than seeking to explain all public-spirited activity in Hamilton's time or our own in terms of a Christian or a classical heritage, we might instead think of the rise of the American nation-state as Hegel thought of the rise of all modern states, in terms of the passage from *Gesellschaft* (civil society) to *Gemeinschaft* (ethical community). Largely because of Montesquieu, Hamilton believed that each nation has its own spirit, ethos, or *Geist*, which creates a fellowship in a political way of life that distinguishes it from other political fellowships. Because the "we-feeling" of modern nationalism is always mysterious, no one is sure how or when Americans developed their own distinctive identity. One certainty is clear, however. Hamilton meant to develop a powerful American national consciousness as quickly as possible, lest sectional, party, and other differences result not only in civil war but also in the militarism that he believed would surely accompany any war among Americans themselves.

We therefore caricature Hamilton if we reduce his statecraft to militaristic state building on the model of Frederick the Great and Bismarck. As a man of parts, as men used to say in the eighteenth century, Hamilton was too complex to fit within any of the schools of thought said to characterize his time. He made use of elements from each one and developed other themes, such as nationalism, which reveal fundamental limitations in these languages. Possessing a synthetic mind, he was a liberal-republican Founder of the American nation-state, or as he often preferred to say, empire, who took responsibility to attach all useful passions, both noble and self-interested, both Christian and secular, to preserve the American Union and to "justify the Revolution by its fruits."

How then was he different from the other great synthetic minds of his age, such as James Madison, Thomas Jefferson, and John Adams? His characteristic emphases on responsibility in statesmen and energy in government constitute a large part of the answer. So too is his general lack of concern with federalism. Yet these were results of a much more profound difference that merits careful attention from historians, political theorists, and students of civil-military relations especially. Scholars as diverse as Isaac Kramnick, Harvey Mansfield, Gerald Stourzh, Julius Goebel, and J. G. A. Pocock have usually said both too much and too little when they have compared Hamilton, the founder of America's republican empire, to Machiavelli, the founder of modernity. Although it is impossible to prove that he read Machiavelli, Hamilton's many observations on human motivation, the effectual foundations of political authority, executive power, international relations, and a host of other issues reveal a style of reasoning for which Machiavelli is justly famous. The problem is that this way of thinking coexists with other dimensions in Hamilton's thought and character (Christianity, natural rights, a sense of honor) that are commonly understood as antithetical to Machiavellian politics. The essential yet paradoxical truth is that Hamilton was much more like Machiavelli than commonly believed and was at the same time fundamentally opposed to a kind of politics that we usually call Machiavellian. Following Machiavelli, Hamilton believed there was no viable alternative to transforming the United States into a great empire; unlike Machiavelli, he meant to found the American empire by means of consent rather than through the force and the fraud that the former assumed were the only effectual foundations of political authority. In his efforts to found the world's first republican empire, Hamilton distinguished himself both as the most Machiavellian statesman of his generation in America and the one most opposed to modern Machiavellianism, as it revealed itself in revolutionary France, for example.[38]

Recent studies suggest that Hamilton's efforts to found a republican empire were strategically necessary but politically premature. They were necessary because the wars spawned by the French Revolution inaugurated the modern age of unlimited war, for which the United States was completely unprepared. They were premature because a domestic constituency to support them was lacking. This mismatch between objective strategic reality and subjective political culture virtually guaranteed that Hamilton's program could not be enacted all at once and would even produce a backlash. His political-economic-strategic program quickly became associated in the minds of many Americans with the competition between the informal court and country parties of eighteenth-century England. Significantly, England's country party usually played the role of a vigilant opposition; the court party commonly had the responsibility of running the government. The country party had agrarian roots and was distrustful of a standing army, monopolies, and a credit economy. It feared tyranny from an executive able to use his wealth and patronage to influence Parliament and control the army. In contrast, the court party generated the arms, the wealth, and the responsible leadership that enabled England to defeat its major adversaries and rule the waves. Perhaps because England was almost constantly involved in wars during the eighteenth century, the fears of the country party apparently did not have significant influence on English politics. Perhaps because Americans were relatively isolated from European wars, the vigilance called for by the country party had much greater influence in America. If only because war is at least as dangerous to liberty as power, the responsibility of the court probably had more than a little to do with the preservation of English liberty in the eighteenth century. Still, few Americans believed this was true, and perhaps even fewer were willing to admit it might be true. Anything that resembled court politics (influence, patronage, standing armies, funded debts, or Hamilton) was seen as a harbinger of tyranny.[39]

The vigilance of the country persuasion dominated debates over declaring independence in America. In turn, that persuasion animated much of the Anti-Federalists' suspicion of the new Constitution, and, still later, the Jeffersonian Republicans' crusade against Hamilton's financial and military policies.[40] Partly because the war Hamilton expected did not happen as quickly as he feared, and partly because his policies produced significant opposition from ever-vigilant subscribers to the country persuasion, the country party won the historical debate in America in 1800. We honor Jeffersonian vigilance as a necessary republican virtue and remain suspicious of Hamiltonian responsibility as a result. Yet this historical victory was by no means a theoretical one. Indeed, in practice, even the historical victory was extremely ambiguous and short-lived. As heirs of Jefferson, we consistently seek to bury Hamilton, but whenever we go to war, we invoke his ghost to provide for the common defense. Our often grudging but consistent recourse to Hamilton in times of danger, when we cannot pretend we can do without his way of thinking, suggests his most important place in American political thought. From his youth to his death, he was the Founder who reflected most deeply and comprehensively on preserving freedom in a world all too frequently at war.

Part One

REVOLUTIONARY

2. Principle and Prudence

Hamilton wrote his first political tract, *A Full Vindication of the Measures of Congress,* at the age of seventeen while still an undergraduate at King's College in New York City. The *Full Vindication* was written seventeen months before the Declaration of Independence under the nom de plume "A Friend of America" in December 1774. Hamilton defended resolutions of Congress calling for a boycott of British goods in America and an embargo on exports to the British Empire. The resolutions were a response to the great political issue of the day: the efforts of Parliament to tax the American colonies without their consent. Hamilton's effort to vindicate the resolutions was a response to a pamphlet, *Free Thoughts on the Proceedings of the Continental Congress,* by the Tory Samuel Seabury, who wrote under the pseudonym A. W. Farmer. Seabury responded to Hamilton with another pamphlet, *A View of the Controversy Between Great Britain and Her Colonies,* which in turn led Hamilton to reply with yet another pamphlet, *The Farmer Refuted.* Seabury argued that Congress had "ignorantly misunderstood, carelessly neglected, or basely betrayed the interests of the colonies." He also defended the "supreme legislative authority of Great Britain" to make laws for its colonies. Seabury's attack on Congress and the sanctions set the terms of the debate. Hamilton was obliged to vindicate the measures of Congress "from the charge of injustice or impolicy."[1]

That practical necessity left an indelible stamp on the character of Hamilton's political rhetoric. From 1774 to the end of his career, Hamilton consistently sought to demonstrate that his policies were both morally principled and politically prudent. Other Founders often employed this rhetorical strategy, but Hamilton was unique in his ability to harmonize revolutionary principles with the practical necessities of a more traditional raison d'etat. With far more emphasis on the latter than on the former, Felix Gilbert, Paul A. Varg, Hans Morgenthau, Charles A. Beard, and many other scholars have often seen Hamilton as the hardheaded, clear-sighted Founder of the realist approach to American foreign policy. Clinton Rossiter, however, objects to treating Hamilton as the father of political realism in America, especially if by that term one means an exponent or practitioner of "amorality in foreign affairs." Although J. G. A. Pocock has suggested that Hamilton's writings on war and foreign affairs exhibited a "preference for success over deservingness" or Machiavellian "*virtu* over virtue," Hamilton's earliest writings set the pattern for his later discussions of war and foreign policy. He sought to show that liberal principles not only allowed but even required American statesmen to take any measures necessary to secure the rights of their own people. The priority Hamilton gave to securing American rights was not the result of realpolitik but a necessary consequence of American revolutionary principles as he understood them.[2]

Hamilton's early writings also reveal the synthetic character of his political thought. According to Stanley Elkins and Eric McKitrick, Hamilton's pamphlets covered "virtually the entire ideological range within which Americans would justify what they would shortly do."[3] That range included not only a theory of the British constitution and a historical examination of the colonial charters but also the Catonic synthesis of natural rights with the radical Whig suspicion of power, which Michael Zuckert and Jerome Huyler see at the bottom of modern liberal-republicanism. As Forrest McDonald has ironically observed, Hamilton in his youth often sounded like his opponents in his maturity. He warned as firmly as any of his future adversaries of the dangers of corruption, patronage, ministerial influence, standing armies, and, above all else, government without the actual consent of constituents. In this respect, his early writings are typical of the political thought of Americans during the Revolution.[4]

Nonetheless, Hamilton was already moving in a significantly different direction from many of his contemporaries. In his view, self-preservation not only trumped American duties to Englishmen and benevolence toward mankind, but it also gave Congress a responsibility to take all necessary measures to secure American rights in the quarrel with England. The necessity of resisting effectively led Hamilton to defend Congress precisely because it had assumed the responsibility of national leadership. Soon after the Revolution began, many Americans turned their vigilance on Congress, but Hamilton took for granted that those men responsible for securing American rights required sufficient power to do so. Moreover, as early as 1774 he understood that Americans would need a force at least as powerful as the British Empire to provide effectively for their common defense. In that respect, his earliest political tracts also defined the great problem of his political career. His task was to reconcile the strategic necessity of empire with the new view of sovereignty, based on the liberal-republican principle of consent, implicit in his defense of Congress in 1774 and 1775.

As a matter of principle, Hamilton had to demonstrate three propositions: first, that Parliament had no right to tax the American colonies;
second, that Congress had a right to enact sanctions against the British and
their dominions; and third, that such sanctions were justified even if they
caused much suffering for ordinary British subjects. The first task led him to
employ the conventional Whig language of vigilance; the second, to speak less
conventionally in terms of responsibility; the third, to explain some of the
harsher dimensions of modern natural rights philosophy in time of war.

To undermine the authority of Parliament to tax Americans, Hamilton
insisted that the quarrel with the British was not about interests but about
the fundamental principles of free government. "What," he asked, "is the
subject of our controversy with the mother country? It is this, whether we
shall preserve the security to our lives and properties, which the law of nature, the genius of the British constitution, and our charters afford us; or
whether we shall resign them into the hands of the British House of Commons, which is no more privileged to dispose of them than the Grand
Mogul." The "only difference between freedom and slavery," Hamilton
declared, is that in "the former state, a man is governed by laws, to which
he has given his consent, either in person, or by his representative; in the
latter, he is governed by the will of another. In the one case his life and property are his own; in the other, they depend upon the pleasure of a master."
Neither the House of Commons nor the Grand Mogul had received the
consent of the American people to tax them. "How ridiculous then is it to
affirm that we are quarreling for the trifling sum of three pence a pound on
tea; when it is evidently the principle against which we contend." Without
actual consent and equality under law, Americans would be reduced from
freemen to slaves, for "when any people are ruled by laws, in framing which,
they have no part, that are to bind them, to all intents and purposes, without, in the same manner, binding the legislators themselves, they are in the
strictest sense slaves, and the government with respect to them, is despotic."[5]

Hamilton's argument rested on his understanding of the natural rights
of mankind, the British constitution (the rights of Englishmen), and colonial charters with the king (the rights of British Americans). Natural rights
were by far the most important foundation of his argument, however. Indeed, they were equally important in Seabury's response to Hamilton, which
suggests that even this classic debate between an American Whig and an
American Tory occurred largely within the confines of modern liberalism.
Thus, for example, Seabury responded to Hamilton by wishing he had made
clearer to the public what he meant by the "natural rights of mankind. Man
in a state of nature," Seabury declared, "may be considered free from all

restraints of law and government; and then the weak must submit to the strong." Evidently, Seabury feared (or pretended to fear) that invoking natural rights in the controversy with England would lead to a return to the state of nature, and "introduce confusion and violence, where all must submit to the power of the mob."

Likewise, the liberal state of nature was also very much on Hamilton's mind, but for different reasons. After wading through numerous documents and colonial charters to demonstrate that American liberty rested on compacts with the king, Hamilton had to admit that Seabury was partly right. Some colonies, such as New York, had no such charters. Hamilton therefore could not invoke them against Parliament, but this did not matter: "The sacred rights of mankind are not to be rummaged for among old parchments or musty records." These rights existed by divine ordinance and could not be changed by mortal power. Therefore, the "nations of Turkey, Russia, France, Spain, and all other despotic kingdoms" had a natural "right to shake off the yoke of servitude (though sanctified by immemorial usage of their ancestors), and to model their government upon principles of civil liberty."[6]

Significantly, Hamilton misunderstood Seabury, or perhaps even deliberately misconstrued his position to strengthen his own. Though Hamilton accused the Tory of being an enemy "to the natural rights of mankind," Seabury did not deny the existence of those rights. Rather, he insisted that "not only Americans but Africans, Europeans, Asiatics, all men of all countries and degrees, of all sizes and complexions, have a right to as much freedom as is consistent with the security of civil society. And I hope you will not think me an 'enemy' to the 'natural rights of mankind' because I cannot wish them more." Seabury merely questioned whether the autonomy of the colonies in internal policy was compatible with civil society and the preservation of the British Empire. Yet Hamilton deliberately portrayed Seabury as an atheistic "disciple" of "Mr. Hobbes."[7] Although this rhetorical sleight of hand was unfair, it makes sense if one recognizes that Hamilton was employing Locke against Hobbes, the straw man to whom he sought to reduce Seabury.

To justify resistance to British authority, Hamilton had to make an essentially Lockean distinction between absolute and arbitrary power. The distinction rested on the premise that moral obligation existed prior to the establishment of civil society. The sovereign might lay claim to all the means necessary to accomplish the ends of civil society and in that sense be absolute, but it had no authority to use its power arbitrarily. That is, it could not act contrary to the ends of civil society, which existed for the sake of preserving preexisting natural rights. In contrast, for Hobbes, Hamilton believed, "moral obligation" was derived not from nature but "from the introduction of civil society." There was "no virtue, but what is purely artificial, the mere contrivance of politicians, for the maintenance of social intercourse." Hobbes formulated this "absurd and impious doctrine" because he rejected "the existence of an intelligent superintending principle, who is the governor, and will be the final judge of the universe." The existence of such a superintending principle, Hamilton observed, "has constituted an eternal and immutable law, which is, indispensably, obligatory upon all mankind, prior to any human institution whatsoever."[8] Thus, no laws contradicting the natural law could be valid; they would violate the moral constitution of the universe.

What was that moral constitution, and what was its basis? Though Hamilton blurred the distinction between natural and divine law, he did not derive the moral order from revelation. Instead, he patronized Seabury, who was many years his senior, by telling him to do his homework. He needed to read the modern works of "Grotius, Puffendorf, Locke, Montesquieu, and Burlamaqui." There were many other "excellent writers" on the subject, but in his "enlightened age" he did not think any others were required to grasp the main points of the natural rights of mankind. Hamilton cited Blackstone most frequently in his formulations of these rights, though it is not immediately clear why. Perhaps it was because even this ardent advocate of parliamentary supremacy argued that the British constitution rested on, or ought to rest on and be limited by, natural rights. Blackstone's conservative authority may thus have bolstered Hamilton's argument that he did not need to rely simply on musty parchment. In any case, Hamilton's conception of natural rights is clearly Lockean in character. It rests on the fundamental right of self-preservation as a limit on arbitrary power and the capacity of individuals to use their own reason to determine how to secure this right. Paraphrasing Locke, Hamilton therefore declared that "the supreme being gave existence to man, together with the means of preserving and beatifying that existence. He endowed him with rational faculties . . . to discern and pursue such things, as were consistent with his duty and interests, and invested him with an inviolable right to personal liberty and personal safety."[9]

Yet there was one intriguing twist in Hamilton's formulation that did not strictly follow the conventional pattern of securing life, liberty, and property. Hamilton wrote not merely of preserving but also of beatifying or achieving some splendid goal with our existence. Natural rights are not privileges. They belong to us by virtue of our common humanity. By nature, they do not depend upon extraordinary behavior—even human vegetables have these rights. Nonetheless, they are not simply egalitarian. They supply a chance for individuals from the lowest stations, like Hamilton, to fulfill their natural potential, to become exceptional human beings, or supremely happy, if not even blessed or beatified, by virtue of extraordinary labors. Beatification thus might be a synonym for the pursuit of happiness, but it is a very Hamiltonian kind of happiness, based on the possibility of rising from obscurity to greatness. In this sense, beatification might be considered a Hamiltonian fusion of liberal principles with work-ethic Christianity, if not more—a vision of political greatness that would enable him and other Founders to rival the lawgivers and statesmen of antiquity.

This interpretation aside, Hamilton was in essential agreement not only with most American Whigs but also with the author of the Declaration of Independence and his future rival, Thomas Jefferson, about the political consequences of our common humanity. By nature, no man had any "*moral power*" or authority to govern another man. Thus, political society had to be artificial, with the consequence that bad governments could and should be replaced by better ones. Legitimate authority could arise only from "voluntary compact, between the rulers and the ruled, for what original title can any man or set of men have, to govern others, except their own consent?" By this standard, Parliament had no authority to make laws for Americans. Parliament usurped their "natural liberty" by assuming an authority Americans had never granted.[10]

At this point, Hamilton started to blend liberal principles with Whig suspiciousness and the science of power. The doctrine that Parliament could tax the colonies without their consent deprived Americans of the "moral security" of being governed by representatives who were bound to their constituents by gratitude and interest (based on elections) and subject to the same laws they made for their people (equality under law). Such security, Hamilton insisted, is the "primary end of society to bestow." Such security could never exist "while it may be the interest of uncontrollable legislators to oppress us as much as possible."[11]

Seabury granted that an Englishman is not bound by any laws but those to which the representatives of the nation have given their consent, but he also accused Hamilton of an "artful change of terms." It "never was true, and never can be true" that a law had no validity for an Englishmen unless he consented to it in person or through his representative. "A great part of the people in England" had "no choice of representatives." They were virtually represented by members of the House of Commons who ostensibly considered themselves responsible for the welfare of the empire as a whole.

Hamilton, however, insisted that virtual representation was no security for American liberties. Like other American Whigs, he associated the House of Commons with the "democratical part" of the British constitution. The Commons was an institution for protecting the people against the abuses of royal prerogative. It was an "undeniable birth-right of every Englishman, who can be considered as a *free agent* to participate in the framing of the laws which are to bind him, either as to his life or property." Representation in the Commons was a means for avoiding the inconveniences of direct participation in national lawmaking, but "no power on earth" could divest Englishmen of their right to consent. With regular elections, "if their representatives have abused their trust, the people have it in their power to change them, and to elect others, who may be more faithful and attached to their interests." Because free agents (with some property) among the English people were represented in Parliament, they could throw their rascals out. Americans, however, had no such hold over the interests of members of Parliament. "Interests, indeed, may operate to our prejudice. To oppress us may serve as a recommendation to their constituents, as well as an alleviation of their own encumbrance." Parliament might follow the pernicious example of ancient Rome in its policies toward its colonies. "The British patriots may, in time, be heard to court the gale of popular favor, by boasting their exploits in laying some new impositions on their American vassals, and, by that means, lessening the burdens of their friends and fellow subjects."[12]

Although a Parliament with supreme power over legislation might govern the American colonies quite well, perhaps even better than they could govern themselves, Hamilton insisted that it was unsafe to rely on the mere virtue of virtual representatives. Indeed, he insisted that Seabury's position was ultimately reducible to a plea for Americans to rely on such virtue. Sounding like the most jaundiced American Whigs, whom Seabury claimed could see "no color but yellow," Hamilton observed that "a fondness for power is implanted, in most men, and it is natural to use it, when acquired." This natural tendency made it "the height of folly to entrust any set of men with power, which is not under every possible control: perpetual strides are made for more, as long as there is any part withheld. We ought not, therefore, to concede any greater authority to the British Parliament, than is absolutely necessary."

Though inconclusive as proof, an English standing army in America, the occupation of Boston, taxation without actual representation, and so on, amounted to suspicious evidence of a predilection to establish British authority on "*fear*" rather than on the "*affection* of their subjects." To Seabury

he protested, "Tell me not of the British Commons, Lords, ministry, ministerial tools, placemen, pensioners, parasites. I scorn to let my life depend upon
the pleasure of any of them." He demanded security against abuses of power.
"Give me the steady, uniform, unshaken security of constitutional freedom,
give me a right to be tried by a jury of my own neighbors, and to be taxed by
my representatives only." Hamilton's demand for security reveals that he and
most of his contemporaries understood despotism not in terms of actual
oppression but in terms of the mere unchecked power to oppress. When any
part of government sought such power, it was only prudent to "apprehend
the worst," or what Locke called a "design" of tyranny. Hamilton thus warned
of the possible "design" of a corrupt ministry that had been "formed and ripening, for several years" to suppress the liberties of Americans.[13]

He explained the necessity of suspecting such a design by quoting David
Hume, another conservative authority who might make the radical American Whigs' call for vigilance more acceptable among his compatriots who
feared a rush toward revolution. "'Political writers,'" Hume observed, "'have
established it as a maxim that, in contriving any system of government, and
fixing the several checks and controls of the constitution, every man ought
to be supposed a *knave;* and to have no other end in all his actions, but *private interest.'*" Though this supposition might be "'false in fact,'" it was "'true
in politics.'" But how could an assumption false in fact also be true in politics? Hume seemed to think it was true in the sense of being the safest political assumption about human nature. To assume the converse, that men
were good by nature, would weaken the arguments for both effective government (public strength) and controls on those who govern (individual
security). Assuming men were naturally good would thus risk the twin dangers of tyranny and anarchy. In contrast, assuming human beings were
knaves suggested ways to provide for security against oppression and to
promote the public good at the same time. If we assume each man is a knave,
Hume concluded, "'by his interest, we must govern him, and by means of
it, make him *cooperate to the public good,* notwithstanding his avarice and
ambition.'" "'Without this,'" Hume declared, "'we shall in vain boast of the
advantages of *any constitution,* and shall find in the end, that we have no
security for our liberties and possessions, except the *good will* of our rulers;
that is, we shall have *no security at all.'*"[14]

For Hamilton, this danger was particularly acute in an empire, and once
again he cited Hume to make his point:

Mr. Hume, in enumerating those political maxims, which will be eternally true, speaks thus: "It may easily be observed, that though free gov-

ernments have been commonly the most happy, for those who partake of their freedom, yet they are the most ruinous and oppressive to their *provinces.*" He goes on to give many solid reasons for this, and among other things, observes that "a free state necessarily makes a great distinction (between herself and her *provinces*) and must continue to do so, 'till men learn to love their neighbors as themselves."

As revealed in a footnote Hume wrote for this passage, his "eternally true" political maxim was a paraphrase of Machiavelli's observation in *The Discourses* that of "all hard slaveries, the hardest is that subjecting you to a republic: first, because it is more lasting and there is less hope of escape from it; second, because the purpose of a republic is to enfeeble and weaken, in order to increase its own body, all other bodies."[15] From this perspective it did not matter that the British had one of the longest traditions of free government in the early modern world. Precisely because they were free, but refused to allow the colonists to share in representation, Americans had to assume the worst case, that they would eventually suffer even harsher treatment from England than the colonies of France and Spain. They might even suffer the repression that England imposed on Ireland and that Rome had forced on its provinces.

Although both Hamilton and Seabury appealed to the example of the Roman Empire, classical allusions were far more illustrative than determinative of their thought.[16] Indeed, in Hamilton's case, Rome served primarily as an example of a reality that Americans, and any other people who subscribed to natural rights principles, simply had to avoid. Seabury argued that

legislation is not an inherent right in the colonies; many colonies have been established and subsisted long without it. It was not 'till the latter period of their republic, that the privilege of Roman citizens, among which, that of voting in assemblies of the people, at Rome, was a principal one, was extended to the inhabitants of Italy. All the laws of the empire were enacted at Rome. Neither their colonies, nor conquered countries had anything to do with legislation.

Hamilton, however, denied that the "practice of Rome, towards her colonies" was relevant to the American quarrel with England. All men were "entitled to a parity" of rights. If Rome's "practice proves anything," he observed, "it equally proves that she had a right to plunder" her colonies as much as possible. "This mistress of the world was often unjust. And the treatment of her dependent provinces is one of the greatest blemishes in her history. Through the want of the civil liberty, for which we are now so warmly contending, they groaned under every species of wanton oppression." If Americans were wise, they would therefore "take warning" from the example of Roman imperialism, "consider a like state of dependence, as more to be dreaded, than pestilence or famine," and act firmly to secure their rights before it was too late to do so.[17]

As Hamilton understood it, Seabury was arguing that it was a "Christian duty to submit to be plundered of all we have, merely because some of our fellow subjects are wicked enough to require it of us, that slavery, so far from being a great evil, is a great blessing." Seabury did not in fact call for American submission, however. Instead, he pleaded for more petitions and remonstrances to Parliament. His ultimate goal was a new compact between England and its North American colonies. He wanted to specify the former's duty to supply protection and the latter's right to local government.[18] Nonetheless, Hamilton's accusation was not entirely unfair. In practice, Seabury was preaching passive resistance. This tactic had failed to secure American rights so far, and Hamilton believed the time for merely verbal appeals had long since passed.

In this respect, the political quarrel between Hamilton and Seabury was a replay of the theological quarrel almost 100 years earlier between John Locke and the divine right advocate Robert Filmer. As Nathan Tarcov has observed, Locke's quarrel with Filmer rested on whether human beings were competent and entitled to preserve their lives and improve their condition, according to the advice of reason, or were required to submit to existing authority as the immutable will of God. Locke insisted that reason was man's "only Star and compass." Though it might reveal the will of God, revelation had to be judged by the standard of reason, which could never allow men to submit to tyranny voluntarily and thereby lose the security essential for their lives, liberties, and properties. "For Men being all the Workmanship of one Omnipotent, and infinitely wiser Maker; All the Servants of one Sovereign Master, sent into the World by his order and about his business, they are his Property whose Workmanship they are, made to last during his, not another's Pleasure." Thus, the law of nature to which Hamilton referred was that "no one ought to harm another in his Life, Liberty, Health, or Possessions." That law could be considered a negative formulation of the Christian Golden Rule. It did not require men to do good for their fellow men, but it did prohibit them from doing harm, so far as possible, unless their own preservation was at stake. When self-preservation and the liberty and property it required were in danger, however, then the law entitled men to "preserve the innocent and restrain offenders." It even allowed preemption (because it was unwise to wait until a suspected design of tyranny was actually accomplished). It therefore justified rebellion as soon as a people had spirit and opportunity enough to succeed in resisting a tyrant or potential tyrant who was in a state of war with his people.[19]

Contemporary Americans might miss the enormous extent to which early modern political writers had to demonstrate that resisting tyranny was consistent with piety, but Hamilton did not. As Alexander Clarence Flick has observed, Loyalism in America was usually blended with Anglicanism. The president of Hamilton's Anglican college, Dr. Myles Cooper, was also the recognized clerical leader of the Tories in New York. Cooper declared in 1774 that the "laws of earth and heaven" forbade rebellion and made it an "unpardonable crime." Hamilton first made a name for himself in New York City by defending Cooper from a Whig mob, which sought to ransack his home; still, he recognized that to justify resistance to England, he had to argue against the authority of his college president. He had to make tyranny seem impious and resistance the will of God. This is perhaps one of the major reasons why Locke was useful in the Christian and primarily Protestant American revolutionary world of the mid-1770s. Faced with the threat of tyranny, a free people would inevitably have to appeal to divine sanctions, but the Lockean appeal to heaven is not mere prayer. It is an appeal to force, with overtones of a medieval trial by combat, and God himself is judge of the conflict.[20] If the law of nature established by the ruler of the universe grants men rights, then Seabury and Cooper were wrong. It is a Christian duty not to submit, but to resist tyrants who aim to destroy the property of God and man.

With this modern liberal sense of Christian duty in mind, Hamilton made a powerful case not only for the right of Congress but also for its responsibility to enact sanctions against the British. Although Seabury had suggested that Congress consisted of traitors who resisted the lawful authority of Parliament, Hamilton argued that it had a responsibility to try sanctions as the last means short of war to secure American rights:

When the political salvation of a community is depending, it is incumbent on those who have been set up as its guardians, to embrace such measures as have justice, vigor, and a probability of success to recommend them: if instead of this, they take those methods which are themselves feeble, and little likely to succeed, and may through a defect of vigor, involve the community in still greater danger, they may be justly considered as its betrayers.

Congress had already attempted to convince Parliament to relent through humble "REMONSTRANCE and PETITION," but these diplomatic means had failed. After years of protest, talk had proved cheap, either because Parliament did not understand the American position, or because it did not care. There was no sign Parliament would ever be persuaded by humble speeches to accept the American position. "This being the case, we can have no recourse but in a restriction of our trade, or in a resistance *vi & armis.*"[21]

Seabury, however, was not satisfied with this argument. He considered Congress, and therefore its sanctions, to be illegal. As Jack N. Rakove has observed, Seabury and other Tories believed Congress usurped the authority of the colonial legislatures. Seabury objected that fewer than a one-hundredth part of the American people had given actual consent to the individuals who supposedly represented them in Congress. Ironically, though he was willing to accept virtual representation of America in Parliament, he tried to turn Whig vigilance against Congress by denying that it was actually representative of the American people. He also asserted that it would be the forum for demagogues whose licentious politics would ultimately breed tyranny. Ironically again, he sounded much like a suspicious Anti-Federalist in 1787 or even a Republican in the 1790s. He feared congressional energy so much that he ultimately defended the authority of the colonial assemblies (states' rights) and strict construction of their laws and charters.[22]

Hamilton could not deny that Congress was, at best, an extralegal body. Nor could he argue that more than a handful of Americans had actually consented to its delegates. He was therefore obliged to make an innovative use of Locke's understanding of prerogative, that is, the authority to act without law or even against it for the public good. Prerogative was traditionally associated with the Crown, but in the case of the sanctions before the Revolution, Hamilton vested it in Congress instead.

> We did not, especially in this province, circumscribe them by any fixed boundary, and therefore as they cannot be said to have exceeded the limits of their authority, their act must be esteemed the act of their constituents. If it should be objected, that they have not answered the end of their election, but have fallen on an improper and ruinous mode of proceeding: I reply, by asking, who shall be judge?

"Extraordinary emergencies require extraordinary expedients. The best mode of opposition" was a "union of councils" to determine American rights and give weight and credit to them in England and America. Though the measures of Congress were illegal, that objection was simply irrelevant. "When the first principles of society are violated, and the rights of a whole people invaded, the common forms of municipal law are not to be regarded. Men may then betake themselves to the law of nature; and, if they but conform their actions, to that standard," they will be justifiable assertions of higher law.[23]

From a theoretical point of view, this novel use of prerogative made perfect sense. Indeed, it was implicit in Locke's justification of rebellion. Just as executives must sometimes rebel against the letter of the law to serve its spirit, so too must representatives, when they are faced with a design of tyranny. Then each must appeal to the people, who are presumed capable of distinguishing between prerogative and usurpation, rebellion and treason. The answer to Hamilton's question, "Who shall be judge?" was the same as Locke's: the people shall be judge. They could and even should pardon the illegality of Congress and the lack of actual consent to its measures as a legitimate acquiescence in the necessity of the times. The fundamental difference, however, is that Hamilton converted a Lockean right of the executive to violate the law in emergencies into the responsibility of members of Congress when faced with the threat of tyranny. Ironically, though we rightly associate Hamilton with support for strong government, and often pit vigilance against it, his first discussion of responsible statesmanship arose from the Whig vigilance that led him to oppose a government he believed was far too strong to be safe for American liberties.[24]

Characterizations of Hamilton as a militarist must be considered in light of his justification of the sanctions. There was no jingoism in Hamilton's rhetoric; rather, he revealed a deep aversion to it. Because the law of nature applies to relations between states as well as rebellions within them, Hamilton was not merely arguing for resisting tyranny. He was also formulating some of the most important principles of the American understanding of just war. That understanding is no less deeply indebted to modern liberal political theorists than is the American understanding of free government.[25] In common with other supporters of Congress, Hamilton suggested a course that would become a traditional American path toward justifying the recourse to war with any nation: do not tolerate invasions of rights, but talk before employing coercion and employ sanctions before violence. Violence is justifiable only as a last resort, when the tools of diplomacy, from persuasion to economic coercion, have failed. Yet it would be unreasonable to wait forever for diplomacy and sanctions to succeed. By then, a foreign aggressor's objectives might already have been accomplished. Thus it is as important not to act too late as it is not to act too soon in resorting to sanctions, rebellion, and war. Precisely because Congress had acted with restraint but also had refused to submit to Parliament, Hamilton believed it had acted as responsibly as the circumstances allowed.

Restraint, however, did not mean pacificism or unwillingness to cause harm or pain to others, including, however unfortunately, the innocent. The purpose of the sanctions was to coerce Parliament by causing subjects in England and within the empire to suffer from the loss of American trade. An opponent might argue that those subjects were not to blame and that it would therefore be unjust to punish or use them when the real knaves were in Parliament. Hamilton regretted that those subjects primarily would feel the pain, and the political leaders much less or perhaps not at all. Nonetheless, he insisted there is "no law, either of nature, or of the civil society in which we live, that obliges us to purchase, and make use of the products and manufactures of a different land, or people." Hamilton acknowledged a "dictate of humanity to contribute to the support and happiness of our fellow creatures," and especially to those tied by "blood, interest, and mutual protection." But he was adamant:

> Humanity does not require us to sacrifice our own security and welfare to the convenience, or advantage of others. Self-preservation is the first principle of our nature. When our lives and properties are at stake, it would be foolish and unnatural to refrain from such measures as might preserve them, because they would be detrimental to others.[26]

Moreover, ordinary British subjects were not necessarily or unequivocally blameless. In a civil society, Hamilton observed, it is the duty of each part to promote not only the good of the "whole community, but the good of every other particular branch: If one part endeavors to violate the rights of another, the rest ought to assist in preventing the injury." If the parts fail to secure the rights of the minority, or fail to secure the individual rights that constitute the common good of each citizen, then the conditional obligations of individuals to their community are dissolved. "Though the manufacturers of Great Britain and Ireland, and the inhabitants of the West Indies are not chargeable with any actual crime towards America," he observed, "they may, in a political view, be esteemed criminal." If citizens "remain neutral, they are deficient in their duty, and may be regarded, in some measure, as accomplices." After all, the purpose of civil society is that the "united strength of the several members" be used to "give stability and strength to the whole body, and to each respective member." Those citizens who remain neutral when one part oppresses another commit the "first breach of an obligation," which in turn justified Congress in considering its obligation to the neutrals "annulled." In Hamilton's view, the annulment rendered Congress even more blameless in adopting sanctions to preserve American rights.[27]

Hamilton's second burden in his quarrel with Seabury was to demonstrate that the sanctions were prudent policy. To be good policy, he observed, the sanctions had to meet three different criteria: "First, that the necessity of the times require [them]; secondly that [they] be not the probable source of greater evils than [they intend] to remedy; and lastly, that [they] have a probability of success." Since these criteria are also fundamental to modern just war theory, they must be taken into account in evaluating conventional interpretations of Hamilton as a militarist.[28]

The necessity of the times justified imposing sanctions because talk had failed to produce action in Parliament. A "restriction on our trade" was the "only peaceable method in our power, to avoid the impending mischief." The sanctions would not cause greater evil than they were designed to remedy because Americans were "threatened with absolute slavery." Innocents within the empire might well suffer because of them, but poverty for some people was nothing compared with the absolute slavery of America. "No person, that has enjoyed the sweets of liberty, can be insensitive to its infinite value, or can reflect on its reverse, without horror and detestation." If liberty does have an infinite value, then Hamilton had already demonstrated that Congress had met the second criterion: the good sought would necessarily outweigh the probable evils. Yet why did Hamilton think liberty had an infinite value? Slavery, he observed, is "fatal to religion and morality." It tends to "debase the mind; and corrupt its noblest springs of action." Slavery "relaxes the sinews of industry, clips the wings of commerce, and introduces misery and indigence in every shape."[29]

Noteworthy in this account is the moral degradation that Hamilton, in common with almost all Americans, associated with slavery. It was, as Locke wrote in the first paragraph of his *First Treatise,* "so vile and miserable an estate" that it was hard to imagine how anyone, whether Filmer in the seventeenth century or Seabury in the eighteenth, could "plead for it."[30] Having grown up on an island where slaves composed 90 percent of the population, Hamilton had firsthand knowledge of its impact on the human character. He believed it made human beings lazy and fatalistic since slaves have no control over their present or their future. Instead of working to improve their condition, they seek to escape work that, after all, benefits only their masters. Though understandable, this desire to escape work also deprives slaves of the will required to act nobly by acting independently. It makes men slaves in spirit as well as by law. Perhaps worse, Hamilton implied, slavery is a natural school of tyrants. It breeds characters who do not consider themselves bound by religion and morality, for who could believe in a just God, and therefore perhaps even in justice itself, if there is no appeal beyond the will of a master?

At this point Hamilton's argument began to bleed into his discussion of the third criterion of sound policy, the probability of success. The mere threat of sanctions might be sufficient to accomplish American objectives, he claimed, so there might be no suffering in England or America. The former appeared to be so dependent on the latter that it either had to grant American demands or resort to force to defend Parliament's supremacy. War would require large numbers of troops and much money. England, however, seemed to be overburdened with debt and taxes. Her advantage in disciplined troops could be matched by the large number of Americans and the tenacious spirit of a people fighting for their liberty. Knowledge that "contests for liberty have ever been found the most bloody, implacable, and obstinate" would then act as a sufficient deterrent against parliamentary military escalation. If Parliament imposed countersanctions, or sought to put a stop to all American trade, Americans could adopt a strategy of autarky and "live without trade of any kind." The colonies had the natural resources for an independent economy. In the long run, English sanctions would give a boost to domestic manufacturing that in turn would render Americans even more formidable in any future conflict.[31]

In later years, however, Hamilton rarely underestimated British military power or financial wherewithal, and he was usually extremely skeptical about the efficacy of sanctions, which he preferred to employ as the last step before war. In light of his later views, Seabury's objections to the sanctions appear sound enough to call into question their value as peaceful instruments of coercion and Hamilton's prudence in defending them in 1774. British North America was not the only part of the world or the empire with which England traded. The British might find substitutes within the empire or elsewhere for the resources denied by Congress. Even if some laborers in the empire were thrown out of work and some merchants were ruined by the sanctions, they might find other employment in time. Hence, the pressure might be merely temporary. Perhaps most important, the English were a proud and free people themselves. The spirit of "Don't tread on me!" was not confined to America. John Bull was more likely to see coercive tactics in America as a form of bullying than as a reasonable assertion of American rights. Consequently, Americans would simply make the British more willing to employ draconian methods. Far from securing rights, the sanctions might polarize the conflict by making the contending parties less willing to listen to each other or to come to any form of compromise. Then the rest of America might feel the wrath England had already unleashed on Boston. This reaction could lead to an actual tyranny worse than the one Americans feared and far worse than the stable government they enjoyed under the protection of the empire.[32]

Yet what was the alternative? When persuasion fails, some form of coercion is the only remaining option. Although it is tempting to think that Hamilton learned from experience and later came to see sanctions as generally inefficacious, it is completely conceivable that even in 1774 and 1775 he doubted that they would be effective. He may well have understood their chief value as symbolic—both to the people at home and to other states. He may have defended using them simply to prove to the American people that all peaceful appeals had been exhausted, including economic coercion. If the sanctions failed, the only option left was war. It is impossible to be certain, but Hamilton's ultimate purpose in these essays was therefore probably not to vindicate the peaceful means of coercion employed by Congress. Instead, it was to prepare his countrymen for the probability that they could not vindicate their rights without going to war.

Nonetheless, war was not inevitable. Nor did Hamilton think it was desirable, if it were possible to preserve American freedom within the most powerful empire of the eighteenth and nineteenth centuries. That empire had protected Americans from attacks from French Canada and American Indians. Some substitute would be necessary to provide for the common defense, no matter what the outcome of the quarrel with England. With luck, the sanctions might have induced Parliament to accept an American interpretation of the ends and means of the British Empire. Although Seabury claimed that Hamilton's denial of parliamentary supremacy was "subversive of that dependence, which all colonies must, from their very nature, have on the mother country," Hamilton averred that his "principles admit[ted] the only dependence which can subsist, consistent with any idea of civil liberty, or with the future welfare of the British empire." Hamilton refused to serve as a slave in a British Empire that ruled America as Rome ruled its provinces. The idea of colony, he declared, "does not involve the idea of slavery. There is a wide difference between the dependence of free people, and the submission of slaves."[33] If the empire deserved to be preserved, it had to combine protection with consent, or power and freedom.

Quite surprisingly, given Hamilton's subsequent reputation, his insistence on rooting authority in consent led Seabury to accuse him of republican principles. "The position that we are bound by no laws to which we have not consented," Seabury declared, "is republican in its very nature and tends to the utter subversion of the English monarchy." Though Hamilton denied that the "commotions in America" arose from a "plan, formed by some turbulent men to erect it into a republican government," Seabury was more right than wrong. To be sure, Hamilton could still speak in quite traditional terms of a compact between "the rulers and the ruled," rather than one among the people. He also portrayed Parliament and the colonial legislatures as limits on the sovereignty of the Crown, not as the embodiments of sovereignty themselves. Nonetheless, there was an enormous tension between the principles Hamilton invoked to justify resistance and the vague compromise he appeared willing to accept. By appealing to the people as the final judge, he had followed Locke in transferring sovereignty to them even before the Revolution had begun.[34] Indeed, that transfer was an important part of his understanding of the dignity and honor of free government (at its best) as a form of rational self-government.

Seabury presented himself as a plain farmer to other farmers. He spoke the language of simple common sense to warn them of the costs of sanctions and the dangers of war. Hamilton detected Seabury's populist rhetorical strategy and therefore appealed to the farmers' pride in order to overcome their concern for their immediate interests. Some people said the farmers were the "most ignorant and mean-spirited set of people in the world," narrow-minded individuals who would sacrifice their liberty to avoid the temporary inconvenience of an embargo and a boycott. "They say that you have no sense of honor or generosity; that you don't care a farthing about your country, children, or anybody else; and that you are so ignorant, as not be able to look beyond the present." In contrast, Hamilton asserted, he would "never entertain such an opinion," unless the farmers verified such words with deeds. "I flatter myself you will convince them of their error, by showing the world, you are capable of judging what is right and left, and have resolution to pursue it."[35] Since Hamilton developed into quite the patrician in later years, some observers might find an odd twist in his appeal to the farmers to deliberate on the justice of the American cause. Still, it is quite consistent with the principles he invoked to justify the measures of Congress. It is also the premise of his myriad newspaper essays, which called on ordinary citizens to serve as judges of political controversies. Hamilton was right to deny that he was a "turbulent" republican, aiming to transfer as much direct power as possible to the people, but he had in fact become a liberal-republican who based all authority on the people's right to judge their laws and those who made them as well.

Even if it were not strictly true that the king's authority over Americans arose, historically, from their consent, such consent was the only way to make British authority legitimate. It might be a lie to say that consent was the historical foundation of American allegiance to the king, but it would serve both American and British interests to say that he was "King of America, by virtue of a compact between us and the Kings of Great Britain." The British could maintain their empire because it would be perceived as legitimate in America, and the Americans could still enjoy its protection.

> The law of nature and the British constitution both confine allegiance to the person of the King; and found it upon the principal of protection. . . . The definition given it by the learned [jurist] Coke is this: "Legiance is the mutual bond of obligation between the King and his subjects, whereby subjects are called his liege subjects, because they are bound to obey and serve him; and he is called their liege lord, because he is bound to maintain and defend them."

Failure to secure American rights from the invasions of Parliament would dissolve the social compact. Yet if the king fulfilled his duty to protect the parts of the empire not only from external dangers but also from the invasions of the other members of the realm, including Parliament, then Americans would still be bound to him. Allegiance to the king, then, would become the bond of the empire.[36]

Seabury found Hamilton's view of the British constitution, as it might be, if the empire were to be legitimate, completely incomprehensible. It was one of those "ridiculous absurdities of American Whiggism," just another "piece of Whiggish nonsense."[37] In "every government, there must be a supreme absolute authority lodged somewhere." If the legislative power were divided within one state, there would be an *imperium in imperio* completely incompatible with effective government. Hamilton did not object to the necessity of establishing sovereign power, "for, otherwise, there could be no supremacy, or subordination, that is, no government at all." Yet it did not necessarily follow that all sovereignty had to be placed in Parliament, or for that matter, in any particular part of the British constitution. "Each branch" of the empire might "enjoy a distinct complete legislature, and still good government may be preserved, everywhere." To be sure, it would be impossible to maintain two supreme legislative authorities in one state, if by one state were meant one distinct community such as New York or England itself. Yet if the same state meant "a number of individual societies, united under a common head," or allegiance to a common king, then there was nothing absurd about multiple legislative authorities that were supreme with respect to the particular ends of their distinct communities.[38]

As Forrest McDonald observes, "Hamilton groped his way toward a workable concept of federalism, and came surprisingly close to finding one." He was not the only revolutionary to try. Others recognized that divided sovereignty was absurd, and a recipe for civil war in any government, but shared sovereignty was at least theoretically possible and might have saved both American liberty and the British Empire. Other American efforts to prove that Americans owed their loyalty to the Crown but not to Parliament failed because the king himself was part of Parliament. To the king in this capacity, Americans owed no loyalty. Still, the king wore many hats. Not only did he serve as a part of the colonial legislatures, through his veto and his governors, but he was also the "supreme executive magistrate" and the "supreme protector of the empire." Significantly, Hamilton chose to stress the strategic offices of the king. "For this purpose, he is the generalissimo, or first in military command; in him is vested the power of making war and peace, or raising armies, equipping fleets and directing all their motions. He it is that has defended us from our enemies, and to him alone," in his capacity as supreme protector of the empire, "we are obliged to render allegiance and submission."[39]

This was quite a sophisticated theory of the empire. Although it clearly anticipated theories of the British Commonwealth after World War II, it was not acceptable in its time. "For want of an idea," McDonald therefore observes, "an empire collapsed." McDonald might have added that from Hamilton's point of view and from that of all other American Whigs, it also deserved to collapse. The consent that they believed was necessary to make British authority legitimate stamped them and future generations with a passionate hatred of imperialism, that is, of government rooted in what Richard Kohn calls the militaristic principle of "force alone." Yet the problem of preserving the Union, not to mention almost inevitable American expansion, virtually dictated that America become not merely a republic but also a great empire. J. G. A. Pocock is therefore certainly right to say that for Hamilton the great question was, "Could America become a republic and an empire at the same time?" Yet Pocock does not explore Hamilton's revolutionary writings. His conclusion that Hamilton was opting for "dominion and expansion" and preferred "success over deservingness, *virtu* over virtue," is inconsistent with his revolutionary stress on consent. If his first political writings serve as any evidence, Hamilton's great moral-strategic problem was to combine the strength required for the Republic to endure with the consent necessary for it to deserve to endure.[40]

He clearly failed in that task in 1774 and 1775. Though quite sophisticated for its time, Hamilton's theory of the British Empire was seriously flawed in ways he himself slowly came to acknowledge. For example, he granted that Parliament had a right to regulate American trade by some earlier, mysterious form of consent from the colonies, but he did not explain how it could possess the right to enforce such regulations without some continuing, regular form of consent. Was the original consent of the earliest colonists to bind all Americans forever? Was change in the original compact impossible? Why trust Parliament with regulating trade when Americans were not represented in the British legislature?

Moreover, Hamilton asserted that Americans had made "liberal and generous" contributions, voluntarily, to the defense of the empire during the Seven Years War (French and Indian War). Parliament had displayed insufficient confidence in the "virtue, or fidelity" of the American colonies in time of war. Kind treatment from England, he protested, would suffice to secure American attachment to the empire through "the powerful bonds of self-interest."[41] Still, what if the parts of the empire did not cooperate voluntarily? Then it might be impossible for the empire and the king to fulfill their responsibility to supply protection to the whole and its parts. As the colonies within the British Empire had done, the American states during the Revolution were also bound by self-interest to wage the war against England. This common good ought therefore to have produced substantial public spirit in America's struggle against England, and in fact it did, for quite a while. Yet Hamilton soon discovered that the very jealousy of power that he and others invoked to justify the Revolution made it extremely difficult to produce cooperation in the struggle against England. When Hamilton traded his college gown for his soldier's sword, he began to wonder if the vigilance required to mobilize opposition to England in 1774 had become a vice that prevented responsible government in time of war.

3. Fit for War

Five years after his efforts to justify resistance to England, Hamilton found himself working at General Washington's field headquarters as a lieutenant colonel and one of the general's principal confidential aides. Hamilton was by then no longer a revolutionary firebrand, but an experienced veteran of many campaigns. He had done more than his share in his adopted country's service, but combat service was not his proper or future role. Though sometimes loathe to admit it, Hamilton discovered that his great talent was not for leading men in battle but for organization and administration, skills that were in short supply both in the army and in Congress throughout the early years of the war. By 1780, Hamilton had carried out most of the functions of a modern staff officer. He was also frequently responsible for communicating on Washington's behalf with the state governments and the Continental Congress. As a result, he was forced to pay as much attention to the political as to the military dimensions of the war. That necessity was the mother of his invention.

A letter the young colonel wrote from Washington's headquarters in September 1780 to James Duane, a friend who was serving in Congress, amounts to a military briefing on the necessity of constitutional and administrative reform to win the war. Duane apparently asked Hamilton for the briefing, so he replied with a passionate account of virtually all the measures he believed were necessary to "save us from ruin." Paradoxically, but also characteristically for Hamilton, the briefing combines a tough-minded sense of the sort of government that he believed Americans simply had to acquire to win the war with almost utopian expectations from Congress during the middle of it. Hamilton himself recognized this odd dimension of his thought, one representative of many of his later writings as well. He feared his remarks would be understood as the "reveries of a projector rather than the sober views of a politician." He knew they were too far ahead of the existing state of public opinion to be accepted in 1780. He therefore advised Duane to make "what use you please of them." If they could not be enacted immediately, Duane might push for them piece by piece, and they still might help to make a difference in the war effort.[1]

Edmund Cody Burnett exaggerated when he asserted that "it was a long way from 1780 to 1787, but it would seem to have been directly, perhaps chiefly, from this implantation by Hamilton, that the Federal Convention of 1787 actually grew." James Madison, James Duane, and James Varnum also submitted proposals for revising the Articles of Confederation in the last years of the war. Though necessary as catalysts, the arguments in Hamilton's briefing were hardly sufficient to sustain the movement for constitutional reform. They bore no fruit until other major issues, for example, faction in the states, commerce between them, and Shays's rebellion became part of the reform agenda. Still, the briefing was one of the first calls for a constitutional convention. It revealed most of the program of the nationalists in the early 1780s and of the Federalists in the 1790s. As Jack N. Rakove has observed, it was the most "innovative" proposal for constitutional and administrative reform produced during the war because it went far beyond piecemeal amendment of the Articles of Confederation. Perhaps no single proposal in the briefing was original to Hamilton, but it synthesized the available options into a comprehensive plan for winning the war, and just as important, for preserving the Union after it was won. It therefore serves as a yardstick of Hamilton's success as a statesman. Its far-reaching objectives virtually guaranteed that Hamilton would not achieve all of them at once. The wonder is that he eventually accomplished almost every one of them.[2]

The most distinctive feature of the briefing is Hamilton's understanding of the relation between arms and virtue, or effective instruments of state power and public-spiritedness in America. That most of Hamilton's program grew from his wartime experience is well known; that it was originally an effort to use the tools of the modern state to revive public spirit is not. Hamilton was a lifelong supporter of energetic government, but it is less well known that he believed energy could have a decisive impact on public spirit. The conventional view of nationalists like Hamilton is that the bitter lessons of the war led them to reject public-spiritedness in favor of self-interest as a foundation of government. As Charles Royster notes, the early years of the war, and 1775 especially, witnessed a remarkable enthusiasm for the cause, or *rage militaire.* Within a few years, however, profiteering in Congress, hoarding among civilians, desertions from the army, speculation among monied men, graft among military contractors, and a host of other common wartime vices made many observers doubt that Americans had the virtue required of republican citizens. Henceforward, then, it is often argued, the nationalists decided to rely on a strong state (rather than on voluntary sacrifice for the cause) to supply the arms and the wealth required for American independence. As Lawrence Delbert Cress observes about the military policy of the nationalists, "Self-interest replaced public virtue in the lexicon of military motivation, and centralization and professionalism were embraced by men vested with responsibility for national security." As Sue Davis concludes about Hamilton's economic policy, "Hamilton believed that the vast majority of the people operated purely on the basis of self-interest. Thus, it would be useless to appeal to the citizenry's sense of civic virtue to act in the interest of the public good; instead, people could be manipulated in a way that could be good for the country while at the same time they could continue to pursue their private interests."[3]

These important half-truths do not come to terms fully with the character of Hamilton's briefing. For Hamilton, public-spiritedness was not merely a moral concept but a real and palpable passion that could be seen in the behavior of soldiers, citizens, and investors. As Clinton Rossiter has observed, Hamilton had a "refreshingly modern grasp of the political significance of 'confidence'" in national morale. As a result, he substantially anticipated Carl von Clausewitz's famous "trinity of war" based on a responsible government, an effective military instrument, and high national morale.[4] Hamilton's briefing was primarily an effort to address this third element, morale. Especially when considered in light of his other major wartime writings, his *Continentalist* essays, his *Unsubmitted Resolution Calling for a Convention to Amend the Articles of Confederation*, his *Report on a Military Peace Establishment*, and his letters to Robert Morris, the briefing supplies a coherent plan for reviving "the hopes of the people" and giving a "new direction to their passions."[5]

Contemporary students of war and international relations commonly understand state power as the product of tangible capabilities and the intangible will to use them. They also recognize that the tangible and intangible dimensions of modern war are mutually dependent. As John Nef has observed, "If the will to war is weak, this is partly for lack of adequate means. If the means are inadequate to produce an annihilating struggle, this is partly because the will is weak."[6] The dramatic and sad story of war in the last 200 years reveals the almost infinite increase in both tangible capabilities and intangible will for war made possible by the rise of the modern nation-state. As the wars of the French Revolution spread over Europe, Hamilton eventually recoiled in horror at this revolution in war. In 1780, however, when his country's independence was at stake, he did his best to make it possible in America.

No one knows clearly why human beings are sometimes willing to risk their lives, homes, families, and wealth in war. This may perhaps explain why Clausewitz treated morale as an irrational element of his trinity.[7] Today we would call it the psychological element, the realm of confidence, stubbornness, and will. Given the proper instruments of governing, Hamilton believed responsible statesmen could harness not only the arms and wealth but also the spirit, or virtue, of the American people for victory. Effective instruments of governance, instead of producing a nation in arms, which was unnecessary at the time and which Hamilton had not yet envisioned, could generate confident citizens, soldiers, and investors. Their faith in their government, discipline in combat, and stake in the Confederation's finances would sustain their will to fight for their independence and liberties.

In this intangible respect at least, the conventional view of Hamilton's attitude toward public-spiritedness distorts the ends and means of his statesmanship. Hamilton took public spirit seriously, not because he was a utopian but because it was unrealistic to hope to win the war without mobilizing the passions of the people. Constitutional and administrative reforms were emphatically not alternatives to public-spiritedness, in his view, but were important means of generating and sustaining it. If mere devotion to the cause was not enough to make citizens, soldiers, and investors contribute to the war, then perhaps their spirit might be fortified (rather than replaced) by a confidence-inspiring national government. In seeking to build public spirit on public confidence (and on private interest, too), Hamilton began to explore the modern rather than the classical foundations of the highly controversial form of civic virtue that we call nationalism.

The fundamental premise of Hamilton's briefing was that soldiers, citizens, and investors had lost confidence in the ability of Congress to prosecute the war. As he explained to Duane, the states' "jealousy of all power not in their own hands," Congress' "diffidence" in exercising its own powers, and its lack of constitutional means to call on the resources of the nation had made the government seem "timid and indecisive" in its resolutions. In turn, the perception of congressional weakness had ruined Congress' "credit and influence with the army," especially. The root of the problem was the very jealousy Hamilton had invoked earlier in order to mobilize resistance to England. In the *Continentalist* essays of 1783, for example, he blamed almost all of Congress' difficulties on the "extreme jealousy of power" that is "attendant on all popular revolutions, and has seldom been without its evils." He then began to develop his own ethic of responsible government as a way to moderate this revolutionary passion. "History," he observed, "is full of examples where in contests for liberty, a jealousy of power has either defeated the attempts to preserve or recover it in the first instances, or has afterward subverted it by clogging the government with too great cautions for its felicity, or by leaving too wide a door for sedition and popular licentiousness." An enlightened partisan of "durable liberty" therefore had to recognize that "no less regard must be paid to giving the magistrate a proper degree of authority, than to guarding against encroachments upon the rights of the community."[8]

One might object that Congress had actually done as well as any new government possibly could under the circumstances. It had begun the war with almost none of the instruments of a modern state. Although Congress lacked the revenue, coercive powers, and undisputed sovereignty to make its resolutions stick, Americans had not yet lost the war. A year after he wrote his briefing, Hamilton admitted this objection was at least partly true. "Congress has been responsible for the administration of affairs, without the means of fulfilling that responsibility." But this objection was also irrelevant. What mattered were perceptions. The colonel observed to Duane that there are

> epochs in human affairs, when *novelty* even is useful. If a general opinion prevails that the old way is bad, whether true or false, and this obstructs or relaxes the operation of the public service, change is necessary if it be for the sake of change. This is exactly the case now. 'Tis a universal sentiment that our present system is a bad one, and that things cannot go right on this account.

By public service, Hamilton meant the willingness to serve the public.

> Men are governed by opinion; this opinion is as much influenced by appearances as realities; if a government appears to be confident of its own powers, it is the surest way to inspire confidence in others; if it is diffident, it may be certain, there will be still greater diffidence in others, and that its authority will not only be distrusted, controverted, but contemned.

If Congress hoped to acquire and maintain the support of the people, the army, and investors, it had no choice but to "inspire . . . confidence" by adopting the measures Hamilton advocated, or others equivalent to them. Then, he asserted, there would be a "new spring to our affairs; government would recover its respectability and individuals would renounce their diffidence."[9]

Though Hamilton based his argument on perceptions, they rested on solid financial and military realities. At the time of the briefing, the army was starving again. Hamilton feared another winter like the one he had experienced at Valley Forge, where soldiers died of disease, hunger, and cold at a rate of over 400 a month. All told, as many as 2,500 soldiers, or about one-fourth of Washington's command, may have perished in the six months the army spent in the camp. Congress had left the post of quartermaster general vacant during the three coldest months of the army's ordeal. Not surprisingly, then, the soldiers tended to blame Congress for their accumulated sufferings. Hamilton suggested the soldiers might become "a mob, rather than an army." They were without "clothing, without pay, without provision, without morals, without discipline." The order of terms in this observation is important. Hamilton progressed from the necessities to the virtues and implied that the latter were succumbing to the former. "We begin to hate our country for its neglect of us," he told the congressman. Just as significantly, he warned Duane, "the country begins to hate us for our oppressions of them. Congress has long since been jealous of us; we have lost all confidence in them, and give the worst construction to all they do. Held together by the slenderest of ties we are ripening for a dissolution." By the end of 1780, many of the soldiers' three-year enlistments would expire. Many wished to go home, but the disintegration of the army was not the worst scenario in Hamilton's mind. The "*worst* of evils," Hamilton explained to his best wartime friend, Col. John Laurens, seemed to be "*a loss of our virtue.*" Bitterly, he declared, "I hate Congress—I hate the army—I hate the world—I hate myself." All that Hamilton may have meant by virtue is unclear, but this much is certain: he feared that Americans were losing the will to fight. As a result, he was beginning to lose his respect not only for Congress but also for the army, and even for himself.[10]

Hamilton had not always spoken thus. As Charles Royster has observed, most Americans began the war with strong faith in the "innate courage" of free citizens, and Hamilton was typical in that regard. When he observed that "contests for liberty have ever been found the most bloody, implacable and obstinate" before the Revolution began, he knew he was not indulging in a romantic vision. The most sober of political realists, Machiavelli himself, had been perhaps the first to recognize that the stake republican citizens have in their liberties often makes them the most stubborn soldiers. In addition to this intangible American advantage, Hamilton recognized that the tangible capabilities upon which Americans might draw were substantially greater than those of England. "The disciplined troops Great Britain could send against us are but few. Our superiority in number would overbalance our inferiority in discipline. It would be a hard, if not an impracticable task to subjugate us by force." "Discipline and military skill" were certainly on the side of the British, but "superior numbers, joined to natural intrepidity, and that animation, which is inspired by a desire of freedom, and a love of one's country, may very well overbalance those advantages."

Hamilton predicted that the British would be unable to send more than 15,000 troops to America. Though this was an underestimate, the "established rule" for determining the potential military manpower of a nation in his time was to calculate one-fifth of its population. With a total of 3 million men in the colonies, Americans had a potential armed force of 600,000. Even assuming Americans were able to raise only 500,000, Hamilton simply could not imagine that their combined tangible and intangible capabilities could fail to produce a military victory. Experience soon taught him that he had overestimated his country's actual strength, however. The advantages of spirit and numbers do not count for much unless a nation has the kind of government that can draw on them and employ them with effect. Indeed, if it lacks such a government, it may not even be able to sustain its spirit. As Hamilton later observed in the *Continentalist,* Great Britain had managed to keep the odds at least even with "little more than fourteen thousand effective men." Nothing but a "GENERAL DISAFFECTION of the PEOPLE, or MISMANAGEMENT in their RULERS" could account for the inability of the Confederation to win the war. Hamilton dared not admit the former alternative, at least not in public, and therefore focused on the mismanagement of the rulers as the cause of declining public spirit.[11]

Of course, not all news about the war was bad, but despite the great American victory at Saratoga and the signing of commercial and defense treaties with France in 1778, French military and economic aid was not forthcoming in large measure in 1780. In common with many others, Hamilton also believed it was both dangerous and dishonorable to depend too much on France or any other foreign power. Worse, the continental currency had collapsed because, as Jack Rakove ironically observes, Americans had a system of representation without taxation. Specie was usually scarce in the colonies before the Revolution, so the colonial legislatures had traditionally financed wars through what E. J. Ferguson first dubbed the system of "currency finance." The colonial assemblies issued notes in exchange for wartime purchases and then accepted them in payment for taxes in order to decrease their circulation and prevent inflation. So long as England assumed the primary responsibility of paying for colonial defense, this system seems to have worked. During the Revolution, however, Congress and the state legislatures began to print large amounts of money, but Congress lacked the means and the states often lacked the will to tax it out of circulation. The result was enormous inflation. By spring 1779 continental bills had depreciated to 5 percent of their original value. By March 1780 Congress was obliged to devalue the currency to a ratio of 40:1 in specie, or 2.5 percent of its original value. This amounted to a de facto repudiation of $200 million of paper money and bills of credit. In 1779 and 1780 the collapse of the currency led to a virtual barter economy in some portions of the country, to price controls, and to largely unfulfilled requisitions for the states to supply the army directly, with food and war materials, instead of currency. By October 1780, a month after Hamilton wrote his briefing, the ratio of paper to specie was 77.5:1; the continental currency had become essentially worthless.[12]

As James Ferguson somewhat immodestly suggests, "one of the most important sources of federal income" during the war was "almost unknown to history" until he began to explore it. Approximately half the cost of supporting the army was paid for by impressment, that is, by confiscating supplies from citizens and issuing certificates promising to pay them later. At first the certificates were handwritten; later, as impressment became common practice, federal officers had printed bills upon which to issue them. Once inflation rose significantly in 1779, almost all military operations were supported primarily through these certificates. According to Timothy Pickering, the quartermaster general in 1781, the army issued certificates for everything from purchases of boots, rations, and horses for the troops to meals and drinks for officers in taverns. No one could object because the army had the guns. It is impossible to be sure how many certificates were issued, but $93 million were in circulation before the siege of Yorktown, excluding certificates issued in the Carolinas and Georgia, which were principal theaters of the last years of the war. The certificates may well have equaled the entire value of continental currency issued during the war. Since they were almost worthless for purposes of trade, impressment differed little in effect from theft. Though many citizens exhibited remarkable patience, their morale was low, particularly among farmers, who felt the injustice of impressment perhaps most. In 1780, Ferguson observes, "Troops marching in Virginia seldom saw a wagon which had not been stripped of its wheels and gear." For fear of being robbed to support the army, citizens hoarded any property of military use.[13]

In the face of this mixed crisis in revolutionary principle, finance, and national morale, Hamilton argued for assuming national responsibility to direct all aspects of the war effort. He wrote his briefing six months before the Articles of Confederation were accepted by all the states in February 1781.

He acknowledged that the pre-Confederation Congress never had "any definite power granted them" and from that perspective, "of course could exercise none." It lacked the legitimacy that arises from a formal delegation of powers and "could do nothing more than recommend." After years of frustration, however, Hamilton found this common explanation for delay and stagnation inexcusable. The same principle that justified the first Congress in asserting the prerogative to act without legal authority at the beginning of the war also justified subsequent Congresses in asserting implied powers to direct it effectively. "The manner in which Congress was appointed," in an extraconstitutional emergency when American liberty was at stake, "and the public good required" that Congress should have done what the Romans did when they appointed a dictator: Congress should have considered itself "vested with full power *to preserve the republic from harm.*"

Congress had already acted according to this principle by declaring independence, forming an army and a navy, establishing diplomatic relations and alliances, and so on. These "implications of complete sovereignty were never disputed" and should therefore have served as the "standard of the whole conduct of the Administration." Until the Articles of Confederation were drafted and accepted, Congress' powers were "discretionary powers, limited only by the object for which they were given . . . in the present case, the independence and freedom of America." As Rakove demonstrates, Congress had actually retreated from the assertions of national sovereignty that had marked its policies at the beginning of the war. By 1780 it allowed much responsibility for the war, especially finance and military recruiting, to devolve again upon the states. Thus Hamilton believed it had made so "many concessions to the states" that it was barely left with the "shadow of power." It thereby became accustomed to the vice of "doing right by halves, and spoiling a good intention in the execution." Since Congress had already acted on the assumption that it possessed complete sovereignty to sustain and direct the war, Hamilton believed there was no legitimate reason for it not to reassert that authority. Indeed, he suggested it was disgraceful that Congress had abdicated its responsibility to the states, which were even less capable of exercising it than Congress.[14]

Hamilton was well aware that asserting complete control of the war might have been "thought too bold by the generality of Congress" to be practical at this time. Moreover, although the Articles of Confederation formalized some of the necessary war powers, he believed the Articles themselves were half measures that did not rise to the necessities implied in declaring independence. They might even provide additional excuses for congressmen to fail to take responsibility. Hence, he argued that nothing was more important than a constitutional convention with plenipotentiary authority to make a formal grant to Congress of "complete sovereignty in all that relates to war, peace, trade, finance, and the management of foreign affairs." It was essential to make the reassertion of congressional responsibility for the war unambiguously legitimate by constitutionalizing it.[15]

Even before the Articles had been accepted by all the states, Hamilton did not believe they would generate sufficient congressional power to restore public confidence. The states had too much control over the vital powers of the purse and the sword. Like Machiavelli, his nearest political kinsman in this regard, Hamilton deplored depending on the uncertain arms and virtue of others, especially the states. The "source of all our military misfortunes," he observed, was the "fluctuating state of our army." Nothing contributed to the ebb and flow of recruiting and retention more than dependence upon the states for supplies, revenue, and troops. This was "too precarious a dependence because the states," particularly those situated in a calm theater of the war, "will never be sufficiently impressed by our necessities." Experience revealed that "each will make its own ease a primary object, the supply of the army a secondary one." The colonel spoke for the whole army when he observed that "we feel the insufficiency of this plan, and have reason to dread under it a ruinous extremity of want."

Hamilton described the Articles as "neither fit for war nor peace." They could not generate sufficient revenue or manpower to sustain the army in the field, and perhaps worse, they invited conflict between the states and Congress that might even issue in civil war (to enforce congressional requisitions, for example). "The confederation gives the states too much influence in the affairs of the army; they should have nothing to do with it. The entire formation and disposal of our forces ought to belong to Congress." Thinking as much of the future as of the present, he added that the army is "an essential cement of the union; and it ought to be the policy of Congress to destroy all ideas of state attachments in the army and make it look wholly up to them. For this purpose all appointments, promotions, and provisions whatsoever ought to be made by them." The same was true of revenue powers, which Hamilton believed had been given "too entirely to the state legislatures . . . , for without certain revenues, a government can have no power; that power, which holds the purse strings absolutely, must rule."[16]

In anticipation of Whig fears that vesting Congress with full control of the military and an independent source of revenue would be "dangerous to liberty," Hamilton made a largely ignored but significant exception for "internal police, which relates to the rights to property and life among individuals and to raising money by internal taxes. It is necessary, that every thing, belonging to this, should be regulated by the state legislatures." Complete sovereignty therefore did not mean unlimited power but complete control in both the states and the national government over the resources required to accomplish their delegated ends. Besides, Hamilton insisted, there was a "wide difference" between a confederation and an "empire under one simple form of government." In the latter case, "the danger is that the sovereign will have too much power to oppress the parts of which it is composed." In a confederation, however, the danger was "exactly the reverse. It is that the common sovereign will not have sufficient power to unite the different members together, and direct the common forces to the interest and happiness of the whole." Hamilton then discussed the weaknesses of earlier confederations in ancient Greece and modern Europe in detail. In each case, their centrifugal tendencies were stronger than their centripetal ones. Responsible statesmanship was a matter of calculating probable, not merely possible, risks. If historical practice was any evidence, there was a far "greater risk" of a "weak and disunited government than one which will be able to usurp the rights of the people."[17]

Even complete sovereignty would not be sufficient to produce victory, however. The wartime government had no separation of powers, and this fact had much strategic importance. Congress ran every aspect of the war, but it was "properly a deliberative corps and it forgets itself when it tries to play the executive." Hamilton both exalted and criticized Congress when he said this. It was responsible to deliberate upon policy; this was perhaps the highest task of government. But Congress was incapable of executing policy against an enemy who might oppose its resolutions. Its members did not serve long enough to learn how to run a nation at war. As Rakove suggests, frequent rotation made it extremely difficult for anyone to assume responsibility for the overall conduct of any part of the war effort, so much so that Congress seemed to begin every task but finish none. Winning the war required instituting a separation of powers that might "blend the advantages of monarchy and a republic in our constitution."[18]

Hamilton was not talking about instituting a monarchy, and certainly not a hereditary one. Instead, he was discussing the advantages enjoyed by monarchies and republics in time of war. According to Montesquieu, combining the strategic advantages of large monarchies (unity and numbers) with the political advantages of small republics (liberty and spirit) is the fundamental objective of all republican federations. Hamilton was therefore talking about how to make federal theory work in practice. The problem with federal theory during the Revolution is that it never explained how federations can have the advantages of monarchy, which literally means the rule of one, without one person actually governing with respect to those matters where one executes policy best.

Contrary to conventional Whig views that power is necessarily corrupting, Hamilton believed that dividing executive power undermines energy and responsibility. Conversely, concentrating executive powers in individuals can actually encourage greater responsibility in them. The boards of war, finance, and so on established by Congress were therefore signs of a "bad plan. A single man in each department would be greatly preferable. It would give us a chance of more knowledge, more activity, more responsibility, and of course more zeal and attention." In contrast, boards "partake of a part of the inconveniences of larger assemblies," chiefly because of their negative impact on ambition. "Men of the first pretensions," that is, those who wish to be acknowledged as first among men, "will not so readily engage in them, because they will be less conspicuous, of less importance, have less opportunity of distinguishing themselves." Though some observers doubted that single men would be willing to undertake such offices, Hamilton stressed that concentrating executive powers in individuals was perhaps the only way to "excite the ambition of candidates." Then, perhaps, the ambitious love of honor, which Montesquieu treated as the animating principle of monarchies, would become the source of energy in the executive, the office that, somewhat paradoxically, Hamilton relied on most to harness the spirit of American republicans.[19]

Though his argument led logically to a unitary executive, an unexpected turn in the briefing is that Hamilton actually proposed several executives for war, finance, marine, and so on. Each would be appointed by and therefore dependent upon Congress. It is unclear why Hamilton advocated such a weak executive. He did "fear a little vanity" had blocked the way of establishing executive power, as though it would "lessen the importance of Congress and leave them nothing to do." Perhaps, then, plural, dependent executives were the ultimate goal he believed he could expect from a Congress determined to defend its authority and fearful of executive power. Nevertheless, he insisted that establishing executive departments would not strip Congress of any essential dignity. "They would have precisely the same rights and powers as heretofore, happily disencumbered of detail. They would have to inspect the conduct of their ministers, deliberate upon their plans, originate others for the public." Thus Hamilton hoped to build an effective division of labor into the government. Indeed, perhaps more than any other Founder, he looked at the separation of powers as a device that could serve multiple ends. For Hamilton especially, the separation of powers was not merely a means to secure liberty by balancing power within government. It was also a mechanism for making government more efficient by concentrating different kinds of powers in different departments, according to their capacities to use those powers well. The tension between these goals helps to explain his later quarrels with his adversaries in the 1790s over the proper role of the executive.[20]

Because separating legislative and executive powers might make the government more efficient, Hamilton believed it could also promote public confidence. After Robert Morris was appointed superintendent of finance in April 1781, Hamilton wrote to him that "an administration by single men" was the "only resource we have to extricate ourselves from the distresses, which threaten the subversion of our cause. . . . It is palpable that the people have lost all confidence in our public councils." Moreover, friends in Europe shared the "same disposition." Neither the people at home nor allies abroad would give "half the succors to this country while Congress holds the reins of administration" as they would if the administration were "entrusted to individuals of established reputation and conspicuous for probity, abilities, and fortune." As Ferguson has observed, such individuals would lend their names to their departments, which would then acquire greater reputation with the public because they would be built on the private reputations of their executives. In turn, greater faith in these institutions would promote greater willingness among individuals to take risks on their country's behalf, not the least of which was accepting the continental currency.[21]

Primarily, the necessity of military impressment explains why Hamilton believed many citizens had begun to hate the army and to withhold their support from it. Its logistical necessities were in grave tension with the moral goal of the Revolution, which was to secure American rights, including rights to property. This fundamental tension also explains Hamilton's sense of urgency about reestablishing credit. If Congress meant to deserve victory, it had to find a way to finance the war without obliging the army to steal. "'Tis by introducing order into our finances—by restoring public credit—not by gaining battles that we are to attain our object," Hamilton wrote to Robert Morris. "'Tis by putting ourselves in the position to continue the war, not by temporary, violent and unnatural efforts to bring it to a decisive issue, that we shall in reality bring it to a speedy and successful one.'"[22] If Morris could revitalize the credit of the Confederation, he could also contribute mightily toward resurrecting declining morale. Not only monied men on the lookout for profit, but ordinary citizens fearful of impressment would be more likely to respect the army and Congress, which could then count on their continuing support.

Hamilton informed Duane that fiscal solvency required a foreign loan, new taxes, and most important, a bank founded on public and private credit. He hoped that Congress would be vested with authority to sell lands in the West. Yet quarrels over those lands among the states made them an unlikely source of revenue for the near and probable future. For the loan, which he hoped would supply the specie to back American bank notes, Hamilton suggested that Americans play France against England, hinting at a possible peace with England if France did not supply aid immediately. He also called for a land tax, a poll tax, and an impost, but left collection to state-appointed officers, a mistake he would not make again. Two years later, he insisted that federal collection was both the only reliable way of collecting such revenue and highly salutary for the future of the Union. "The reason of allowing Congress to appoint its own officers of the customs, collectors of taxes, and military officers of every rank, is to create in the interior of each state a mass of influence in favor of the Federal Government." To many observers, this approach no doubt appeared to be a vulgar endorsement of the court policies of patronage and influence that they (and Hamilton) had objected to in 1775. Hamilton believed the circumstances were different, however. If the "great danger" was a lack of power to preserve the Union, not the Union becoming "formidable to the general liberty," nothing was more important than consolidating its hold on the passions and interests of Americans.

> A mere regard to the interests of the confederacy will never be a principle sufficiently active to curb the ambition and intrigues of different members. . . . The application of force is always disagreeable, the issue uncertain. It will be best to obviate the necessity of [civil war to preserve the Union] by interesting such a number of individuals in each state in support of the Federal Government, as will be counterpoised to the ambition of others; and will make it difficult for them to unite the people in opposition to the just and necessary measures of the union.

Hamilton therefore tended to regard this influence as a source of civic health.[23]

Hamilton's discussion in the briefing of banking and credit reveals the essence of his strategy, which was to create confidence-inspiring illusions. Credit is not merely an economic concept. It comes from the Latin *credere*, to believe. Credit is about having faith in the promises of others, including those of governments. It is therefore fundamentally a matter of honor.

Governments lose the faith of their people not only when they break their trust, which is presumably what justified the revolution against England, but also when they are so weak that they cannot inspire confidence. The latter concern animated Hamilton's call for a bank and a new constitution. When the people trust their government, they give it credit not merely by lending money but also by paying taxes, obeying laws, serving in the military, and accepting its currency. By seeking to reestablish credit, broadly understood, Hamilton was therefore also seeking to produce the kind of citizens required to win the war.

Hamilton declared that it was the business of the government to inspire "confidence by adopting the measures I have recommended." Under a "good plan of executive administration" capable of putting his proposals in a "train of vigorous execution," he told Morris that he was bound to raise national morale. "All we have to fear," Hamilton observed, was quite close to what Franklin Roosevelt later called fear itself. Morris had to fear only "a general disgust and alarm," which could lead the army to disband or the people to clamor "for peace on any terms." If Morris proposed and Congress adopted a national bank offering investors a significant return for their risk, then Hamilton believed public and private credit could be united and multiplied. In a crisis, Congress might borrow from the bank to help pay for the war, as the British did from the Bank of England and as all successful modern republics had done since Renaissance Venice. Nonetheless, the fundamental purpose of the bank was not to fund the war, at least not directly. Especially if the bank's notes were both financed by and lent to the leading monied men in the nation, the notes would supply a substitute for money, which could be traded and used to spur industry. By supplying a trustworthy medium of exchange, the notes could resurrect public confidence, help investors to produce the material goods necessary for a war economy, and generate profits that Congress could tax to fund the war and the Confederation's enormous debts.[24]

The dependence of public spirit on effective finance was virtually unknown to Americans of Hamilton's time, and most contemporary scholars of the Founding era pay little attention to it. Yet Hamilton was not the only innovative statesman of his time to reflect on how a finance minister might influence the morale of his people. Jacques Necker, the minister of finance in France during the war and something of a model for Hamilton as well, observed that such a minister must

above all, by active and continual anxiety, excite confidence, that precious sentiment which unites the future to the present . . . and lays the foun-

dation of the happiness of the people. Then everyone will look on the contributions which are demanded of him, as a just assistance afforded to
the exigencies of the state, and as the price of the good order which sur-
rounds him, and the security which he enjoys.

By such means, the minister may recall the "ideas of justice and patriotism"
among the people. If they lose their confidence, however, "private interest
will be everywhere opposed to the public welfare." A "skillful administration," he observed, has the "effect of putting in action those it persuades, of
strengthening the moral ideas, of rousing the imagination, and of joining
together the opinions and sentiments of men by the confidence it produces."
It therefore could have the "greatest influence over the social virtues and
morals." Necker thus argued that it is the "fault of the administration," and
especially its finance minister, "if these natural dispositions, so adapted to
PATRIOTISM" are not produced by and attached to the government.[25]

The fundamental cause of Congress' difficulties in sustaining confidence
was the lack of specie; there was not enough to back its paper. The specie
supply would not increase merely through Congress' establishing a bank.
Yet if the notes were backed by a foreign loan, securities on land, gifts of
plate and silver from citizens, specie subscriptions from private investors,
and denominated in the old forms of pounds and shillings rather than
worthless dollars, the people might believe the bank's assets were as available as specie in the Bank of England. The "illusion" of solidity would then
produce confidence in the bank notes. In time, perhaps, the credit bubble
would burst, especially if someone without Hamilton's administrative skills
managed it, but if it lasted long enough to fund the war, Americans would
be independent. This alone would justify the risk. Yet Hamilton understood
that the "real wealth" of a nation is not its specie but its "labor and commodities." If investor confidence could last beyond the end of the war, re-
suscitated credit could even promote a new kind of economy of industrious
increase, which John Nef and many other scholars have recognized as the
most important foundation of modern military power.[26]

In a bow to radical Whig prejudice, Hamilton admitted that a bank and
prosperity might produce "insolence, an inordinate ambition, a vicious
luxury, licentiousness of morals, and all those vices" that Americans commonly believed served to "corrupt government, enslave the people, and
precipitate the ruin of a nation." Still, Hamilton saw no practical alternative. "No wise statesman will reject the good from an apprehension of the
ill. The truth is in human affairs, there is no good, pure and unmixed; every
advantage has two sides, and wisdom consists in availing ourselves of the

good, and guarding as much as possible against the bad." The great good promised by the bank was generally unavailable to the republics of antiquity: a combination of public strength and private security. David Hume had been the first to notice this modern phenomenon in his writings on commerce, in which he insisted that the ancients had no choice but to sacrifice private rights and happiness to the survival of their cities in time of war. Hamilton extended Hume's argument to banks:

> The tendency of a national bank is to increase public and private credit. The former gives power to the state for the protection of its rights and interests; the latter facilitates and extends the operations of commerce among individuals. Industry is increased, commodities are multiplied, agriculture and manufactures flourish, and herein consist the wealth and prosperity of the state.

England was indebted for her many "successful wars essentially to that vast fabric of credit" raised on the basis of a bank. "Tis by this alone," Hamilton believed, "she now menaces our independence." The choice, it seems, was between losing the war (while continuing to steal from citizens) or establishing credit, based on a bank, with all the ills a prosperous, credit-based economy might produce.[27]

Promoting confidence was also important in Hamilton's arguments for regulating trade. He regarded trade, like credit, as a source of both individual prosperity and national strength. He hoped a constitutional convention would vest Congress with power to regulate trade, but to explain why, he had to attack the "cant phrase" that "TRADE MUST REGULATE ITSELF." If the assertion meant that trade had its "fundamental laws" and that "any violent attempts in opposition to these would commonly miscarry," Hamilton had no objection to the maxim, but he feared a doctrinaire application of it far beyond the intentions of those, like David Hume, who were among the first to develop it. On the one hand, the "avarice of individuals may frequently find its account in pursuing channels of traffic prejudicial to" the public interest; on the other hand, there might well be numerous sorts of trade of great benefit to the public that might not arise without substantial confidence in a profit on a risky investment. Virtually every industry relevant to war (mining coal and iron, forging cannon and other weapons) fell under the latter category. "Though accompanied with great difficulties in the commencement," such industries would still "amply reward" the nation for "the trouble and expense of bringing them to perfection" through modest bounties and tariffs.[28]

Hamilton's chief goal, however, was for Congress to professionalize the army. This too was a matter of confidence, but quite a special kind. In an effort to convince the Pennsylvania Executive Council to call out the militia to suppress some mutineers in 1783, Hamilton made some intriguing remarks on courage:

> Nothing can be more contemptible than a body of men used to be commanded and to obey when deprived of the example and direction of their officers. They are infinitely less to be dreaded than an equal number of men who have never been broken to command, nor exchanged their natural courage for the artificial kind which is the effect of discipline and habit. Soldiers transfer their confidence from themselves to their officers, face danger by force of example, the dread of punishment, and the sense of necessity. Take away these inducements and leave them to themselves, they are no longer resolute 'till they are opposed.

Though he believed the natural courage of the militia would be superior to the passions of mutineers, Hamilton implied that the "artificial" courage of professional soldiers would normally be superior to that of ordinary citizens in the militia. The professionals had the advantage of experience, or habituation to the confusion and danger of war. Professional soldiers acquire confidence in the use of arms and in working together in large groups through repetition of essentially mindless tasks. Though free-spirited members of the militia would normally balk at such tedium, professional officers would compel their troops to practice such tasks until they were second nature and the men had acquired artificial courage. Hamilton also implied that professional soldiers borrowed their courage from their officers. If so, the better trained the officers, the more courageous the soldiers would become. The natural courage of free citizens was a product of enthusiasm, which waxed and waned, according to the fortunes of war; but the confidence of professionals, who acted bravely in combat because they had performed the same tasks a thousand times before in drill, was much more reliable.[29]

The first step in producing such a professional army, Hamilton explained to Duane, was to replace the customary method of gaining recruits through bounties for short-term service with a draft for three years. This would not only increase the numbers of the army but also give veterans time to train recruits to be confident soldiers. The second step was to establish a pension plan of half-pay for life for the officer corps, a proposal that was eventually adopted by Congress. Some members feared pensions would corrupt the army by making it dependent on Congress rather than on the states. Corruption, however, must to some extent be in the eye of the beholder. Hamilton had little but contempt for such doctrinaire reasoning in the middle of a war for the nation's existence. The pensions would secure the "attachment of the army to Congress. . . . We should then have discipline, an army in reality, as well as in name." Without such attachment, Hamilton was well aware that the army would be ineffective in the field and dangerous to the liberties of the American people. "Already," he warned Duane, "some of the lines of the army would obey their states in opposition to Congress notwithstanding the pains we have taken to preserve the unity of the army." If Congress meant to avoid a civil war, it had no choice but to assert complete control over the army.[30]

Though Hamilton stressed developing professional confidence, enthusiasm for liberty remained an important element in his wartime discussions of morale. Thus, for example, he hoped to enlist slaves in the South and to promise them their freedom with their muskets. To John Jay in Congress in 1779, he had written that the promise of freedom would "secure their fidelity, animate their courage," and have a "good influence" on those who remained in bondage by "opening the door to emancipation." Their habits of obedience coupled with their new spirit of liberty might make them the most disciplined and courageous soldiers America could produce. As the South became the primary theater of the war in the last years of the Revolution, such soldiers were at a premium because there were extremely few whites who could be pressed into service. Yet Hamilton observed that the offer of emancipation followed from both "the dictates of humanity and true policy." It had "no small weight" to Hamilton that employing this "unfortunate class of men" might open the door to freedom for all. He may therefore have disguised humanity as good policy. Speaking soberly, or rather in a manner calculated to inspire terror in the hearts of all slave owners, he argued that if the southerners did not emancipate and arm their slaves, the "enemy probably" would. The "best way to counteract the temptations they hold," he suggested, would "be to offer them ourselves."[31] Hamilton's plan had almost no support from the South, however, and went nowhere in Congress.

The difficulties that Hamilton and other nationalists faced in generating support for these fiscal and military reforms form the background for his most problematic activity as a revolutionary nationalist: his ambiguous role in the conspiracy between some members of Congress and some officers in Washington's camp at Newburgh in the first months of 1783. The conspiracy makes sense only in relation to several important developments subsequent to Hamilton's briefing for Duane. After the siege of Yorktown in 1781, Hamilton left the army for good and began to serve in Congress. By then, nation-minded men like Robert Morris were in the ascendant. Hamilton joined them because they were thinking at least as much about the future of the Confederation as about winning the war. To cement the Union as much as possible, Morris planned to fund the Confederation's enormous war debts, which would unite the nation's creditors in its support. To accomplish these goals, Morris and his supporters proposed a new system of national finance, including an impost and a land tax. These fundamental changes in the revenue powers of the Confederation required the approval of all the states. The conspiracy occurred in the last months of the war, when a peace treaty with England was expected any day. By late 1782, twelve of thirteen states had agreed to a 5 percent impost. Yet if peace were declared, financial reform would lose its urgency, and years of hard work might amount to nothing. The Morrisites began to grow desperate at the end of 1782 when the Rhode Island delegation in Congress began to oppose the impost. Perhaps because Rhode Island stood to lose significant revenue from the impost, or perhaps because its leaders seriously feared it would threaten the liberty of their people, or both, the Rhode Island legislature also voted unanimously against the impost; and Virginia soon followed by repealing it in December 1782.[32] For those men who believed effective political power was based on the power of the purse, such extreme jealousy made it unlikely that the Union, deprived of an independent source of revenue, would endure beyond the end of the war.

Discontent in the army nonetheless seemed to offer the Morrisites one last opportunity to achieve their objectives. A deputation from Washington's camp consisting of Maj. Gen. Alexander McDougall, Col. John Brooks, and Col. Mathias Ogden arrived in Congress on 29 December 1782 and warned of "fatal effects" if Congress failed to do "justice" to the army's demands for back pay. They also hoped to have their promised pensions converted to a lump-sum payment to help them adjust to civilian life. In private, Robert Morris told the delegation in the first weeks of January 1783 that he could not advance the army's pay unless it cooperated with the creditors on behalf of his financial program. He thus sought to combine the army and the creditors into a powerful coalition, with the dual objective of increasing pressure on Congress to push for his financial plan and of eliciting support from the state governments. Together with Hamilton, he deliberately manufactured a crisis; not a mutiny, but the threat of a mutiny in the army. Just as Hamilton sought to use the illusion of solvency to foster public credit, so too did he and Morris seek to use the illusion of a mutiny to pressure Congress to try one more time to establish an independent source of revenue for the Confederation. "The claims of the army," Hamilton wrote to Washington at Newburgh on 13 February 1783, "urged with moderation, but with firmness" too, "may operate on those weak minds which are influenced more by their apprehensions than their judgments."[33]

Throughout February, Hamilton spread rumors in Congress that the army might refuse to disband if Congress failed to honor its claims. Adding to the drama, on 24 January 1783, Robert Morris told Congress he would resign as superintendent of finance by May 1783 unless his program were enacted. Probably at the behest of the Morrisites, McDougall wrote Gen. Henry Knox at Newburgh that the army should resolve not to disband unless Congress provided for back pay and commuted the officers' pensions to a lump sum. Though Knox thought it laughable that the soldiers would risk mutiny (a capital crime) for the sake of the officers' pensions, the messages back and forth between Congress and Newburgh did create an atmosphere of crisis, exactly what the Morrisites wanted. Perhaps as part of their plan, Hamilton also wrote Washington, warning him to "keep a *complaining* and *suffering army* within the bounds of moderation." He apparently wished the general would press the army's grievances firmly enough to add its weight to that of the creditors but also to "guide the torrent, and bring order, perhaps even good, out of confusion."[34]

In the meantime, opponents of the impost began to complain of a campaign of military terrorism to force them to support the amendment. Rhode Island's delegates spoke of a conspiracy to oblige it to sacrifice its sovereignty for the sake of the Union. At the beginning of March, events looked as if they might get out of hand. Officers associated with Washington's chief rival for command of the army, Gen. Horatio Gates, began to circulate rumors that Congress would do nothing for the officers. Gates's aide, Maj. John Armstrong Jr., wrote two unsigned addresses, one calling for a meeting of the officers to discuss relations between Congress and the army and another calling on the officers to declare that they would not disband unless they obtained justice. Because the first address called for a meeting without Washington's permission, it violated army regulations. The second was a public threat to Congress. Washington put a stop to the disturbance by appearing (quite ironically) at the Temple of Virtue, the meetinghouse in the camp, where the officers had been asked to assemble to discuss their grievances. In effect, Washington took charge of the meeting and forced the agitators to confront him publicly or be silent. None wished to challenge the general, and the mutiny, such as it was, came to an end. To avoid future disturbances, Washington then wrote Congress, begging it to provide for the army. On 12 March, Congress learned of a provisional peace agreement with England. On 24 March came news of a general peace, and then the Morrisites' hopes of forging a coalition of creditors and soldiers fizzled out. Congress agreed to commute the officers' pensions to a lump-sum payment of five years' salary but had no money to do so. The army was furloughed, and most soldiers disbanded quickly, even before three months' back pay arrived at the camp. On 18 April Congress did pass an impost. Hamilton refused to support it, however, both because it was meant to be a temporary rather than a permanent source of revenue, and because it called for state rather than federal revenue collectors. The impost floundered in limbo from 1783 to 1786 as different states debated it, amended it, and made it unacceptable to Congress, which relied on a trickle of requisitions from the states for revenue instead. Robert Morris eventually resigned. He was then replaced by a board of finance to ensure that no individual gained too much power over the Confederation's finances.[35]

A major question arises from this confusing affair: How far were Hamilton and his allies willing to go to secure adequate revenue powers for the Confederation? According to Forrest McDonald, the Morrisites "did not actually intend to employ the force of a rebellious army, for the practical reason that it was not likely to work." Richard H. Kohn, however, claims the Morrisites had precisely that intent: they hoped to "incite a mutiny" among the officers surrounding General Gates in order to increase pressure on Congress. Then, in an act of deliberate treachery, they hoped to "make sure it was immediately snuffed out." For Kohn, this extraordinary duplicity reveals the beginning of the militarism that he attributes to the Federalists in the 1790s. Kohn asserts that the Morrisites not only lacked the traditional American fear of standing armies but also were attracted to their power and were even willing to use them in ways antithetical to the American political tradition, by which he means military subordination to the civil authorities.[36]

In Hamilton's case at least, a third interpretation is much more plausible. In June 1783, three months after the Newburgh affair, he took a leading role in attempting to suppress an actual mutiny of soldiers who marched on and surrounded Congress while it met in Philadelphia. Though Kohn says nothing about this, it is not the sort of role one would expect from a statesman who allegedly fomented mutinies for political gain.[37] Hamilton did hope to keep up the illusion of a threat to Congress from the army. His well-known personal enmity toward General Gates, however, suggests that he would not have been involved with him in plotting an actual mutiny. Moreover, his explicit reservations against actually using the army against Congress were much stronger than either McDonald or Kohn reveals. Writing to Washington, in March 1783, he asked, "Supposing the Country ungrateful what can the army do? It must submit to its hard fate. To seek redress by arms would end in its ruin. The army would molder of its own weight and for want of the means of keeping together. The soldiery would abandon their officers," a perception that confirms McDonald's suggestion that Hamilton believed an actual mutiny was not practicable. Yet Hamilton then added an insight missing from McDonald's pragmatic account and contrary to Kohn's more sinister one. "There would be no chance of success without having recourse to means which would reverse our revolution." Kohn cites this passage, but interprets it as a frank recognition that the actual use of force would destroy the Confederation Hamilton hoped to preserve. If so, Kohn himself supplies good reason to doubt that Hamilton actually intended to incite a mutiny. Yet Kohn's interpretation is inconsistent with what Hamilton actually said. He was not talking about preserving the Confederation. Nor was his nationalism an end in itself. Instead, it was a means to serve the principles of the Revolution as he understood them. The impact of those principles on the character of the soldiers was the reason he believed they would not support a mutiny. In truth, Hamilton was considering the moral price of a successful mutiny and rejecting it because it was too high. For mutiny to succeed, force would have had to replace consent as the basis of American government. Hamilton rejected this option because it would have meant a complete reversal of the principles he had invoked to justify the Revolution. "Could force avail," Hamilton wrote Washington in a moment of despair, "I should almost wish to see it employed," but that is quite different from actually intending to use it. Hamilton went to the brink of disloyalty to produce an illusion he believed might help save the Union, but his words reveal that he was unwilling to sacrifice the goals of the Revolution to the means of preserving the Confederation.[38]

Hamilton had enormous disdain for superficial moralism, and perhaps so too should we. The moral problem in this affair is not that Hamilton believed the end justified the means, for if the end does not justify the means, what does? Instead, the problem is whether the end was weighty enough to justify Hamilton's means and if the means were proportional to the end. Unfortunately, American liberty in this crisis depended on many different components, and some of them were in conflict. The taboo against military intervention in politics was not the only safeguard to liberty at stake in 1783. In the long run, the Union was at least equally important to preserve American freedom. The danger of poisoned civil-military relations must therefore be balanced against the risk that the Confederation, lacking an independent source of revenue, would have gone the way of almost all war-time alliances and eventually collapsed. Writing in the mid-1970s, Kohn was able to take for granted a durable Union that simply did not exist in 1783. Hamilton could not assume that four years after the Newburgh affair Americans would adopt a new constitution that included most of the reforms he advocated in his briefing for Duane. Indeed, he regarded it as somewhat miraculous that the Federal Convention was able to meet. To the extent that Hamilton's part in the Newburgh affair resulted from his desire to preserve the Union without relying on miracles, it could well be understood as an act of responsible statesmanship, which is often a matter of balancing different risky courses of action. This does not necessarily mean Hamilton was right, but the stakes were so high and the nature of prudence so unclear at the time that it is impossible to say with certainty that he was wrong.

Not surprisingly, because of the machinations at Newburgh, Congress was in no mood to enact any plans for a military peace establishment when Hamilton and other nationalists proposed one in June 1783. Hamilton's efforts to take responsibility to preserve the Union may therefore have done nothing more than increase the vigilance of his adversaries, a dynamic that occurred quite frequently in his career. In the nationalists' view, however, if Americans were to win the peace as well as the war, there was no responsible alternative to some permanent force for coastal and frontier defense.

Their view collided with traditional Whig vigilance against a standing army, which triumphed in 1783. As Charles Royster observes, American Whigs were generally more interested in finding ways to control military power than in devising means to generate and sustain it. Their vigilance had many different roots: in James Harrington's (grossly inaccurate) gloss on Machiavelli's advice for princes and republics to depend on their own arms and virtue rather than on mercenaries; in fears that reliance on a permanent force would imply that Americans were too soft and corrupt for a virtuous defense of their liberty; and perhaps chiefly in American perceptions of the role of a standing army in eighteenth-century England. Such an army seemed to be composed of the dregs of society, rootless men whose loyalty could be bought and sold. With support from the Treasury and opportunities for court patronage through appointments to the officer corps, such an army also apparently embodied all that Americans of the country-party persuasion understood by corruption. When both the officers and the enlisted ranks were completely dependent on the central political authorities for their subsistence and prosperity, it seemed that a standing army was the perfect instrument by which those authorities could perpetuate their hold on power. In contrast, a militia, presumably composed of independent freeholders, would not be subservient to centralized authorities. For the vigilant, the militia thus seemed to offer a greater security against the emergence of a government that rested on military force alone for its authority.[39]

The men who had been most responsible for the military conduct of the Revolutionary War, however, marched to the beat of a radically different drummer. In mid-1783, after the receipt of preliminary articles of peace with England, Hamilton chaired a congressional committee that asked for postwar plans from Washington and his staff for the "interior defense" of the states compatible with "the principles of our governments." Washington received advice from Insp. Gen. Friedrich von Steuben, Chief of Artillery Henry Knox, Q.M. Gen. Timothy Pickering, Adj. Gen. Edward Hand, Gen. Rufus Putnam, once the army's acting chief engineer, and George Clinton, the governor of strategically important New York and a former brigadier general. As Lawrence Delbert Cress observes, these men, with varying degrees of success, sought to reconcile the "ideal of the citizen-soldier with the demonstrable effectiveness of a professional army." Some, like Pickering, evidently shared fears of standing armies so much that they insisted the militia be the first line of national defense and sought to keep the regular force as small as possible (about 800 officers and men in Pickering's case). Others, like von Steuben, recognized that a lack of uniform training and discipline was a principal cause of "that want of confidence in themselves—that reluctancy to come out—that impatience to get home" and of the destruction of public and private property, which "has ever marked an operation merely militia." More from the necessity of devising a plan acceptable to Congress than from his own convictions, von Steuben advocated classifying and training the militia in regional legions. He also called for a professional force of 3,500 soldiers, however.

Washington then synthesized their advice for Hamilton's committee. He insisted on classifying the militia according to age and advocated extra training based on national standards for men eighteen to twenty-five years old. He also called for a war department, a military academy, and a professional force of 2,631 professional officers and men. In turn, Washington's combination of a small professional force and specially trained militia units became the basis of Hamilton's proposal to Congress for a military peace establishment, but with one fundamental difference: the elite units would consist of volunteers paid, armed, supplied, and directed by the national government. Washington and his advisers were thinking in terms of a state-controlled national guard, but Hamilton was advocating the functional equivalent of a national army reserve as an expandable adjunct to his country's first line of defense—a highly trained though small professional army.[40]

In addition to its defensive value, Hamilton saw a professional army as a way to avoid two great dangers. First, one state, in control of one of the "keys to the United States," like West Point or Pittsburgh, might lack the will or means or both to defend it effectively. It might thereby endanger the safety of the Union through its negligence. Second, without a peacetime professional army, the states would be compelled to raise forces of their own to defend themselves against Indians, England, and Spain. A "considerable force in the hands of a few states" might then "have an unfriendly aspect on the confidence and harmony which ought to be maintained between the whole." The danger of a civil war loomed large in Hamilton's thought from the time of his briefing for Duane until the end of his career. To minimize that danger, he apparently believed it was best to disarm the states and to rely on national forces as much as possible.[41]

Hamilton's own proposal for a military peace establishment was both an evolutionary consequence of his experience in the Continental Army and a conceptual breakthrough in the American understanding of a permanent military power. As Royster observes, at Valley Forge and increasingly thereafter, the Continental Army began to develop a unique martial character, a mix between the natural but unreliable courage of the militia and the more reliable but artificial courage of a European army. The "spirit of 1775 was buttressed by the spirit of military professionalism."[42] The former supplied devotion to the cause; the latter, based on pride in shared suffering and skill in the use of arms, led the soldiers, and perhaps the officers especially, to consider themselves a repository of American patriotism. Because this patriotism was inextricably bound up with devotion to the Revolution, the army's new sense of identity had the potential to blend the loyalty hitherto expected only of militias with the competence of professionals.

Hamilton's immediate priority was to maintain the discipline and confidence that the Continental Army had acquired during the war. He also believed that the army was the strongest embodiment of an American national consciousness, in which citizens of different states set aside their differences for the common cause. Hence, it was an "axiom" for him that "in our constitution an army is essential to the American union." He called for approximately 3,000 career officers and enlisted ranks serving for six years, or for the duration if a war broke out during their time in service. Unlike the members of the militia, who served only a few days a year, the professionals would have the time to train to become confident soldiers; unlike mercenaries, with whom Americans easily confused professionals, these soldiers would also be citizens, with a strong attachment to the freedoms that they hoped they and their children would continue to possess. This attachment was one of the reasons Hamilton believed that, all else being equal, free citizens did in fact exhibit greater public-spiritedness than subjects in other regimes. Even in 1780, when he believed morale had hit bottom, Hamilton wrote to Duane that "where the public good is evidently the object more can be effected in governments like ours than in any other. The obedience of a free people to general laws however hard they bear is ever more perfect than that of slaves to the arbitrary will of a prince."[43] The new army would not forsake this fundamental intangible advantage but combine it with professional confidence. Just as the artificial courage of professionals would be superior to the natural courage of the militia, the combination of national loyalty and professionalism could make the regular force superior in zeal and at least equal in confidence to a European army.

Ideally, the total force was to be capable of almost infinite expansion, which Hamilton hoped would be controlled by nationally appointed officers according to national regulations (for the sake of compatibility among the units in training and equipment). Single and married male citizens could be classified and serve in various kinds of reserve and militia units, which Hamilton planned to maintain at several different levels of readiness. Except during an emergency, however, only the professionals and militiamen in an elite reserve corps, which Hamilton called the "train bands," would spend much time in service. As a quite welcome result for Hamilton, the militia would be the last rather than the first line of defense, but the total force could be mobilized, processed, and trained quickly, according to the degree and kind of military threat. If war threatened, more civilians could be drawn into service; as a threat dissipated, the nonprofessionals could be released from duty. Expenses could be kept low, but only if the professionals were kept at the highest level of training and readiness. Anticipating the frustration and boredom that normally accompanies peacetime military service and that often leads to alcoholism, negligence, and mediocrity in all ranks of the military profession, Hamilton tried to create a compromise between promotions based on seniority (as an inducement to lengthy service) and merit on "account of brilliant services or peculiar talents." Then, perhaps, dedicated officers like himself would remain and rise in the service instead of resigning in frustration from seemingly endless waiting to command. For the same reason, he sought to keep the officers' pay high and their commands as large as the tiny force would permit (to serve their pride as much as their pocketbooks). Likewise, he advocated a large number of noncommissioned officers, whose pride in their little commands would help maintain their professionalism.[44]

Generally, the only ingredients of a modern, professional army missing from Hamilton's plan were a military academy and a general staff, both of which seemed too expensive at the time. For fear of depending on foreign soldiers of fortune, however, Hamilton did stress the need for developing trained artillery and engineering officers, one of the principal reasons military academies had begun to develop in Europe. He even called for attaching civilian professors to the army's regiments to supply such technical training. He also called for a board of officers to revise the regulations and training doctrine of the army, a task that has been one of the traditional missions of general staffs. Finally, he recommended developing fortifications, arsenals, magazines, foundries, and manufactories. This recommendation reveals the fundamental objective of his plan for reorganizing the American military—one that would later be a cornerstone of his financial policies as well. So far as possible, "Every country ought to have within itself all the means essential to its own preservation" in time of war. Otherwise, it would "depend upon the casualties of foreign supplies." Or worse, it might depend on foreign arms and thus not be truly independent.[45]

Despite Whig fears that such a force was incompatible with free government, Hamilton was remarkably faithful to the mission of his committee, to devise means of defense compatible with "the principles of our governments." He suggested how Americans might combine the skill of professionals with the numbers and spirit of republican citizens without impoverishing themselves or turning their country into a military despotism. Naval power was an important element of his solution. In *Continentalist* 6, for example, he suggested that Americans would probably be little exposed to wars on land if they remained united. If they also developed a navy, they would usually need nothing more than the small force he advocated. However useful that force might be in a legitimate crisis, it would be too weak to support schemes of "usurpation" against either Congress or the states.[46]

Though Hamilton was deeply involved in the Newburgh affair, both during and immediately after the Revolution he was clearly thinking carefully about ways to enable his country to generate effective military power and to safeguard its liberty. The conventional view of his labors during and shortly after the war is that he pursued constitutional and administrative reforms because he had come to think it was utopian to rely on appeals to public-spirited citizens. This is a half-truth that emphasizes state building at the expense of nation building in Hamilton's thought. It obscures the role of public-spiritedness in Hamilton's nuanced understanding of the relation between the tangible and intangible elements of state power. His briefing for Duane was not simply a plan to establish a powerful American state. Especially when viewed in light of his other wartime writings, it was also an effort to produce and sustain public spirit by restoring confidence in the government, in its currency, and within the army. Though the experience of the war left Hamilton at times skeptical of the virtue of Americans, he never lost hope. The national spirit most important to him depended on the capacity of the government to attach the passions of the American people to its cause. Because those passions are rarely altogether pure, the new kind of public spirit Hamilton felt obliged to generate would rarely be so, either. Nonetheless, that national spirit is the most significant intangible force in modern warfare. With that half-understood revolutionary insight, Hamilton was far ahead of his time. By the end of 1783 he had little but contempt for idealized images of the people as repositories of unlimited public-spiritedness. Yet he had also begun to tap into and develop the spirit of nationalism, the new form of civic virtue that has produced many of the greatest glories and worst evils of modern warfare.

4. Safe for Liberty

Hamilton's transformation from a fairly ordinary American revolutionary stressing vigilance in 1774 to an ardent nationalist stressing responsibility in 1780 certainly gave a distinctive cast to his thought, but we ought not to confuse it with a turn from revolutionary principle to Prussian-style militarism. The interpretation of Hamilton as a militarist becomes ever more untenable when we investigate his efforts to ensure that Americans did not sacrifice the goals of the Revolution to the means and passions required to wage the war. During and after the war, Hamilton became increasingly worried that the American Republic would become as dangerous to liberty as the Confederation was unfit for war. He was especially worried about the twin dangers of democratic despotism at home and republican imperialism abroad. To avoid both, he invoked the same principles he had employed against England in 1774 and 1775, but with one fundamental difference: they were directed against the government of New York.

His policies toward suspected Tories in New York during and after the Revolutionary War and his postwar policy toward Vermont, which seceded from New York during the Revolution, are important measures of the growth of his thought on war and free government. Establishing the supremacy of a written constitution and revealing the incompatibility of imperialism with the liberal-republican principle of consent were his means of preventing Americans from basing the authority of their government on "force alone," the principle that Richard Kohn treats as the defining characteristic of militarism. Hamilton's policies toward suspected Tories in New York and Vermont's independence represent an important though rarely examined antimilitaristic dimension of his politics.

With the receipt of definitive articles of peace in September 1783, New Yorkers had to decide how to deal with perhaps as much as one-half of the state's population, whose members had collaborated openly, clandestinely, tacitly, or reluctantly with the British.[1] The Treaty of Paris obliged the British to evacuate occupied territory, including and especially New York

City, where as many as 50,000 active Loyalists and Tory refugees had been concentrated throughout the war. Before the evacuation, inflammatory articles appeared in many Whig newspapers, with threats of a "bitter and *neckbreaking* hurricane" for Tories who remained after the British army left New York City.[2] Since Tories found within American lines often suffered from vigilante violence, these threats of vengeance were taken seriously in New York City. Most residents considered emigrating, and the British military governor delayed his military evacuation until 25 November to give them a chance to do so. At the end of 1783, 29,000 Tories (and others who feared being accused as Tories) sailed from New York City to England, Nova Scotia, Canada, and Bermuda. A total of 35,000 eventually sailed from the city's harbor; perhaps as many as 100,000 left from other ports and British bastions, such as Charleston in South Carolina.[3]

Hamilton's initial reaction was to stress the impolitic nature of forced emigration. "Our state," he declared, "will feel for twenty years at least, the effects of the popular frenzy" against the Tories. Although most Tories were individuals of no political consequence, many merchants would "carry away eight or ten thousand guineas" that might otherwise have been used for reconstruction in America.[4] Forced emigration was even ignoble because, as Robert Livingston suggested to Hamilton, the arguments of many of those who called for it were

> almost unmixed with pure or patriotic motives. In some few it is a blind spirit of revenge & resentment but in more it is the most sordid interest. One wishes to possess the house of some wretched Tory, another fears him as a rival in his trade or commerce, and a fourth wishes to get rid of his debts by shaking off his creditor or to reduce the price of Living by depopulating the town.[5]

John Jay, one of the Americans negotiating peace with England, wrote Hamilton from Paris in September 1783 that the Tories were "almost as much pitied" in Europe as they were "execrated" in America. "An undue Degree of Severity toward them," Jay observed, "would therefore be impolitic as well as unjustifiable," or rather, it would be impolitic because it would be unjustifiable. To involve a "whole Class of Men in indiscriminate Punishment and Ruin" would amount to an "unnecessary Rigor and unmanly Revenge without a parallel except in the annals of Religious Rage in times of Bigotry and Blindness." It would be far safer and more profitable, Jay asserted, to see the sweat of the Tories "fertilize our Fields, than those of our Neighbors" in Canada, for example. Forced emigration could produce not only "Seeds of Hatred" but also consequences that are obliterated in the copy of the letter. They might well have included the formation of an émigré army in Canada, which could have become a substantial security threat later. Most important, Jay pleaded that the "glory of the Revolution" not be sullied by cruelty, lest it become an argument against the American Revolution and similar ones elsewhere.[6]

The fears of Jay and Livingston, and more, are at the heart of Hamilton's *Letters of Phocion* in 1784, when he became alarmed at efforts to punish suspected Tories as a class. As early as 1775 the New York legislature had sequestered Tory property. Subsequent laws disenfranchised the Loyalists, provided for the banishment or imprisonment of dangerous adherents to the king, and disbarred Loyalist lawyers. Confiscation was provided for by an act of 22 October 1779, which attainted many Loyalists and made their estates forfeit. Under Article 4 of the Treaty of Paris, however, both Loyalist and Patriot creditors were supposed to meet with no impediment in collecting debts from each other. Article 5 earnestly recommended that each state act to restore real and personal property confiscated from Loyalists. Article 6 prohibited the states from enacting laws against either the political or the civil liberties of Loyalists. No person was to suffer any "future loss or damage, either in his person, liberty, or property" for his part during the war. Unfortunately, virtually all the states ignored these provisions, so that the threat posed to the liberties of the Tory minority was also a threat to the treaty power of the Confederation.[7] Hamilton's *First Letter of Phocion* in January 1784 criticized the New York legislature and the city of New York for refusing to abide by the treaty's provisions. Hamilton's *Second Letter of Phocion* in April 1784 opposed a bill, then being debated in the legislature, that made aliens of citizens who had continued to reside in occupied territory during the war.[8]

Hamilton took aim at a Whig Society in New York City that had called on aldermen to take action against the Tories. As a former soldier and congressman who had a "deep share in the common exertions" of the Revolution, Hamilton's first step was to call their Whiggism into question. The members of the Whig Society, Hamilton declared, "pretend to appeal to the spirit of Whiggism, while they endeavor to put in motion all the furious and dark passions of the human mind." He therefore did not judge them by the principles they preached, which were on everyone's lips, but by the passions they excited and the practices they encouraged. "The spirit of Whiggism" was "generous, beneficent, humane, and just," but these proto-Jacobins encouraged "revenge, cruelty, persecution, and perfidy." The spirit of Whiggism cherished legal liberty and due process and held the rights of individuals sacred, but the members of the Whig Society advocated exiling a large number of citizens without a trial, or failing that, disenfranchising them. In turn, disenfranchisement meant they would be taxed without representation. Ironically, then, New Yorkers would be practicing the same tyranny against suspected Tories that they themselves had opposed from Great Britain. In Hamilton's view, the Whig Society therefore did not consist of Whigs but of the most dangerous kind of counterrevolutionaries. Without their comprehending the principles of Whiggism, Hamilton implied that they were fanatics who would use the rhetoric of the Revolution to subvert its principles.[9]

Hamilton shared John Jay's fears of a new age of political bigotry that would rival earlier ages of religious bigotry, observing,

> There is a spirit of bigotry in politics, as well as in religions, equally pernicious in both. The zealots, of either description, are ignorant of the advantage of the spirit of toleration: It was a long time before the kingdoms of Europe were convinced of the folly of persecution, with respect to those, who were schismatics from the established church. . . . While some kingdoms were impoverishing and depopulating themselves [through forced emigration and religious civil wars] their wiser neighbors were reaping the fruits of their folly, and augmenting their own numbers, industry, and wealth, by receiving with open arms the persecuted fugitives. . . . There is not an enlightened nation, which does not now acknowledge the force of the truth, that whatever speculative notions of religion may be entertained, men will not on that account, be enemies to a government, that affords them protection and security. The same spirit of toleration in politics, and for the same reasons, has made great progress among mankind, of which the history of most modern revolutions is a proof.[10]

Hamilton's politic stress on enlightened self-interest reveals a good deal about his understanding of the effectual foundations of loyalty to a republic. The position of the Whig Society was that the suspected Tories were traitors, a potential fifth column, unsafe to live with. As monarchists, the Tories not only lacked republican virtue; they were also emphatically hostile to the republic of New York. In contrast, Hamilton extended the political psychology of public-spiritedness he had developed during the war even to suspected Tories. If the goal of the Whig Society was to generate and preserve loyalty to the republic in New York, then nothing was more important than to give suspected Tories a stake in it. He declared that the safest reliance of every government is on men's interests. This is a principle of human nature on which all political speculations to be just, must be founded. Make it the interest of those citizens, who during the Revolution, were opposed to us to be friends to the new government, by affording them not only protection, but participation in its privileges, and they will undoubtedly become its friends.

The alternative, to deny the Tories protection (civil liberty) and participation (political liberty), would produce "a large body of citizens" who would "continue enemies to the government, ready, at all times, in a moment of commotion, to throw their weight into that scale which meditates a change whether favorable or unfavorable to public liberty."[11]

Enlightened Whigs needed to consider that "either the number of malcontents in the state is small or it is considerable." If it were small, there was nothing to worry about: an individual or two might cause a commotion, but the minority would be too weak to be dangerous. If the number were large, opposition could be overcome only by winning its friendship or by "extirpating them from the community," a view that anticipates the horrors of genocide and ethnic cleansing in our own age. "A middle line which will betray a spirit of persecution in the government, but will only extend its operation to a small number, will answer no other purpose than to disable a few, and inflame and rivet the prejudices of the rest." A middle line would amount to nothing less than a constant state of war, a policy as undesirable as extirpation was criminal. Hamilton thus presented his readers with three alternatives, two of which were completely unacceptable. The first policy of humanity was best because it avoided the injustice of extirpation and the imprudence of the seemingly "moderate" position.[12]

As Gordon Wood has observed, during the war and increasingly thereafter, many of the Founders, and James Madison especially, were shocked that the new republics in the states had become forums for legalized tyranny.[13] Quarrels between debtors and creditors and members of established churches and dissenters constitute a large part of that story, but so too does the persecution practiced by American Whigs against suspected Loyalists. Hamilton's fundamental concern was that, by degrees, the rhetoric of virtuous republicanism would issue in the reality of vicious despotism. "Nothing is more common than for a free people, in times of heat and violence, to gratify momentary passions, by letting into the government, principles and precedents, which afterwards prove fatal to themselves." Disenfranchisements, disqualifications, and confiscations fell under this heading, for if the legislature could "disenfranchise any number of citizens at pleasure by a general description," it could soon confine all the votes to a "small number of partisans" and thus effectually transform republican government into the rule of the few rather than the many. Moreover, if it could banish anyone without hearing or trial, no man could be safe or know when he might be "the innocent victim of a prevailing faction." The "name of liberty" applied to such a republic, would be "a mockery of common sense." In the worst case, such a republic would lose the popular support necessary to perpetuate itself. "A disorderly or violent government" could "disgust the best citizens, and make the body of the people tired of their Independence." If the people of America were to ask with one voice what they should do to perpetuate their liberties, then Hamilton's answer was "'govern well'" and they would have "nothing to fear either from internal disaffection or external hostility." But if the "wanton use" of liberty showed that "despotism may debase the government of the many as well as the few," then the abuse of republican liberty would be "the forerunner of slavery."[14]

The American Phocion then appealed as much to the pride as to the mercy and interests of his people. The stakes involved in their republican experiments were not confined to America alone:

> The world has its eyes on America. The noble struggle we have made in the cause of liberty, has occasioned a kind of revolution in human sentiment. The influence of our example has penetrated the gloomy regions of despotism, and has pointed the way to inquiries, which may shake it to its deepest foundations. Men begin to ask every where, who is this tyrant that dares to build his greatness on our misery and degradation? What commission has he to sacrifice millions to the wanton appetites of himself and a few minions that surround his throne?
>
> To ripen inquiry into action, it remains to us to justify the revolution by its fruits.
>
> If the consequences prove, that we really have asserted the cause of human happiness, what may not be expected from so illustrious an example? In a greater or less degree, the world will bless and imitate!
>
> But if the experience, in this instance, verifies the lesson long taught by the enemies of liberty, that the bulk of mankind are not fit to govern themselves, that they must have a master, and were only made for the rein and spur: We shall then see the final triumph of despotism over liberty. The advocates of the latter must acknowledge it to be an *ignis fatuus,* and abandon the pursuit. With the greatest advantages of promoting it, that ever a people had, we shall have betrayed the cause of human nature.[15]

Anticipating the rhetorical strategy of many of his later writings, Hamilton flattered citizens of New York at the same time that he sought to shame them. If their experiment succeeded, the world might bless or imitate their example. If it failed, Americans would have betrayed not only themselves but mankind as well by proving that force was the only effectual foundation of government. The choice, it seems, was up to them. Indirectly, but quite powerfully, he appealed to the religious character of the American people by portraying the treatment of the Tories as a potential millennium or apocalypse for republican government, if not for mankind. American nationalism might thereby derive great strength from the conviction that Americans are, or ought to be, different from other peoples. Though the principles of the Revolution (equality, rights, consent, revolution) are universal, and meant to apply to all men, Americans were the first to choose them as their own principles. In that respect, they were a self-chosen people, or might at least come to understand themselves that way. By making it the unique mission of the American people to "justify the revolution by its fruits," Hamilton was self-consciously synthesizing liberal principle with religious conviction to build a national consciousness. While his wartime writings usually sought to unite Americans through confidence and private interest, his postwar efforts to prevent legalized tyranny against suspected Loyalists also sought to define what Americans would stand for, and therefore, what they might be willing to fight against. In turn, Hamilton hoped, this national identity would provide greater support for a stronger Union based on the supremacy of a written constitution.

Establishing that supremacy required the soldier-statesman to leave the sword and saddle behind and don the robes of a jurist. The immediate legal issues in the *Phocion* letters were whether the legislature was bound to restore property confiscated during the war, desist from future confiscations and acts of vengeance against the Tories, and extend the franchise to its former enemies. In support of these propositions, Hamilton pursued two alternate and independent, but also mutually supportive, lines of argument. The first concerned the rights of citizens stated in the New York Constitution. Under it, rights could not be forfeited without benefit of trial and conviction. Therefore, no one could lose the protection of the government or the franchise without trial for an individual act committed as a violation of public law. Although it was the policy of the Revolution to encourage citizens to flee the occupied territories and thus to leave the British with a scorched earth, merely remaining in occupied territory was no crime. To claim that citizens who remained behind to protect their property were traitors would be to "convert misfortune into guilt; it would be in many instances, to make the negligence of the society, in not providing adequate means of defense for the several parts, the crime of those parts which were the immediate sufferers by that negligence."

To be sure, those who went beyond protecting their property and actively aided the enemy were subject to the penalties of treason, but in that case there was no ground to declare them aliens. Treason applies only to citizens. Therefore, if they were accused of treason, they could not be denied the protection and participation of citizens until they were convicted of the crime. To say otherwise, that anyone who remained in occupied territory had ipso facto lost the protection of the laws, would be to "confound one third of the citizens of the state in promiscuous guilt and degradation, without evidence or inquiry. It would be to make crimes, which are in their nature personal and individual, aggregate and territorial." New York's Constitution required that crimes be tried individually and personally, however. Therefore, the acts of confiscation and disenfranchisement on the mere basis of residence were strictly unconstitutional. Hamilton's second line of argument was that confiscations and disenfranchisements were equally as forbidden under the Articles of Confederation as under New York's Constitution. Under the Articles, Congress was responsible for negotiating treaties, and Hamilton understood the treaty power as plenipotentiary. If so, the states had no constitutional right to obstruct enforcement of the treaty.[16]

Hamilton's appeals to the New York Constitution and to the treaty power of the Articles rested on the cardinal premise of American constitutional government: that constitutions are superior to ordinary acts of legislation. Why should they be? Is not a constitution the mere "creature of the people?" Does not their "sense with respect to any measure, if it even stand in opposition to the constitution, sanctify and make it right?" Hamilton argued that a constitution was a special kind of popular creation, a "compact between the society at large and each individual" for the purpose of securing both and was equally binding on both. If the constitution were not equally binding, then either society or individuals would be above the law. This imbalance would result either in the dissolution of government or convert it "into a government of *will* not of *laws*." When understood as the rule of law, republican government would thereby come to an end. Until the fundamental compact was "dissolved with the same solemnity and certainty with which it was made, the society," as well as individuals, had to be bound by it.[17] The practical significance of this interpretation of the fundamental law was clear: it was impossible for individuals to be citizens for the sake of punishment but not for rights and privileges. Resident aliens might sometimes be a different, special case, but if citizens were subject to punishment, they were equally entitled to the protection of the law, especially trials, and to participate, however indirectly, in making the laws to which they would be subject.

The grounds for the legislature's disregarding the constitution were even less sufficient because the legislature was not the people. It was not even the solemn sense of the people expressed in the constitution but a creature of the constitution, and thus two steps removed from the people. Consequently, if the legislature did claim authority to deny one portion of the community protection and participation, then Hamilton declared that it would be a "treasonable usurpation of the power and majesty of the people." If the legislature claimed that it had the people on its side, this would only be a "pretext" for treachery, for the sense of the people is most "explicit and authoritative" in their constitution. To disregard the existing constitution would therefore be to change the form of government without asking for the "explicit and authoritative" sense of the people. Such an act in turn would violate the liberal-republican principle of popular sovereignty that the legislature invoked to justify dispensing with the rule of law. Consequently, the real traitors were not the unfortunate citizens who remained in their homes during the British occupation but the so-called Whig Societies and their friends in the legislature, who were willing to violate their own constitution to stamp out and punish traitors.[18]

Yet who decides whether a legislature has exceeded its powers; that is, who defends the solemn and authoritative sense of the people against the pretexts urged by the legislature? For Hamilton, there was one obvious answer, rooted in the arguments he had made to justify resisting England before the Revolution and in the Lockean theory of the social compact: ultimately, the people shall be judge. That answer, however, which issues in a call for revolution, was impractical except in time of revolution.[19] Or rather, to make the people, or even their elected representatives, the final judge of every constitutional question would amount to a permanent revolution incompatible with the constitutional rule of law. Between the solemn and authoritative enactment of a constitution and the invocation of the right to revolution, some other part of the government would therefore have to judge, but which part was most fit for this responsibility?

Hamilton's legal arguments in the case of *Rutgers v. Waddington* in 1784 supply the beginning of an answer. The basic facts in this case are that Elizabeth Rutgers, who was one of the thousands of Americans to flee New York City when it was captured by the British in 1776, brought suit against Joshua Waddington for using her brewery during the occupation without paying compensation. Popular passions were deeply involved in this case because much of New York City had been burned to the ground. The British had also occupied the best accommodations in the city during the war. Since many Loyalists had fled into the overcrowded city, they were forced to occupy homes and workplaces deserted by other Americans. The British at least were not scrupulous about the upkeep of the occupied buildings and stripped the farms and businesses of known Whigs to supply their army without paying any compensation to them. Thus loyal Whigs paid dearly for deserting their property, which they had been urged to do by their government. Nothing could be done against the British army, but no one was in the mood to let Loyalists go unpunished for trespassing on the deserted property.

Rutgers brought her suit under the postwar Trespass Act of New York, which allowed citizens to seek compensation for the use of their deserted property during the occupation. It also stated that military orders from the occupying authorities would not excuse trespassers of responsibility for the crime. When suit was brought, Waddington hired Hamilton as his attorney. Since Rutgers was an eighty-year-old widow who depended on the brewery for income but had apparently sacrificed all for the cause, her case was extremely well-suited to invoke popular sympathy. Hamilton had his hands full defending a very unpopular person against a woman whose virtue seemed to embody all that was best in the republican spirit.[20]

Once again, Hamilton pursued two independent, yet mutually supportive, lines of argument. First, he argued that the Trespass Act violated the laws of war, which absolved civilians of trespass if they had military authorization. Waddington had such authorization from the British commander for most but not all of the period in which he used the brewery. Hamilton could do virtually nothing to defend Waddington for the period in which he lacked military authorization, but the New York Constitution did supply a means to defend him during the period when he had such authorization. The New York Constitution incorporated the common law. Hamilton argued that the common law also included the laws of nations, and thus, the laws of war. If the court could be convinced that the laws of war had been made part of the New York Constitution through the common law, then it would have to admit that the Trespass Act violated the state constitution.

Hamilton's second argument was that only Congress was authorized to negotiate treaties under the Articles of Confederation. If the Confederation were to serve its ends, then the states had to be bound by those treaties. If Hamilton were right in understanding the treaty as a "general amnesty" for crimes committed during the war, then the statute violated the Articles as well.[21] The case was tried in New York City, where Hamilton's old friend from the war, James Duane, was the presiding judge. If the court upheld the treaty against the New York legislature, then it might be possible for the courts gradually to evolve as instruments to enforce the Articles of Confederation against the states. If so, judicial review might supply the means to uphold acts of Congress against the states and preserve the Union in the process. Hamilton's task was to convince the court that, in the face of such conflict in the laws, it had not only the right but also the responsibility to review the laws and to remove the conflict. This was no easy task. The judges were not federal officers and owed their primary allegiance to the State of New York. Although they might have agreed that they were responsible for reviewing conflicts in the laws of New York, they were far less likely to agree that they were also responsible for holding New York accountable to the Articles.[22]

Because our only records of Hamilton's arguments before the court are in sketchy briefs, we may never know exactly what Hamilton said to persuade the court to accept such a responsibility. Only a somewhat well-informed hypotheses can be established. The fundamental assumption of Hamilton's argument, which is never explicitly stated in the briefs, apparently asserts that it is the responsibility of the courts to interpret the laws. This would not deny that interpretation might also be necessary to legislation or execution, but for the other branches, interpretation is a means to an end; for the judiciary, interpretation is its only legitimate end. Thus failure to interpret the law would amount to an abdication of judicial responsibility. The problem for the court in Hamilton's time, as it continues to be in our own, was how to fulfill this interpretive responsibility without assuming legislative powers.

Hamilton offered two different options to enable the court to confront the problem. First, it could assume that constitutions, which form the fundamental compacts of societies, are the most authoritative expressions of positive law. Then, on the assumption that its function was to declare the meaning of the law, the court could assert that the higher law of the state and federal constitutions took precedence over a mere statute of New York. The court would then be obliged to declare the Trespass Act null and void. To give this innovation in judicial responsibility the respectability of traditional republican practice, Hamilton appealed to ancient precedent. He cited Cicero, who set down the "rule, that when two laws clash, that which relates to the most important matters ought to be preferred."[23] This approach would not assert a power for the court to make law, but it would affirm that the legislature itself was bound by the fundamental law.

If the court did not wish to be so bold, however, Hamilton offered a second alternative. It could also follow the common law practice of interpreting conflicts in the law in light of the presumption that a legislature making new laws does not intend to repeal other laws, unless that body explicitly says so. Since the New York legislature did not say it meant to overturn the laws of war, the laws of nations, the common law, the constitution of New York, or the treaty power of the Articles, then the court could reasonably infer that the legislature had not intended to do so. This somewhat disingenuous alternative did not require the court to overturn the Trespass Act but only to assume that the legislature did not mean to deny that military authorization absolved civilians of responsibility for trespass. Rather than accuse the legislature of acting despotically, the court could politely suggest that it was confused. The rest of the Trespass Act would remain in full standing, but the offensive clause would be treated as unintelligible and without meaning. Not surprisingly, the court adopted Hamilton's second, more politic alternative. It did not go so far as to assert a judicial power to declare laws null and void, particularly state laws contravening the Articles, but it did oppose the anti-Tory sentiment of New York by allowing military authorization as an excuse for trespass.[24]

These legal niceties must now be put in their proper context to reveal their full political significance. In his briefing for Duane, Hamilton described the Articles of Confederation as fit neither for war nor peace, but he stressed their unfitness for war at the time. This was a case revealing their unfitness for peace. Although the states might wish to deny that the treaty with Great Britain was a general amnesty (because some of its provisions were only recommendations for clemency toward Loyalists), the British did interpret it as an amnesty. Congress also took the treaty in this spirit when it recommended compliance among the states. In "law as in RELIGION THE LETTER KILLS," Hamilton declared, but the "SPIRIT MAKES ALIVE."

Yet Congress had no means to enforce the treaty and thereby to give life to the spirit of the law. To allow the states to interpret the treaty as they wished would kill the spirit of peace between Americans and the British. A "judgment contrary to the laws of nations" would be a "good cause of war," which would "endanger the peace of the union." Hamilton wanted the Trespass Act declared null and void not only because it violated the New York Constitution but also because it infringed on an essential power of national sovereignty, the power to make peace. Ultimately, it affected much more, including the power to form alliances, for violating the treaty would prove that the United States was an unreliable partner, with whom few nations would wish to associate. Violating the treaty would lead Americans to suffer "a loss of character in Europe," and become the "scorn of nations."[25] A lasting peace depended on making the treaty stick, which was impossible unless the courts assumed the responsibility to enforce it against the state governments.

Yet there was a fundamental paradox in Hamilton's defense of a written constitution. He concluded his *Second Letter of Phocion* by observing that in a "doubtful case, the constitution ought never to be hazarded, without extreme necessity." Hamilton was clearly hedging his bets. He was too much the soldier to think that mere law-abidingness would be sufficient to preserve the Republic from harm. He was also too much the liberal lawyer to countenance disregard of the law in any case where the necessity was doubtful. Hamilton thus revealed that there are dangers on both sides of the rule of law. Strict construction, against which he fought throughout the Revolutionary War and for the rest of his career, might tie the hands of the government in time of danger, but violations of the Constitution might ultimately destroy respect for the rule of law itself. Hamilton had no solution for this dilemma in 1784, which is not at all surprising. Though probably first explored by Machiavelli, the dilemma was also addressed by most significant constitutional theorists of the seventeenth and eighteenth centuries. In time, it would become the fundamental problem that Hamilton's philosophy of broad construction of the Constitution and especially of executive power was meant to solve.[26]

During the last years of the war, Congress was consistently plagued with a troublesome problem: Vermont's declaration of independence from New York and New York's persistent demand for aid in recovering its territory. The problem was peculiarly vexing because Vermont had made diplomatic overtures to the British during the war. This tactical expedient split the state into competing factions of Whigs, who wished to join the Union as an independent state, and British sympathizers, who desired some kind of association with the British Empire. Reunion with the British might have been the sine qua non of protection for Vermont against the confederation. Situated along Lake Champlain, its southern tip pointed directly at Massachusetts and New York, Vermont was ideally located for a British attack through Canada, which could have split the Union in two. This danger made those members of Congress whose states did not have claims on the territory of Vermont anxious to get it into the Union at all costs.[27]

A moral problem arising from the principles by which Americans had declared themselves free and independent states compounded the strategic problems posed by Vermont's independence. If Americans could declare their independence from Great Britain, why should Vermont be denied the right to declare its independence from New York? Congress had no desire to wrestle with this fundamental problem of liberal principle and ignored the requests of New York for aid against Vermont throughout the war. Yet after the war, Vermont's independence became intimately tied to the vexing question of what to do about conflicting land claims in the Western territories among the states and between their citizens. The Articles of Confederation provided for arbitration of such claims, but this procedure would work only if Vermont were in the Union. Those states that wanted the Western territories ceded to the Union generally supported Vermont's independence and its admission to the Union. Those states whose citizens had claims on land in Vermont feared that admitting it would make settling their claims much more difficult. Hamilton himself feared that Congress would do nothing about the claims of citizens of New York, New Hampshire, and Massachusetts on Vermont territory. He used Vermont's example as evidence of the need for constitutional reform: "While they have a discretion they will procrastinate," he told Gov. George Clinton of New York in 1783; "when they are bound by the constitution" to settle the land claims, "they must proceed."[28] Until then, the presence of these conflicting claims risked a civil war.

On 24 March 1787 the New York legislature received a petition from several persons owning land in Vermont who objected to a bill, then being considered by the legislature, to acknowledge Vermont's independence. On 28 March Richard Harison, a prominent New York lawyer, spoke on behalf of the petitioners. Harison argued that "the social compact, to which all the members of society are parties, and by which all of them are bound was first formed to preserve the rights and properties of each, by the united strength of the whole; and the social compact must suffer the grossest violation, whenever the rights and properties even of the meanest individuals are sacrificed without the most pressing necessity." Hence, to acknowledge the independence of Vermont would amount to a violation of the social compact, unless of course those who claimed to own land there were compensated by the legislature when independence was acknowledged. Harison also asserted that Americans should prove themselves as valiant as the Romans. Then, quite ominously, he asked what the Romans would have done "if an inconsiderable part of their citizens had presumed to declare themselves a separate and independent state."[29]

Harison's suggestion, that New Yorkers ought to consider reuniting the rebel territory by force, compelled Hamilton, who was then serving in the

New York legislature, to confront the same problem of reconciling consent with national security he had addressed in his discussions of the British Empire in 1774 and 1775. This time, however, he cast New York in the role of England against Vermont. As a result, he wrestled with the moral and strategic justifications of imperialism, which do not appear to have changed much in 2,500 years. Thucydides first ascribed the growth of the Athenian empire to the passions of fear, honor, and the love of gain. These three passions remain at the center of contemporary discussions of imperialism, with Marxists and other radicals emphasizing economic interests and class conflict, others stressing pride and prestige, and still others the various dilemmas of security that sometimes make statesmen believe their countries' safety depends on dominion and hegemony. With respect to these motives, Hamilton's position was complicated but also a model of his understanding of the relation between liberal principle and political prudence in foreign policy. Neither the economic interests of New Yorkers nor their honor sufficed to justify a war by New York to force Vermont to join the Empire State. Indeed, war based on such motives would be incompatible with the principles of the Revolution. The appropriate moral-strategic alternative to imperialism was federalism, based on Vermont's voluntarily agreeing to join the Union. Yet if Vermont refused to do so, fear of its alliance with Great Britain would justify a war of the Confederation against Vermont to preserve American independence. Though neglected by Hamilton's partisans and critics alike, his short speech deserves to be considered as one of the classic American discussions of imperialism.[30]

On 28 March Hamilton advocated recognizing Vermont's independence on condition that it join the Union. In response to Harison's suggestion that New Yorkers emulate the Romans, he asked his fellow New Yorkers to reflect on the differences between ancient and modern republics. They needed to calculate their interests rather than nurse their wounded pride: "Neither the manners nor the genius of Rome are suited to the republic or age we live in. All her maxims and habits were military, her government was constituted for war. Ours is unfit for it, and our situation still less than our constitution, invites us to emulate the conduct of Rome, or to attempt a display of unprofitable heroism."[31] Though Hamilton did his best to give his nation a constitution fit for war, he denied that Rome should be a model for America because the Roman government was constituted completely for war. He was not debunking the heroic virtues so much as the willful pride of the Romans. Unprofitable heroism abounds in ages of pride, in which men display their power through dominion; the age Americans lived in was, or ought to have been, devoted to universal liberty and prosperity. The spirit of the modern age was therefore incompatible with that of the ancients. It called into question not only the practicality but also the desirability of such proud displays of unprofitable valor.

Hamilton nonetheless chose not to make the injustice of imperialism the central issue of the debate. Perhaps because he feared offending the pride of New Yorkers, who would resent being told that conquering Vermont would be unjust, he spoke of repression as impolitic instead. He did not deny Harison's principle that the united strength of New York was pledged to secure the rights of its citizens, but he did deny the scope of the principle, or rather, he raised questions about how it could be put into practice. The united strength of the community ought to be exerted to defend the rights of individuals but only "so far as there is a rational prospect of Success" and "so far as it is Consistent with the safety and well being of the whole."[32] The fundamental issues were therefore, first, whether it was practicable for New York to reduce Vermont to obedience to the former's laws, and second, whether satisfying the claims of a few individuals in New York outweighed the costs of war to that state as a whole.

Could New York defeat Vermont? Since Vermont had already made overtures to Great Britain during the war, it was reasonable to suppose that it had made some defensive agreement with the empire. An attack on Vermont might therefore issue in a renewed war with the much more formidable forces of Great Britain. Since Vermont was readily accessible to Britain through Canada, and since the British used powerful Indian tribes to buttress their frontier forces, this was no small strategic consideration. Moreover, Vermont had declared itself tax free to encourage immigration, and its population and wealth had grown substantially during the war. New York, however, had been the "principal seat of the war," and the state was "exhausted by its peculiar exertions and overwhelmed in debt." There is also a vast difference between defensive and offensive operations. The "mountains, the wildernesses, the militia, sometimes even the poverty of a country will suffice" for defensive operations, and these circumstances were present in Vermont. In contrast, offensive war requires "an army and a treasury," neither of which New York had. There was no reason to believe New York's strength relative to Vermont's would improve in the future. Hamilton believed Vermont's population was at least one-half of New York's; immigration was continuing to increase it; and a "country possessing a fertile soil exempt from taxes cannot fail to have rapid growth." Indeed, much of the growth would come at the expense of New York, where high taxes to pay off war debts gave impoverished frontiersmen ample incentive to vote with their feet.[33]

New York could of course call in allies, but Hamilton considered that policy impracticable, and his reasons subtly called into question the justice of war against Vermont. The longer Vermont remained independent in fact from New York, the more the rest of the world would be inclined to think that its independence was a settled matter of right. The other northeastern states had "uniformly countenanced the independence" of Vermont, and their opinion of the origins of the controversy was not "generally in our favor." Most important, a "scheme of coercion" would be ill-suited to the "disposition of our own citizens; the habits of thinking, to which the revolution has given birth, are not adapted to the idea of a contest for dominion over a people not inclined to live under our government." One of two possibilities would therefore result from an attack on Vermont: the character New Yorkers had acquired during the Revolution would render them unwilling to fight (which implied an attack was doomed to fail from the start), or an attack on Vermont would corrupt their character by giving them a taste for dominion. For both strategic and moral reasons, then, it was "not the interest of the state ever to regain its dominion over [Vermont] by force." Even if Vermont were conquered, it would have to be occupied. Because contests for liberty and dominion are both bloody and obstinate, Hamilton suggested the costs of pacification could be even higher than conquest. Consequently, if war were waged, both the moral and material welfare of the whole of New York would be sacrificed to securing the questionable rights of a few individuals to land in Vermont.[34]

A second issue was the constitutionality of acknowledging Vermont's independence, and thus, of surrendering some of the territory of New York. New York's Constitution did not provide for sacrificing its territory in time of war; indeed, no constitution ever does. Yet such a sacrifice is often essential to make peace. This strategic consideration required Hamilton to develop one of the main features of his philosophy of broad construction of constitutions: his doctrine of implied powers. Since no "express power" was granted the legislature to dismember any part of the state, opponents of Vermont's independence argued that the "silence of the constitution" was a "tacit reservation of that power to the people." Hamilton, however, began with Harison's premise, that the chief object of government was to secure rights through the united strength of the community. For this end, the "sovereignty of the people" was represented in the legislature, the Senate, and the New York Council of Revision. Thus the government was entitled to act like any other responsible sovereign, and "dismembering the state under certain circumstances is a necessary appendage of the sovereignty." Indeed, even today it would be difficult to justify the independence of New

York, or any of the original American colonies, if that aspect of sovereignty had not been implicitly vested in the British government, which also lacked an expressed power to sacrifice territory for peace.[35]

The "inference from the silence of a constitution" was therefore the "inverse" of what Harison claimed. For constitutions to endure the stresses of war, their silences should be interpreted in light of the practices of sovereign nations. It was a custom of nations, imposed by the necessities of war, to recognize a difference between the voluntary and involuntary dismemberment of "an empire," like Great Britain, or even of an empire state, like New York. Perhaps no sovereign could voluntarily accede to the dismemberment of the society it was responsible to protect, but where "a part of an empire is actually severed by conquest, or by revolution, the prince or body, vested with the administration of the government, has a right to assent to and ratify the separation." In doing so, it does no more than acknowledge an existing fact, which it may not be able to change without unjustifiable sacrifices. The "safety of society" may require such policy, when the "sacrifice of a part is essential to the preservation or welfare of the rest." Otherwise, there would be no end of wars as sovereign states struggled forever under obligations to regain their lost territories.[36]

Yet if Vermont could secede, why not Long Island, or Harlem, or Albany? If Long Island or any other part of New York could vindicate its independence, then, Hamilton argued, the "same circumstances concurring, the same consequences would result, but no sooner, and it will be the duty of the state to endeavor to prevent a similar extremity." Since Hamilton dedicated much of his career to strengthening the Union, his position on secession bears some scrutiny. Was he justifying an anarchic precedent incompatible with any durable political union? When it comes to revolutions, Hamilton suggested it was imprudent to reason too much about the danger of bad examples:

> Pernicious examples have little to do with the revolutions of empire; wherever such a state of things exists as to make it the interest or the inclination of a large body of the people to separate from the society with which they have been connected, and at the same time, to afford a prospect of success, they will generally yield to the impulse, without much inquiry or solicitude about what has been done by others, or upon other occasions; and when it is not the case, precedents will rarely create the disposition.

His analysis is broadly consistent with Locke's famous conclusion that the people shall be judge, not only as a matter of right but as a matter of almost physical necessity. When they are made "miserable under any government," they will be "ready upon any occasion" to rebel. After a long train of abuses, they "will wish and seek" a change of government, as soon as they have courage and opportunity to do so.[37]

Before the Revolution began, Hamilton observed that

> the experience of past ages informs us, that when the circumstances of a people render them distressed, their rulers generally recur to severe, cruel, and oppressive measures. Instead of endeavoring to establish their authority in the *affection* of their subjects, they think they have no security but in *fear*. They do not aim at gaining their fidelity and obedience, by making them flourishing, prosperous, and happy, but by rendering them abject and dispirited. They think it necessary to intimidate and awe them, to make every accession to their own power, and to impair the people's as much as possible.[38]

In 1775 Hamilton directed popular vigilance against Parliament, but in his debate with Harison, he was directing it against New Yorkers themselves. If they meant their state to endure, then their principal task was to govern well, gain the affection of the people, and thereby prevent the inclination to secede. Since the time for producing such affection between New York and Vermont had passed, union with Vermont could be established by force alone. Yet if Vermont were united by force, there would be no moral difference between the New York legislature in 1787 and the British Parliament in 1776.

Nevertheless, Hamilton wanted real concessions from Vermont, which was not simply a little David fighting Goliath. The Green Mountain men were also pursuing an opportunistic policy that was truly dangerous to the United States. The quid pro quo for acknowledging Vermont's independence was that it join the Confederation. Outside the Confederation, Vermont had little choice but to ally itself with Great Britain. Indeed, Ethan and Ira Allen had already engaged in negotiations with Gen. Frederick Haldimand, the governor of Quebec, to explore the possibility of a separate peace and an alliance. Given the hostility of New York, which was already taxing landlocked Connecticut and New Jersey indirectly through its tariff policies, an independent Vermont could not expect its trade to enter or exit profitably through New York. Its "inland situation" forced it to depend on trade with Canada. In turn, the British had ample reason to relish the prospect of an alliance. Although American violations of the peace treaty gave the British a "pretext" not to evacuate posts in the Northwest Territories, the real reason was the "prodigious advantage which the monopoly of the fur trade" gave to their commerce. Vermont was ideally situated to hamstring American expansion and thus to help secure the British monopoly in the future.[39]

If Vermont agreed to join the Union and had the right to trade freely through New York, however, the obstacle to expansion and the fur trade could be eliminated; just as important, it would be united to the Confederation on the basis of choice and affection rather than to New York through fear. Indeed, even if Vermont refused to join the Union, offering the quid pro quo would still be advantageous. Vermont's refusal to join the Union would be evidence of a "determined predilection to a foreign connection, and it would show the United States the absolute necessity of combining their efforts to subvert an independence, so hostile to their safety." Here, Hamilton changed his policy, but not his principles, because different circumstances would require a different policy to serve the same principles. It was desirable to have Vermont in the Union by its consent, but if necessary, it would have to be united by force. The existence of New York was not immediately at stake in the independence of Vermont, but the existence of the United States was at risk in a legal independence that would almost necessarily result in Vermont's political dependence on Great Britain. If Vermont refused to join the Confederation, both justice, the first principle of self-preservation that Hamilton had invoked in 1774, and policy would argue in favor of a war of national preservation (rather than one to increase the empire of New York).[40]

Hamilton's final consideration was the problem of compensating New Yorkers who claimed to own land in Vermont. Where rights exist, there ought to be a legal remedy to vindicate them. New Yorkers, however, were more likely to secure compensation if Vermont were in the Union rather than out of it. If Vermont joined the Union, the arbitration procedures of the Articles of Confederation would be available, although this argument may have been somewhat disingenuous. Even with Vermont in the Union, some states might have opposed arbitration for fear that their own citizens would lose. This fear may explain why Hamilton associated admission of Vermont with a new constitution. Settling these kinds of disputes appeared to require federal courts that did not depend on the states for the authority to preside over them.

Yet Hamilton went even further. New York itself was not bound to compensate its citizens for their losses in Vermont. If New York had surrendered the territory voluntarily, then it would owe compensation, but sovereign states cannot be held responsible for losses caused by wars and revolutions that are beyond their power to control. "In wars between states, the sover-eign is never bound to make good the losses which the subject sustains by the captures or ravages of the enemy." When nations make peace, they ought to try to provide for compensation to civilians who have suffered from the war, but it is not always in the power of nations to win such terms from their opponents or to supply them by themselves. "The resources of nations" may not be "adequate to the reparation of. . . extensive losses." It would be "con-trary to the general good of society" to make a war-ravaged state, already deeply in debt, responsible for reparations. "Generosity and policy" might dictate compensation in some instances, but policy should govern to avoid sacrificing the welfare of the whole people to the demands of their wounded parts.[41]

These were harsh truths, which might seem to reveal Hamilton as an unprincipled practitioner of realpolitik; in fact, however, they establish his bona fides as a statesman who treated liberal restraints upon the use of force seriously. Hamilton anticipated one of the classic American arguments against imperialism in William Graham Sumner's *Conquest of the United States by Spain*. Writing after the Spanish-American War, on the eve of American annexation of the Philippines, Sumner warned Americans that their military victories could lead to a severe moral defeat:

Spain was the first, for a long time the greatest, of the modern imperialist states. The United States, by its historical origin, its traditions and its prin-ciples, is the chief representative of the revolt and reaction against that kind of state. I intend to show, by the line of action now proposed to us, which we call expansion and imperialism, we are throwing away some of the most important elements of the American symbol, and are adopting some of the most important elements of the Spanish symbol. We have beaten Spain in a military conflict, but we are submitting to be conquered by her on the field of ideas and policies.

Like Sumner, who was one of his nineteenth-century biographers, Hamilton suggested that New Yorkers, having bested England on the field of battle, would be conquered by it in the field of ideas and policies. "For my part," Hamilton observed, "I should regard the reunion of Vermont" by force with New York "as one of the greatest evils that could befall it, as a source of continual embarrassments and disquietude."[42]

Hamilton's remarks may have helped induce the New York Assembly to pass a bill recognizing the independence of Vermont on 11 April 1787, but his comments were not enough. The Senate rejected the bill, and the status of Vermont was left unresolved until after the ratification of the Constitution. Nonetheless, characterizations of Hamilton as "the personification of American militarism" need to be evaluated in light of his policies toward suspected Tories and Vermont. If Richard Kohn is right to suggest that the defining quality of militarism is a disposition to govern "by force alone," such a disposition is clearly absent in Hamilton's writings at the beginning, during, and after the Revolution.[43] The evidence indeed points in the opposite direction—toward a growing sophistication in Hamilton's understanding of war and free government, which would make him substantially ahead of his time, not just in his ideas about how to generate military power but also how to control it.

By the time of the Vermont debate, only three months before the Federal Convention of 1787, war had made Hamilton a revolutionary three times over: first, when he employed the conventional Catonic synthesis of Whig vigilance and Lockean liberalism to justify resistance to England; second, when he steered his own course by advocating a responsible, confidence-inspiring national government to increase the tangible and intangible capabilities of the Confederation during the war; and third, when he returned to the first principles of the Revolution to oppose democratic despotism and republican imperialism in New York. Though he shared the first revolution with his contemporaries, the second made him think not less but more about the effectual foundations of modern public-spiritedness in time of war; and the third sometimes made him wonder whether durable liberty was possible in a merely republican form of government. The second instance brought him to advocate a new constitution as a means to wage war effectively, but the third led him to interpret the New York Constitution and the Articles of Confederation so as to make them safer for liberty and a more durable Union. As a result of these intellectual revolutions, his most important contributions to American political thought arose from the different ways in which he began to suggest a new constitution could enable Americans to wage war effectively without succumbing to militarism.

Part Two
CONSTITUTIONALIST

5. Republican Empire

Americans have been quarreling about Hamilton's use or abuse of the Constitution for over 200 years, so anyone who enters this battle zone must do so with great trepidation. What new can be said? What value can it have to the larger debate over Hamilton and the Constitution? What light might it shed on Hamilton's alleged militarism?

To begin with the last question, both in *The Federalist* and at the New York Ratifying Convention, Hamilton took great pains to explain some of the paths that the United States might follow in order to become a great power without becoming a military despotism.[1] Because we today often take this possibility for granted, the many essays and speeches Hamilton wrote about it are commonly ignored, especially by readers who wish to discover the entire genius of the Constitution in *Federalist* 10 and 51. Yet neither Hamilton nor his opponents in the struggle to ratify the Constitution could assume that great power and liberty would necessarily flourish together in the United States. For vigilant American Whigs, most of the historical evidence from modern Europe and antiquity seemed to point in the opposite direction. By demonstrating the necessity of energy to secure liberty, Hamilton began to turn the conventional opinions of American Whigs upside down.

As revealed in the first paragraph of *The Federalist*, Hamilton regarded the American "empire" as one of the "most interesting" in the world because Americans were attempting to establish it in an entirely new way, through popular "reflection and choice" rather than through the traditional modes of sheer "accident" and military "force."[2] This hope to combine power and consent was present even in his earliest political tracts, but during the struggle to ratify the Constitution it became a call to national greatness. This was not the only reason he presented the act of establishing a new Constitution as a test of the principles of the Revolution, however. The rhetorical necessities of the debate over ratification left him no alternative.

The opponents of the Constitution, the Anti-Federalists, often argued that a national government could uphold its authority only through military force. By allowing standing armies in time of peace, congressional regulation of the militia, the suspension of habeas corpus in time of rebellion, and unlimited powers to raise revenue and troops, the Constitution appeared to supply the means to establish a military despotism. Federalist talk of upholding national honor in relations with other nations also seemed to be a suspicious sign of a motive for military adventurism.[3] For Hamilton's vigilant opponents, the coincidence of the means of oppression with dangerous signs of imperial ambition indicated that government by force alone would replace the consent of a free people and degrade their character as standard-bearers of the rights of mankind. These sorts of fears continue to influence our understanding of the debate over ratifying the Constitution. Thus, for example, Douglass Adair, one of the most influential scholars of the Founders in this century, has portrayed Hamilton as virtually obsessed with the idea of a "continual use of military force to keep the rebellious poor in their place."[4]

Hamilton could not leave unanswered his opponents' accusations that the Constitution was the "offspring of a temper fond of despotic power and hostile to the principles of liberty."[5] He turned the tables on his opponents by arguing that national weakness, not energy, was most likely to lead to civil war, arms races, martial law, prerogative, and military despotism. Hamilton did not limit his analysis merely to procedural safeguards against abuses of power. He also took into account both the geopolitical setting of the United States and (quite surprisingly) the necessity of preserving the vigilant spirit of liberty as a bulwark against militarism. As much by necessity as by design, his confrontation with the Anti-Federalists led him to develop his three most important contributions to the American understanding of war and constitutional government: his vision of an American republican empire, based on consent, but able when necessary to generate virtually unlimited military power; his defense of an energetic executive to avoid the extremes of constitutional weakness on the one hand and unconstitutional prerogative on the other; and his defense of an independent judiciary, which Hamilton had the temerity to refer to as the imperial chamber of the Union.

Hamilton's vision of a republican empire deserves special attention here because its character is still inadequately understood. Like Thomas Jefferson's empire of liberty and James Madison's extended republic, Hamilton's republican empire was meant to be big, but there are significant differences among these three visions. The agrarian frontier, the famous safety valve, was among Jefferson's fondest hopes to escape the necessity of an energetic government and the commercial society advocated by Hamilton.[6] As Gerald Stourzh observes, however, Hamilton was quite fearful of expanding too rapidly, lest expansion sow the seeds of disunion. In this regard, his position was completely opposed to Jefferson's. The "strongest argument in favor of an energetic government" was that none other could "preserve the Union of so large an empire" as the United States.[7] Although Hamilton sometimes made use of Madison's theory that the greater diversity produced by a larger republic might moderate the abuses of faction, he did not believe this was sufficient to control faction or to avoid the seditions that commonly lead to civil war in republics.[8] Madison supported not merely an extended but also a compound republic, with the states able to check the national government and vice versa.[9] He was much more a nationalist than perhaps most members of the Federal Convention of 1787, but as Lance Banning observes, federalism was still a necessary component of his vision of constitutional balance.[10] Hamilton, however, tended to regard the states as the greatest threat to continuance of the Union, and consequently, to durable liberty as well.[11] To confront this danger, he had to focus as much on nation as on state building. His solution to the interrelated problems of the common defense, domestic tranquillity, and durable liberty was to change the balance of power in the Union by changing the balance of loyalties of the American people. He meant to use the tangible instruments of state power to help build the intangible American national identity required to produce voluntary acceptance of national authority and thereby avoid a civil war.

Empire comes from the Latin *imperare*, to rule. When combined with the liberal-republican principle of consent, this sense of empire made Hamilton's vision unique—and quite different from that attributed to him by Gerald Stourzh, the scholar who has paid most attention to empire in Hamilton's thought. Empire was both a psychological and a political concept for Hamilton. It clearly meant powerful, but contrary to Stourzh, it did not mean imperialistic, in the modern sense of ruling by force alone.[12] It meant the ability to direct and attach the passions of the people to the national government. Although much has been written about the political psychology of the Founders and of *The Federalist* especially, scholars have usually focused on the problem of deriving a rule of reason from men governed by passion.[13] Because this task sounds like a contradiction in terms, the puzzle is certainly one of the most theoretically interesting problems raised by Hamilton and others in his time. Nonetheless, Hamilton's immediate, practical goal was to establish the authority of the government in a manner consistent with civil and political liberty. For that end, he rested his hopes on an essentially Machiavellian political psychology of confidence, fear, love, and hate. After explaining how the national government could establish its authority or empire within the hearts and minds of Americans, he turned his attention to making that authority effective in time of war by defending vigor in the House of Representatives and responsibility in the Senate.

Hamilton's career as one of the leading constitutional thinkers of his time did not begin auspiciously. Despite his labors to bring about a constitutional convention, he was not especially effective at the Federal Convention of 1787. To be sure, along with Madison, he did succeed at the Annapolis Convention in 1786 in drafting the call for another convention to render the Confederation "adequate to the exigencies of the union." Because this broad language could be construed to supply the moral authority to go beyond mere reform of the Articles of Confederation, it was perhaps Hamilton's most significant contribution to the Convention in 1787. Yet Gov. George Clinton of New York sent Robert Yates and John Lansing, two staunch opponents of a stronger national government, along with Hamilton to Philadelphia to ensure the archnationalist did not sacrifice any of the rights and interests of New York. Thus Hamilton was shackled with the delegation, which was perhaps the most suspicious of a national government at the Convention. Technically, he had one of three of New York's votes, but since the state voted as a delegation, he usually had no vote at all. He may have contributed some ideas in private, in the taverns after the daily meetings, but we will never know; he usually did not speak much in the official proceedings. As a rule, Hamilton did not reveal his frustration, either with his delegation or with the work of the Convention. On 18 June 1787, however, he presented one of the most brilliant, though also unsuccessful, speeches of his career.[14]

This part of the story is well known. With its proposal for a national government, including a separation of powers among the legislature, executive, and judiciary, Madison's Virginia Plan (introduced by Edmund Randolph) set the agenda for the Convention. Because Madison supported representation by population rather than by the states, however, the smaller states feared domination by the larger ones. On 15 June William Paterson of New Jersey introduced an alternative, the New Jersey Plan, which enhanced the revenue powers of the Confederation but vigilantly retained equal representation of the states. On 18 June, Hamilton introduced his third plan. Some scholars suggest it was deliberately designed to stake out an extreme nationalist position in order to make a much-reformed Virginia Plan seem like a moderate alternative to both Paterson's and Hamilton's.[15] It is far more plausible, however, to see it as a mixed result of Hamilton's frustration and the weakness he saw in both the other plans. Like the Continental Congress he described in his letter to Duane, the Convention seemed to be paying far too much attention to measures the delegates hoped the people would accept and not nearly enough to the institutions Hamilton believed they would ultimately need. Both in his speech and in his more formal plan of government, he therefore reacted in exactly the opposite way.[16]

Thus, for example, Hamilton called for vesting full sovereignty in the national government, establishing a Senate and an executive serving for good behavior (and thus, practically speaking, for life), and instituting nationally appointed governors with a right to veto state legislation. Though he did not propose abolishing the states, he saw no reason not to do so other than the danger of shocking public opinion. He also expressed an old-fashioned view of politics as the conflict between the few and the many and displayed a willingness to tolerate some of the newer, seamier sides of English politics (influence, patronage, and so on) as necessary supports of an effective new government. To cap it off, and to ensure a warm reception of his ideas, he indiscreetly quoted Jacques Necker's praise of the British constitution as the best in the world *so far* because of its unrivaled combination of "'public strength'" and "'individual security.'" It is impossible to be certain how seriously he meant the Convention to take these proposals. He said he "did not mean" to offer them as a "proposition" but to give a more correct view of his ideas and to suggest amendments to the Virginia Plan. This much is clear, however: without "*strong organs*" to uphold national authority and to lead within the national government itself, Hamilton believed the "representative democracy" developed by the Convention would inevitably be "feeble and inefficient." And just as inevitably, it would fail.[17]

To most members of the Convention, Hamilton's plan probably looked like the Second Coming of the British Empire. In effect, Congress would stand in place of Parliament with a right to make "all *laws whatsoever*" for the Union. For Hamilton, however, who never objected to Parliamentary supremacy but to Parliament's making laws arbitrarily, without the consent of the American people, there was an enormous difference between his plan and the British Empire. One way or another, all authority in his plan arose from consent, but by stretching republican principles as far as they would "admit," he also hoped to energize and balance the new government.[18] Indeed, Hamilton groped his way toward an important insight in this speech, which played an increasingly significant role in his subsequent discussions of the Constitution. Consent, the fundamental principle of representative democracy, did not necessarily have to result in weakness, as he believed it had during the Revolutionary War. As he had indicated in his

Phocion essays in 1784, consent might even be a source of enormous energy because it could legitimize the strong organs of government he believed were necessary. Because of its traditional character, Hamilton's proposal is usually regarded as the least republican plan offered at the Convention, but as all too often happens in Hamilton's case, this conclusion is only half true. Because he employed consent to legitimize energy (rather than simply to limit power), his plan was also a radical innovation in American republican theory.

Hamilton may not have understood all the implications of his strategy, but as he groped his way toward a means to circumvent the jealousies of the states, he found that he could often trump them with the liberal-republican principle of consent. Because the national government could also lay claim to the consent of the people, it could have at least equal moral authority with Americans during the Founding era, and perhaps much more as it acquired the invaluable support of custom and habit. Despite these liberal-republican innovations, the similarities between Hamilton's plan and the British Empire were probably more impressive to the delegates than the differences. As a result, Hamilton's speech, though applauded by many, was supported by none. Though he contributed to some important committees and sometimes spoke up on the floor of the Convention, he must therefore have felt useless in Philadelphia. He left on 30 June, returned without Yates and Lansing on 13 August, and then left the next day. He forced himself to return again on 5 or 6 September, when he gave Madison a second version of his plan. The second draft incorporated the features of the Convention's work that he approved but also retained the elevated tone of the first.[19]

Despite his misgivings, Hamilton forced himself to sign the Constitution and encouraged all others present to do so because he believed it would be irresponsible not to. The chance of good to be obtained from it outweighed the anarchy and disorder he feared without it. He also took some encouragement from the probability that George Washington would be the first president, with himself perhaps as his former chief's principal adviser. He believed that the success of the government would depend upon good habits, which in turn would depend upon a successful administration. He thus seems to have pinned all his hopes for the Constitution on its first years, when good results might "conciliate the confidence and affection of the people" in its favor.[20] Thus, though he failed at the Convention, he did not give up hope of accomplishing his objectives. His goals were not to transform the United States into another England, with king, lords, Commons, and corruption to boot, but to make the Constitution a workable instrument of government. Because the Convention rejected his plan for an executive and a Senate during good behavior, he never advocated them again, at least not in any of his collected writings. Yet he never gave up on his larger goal of endowing the Republic with the public strength and individual security that had enabled England to become both the greatest power and the freest nation of the eighteenth century. Indeed, he sought to turn even the most popular or democratic features of the Constitution to serve this end. As a result, he and other Founders consistently provoked enormous opposition, especially when they spoke about national greatness.

At the Federal Convention, for example, Charles Pinckney anticipated many of the Anti-Federalists' worst fears about the new Constitution, observing that

> our situation appears to be this—a new extensive country containing within itself the materials for forming a government extending to its citizens the blessings of civil and religious liberty—capable of making them happy at home. This is the great end of Republican Government. We mistake the object of government, if we hope or wish that it is to make us respectable abroad. Conquest or superiority among other powers is not or ought never to be the object of republican systems.

So far as practicable, Pinckney wanted to turn his back on the obsession with military power of traditional European states. If the American republics were "sufficiently active and energetic to rescue us from contempt & preserve our domestic happiness and security, it is all we can expect from them. It is more than almost any other Government ensures its citizens."[21]

A thoughtful Anti-Federalist, Brutus, developed Pinckney's objection much further in a manner that also testifies to the liberal-republicanism of even Hamilton's most determined opponents. By writing as Brutus, he implied the Federalists were embryo Caesars. Though he put on a republican toga, he was no more a classical republican than Publius-Hamilton. Few classical statesmen, whether Brutus or Cato or Cassius or Publius or Phocion or Pericles, ever objected to imperialism when they could get away with it. Yet the American Brutus objected to imperialism as a matter of principle, because it was incompatible with the most important innovation in political and moral theory in his time, the universal rights of mankind. Why should Americans, removed as they were from Europe, care about respectability and military power? "European governments are almost all of them framed, and administered with a view to arms, and war, as that in which their chief glory consists; they mistake the end of government." According to the law of nature, "It was designed to save men's lives, not destroy them."

Americans had to beware of the imperial temptation not only because it contradicted the liberal principles of their Revolution but also because experience suggested that imperialism was the traditional ruin of republics:

> History furnishes no example of a free republic, anything like the extent of the United States. The Grecian republics were of small extent; so also was that of the Romans. Both of these, it is true, extended their conquests of large territories of country, and the consequence was that their governments were changed from free governments, to those of the most tyrannical that ever existed in the world.

Brutus was especially suspicious of individuals who spoke of honor and glory, which he treated as the primary motives of imperialism. Yet to wean his countrymen from the love of martial glory, he also felt obliged to hold out a different kind of honor as a source of American pride and self-restraint. In effect, he accomplished a transvaluation of the meaning of honor by synthesizing the Puritan vision of the city on a hill with the liberal principles of mutual preservation and consent. "We ought to furnish the world with the example of a great people, who in their civil institutions hold chiefly in view, the attainment of virtue, and domestic happiness among themselves." He then added with enormous contempt for the martial ways of the Old World, "Let the monarchs of Europe share among them the glory of depopulating countries. . . . I envy them not the honor, and I pray this country will not be ambitious for it."[22]

In Virginia, Patrick Henry voiced both the political and the moral worries of Brutus and Pinckney with almost biblical passion. Were Americans beginning to worship the golden calf of power? He did not know, but he suggested they had to be vigilant against this dark passion in themselves lest it corrupt them and make them like the heathens of the Old World. There was too much talk of Americans becoming a "contemptible people" because of their allegedly "feeble Government." This was not the way Americans spoke at the beginning of their Revolution. "When the American spirit was in its youth, the language of America was different: Liberty, Sir, was then the chief object." How low Americans had fallen since that time! The true "American spirit has fled from hence: It has gone to regions where it has never been expected. It has gone to France in search of a splendid government—a strong energetic Government." He heard from the Federalists only that "some way or other we must be a great and mighty empire: we must have an army, and a navy, and a number of things" that no original leader of the Revolution had considered necessary for liberty. If Americans became

animated by a taste for the splendor and respectability "of one great consolidated empire of America," they would inevitably sacrifice the soul of their
Revolution. Either the Union would be too weak to maintain itself, or the
instruments of state power allowed by the Constitution would substitute
the rule of force for the consent that had maintained the Union so far. Like
an Old Testament prophet, Henry warned that "those nations which have
gone in search of grandeur, power and splendor, have also fallen a sacrifice,
and been victims of their own folly. While they acquired those visionary
blessings, they lost their freedom."[23] As Herbert Storing has observed, the
sum of these Anti-Federalist objections was that Federalists seemed to want
Americans to be just like other nations. For the Anti-Federalists, however,
that was precisely what they could not be if they were to remain true to the
revolutionary principles that gave them a unique title to honor among all
nations.[24]

The Anti-Federalists were a diverse group, so it is difficult to generalize
about them, but equally as important to some of them as the danger of
American imperialism abroad was the threat of military despotism at home.
Much of this fear arose from their well-known preference for small, homo-
geneous republics, where citizens know their representatives not only by
name but also by character. Thus, for example, the Federal Farmer observed
that within each state, "Opinion founded on the [citizen's] knowledge of
those who govern, procures obedience without force. But remove the opinion, which must fall with a knowledge of characters in so widely extended a
country, and force then becomes necessary to secure the purposes of civil
government." In addition to popular suspicion of unknown and perhaps
unresponsive representatives, the great diversity of American manners, interests, and opinions seemed less likely to moderate than to produce faction and even civil war. "In a republic," Brutus observed, "the manners,
sentiments, and interests of the people should be similar. If this be not the
case, there will be a constant clashing of opinions; and the representatives
of one part will be constantly striving against those of the other. This will
retard the operations of government, and prevent such conclusions as will
promote the public good." Precisely because there were not sufficient bonds
of community to unite Americans by affection and consent, the Federal
Farmer concluded that the new government could not accomplish its responsibilities "without calling to its aid a military force, which must very
soon destroy all elective governments in the country, produce anarchy, or
establish despotism" through a standing army.[25]

Hamilton confronted these objections, first by stressing the dependence
of domestic happiness on respectability abroad, and then by suggesting that

a weak Union was bound to produce his opponents' worst nightmares. Responding to Pinckney at the Convention, he observed that "it has been said that respectability in the eyes of foreign nations was not the proper object at which we aimed; the proper object of republican Government was domestic happiness and tranquillity. This," Hamilton observed, was "an ideal distinction. No government could give us tranquillity and happiness at home, which did not give us sufficient stability and strength to make us respectable abroad." The United States could not remain safe for liberty unless it also became fit for war. Hence, the dispute between Hamilton and most Anti-Federalists was not over the ultimate objective but over the best means to pursue it: an energetic national government or a more traditional confederation of states.

For Hamilton, conquest and imperialism were as unacceptable as objects of national policy as they were for New York against Vermont, but that did not mean the United States could turn its back on European quarrels. He had his eyes on a gathering storm in Europe that might soon cross the Atlantic. A "cloud has for some time been hanging over the European world. If it should break forth in a storm, who can insure us that in its progress, a part of its fury would not be spent upon us?" Hamilton observed that "peace or war will not always be left to our option. . . . However moderate or unambitious we might be, we cannot count upon the moderation, or hope to extinguish the ambition of others." At the close of the Seven Years War, it was impossible to imagine that exhausted England and France would go to war little more than a decade later during the American Revolution. Nonetheless, America was a pawn, or rather, the vulnerable and strategically vital king in the chess games that these two empires played across the globe. Judging from recent history, indeed from the "history of mankind," it seemed to Hamilton that the "fiery and destructive passions of war" are far more powerful than the sentiments that support peace. Therefore, "to model our political systems on speculations of lasting tranquillity" would be "to calculate on the weaker springs of human nature."[26]

Hamilton did not believe the United States could always isolate itself from Europe's wars. The ocean was a highway as well as a barrier to the Western Hemisphere, but "the rights of neutrality will only be respected when they are defended by an adequate power. A nation, despicable by its weakness, forfeits even the privilege of being neutral." As if he were predicting the first twenty-five years of the Republic's maritime history, he observed that American military insignificance would make American "commerce prey to the wanton intermeddlings of nations at war with each other; who, having nothing to fear from us, would with little scruple or remorse supply their wants by depredations on our property, as often as it fell their way."[27] The need to prepare for such wars and to prevent civil war in America then led Hamilton to develop a critique of confederations from which they have never recovered.

The "great and radical vice" in the Articles of Confederation was the great and radical vice of all merely federal governments and the one most responsible for American military weakness during the Revolution. It was "the principle of LEGISLATION for STATES or Governments, in their CORPORATE or COLLECTIVE CAPACITIES and as contradistinguished from the INDIVIDUALS of whom they consist." In theory, the existing Confederation was well-suited for war. It had an "indefinite discretion to raise men and money," but in practice, it had "no authority to raise either by regulations extending to the individual citizens" of America. In "theory" its "resolutions concerning those objects are laws, constitutionally binding on the members of the Union, yet in practice they are mere recommendations, which the states observe or disregard at their option."[28] The Articles gave the legislative power in time of war to Congress, but the executive power over individuals remained with the states. This overjealous separation of powers ensured that the Confederation's powers would be executed only when it served the interests of the individual state governments.

A confederation is a species of alliance "depending for its execution on the good faith of the parties. Compacts of this kind exist among all civilized nations subject to the usual vicissitudes of peace and war, of observance and nonobservance, as the interests of the contracting powers dictate." The parallelism in this sentence is striking. Observance went with peace, nonobservance with war. Confederations were effective when least needed, and useless when most necessary. Europe in the eighteenth century was possessed by an "epidemical rage" for this "species of compacts," but they were "scarcely formed before they were broken, giving an instructive but afflicting lesson to mankind how little dependence is to be placed upon treaties which have no other sanction than the obligations of good faith; and which oppose the general considerations of peace and justice to the impulse of any immediate passion or interest."[29]

Hamilton was confronting two different but interrelated strategic problems at the same time: first, the imbalance of power between Europe and the United States, and second, the imbalance of power between the states and the federal government. He recognized not only that an effectual balance between the United States and Europe depended on correcting the imbalance between the states and the federal government, but also, and far more important, that the root cause of the domestic imbalance arose from the greater loyalty of citizens to their states than to the Union. In quarrels between the Union and the states, the states had "one transcendent advantage," the "ordinary administration of criminal and civil justice." Hamilton called this advantage "the most powerful, most universal, and most attractive source of popular obedience and attachment." Men love their benefactors and are therefore attached to them, but they fear and therefore obey those who can do them harm. The states' utility in enabling victims to obtain justice would secure attachment while their ability to punish and deter criminals would ensure obedience. Their "benefits" and "terrors" would be constantly before the "public eye." Their role as the "immediate and visible guardian of life and property" would contribute "more than any other circumstance to impressing upon the minds of the people affection, esteem, and reverence toward the government." Hamilton therefore called the states' ability to distribute benefits and to inspire terrors the "great cement of society," which, "independent of all other causes of influence, would ensure them so decided an empire over their citizens, as to render them at all times a complete counterpoise, and not infrequently dangerous rivals to the power of the Union."[30]

This was not the first time Hamilton spoke of empire. On the back of the pages of his military pay book during the Revolutionary War, he took notes on Plutarch's account of the life of Numa. He was particularly impressed by Numa's use of religion to mold the character of the Romans. This "alone could have sufficient empire over the minds of a barbarous and warlike people to engage them to cultivate the arts of peace." During the Revolution, he observed that the "particular governments will have more empire over the minds of their subjects, than the general one, because their agency will be more direct, more uniform, more apparent. . . . The people will be habituated to look up to them as the arbiters and guardians of their personal concerns, by which the passions of the vulgar, if not all men are most strongly affected."[31] For Hamilton, the fundamental advantage of the states was that they had empire, or rule over the minds of their citizens already, while the distant, remote, and invisible general authority did not possess such empire, and in any merely federal system, depending on the cooperation of the states, could not acquire it. In sum, *imperium in imperio* was a necessary consequence of any merely federal system because the central authorities had no chance of competing effectively with the states for the loyalties of their citizens.

Hence, the general pattern of federations was that "weakness at the head has produced resistance in the members. This has been the immediate parent of civil war: auxiliary force has been invited" from abroad, "and a foreign power has annihilated their liberties and their name." This pattern did not justify the inference that "republics cannot exist"; but to Hamilton at least, it strongly suggested republics could not exist for long on merely federal principles. One of two consequences would follow from continuing the Confederation: either it would go the way of almost all wartime alliances and collapse into competing states or alliances of states, or it would impose its authority by military force. The reason: government implies the power of making laws, and laws require a sanction, a penalty or punishment for disobedience. Without a penalty, laws are not laws, but mere advice or recommendations.

There are only two ways of inflicting a penalty: through "Courts and Ministers of Justice, or by military force; by the Coercion of the magistracy, or by the COERCION of arms. The first can evidently only apply to men—the last must of necessity be employed against bodies politic, or communities or states." Contrary to Douglass Adair's argument, Hamilton had no intention of upholding the authority of the Union by means of a "continual" resort to force; instead, he showed that the continual use of force was the only way the Confederation could overcome the empires of the states. Though the states ought not to "prefer a national constitution" that "could only be kept in motion by the instrumentality of a large army," this was the "plain alternative" for opponents who would "deny it the power of extending its operations to individuals." Republican government requires the rule of law, but the confederal form of union denied Congress the means of establishing the rule of anything but martial law. Either an army must put down resistance, or the government could not uphold its law. Either the Confederation would become a military despotism, or it would collapse, and the American states would become even more vulnerable to foreign powers.[32]

As David Epstein suggests, this observation was the foundation of Hamilton's most devastating critique of Montesquieu, if not of all early advocates of confederations. Montesquieu's cure for both anarchy (the rule of chance or "accident") and hegemony (the rule of "force") in a federation was to subdue those states that resisted its authority in a civil war. Neither Hamilton nor Madison ever ruled out this possibility, but Hamilton also revealed that Montesquieu's strategy was absurd as a first principle of day-to-day government. "Such a scheme," Hamilton observed, "if practicable at all, would instantly degenerate into a military despotism, but it will be found in every light impracticable. . . . A project of this kind," he declared, "would be little less romantic than the monster taming spirit that is attributed to the fabulous heroes and demi-gods of antiquity."[33] The reason: the imbalance of loyalties favored the states, which were more likely to resist than to enforce confederal authority and much more likely to win in quarrels with the Confederation as well. As a result of this imbalance, Hamilton strongly suspected that the existing Confederation would quickly disintegrate into several regional alliances.

As Gottfried Dietze observes, if the Confederation did collapse, Hamilton believed a variety of actual or potential quarrels over trade, tariffs, land in the West, and the apportionment of the national debt, not to mention the passions of human nature and mere circumstance of geographical propinquity, made civil war almost inevitable and foreign intervention highly probable.[34] If the states were continually at war, or in fear of war with each other, then the Anti-Federalists' worst fears would come true. As Hamilton observed,

> Safety from external danger is the most powerful director of national conduct. Even the ardent love of liberty will, after a time, give way to its dictates. The violent destruction of life and property incident to war, the continual effort and alarm attendant on a state of continual danger will compel nations the most attached to liberty to resort for repose and security to institutions which have a tendency to destroy their civil and political rights. To be more safe, they at length become willing to be less free.

This famous passage should not be taken as a description of the motives that induce men to move from a Hobbesian state of nature toward an uncontrollable Leviathan state. Instead, it was a warning that Americans could preserve neither the forms of free government nor the spirit of a free people unless they took all necessary steps to maintain the Union and peace within it. Standing armies

> must inevitably result from the dissolution of the confederacy. Frequent war and constant apprehension must produce them; the weaker states or confederacies, would have first recourse to them, to put themselves upon an equality with their more potent neighbors. They would endeavor to supply the inferiority of population and resources, by a more regular and effective system of defense, by disciplined troops and fortifications.

In addition to raising the standing armies dreaded by the Anti-Federalists, "they would, at the same time, be necessitated to strengthen the executive arm of government; in doing which, their constitution would acquire a progressive direction towards monarchy."[35]

Fears of civil war would produce not only an arms race but also a race toward military despotism. The smaller states would be the first to militarize their communities, but they would not be the last:

> Small States, or States of less natural strength, under vigorous governments, have often triumphed over larger States, or States of greater natural strength, which have been destitute of these advantages. . . . Neither the pride, nor the safety of the more important states, or confederacies, would permit them long to submit to this mortifying and adventitious inferiority. They would quickly resort to means similar to those by which it had been effected, to reinstate themselves in their lost pre-eminence. Thus we should see in little time established in every part of this country, the same engines of despotism, which have been the scourge of the old world![36]

As Frederick Marks demonstrates, this argument *ad horrendum* was not overwrought. In light of the existing independence of Vermont and of secessionist talk in Kentucky, dissolution and civil war, with the intervention of perhaps both England and Spain, were quite possible.[37] If Americans meant to avoid the "same engines" of military despotism of the Old World, they had to move significantly beyond any previous conception of federal union. But how?

The most obvious answer was to make prudent use of the accidents of geography. Despite Hamilton's derogatory remarks in his youth about British standing armies, he and most of his contemporaries knew that England was an exception to European history because sea power was generally more favorable to free governments than land power. They knew there was "a wide difference . . . between military establishments, in a country seldom exposed by its situation to internal invasions, and one which is often subject to them, and is always apprehensive of them."[38] For land powers surrounded by hostile neighbors, like Germany in the nineteenth and twentieth centuries, for example, the "perpetual menacings of danger oblige the government to be always prepared to repel it—its armies must be numerous enough for instant defense. The continual necessity for their services enhances the importance of the soldier, and proportionately degrades the condition of the citizen." Land powers, then, tend to become military despotisms:

> The military state becomes elevated above the civil. The inhabitants of territories, often the theater of war, are unavoidably subjected to frequent infringements of their rights, which serve to weaken their sense of those

rights; and by degrees, the people are brought to consider the soldiery not only as their protectors but as their superiors. The transition from this disposition to considering them as masters, is neither remote, nor difficult.

When the people habitually sacrifice their liberty for security, it then becomes almost impossible to encourage them to "make a bold or effectual resistance, to usurpations, supported by the military power."[39] Even for Anti-Federalists who understood vigilance as the virtue most essential to keep Americans free, it was of prime importance to prevent wars between states that would make the people themselves willing to accept a military despotism. The argument was brilliant, first because it turned the Anti-Federalists' most cherished virtue against their strongest prejudice, and second because it was probably true. If the spirit of liberty depends upon a sense of security that is more likely to arise in maritime than in land powers, it necessarily depended upon a government strong enough to unite the strength of all the members of the Union, so that they could become allies rather than adversaries.

The best strategy for avoiding a military despotism while simultaneously providing for the common defense was therefore to preserve the Union at almost any cost and to transform the United States into a sea power as quickly as possible. Sea powers "can have no good pretext, if they are even so inclined, to keep on foot armies so numerous as must be maintained" by land powers. Consequently, the people can be in "no danger of being broken into military subordination. The laws are not accustomed to relaxations, in favor of military exigencies—the civil state remains in full vigor, neither corrupted nor confounded with the principles or the propensities of the other state." When nations do not have to fight on their own territory and rely more on sea than on land power,

> the smallness of the army renders the rest of the community an overmatch for it; and the citizens, not habituated to look up to the military for protection, or to submit to its oppressions, neither love nor fear the soldiery: They view them in a spirit of jealous acquiescence in a necessary evil, and stand ready to resist a power which they suppose may be exerted to the prejudice of their rights.

"When a nation has become so powerful by sea, that it can protect its dock-yards," and the rest of the nation as well, "by its fleets, this supersedes the necessity of garrisons for that purpose." Then, the usually small army

Hamilton had been advocating since 1783, though it might "usefully aid the magistrate to suppress a small faction, or occasional mob, or insurrection," would be "unable to enforce encroachments against the united efforts of the people."[40]

To produce this optimum defense posture (which, we should never forget, was also necessary to preserve the vigilant spirit of free citizens), the prime necessity was to change the balance of power in the Union. Or rather, if the fundamental source of the Union's weakness arose from the empires that the state governments possessed over the minds of their citizens, the necessary solution was to change the balance of power by changing the balance of loyalties. The national government's own empire must be established over their passions. As Machiavelli, the first great state-and-nation-builder of the modern world, argued, the new government would have to produce affection among most citizens, instill fear in the lawless, and avoid inspiring hatred for its authority.[41] As Hamilton well understood, the first objective required the ability to have a material impact for the better on the daily lives of ordinary citizens; the second, the power to punish individuals through the courts; and the third, popular belief in the legitimacy of the government's authority.

The first objective led Hamilton to discuss the dependence of public spirit upon public confidence once again. Although some observers presumed that public spirit and devotion to liberty in America had declined since the war, Hamilton observed that the people's devotion to liberty, their "Spirit of Patriotism" was as "high as ever," but their attachment to the weak and ineffective government produced by their own "extreme jealousies" was indeed in decline. No power on earth, Hamilton observed, would "be capable of making a government unpopular, which is in its principles a wise and good one, and vigorous in its operations."[42] As a "general rule," Hamilton believed the people's "confidence" in and obedience to a government will "commonly be proportioned to the goodness or badness of its administration." "The confidence of the people will easily be gained by a good administration. This is the true touchstone." For a number of reasons, ranging from the probability that national councils would be less prone to faction than those of the states to the likelihood that Washington would be the first president, Hamilton believed there was a "probability that the General Government would be better administered than the particular governments."[43] Consequently, Hamilton hazarded an

observation which will not be the less just, because to some it may appear new; which is, that the more the operations of the national authority are intermingled in the ordinary exercise of government; the more the citizens are accustomed to meet with it in the common occurrences of their political life; the more it is familiarized to their sight and to their feelings; the further it enters into those objects which touch the most sensible chords, and put in motion the most active springs of the human heart; the greater will be the probability that it will conciliate the respect and attachment of the community. Man is very much a creature of habit. A thing that rarely strikes his senses will generally have but little influence on his mind. A government continually at a distance and out of sight, can hardly be expected to interest the sensations of the people. The inference is, that the authority of the Union, and the affections of the citizens towards it, will be strengthened rather than weakened by its extension to what are called matters of internal concern; and it will have less occasion to recur to force in proportion to the familiarity and comprehensiveness of its agency. The more it circulates through those channels and currents, in which the passions of mankind naturally flow, the less will it require the aid of violent and perilous expedients of compulsion.[44]

Although the Anti-Federalists argued that a powerful and distant national government would breed such distrust that it could uphold its authority only by means of military coercion, Hamilton turned the tables on them once again. In general, the more active and effective the government, the more it would be able to rely on affection. To be sure, confidence would be lowest in the beginning; therefore Hamilton staked most of his hopes for the Constitution on a successful initial administration of the new government. Yet over time, citizens would become habituated to its authority, and perhaps even grateful for its advantages. The more durable, tangible, and visible the advantages, the more the loyalty of the people would solidify and increase. Sadly, this process suggests that some form of military coercion was most likely to be necessary in the beginning, but it also implies that as the government acquired the respectability that comes with age, such coercion would become ever less necessary. The more the government could rely on habitual obedience to its laws and on affection for its blessings, the less likely it was to become a military despotism.

Popular attachment would not be enough to change the imbalance of loyalties in the Union, however. To become a respectable, confidence-inspiring government, rather than a mere alliance, the national government would also have to produce respect for its authority. It had to be able to employ judicious doses of legitimate terror against the lawless. It needed to address the "hopes and fears of individuals, and to attract to its support, those passions, which have the strongest influence on the human heart. It must in short, possess all the means and have a right to resort to all the methods of executing the powers" that had enabled the state governments to acquire empire over the hearts and minds of their citizens. To overcome the great and radical vice of the Confederation, the principle of legislating for the states rather than for individuals, the national government required the ability to use coercion against individuals through courts and magistrates. For Hamilton, this measure was the only way to uphold the authority of the Union without recourse to the monster-taming and ultimately despotic means of military coercion suggested by Montesquieu.[45]

The great problem was to produce this respect without inspiring hatred. Judicial process was certainly more likely to avoid producing hatred than military enforcement of the laws of the Union, but that was hardly enough to accomplish the task. The problem of establishing governmental authority had been addressed by most modern political theorists from Machiavelli to the American Founding, and by Hamilton's time something of a consensus had emerged: authority had to be rooted in freedom. Man was born free, but everywhere he is in chains, or subject to laws, both just and unjust, said Rousseau. He did not know how this transformation occurred and doubted that anyone else did either, but he thought he could explain how to make authority legitimate. Hamilton agreed with Rousseau about the foundation of legitimate authority: consent. Indeed, Rousseau's famous formula for legitimate government, that the citizen be to the government as the government is to the subject, is also useful in describing Hamilton's strategy for establishing the empire of the national government. For the sake of legitimacy, authority would arise from the people, collectively, as citizens; both for the sake of effectiveness and to avoid military enforcement, power would then be applied to them individually, as subjects of the laws, through the courts.[46]

Fundamentally, Hamilton believed consent was necessary to give the Constitution true empire over the minds of the American people. If it were perceived as the product of an external will, it would lead to disunion and civil war. It had to be seen as the result of popular sovereignty, or it would have no authority at all. He therefore concluded his critique of the Confederation in The Federalist by questioning the legitimacy of the authority exercised by Congress under the Articles. He observed that "it has not a little contributed to the infirmities of the existing federal system, that it never had a ratification by the people." In principle, this lack called into question the "validity of its powers" over a people who had not consented to give it any powers at all; in practice, it called into question the ability of the Confederation to govern by giving "birth to the enormous doctrine of legislative repeal" (or nullification and even secession) by the states. To avoid that grave danger, Hamilton argued that the fabric not of an American federation but of "the American Empire ought to rest on the solid basis of the CONSENT OF THE PEOPLE. The streams of national power ought to flow immediately from that pure original fountain of legitimate authority."[47] As a result, the American empire would be different from all others before it. It would be the world's first republican empire because it would be the first empire founded in consent.

In the best case, consent might even produce popular affection for the new government and a sense of national identity, by attaching the people's passions to a principle and vision of themselves that they believed to be fundamentally good. Hamilton invoked some of Hume's skepticism about the possibility of establishing a government by consent in order to turn this task into a national challenge. He concluded *The Federalist* by observing that the establishment of a Constitution, "by the voluntary consent of a whole people" was a political "PRODIGY" of the greatest magnitude, the sort that could bind the nation more by its pride than by its interests and fears.[48] Though Hamilton shared Brutus's hope that the United States might lead the world by its "conduct and example," his vision of his country's role in the world was also much more active and far grander than his fellow New Yorker's. He hesitated to enter too far into "regions of futurity," especially in a newspaper discussion, but he did suggest that "our situation invites and our interest prompts us to aim at an ascendant in the system of American affairs." He was no longer talking about the United States alone, but the Western Hemisphere as well. "Europe by her arms and by her negotiations, by force and by fraud," had established its dominion over most of the world, including the New World. Serving as an exemplary republic would not be enough to resist the great empires of Europe, with all their power and their exalted claims of "superiority" to the rest of mankind. The United States would also have to become a forceful republic, and sometimes even make common cause with other countries. Hamilton declared that "it belongs to us to vindicate the honor of the human race, and to teach that assuming brother moderation." The means to resist the Europeans was not a mere union of the thirteen states but "a great American system," which would include most of a New World, presumably after it followed the American example and rebelled against its colonial masters. Such an alliance would be "superior to all transatlantic force or influence and able to dictate the terms of the connection between the old and the new world!"[49]

The seeds of the Monroe Doctrine as a vehicle for resisting European imperialism are clearly latent in this passage, which, unfortunately, also leaves some disturbing questions unanswered. Hamilton did not explain how Americans could lead the New World without dominating it, like an Old World empire. Yet his omission does not justify Gerald Stourzh's conclusion that his "call to greatness" was "only superficially clothed in the language of self-determination."[50] Hamilton did not employ the language of consent ad hoc, merely for the sake of making debating points. It was an essential component of his political writings from their beginning in 1774 until his death. Reconciling leadership with consent is a fundamental problem of all alliances and must be worked out over time. There was no possible way for Hamilton to offer prescriptions when the Latin American colonies had not yet won their independence. His critique of confederations (alliances) reveals the enormous difficulty of blending leadership with consent, but he was not encouraging imperialism in this passage. Instead, he was taking American exceptionalism more seriously or romantically than anyone had before. Nationalism has many deservedly ugly connotations in our time, but since the beginning of the American Revolution, American nationalism has always been an odd bird in world politics. Its most important foundation may well be allegiance to principles that Americans at least believe to be universal, for example, equality, rights, consent, and so on. Though such allegiance can lead to great self-deception and more than a little self-righteousness, the hope of being an exception to the practices of other nations has almost always been at the center of Americans' understanding of their role in the world; this was true of Hamilton as well. At the end of *Federalist* 11, he was almost daydreaming of an anti-imperial alliance that would supply great regard to his country as a champion of the honor (equal rights) of the human race.

In truth, with a remarkable blend of liberal principle and geopolitical prudence, Hamilton supplied an almost utopian vision of national greatness, still rooted in consent, which is much closer to his countrymen's understanding of their role in the world in the twentieth than in the eighteenth century. American ascendancy could lead to imperialism, as it did in the late nineteenth century especially, but it did not have to do so. Under no circumstances should we conclude that imperialism was a necessary or desired outcome of any of the Founders' visions of the United States. It was much easier to preach than to practice anti-imperialism, but late-nineteenth-century views of imperialism as a positive benefit for peoples subjugated by Americans were as much a corruption of the Founders' thought as were views of slavery as a positive good before the Civil War. In the best case, Hamilton hoped the United States would become a force not merely in the hemispheric but also in the world balance of power, with modern liberal-republican opposition to a government rooted in force and fraud (not a crusade for democracy) at the center of the national purpose.

Sooner or later, Hamilton believed his country would come into conflict with the Old World, and he meant to do everything he could to prepare for it. Yet his moral-strategic calculus ought not to be confused with militarism. He concluded *The Federalist* by warning the sincere lovers of the Union against "hazarding anarchy, civil war, perpetual alienation of the States from each other, and perhaps the military despotism of a victorious demagogue, in the pursuit of what they are not likely to obtain, but from TIME and EXPE-RIENCE."[51] He had to agree with Hume that Founding was not simply a matter of reflection and choice but also of custom and habit. Time, experience, feeling, and (Hamilton did not say) good luck as well seemed necessary to produce the union of sentiments, interests, and opinions required to make consent an effectual principle of American national government. Because he took the lead in early American efforts to transform the United States into a great power, it was perhaps inevitable that he would be accused of militarism. Nonetheless, his own determination to avoid any government resting on "accident and force" is as apparent on the last page as it is on the first of *The Federalist.*

For Hamilton, the fundamental question in 1787 was whether a representative democracy, a term he may well have coined, could generate the leadership required to build and sustain a great empire. It was not that he valued the latter more than the former but that he saw the fates of the republic and the empire as mutually dependent. Though he was not sure that the American Republic was capable of empire, and doubted its capacity to survive and flourish as a consequence, his discussions of bicameralism reveal the two qualities he believed most essential to build a republican empire: vigor in the House of Representatives and responsibility in the Senate. These qualities merit attention not merely because of their value for war. They also deserve it because of a common tendency either to see Publius as the author of an inefficient government unsuited to the needs of modern democracy or to concede that such inefficiency has sometimes been the result of his vision, but with the protest that it is the price we must pay for freedom.[52] If we are comparing the United States to a parliamentary system, there is some justice in the latter view especially. Yet Hamilton was not comparing the Constitution to a modern parliamentary system. Instead, his reference point was the Articles of Confederation. Compared to the Articles, the Constitution was not only intended to build but actually resulted in an enormous increase in the vigor of Congress.

Largely because the states retained control over the police powers of health, safety, welfare, and morals within their territories, Hamilton believed the role of the national government would initially be quite limited—except when it came to national defense, for which vigor was essential. The principal powers of Congress were to "provide for the common defense," to "regulate commerce," to "declare war," to "raise and support armies," to admit new states, and to dispose of the Western territories. These tasks required money, but none more so than defense. The "chief sources of expense" in every government are "wars and rebellions," and "the great and leading objects of the federal government, in which revenue is concerned, are to maintain domestic peace, and to provide for the common defense." Hamilton observed that "fourteen-fifteenths" of the British budget was "absorbed in the payment of interest of debts, contracted for carrying on wars, in which that nation has been engaged, and in the maintenance of armies and fleets" in time of war and peace. Especially when the United States' civil list was in its infancy, the same or greater proportion of revenue would go to pay for defense and the debts incurred to support it.[53]

Hence, Hamilton objected to proposals from some Anti-Federalists in New York to amend the Constitution to require a two-thirds majority to borrow money. Their premise was that the easier it was for Congress to borrow to pay for war, the easier it would be for Congress to go to war. It could then push the responsibility for paying for it onto future generations rather than onto its own constituents.[54] Like Montesquieu, who feared "infinite delays" and the possibility that "on the most urgent and pressing occasions, the wheels of government might be stopped by the caprice of a single person," Hamilton worried that a combination of jealousy and moralism would deny Congress the vigorous revenue powers essential to the common defense. Supporters of the Anti-Federalists' amendment clearly feared their own government more than potential enemies. Yet which, after all, was to be "preferred, to trust a majority of your whole Govt. and president to enter into a war of Ambition—or to put it into the power of a minority to prevent your own defense against Ambitious War" from abroad? Were the Anti-Federalists so jealous of ambition, even in the House, that they would deny the government the means to defend the rights of the American people? If so, and it should "become a steady principle not to make war for rights," the people would "soon have no rights." At all times, Hamilton insisted, "it should be in our power to enforce a defense and assert the Rights of the Nation."[55]

This constitutional requirement for Hamilton's geopolitical strategy raises the question of how much energy he believed would be necessary for Congress to provide for American defense. His answer was unequivocal, and almost as shocking today as it must have been in 1787: unlimited energy. He was not talking about arbitrary, but absolute, power. If the end of defense was legitimate, it required as much power to raise ships, troops, and revenue as might be necessary. The degree of revenue and amount of manpower and equipment that might be required for defense was not and never could be subject to American control. It depended upon the degree of power employed by American enemies. "Long and ruinous wars may require all the possible abilities of the country." This might not be true of every war, but it could be true of some and would in fact prove true in the great wars of the nineteenth and twentieth centuries, when Clausewitz's merely theoretical vision of total war came close to becoming a practical reality. "A constitution cannot set bounds to a nation's wants; it ought not therefore to set bounds to its resources." A constitution meant to endure for the ages had to be prepared for all contingencies. "The circumstances that endanger the safety of nations are infinite; and for this reason no constitutional shackles can wisely be imposed on the power to which the care of it is committed." Thus, for example, Hamilton objected to the "novel and absurd experiment in politics, of tying up the hands of government" even from "offensive war, founded upon reasons of state." Especially for a maritime power seeking to keep war at a distance, there might be times when the best defense would be a good offense. Hamilton therefore refused to allow well-intentioned moralism to limit either the resources or the strategies that might be employed in time of war or imminent war. In general, he was against "every project that is calculated to disarm the government of a single weapon, which in any possible contingency might be usefully employed for the general defense and security."[56]

Once again, Hamilton turned the tables on his opponents. Like Machiavelli, he recognized that some constitutional limits are more dangerous to the constitutional rule of law than no limits at all. This circumstance was especially true with regard to the means necessary for defense. To ban a standing army, for example, or to limit it to a certain number in time of peace, or to say that only some revenues but not others could be appropriated to the military was a "violent policy, contrary to the natural and experienced course of human affairs." It would therefore defeat itself. Pennsylvania had banned a standing army in time of peace, but in consequence of disorders in its counties, had raised a body of troops and would in all probability keep them up "as long as there was an appearance of danger to the public peace." Pennsylvania's ban thus led it to violate its own constitution. Likewise, Massachusetts, which had no such ban, nonetheless raised troops without consent of Congress (as required by the Articles of Confederation) in order to crush the Shays's Rebellion. It was still maintaining them in time of peace to deter further revolt. These acts revealed to Hamilton "how unequal parchment provisions are to a struggle with necessity." In general, "Nations pay little regard to rules and maxims calculated in their very nature to run counter to the necessities of society." Prudence dictated imposing no such limits, because if broken in time of necessity, that action would set precedents for violating the Constitution when the necessity was less pressing. In turn, this practice risked destroying that "sacred reverence, which ought to be maintained in the breasts of rulers towards the constitution of a country."[57] If possible, then, it ought never to be necessary for representatives to violate their constitution in time of war or imminent war. The best way to prevent that necessity (and to preserve the rule of law at the same time) was to grant unlimited powers to spend, tax, borrow, and raise troops for war.

To possess these powers, however, Americans would have to risk that they might sometimes be abused. It was imprudent to attempt to prevent unjust, offensive wars by banning the means of providing for just, defensive wars. It was better to rely on the republican principle of majority rule as a means of empowering the national government to do good, and a locally rooted, usually jealous and vigilant House to prevent evil. That principle put it in the hands of the people, through their representatives, to judge whether wars were defensive or ambitious, just or unjust, essential to the public good or an inexcusable waste of life and a drain on the public revenue. It was both strategically necessary and politically proper for a free people to rely on the reflection and choice of a majority of Congress to provide for their security while also guarding against a dangerous ambition that could lead to ruinous wars. To address the danger of abuses of power, Hamilton relied far less on written limits to the government's power than on the "internal structure" of the government: representation, separation of powers, and so on. "When you have divided and nicely balanced the departments of government; when you have strongly connected the virtue of your rulers with their interests," through elections and equality under law, "when, in short, you have rendered your system as perfect as human forms can be," you have no choice left but to confront the dangers that war poses to liberty as well: "You must place confidence; you must give power."[58]

One of Hamilton's objections to the Confederation was that the "important powers of declaring war, making peace, &c., can only be exercised by nine states." Vigorous powers in Congress were as essential to establishing peace as they were to declaring and waging war. Under the Confederation, when a majority had decided that war or peace was just and wise, it could be frustrated by a minority of states that might consist of an even smaller minority of the people. The requirement for a three-fourths majority to declare war or to make peace was also an open invitation to foreign influence. It was not impossible that a foreign power, by force, fraud, or corruption, could gain control of the votes of a few states and "totally prevent a measure, essential to the welfare or existence of the empire." By such a means, a nation at war with the United States might then make "the efforts of a majority totally vain."[59] Or an ally of the United States, fearing a separate peace with the common enemy, might involve the nation in a war or an alliance longer than a majority of the people and their representatives believed was wise or just. In contrast, the only way a foreign power could prevent Congress from declaring war or concluding peace under the new Constitution would be to attempt to corrupt a majority of the Congress, a project that Hamilton implied would have been both dangerous and utopian.

Persuading statesmen to step forward and take responsibility for the welfare of the whole nation required more than the constitutional power to act with vigor, however. As David Epstein and Harvey Flaumenhaft reveal, responsibility emerges as an honor-loving substitute for or approximation of public-spirited virtue in the writings of Publius. This is especially true of Hamilton.[60] He invented what might be called "Hamilton's rule" of responsible government: individuals will take responsibility for important and risky measures in proportion to their ability to understand what needs to be done and to pursue their objectives consistently over time, and to the degree to which they will be held personally accountable for failure or success. Responsibility is generally directly proportional to the amount of time a representative has to accomplish a task, and inversely proportional to the number of representatives who can share blame or take credit for the task. For Hamilton, it was "unquestionable" that the people desired the prosperity and security of their country, but it was "equally unquestionable that they do not possess the discernment and stability necessary for systematic government." Discernment arises from a lifetime of political experience and stability from the leisure to devote one's life to politics and nothing else. Consequently, the people, and even their closest representatives in the House, could never supply the wisdom and stability necessary to make the Republic endure or to provide a solid foundation for a growing American empire. This inability was most especially true in foreign affairs. "The branch of administration especially, which involves our political relations with foreign states, a political community will ever be incompetent to." Especially in foreign affairs, the business of the Senate was to balance the responsiveness of the House with the guidance of a more politically responsible elite. The Senate was to form a more "permanent body" than the House to "correct the prejudices, check the intemperate passions, and regulate the fluctuations of a popular assembly."[61]

If the Senate were to correct the imperfections of the House, it had to "exclude as much as possible from its own character, those infirmities and that mutability it was designed to remedy." This task required extending the term and decreasing the number of senators. To a large extent, stable policy would result merely from the same individuals making it for a "considerable period." In turn, a longer time to make policy would also help the Senate become a "center of political knowledge." Together with the executive, the senators were to "manage all our concerns with foreign nations. They must understand their interests and systems. This knowledge is not soon acquired. But a very small part of it is gained in the closet," or library; most had to come from experience. The longer the term, the greater were the chances that the senators could learn something useful from experience. Plans to promote the strength and prosperity of the empire in its relations with other nations required "time and diligence to bring to maturity." This was partly because senators would not undertake such plans unless they were confident they could succeed. They would not be confident unless they had benefited from the lessons of experience and could "make their calculations accordingly." Yet to succeed, such plans also required a custodial superintendence, or day-to-day supervision over time. Since few, if any, prudent senators would risk their careers on measures for which they might be held accountable unless they could also take personal credit for their success, they could "never have that responsibility which is so important to republican government" without a lengthy term. The odds in favor of responsible government increased when a small number was combined with a long term in the Senate. "Senators," Hamilton observed, "will not be solicitous for the reputation of public measures, in which they have a temporary concern, and will feel lightly the burden of public disapprobation, in proportion to the number of those who partake of the censure."[62] The more senators there were, the easier it would be for them to blame others for failure or to do nothing, and the harder it would be to discover who was personally responsible for attempting an evil action or accomplishing a good one.

Above all, Hamilton wanted each senator to consider himself "an agent of the union," as "bound to perform services necessary to the good of the whole, though his state should condemn them." He knew that foreign nations would be watching the deliberations of Congress. Manifest evidence that no one would take responsibility for the good of the whole empire would undermine the "national character" or reputation abroad, and "forfeit the respect of foreigners." Responsibility is not the same as wisdom, but to "political rivals" abroad, irresponsible government would appear as evidence of "deficient wisdom." Consequently, they would be "little apprehensive of our arriving at any exalted station in the scale of power."[63] And if they had no reason to fear the United States, they might begin to think of exalting their own station in the scale of power at America's expense.

This hope that senators would consider themselves responsible for the welfare of the empire as a whole reveals a significant tension between the fundamental ends and necessary means of republican government. The end is the public good, but the means require accountability. In the Founding era, the vigilant recognized that the means required dividing power among many hands and keeping those in power dependent upon the electorate through frequent elections; Hamilton, however, understood that the end required statesmen to be substantially independent of popular control through a lengthy term. It also required concentrating power in a few hands to excite their ambition to use their power well. From the standpoint of ends, Hamilton's hopes for the Senate were clearly republican; from the standpoint of accountability, they were much less so. The great irony is that the Convention's rejection of Hamilton's *Plan of Government* probably made it easier for him to carve out some room for responsibility in the Senate. If consent was necessary to legitimize senatorial responsibility as well as congressional vigor, then a responsible Senate was more likely to receive popular support from the plan of the Convention than from Hamilton's original proposal. Paradoxically, the Senate could add a high degree of responsibility to Congress precisely because it was more accountable and tailored to the spirit of American republicans than the senate Hamilton originally envisioned. In the long run, however, Hamilton was well aware that even the most national-minded senators would be so tied to their states that they could never consider themselves merely as representatives of the nation. For that end, Hamilton relied chiefly on the executive.

6. Executive Energy and Republican Safety

As is true of his labors in Philadelphia in 1787 in general, Hamilton seemingly did not have a significant impact on the executive proposed by the Federal Convention.[1] He did serve on the Committee on Style and may have contributed to the lean language of Article 2 of the Constitution, but we shall never know and need not care. He wrote all the essays on the executive in *The Federalist*. When these are combined with his interpretations of executive power in the 1790s, he wrote more of enduring relevance about the theory and practice of the presidency than any other Founder. Accordingly, Edward S. Corwin has observed, the "modern theory of presidential power" has been the "contribution primarily of Alexander Hamilton." Corwin's student, Clinton Rossiter, later wrote that Article 2 of the Constitution is "thoroughly Hamiltonian today." Jeffrey K. Tullis is quite specific about practical matters: the modern executive's initiation and supervision of a legislative program, his use of the veto for partisan purposes rather than as a matter of constitutional propriety, the growth of a large executive staff, assertions of executive privilege in matters of national security, executive agreements with foreign governments, and even actual presidential command of the armed forces were "constituent features of Alexander Hamilton's theory of governance."[2]

Not everyone agrees that the modern presidency is chiefly Hamilton's legacy, however. Forrest McDonald argues that "the presidency has been responsible for less harm and more good, in the nation and in the world, than any other secular institution in history." Yet he leaves little doubt that the sometimes unmanageable national government that evolved from presidential leadership during the New Deal and the cold war is quite far from Hamilton's vision of energetic government. When presidents try to do everything, they are sometimes unable to accomplish much of anything. In that respect, the modern presidency seems to have little to do with Hamilton's original vision, which was more energetic than the contemporary presidency precisely because it was more limited.[3]

Even more than McDonald, Richard Loss takes care to distinguish between Hamilton's energetic executive and the more clearly modern, potentially unlimited theories of national government and executive power developed by Woodrow Wilson and Theodore Roosevelt. In Loss's view, Roosevelt's Stewardship Theory of the presidency was a license for presidential lawlessness. It allowed the Rough Rider to presume the president was subject "only to the people, and under the Constitution, bound to serve the people affirmatively in cases where the Constitution does not explicitly forbid him to render the service."[4] Loss also claims that Woodrow Wilson was a proponent of unlimited presidential power because of his endorsement of a living Constitution, which is not to be understood in terms of the opinions of the men who made it but in light of the "spirit of the age." After all, Wilson had the audacity to write that "the personal force of the President is constitutional to any extent to which he chooses to exercise it."[5] The true Hamiltonian of the early twentieth century, Loss suggests, was Robert Taft, who was enormously suspicious of the virtually unlimited executive powers claimed by Roosevelt and Wilson. Loss, in other words, fears that by exalting Hamilton's influence, Corwin, Rossiter, and other scholars may also have damaged his reputation as a constitutionalist. Or perhaps worse, by lending the authority of one of the leading Founders to unlimited visions of presidential power, they may well have encouraged the lawlessness that Loss believes Hamilton meant to avoid.[6]

Can one have it both ways? Can one support energy in the executive yet not be a spokesman for unlimited executive power? Could Hamilton be the most important original source of the modern presidency but still deserve to be seen as a faithful servant of the Constitution as he understood it? Bearing in mind that Hamilton's chief rivals in the 1790s, Thomas Jefferson and James Madison, accused him of the same unlimited views of executive power that Loss attributes to Theodore Roosevelt and Woodrow Wilson, these questions merit serious investigation. Though J. G. A. Pocock appears to know Hamilton's works only indirectly, through the writings of Gerald Stourzh, he helps sharpen these questions by compelling us to take into account the impact of time or change on any republic. As both Stourzh and Harvey C. Mansfield Jr. suggest, Hamilton sought to carve out some room for Machiavelli's dynamic and adaptable *virtu* in the executive. Among other things, this room for maneuver was meant to supply the innovative leadership the republic would inevitably require in time of war. Yet nothing is more characteristic of those individuals Pocock associates with the Atlantic Republican Tradition than their fear of innovation, or "dread of modernity."

As Machiavelli was well aware, a strong executive helped Rome to conquer the world, but at the price of an enormous transformation in the social and political basis of the Roman regime. The development of private
armies more loyal to their commanders than to the republic, for example,
suggests that the innovations by which the Roman republic sought to confront the necessities of war also became the instruments of its destruction.
Yet Machiavelli believed that had the Romans not developed a strong executive, their republic probably would have fallen victim to foreign and civil
war much sooner than it did. For Machiavelli at least, innovation was not
synonymous with corruption. As both Hamilton and Machiavelli knew quite
well, innovation is no less necessary to a republic's survival than stability.
For both men, the great task for republics was to change according to the
predictable necessities and unpredictable fortunes of war while preserving
the principles of consent and the rule of law that keep a republic free.[7]

For Machiavelli, the best solution was the Roman dictatorship, which he
believed did far more good than harm in Rome. It was not a vehicle for
strong men to rule by force alone, but a constitutional and consensual means
to subdue rebels and confront foreign enemies in crises when the ordinary procedures of lawmaking were too slow or weak to suit the occasion.
Hamilton never endorsed this strategy; indeed, his principal contribution
to the modern understanding of executive power may well have been his
efforts to find ways to produce energy without resorting to a Machiavellian
or Roman dictatorship.[8] Nonetheless, Hamilton would undoubtedly have
agreed with Machiavelli that in republics great "harm is done by magistrates
that set themselves up and by power obtained in unlawful ways, not by power
that comes from lawful ways."[9] For both Hamilton and Machiavelli, the
extremes to be avoided in the executive were constitutional weakness on
the one hand and lawlessness on the other. Executive energy was the mean
between impotence and usurpation, the extremes that Hamilton believed
would necessarily result from a strict construction of executive power.
Where, then, was the path of moderation?

Despite recent efforts to disassociate Hamilton from John Locke, his
efforts to produce energy, understood as moderation, in the executive,
probably owe more to Locke than to any other modern political theorist.[10]
Following Locke and Montesquieu, Hamilton assumed there were not three,
but five powers of government: legislative, executive, judicial, federative,
and prerogative. The first made laws, the second executed them, and the
third interpreted them. Together, these three powers implied legislative
supremacy in domestic policy, subject to the important constraints of the
executive's qualified veto and judicial review. Unless the constitution speci-

fied otherwise, however, the federative power, or power to make war, form alliances, and conclude peace, was usually not subject to the legislature. For Locke, the federative power was a prudential, discretionary power for the executive to provide for the common defense. Although Montesquieu confused the matter by calling the federative power executive, and Hamilton followed him in doing so, both Montesquieu and Hamilton agreed with Locke about the high degree of discretion required to make the executive power effective in its federative role. This was not because any of them were advocates of arbitrary power but because placing this power in the executive was the best way to avoid a civil war (arising from two rival armed forces within a single state). Especially in time of war, it was also essential to supply the executive the flexibility to address the variations and designs of other nations.

This federative power must be distinguished from prerogative, a term Hamilton rarely employed in his discussions of the executive.[11] Locke defined prerogative as the power to "act according to discretion, for the publick good, without prescription of the law, and sometimes even against it." By Locke's definition, prerogative was not one of the traditional privileges of the British Crown. Instead, it was an unconstitutional but nonetheless legitimate power reserved for various crises, when the legislature was incapable of acting effectively for the public good. By thus defining prerogative, Locke generally sought to narrow its scope, but he could not bring himself to deny its occasional necessity. He therefore left it to the people to decide when or whether princes who invoked this power were justified.[12]

Like Locke, Hamilton recognized that mere lawmaking would not always be sufficient to preserve the Republic from harm; but like Machiavelli, he wanted a constitutional and consensual foundation for the executive to take the initiative in war and foreign policy. Hamilton's strategy to avoid constitutional weakness on the one hand and prerogative (or even worse, dictatorship) on the other was as simple as it was bold. He incorporated the elements of Locke's federative power that had not been specifically transferred to Congress into the executive power of the president. The federative power was traditionally associated with kings; therefore Morton J. Frisch is clearly right to suggest that the "great originality of the American regime" was Hamilton's "incorporation of monarchical or executive power within the framework of traditional republicanism, a blend now referred to as presidential government." Since Hamilton did so, however, J. C. Vile was wrong to mention Hamilton only twice in his apparently comprehensive account of modern constitutionalism and the separation of powers. Because Hamilton developed ways for the executive to act with vigor in time of war without resorting to prerogative, his contribution to creating an energetic executive compatible with the rule of law cannot be underestimated.[13]

To understand why, it is most helpful to compare Hamilton's theoretical defense of an energetic executive in *The Federalist* with his later, more practical interpretations of the executive power in the Washington administration. Though control of most of the federative power was necessary for the executive to steer between the Scylla of weakness and the Charybdis of prerogative, Hamilton was well aware that there is a great difference between parchment, theoretical powers and real, practical powers. In addition to competent powers, Hamilton argued in *The Federalist* that executive energy depended on unity, substantial duration in office, and adequate support (salary). Once again, Hamilton's rhetorical necessities in confronting the Anti-Federalists compelled him to innovate. He had to prove that these components of executive energy were compatible with the safety of a republic, understood in terms of a "due dependence" upon the people and a "due responsibility" for their welfare.[14] And yet again he countered his opponents by arguing that executive energy was more necessary than dangerous to republican safety. He no doubt believed that the executive established by the Federal Convention was too dependent upon the people to take adequate responsibility for their welfare. In his defense of Washington's initiatives during the Whiskey Rebellion, however, he turned this dependence into a political advantage. The executive could have not only the constitutional but also the moral authority to preserve the Republic from harm because he was the only elected member of the government who could claim to act for the people as a whole. By republicanizing the basis of the executive's authority, Hamilton thereby increased his ability to act energetically. Although James Madison confused Hamilton's invocation of the executive's federative powers with prerogative, Hamilton also constitutionalized the federative power in his defenses of Washington's Neutrality Proclamation and the Jay Treaty. He thereby earned the right to be called the most important author of the modern presidency.

Although some Anti-Federalists suggested that a "vigorous executive is inconsistent with the genius of republican government," Hamilton replied that the "enlightened well wishers" of republican government could not admit this premise without condemning their own principles. "A feeble executive implies a feeble execution of the government. A feeble execution is but another phrase for a bad execution: And a government ill executed, whatever it may be in theory, must be in practice a bad government." For

Hamilton, energy was essential to four fundamental tasks of any good government: first, to preserve the community against foreign attacks (Locke's federative power); second, to enforce the law against criminals and thereby guarantee individual security (Locke's executive power); third, to protect property against those who sometimes interrupt the ordinary operation of the courts of justice; and fourth, to secure liberty against the assaults of ambition, of faction, and of anarchy in the republic.[15] Thus, one of the extremes to which Hamilton opposed energy was weakness, but it was not the only one.

Perhaps because foreign and civil wars are at the center of three of the four chief responsibilities that Hamilton assigned to the executive, he had the temerity to remind "those conversant in Roman story how often that republic was obliged to take refuge in the absolute power of a single man, under the formidable title of dictator" to guard against ambition, sedition, and "invasions of external enemies, who menaced the conquest and destruction of Rome."[16] Hamilton was not calling for dictatorial power in the president but was reminding his readers of the other extreme to which executive energy is opposed, the unlimited power of a dictator. Especially in time of war, the great question was how to produce the strength that enabled the Roman dictators to preserve their republic from harm without entitling the president to rule by decree.

Part of the answer was unity. Of "all the cares of government," Hamilton observed, "the direction of war most peculiarly requires those qualities which distinguish the exercise of power by a single hand. The direction of war implies the direction of the common strength; and the power of directing and employing the common strength forms a usual and essential part in the definition of the executive authority." Unity favored "promptitude of decision," which is "oftener an evil than a benefit in the legislature," whose task is to promote "deliberation and circumspection." The more vigorous the powers of the legislature in a republic, the more important it is to slow the legislature down, so that its members can deliberate carefully about how to make the laws good. Yet the same reasoning is usually "unnecessary" and "unwise" for the executive branch in a republic. The different branches have different kinds of work to do. The most important work of the executive is not deliberative but active. Consequently, the "most important ingredients in its composition" are "vigor and expedition." Denying it these qualities would prevent it from performing its work without producing any "counterbalancing good." Once again, war was central to Hamilton's justification for the quickness favored by unity in the executive. "In the conduct of war, in which the energy of the executive is the bulwark of national security," everything would depend upon its vigor and expedition.[17]

Even in dangerous times, which enforce a kind of unity among a number, "plurality" of authority always increases the "danger of differences of opinion." Whenever plurality causes "bitter dissensions" among those who govern, those dissensions serve to "lessen the respectability, weaken the authority, and distract the plans and operations of those whom they divide." Among "men clothed with equal dignity and authority, there is a peculiar danger of personal emulation and animosity." Such men often oppose each other out of spite, merely because they have "had no agency in planning" the measures proposed. Even or especially if they have been consulted, opposition may seem to them to be an "indispensable duty of self love. They seem to think themselves bound in honor, by all the motives of personal infallibility, to defeat the success" of their rivals, however worthy they may be. This "despicable frailty, or rather detestable vice in the human character" was so strong that it could well "impede or frustrate the most important measures of the government in the most critical emergencies of state."[18]

The most startling turn in Hamilton's discussion of executive energy was his effort to confront the Anti-Federalists by suggesting that unity was no less essential to republican safety than it was to executive energy. The great danger to a republic from plurality in the executive is that rivalry may issue in civil war. Avoiding that danger was a major reason for Locke's call for uniting the executive and federative powers in one person. It was also an important reason that, in time of crisis, the Roman republic took the executive power from two consuls and gave it to one dictator. For Hamilton, it was a "matter of astonishment" that the dissensions inherent in the Roman republic's plural executive were not "more frequent, or more fatal" than they actually were. The only explanation he could find for the failure of the division of executive power to issue always in civil war was that the consuls were patricians, who were usually united in a desire to preserve the privileges of their class against the plebs. Later, after Rome expanded, however, he noted that the consuls tended to divide the administration. One was responsible for governing Rome, and the other took command in the provinces.[19] In effect, the Romans divided Locke's executive and federative powers between two different commanders. In time, the division was in fact fatal to the republic because it pitted Caesar and Pompey, and later Octavius, Anthony, and Lepidus against each other in a titanic struggle from which only one could emerge, and only by rendering everyone else completely dependent upon his will.

Though it was a "maxim of republican jealousy" that power is "safer in the hands of a number of men than of a single man," the maxim did not apply to the executive. Taken as an argument for balancing the powers of government and especially for dividing the legislative power among many, the maxim was undoubtedly true. With respect to the executive, however, Hamilton suggested that it is "more safe that there should be a single object for the jealousy and watchfulness of the people; and in a word that all multiplication of the executive is rather dangerous than friendly to liberty." When there is only one executive, there is only one to watch. He therefore cannot hide in the anonymity of a crowd. "Hamilton's rule" of responsible government applied to the executive even more than to the Senate. If responsibility increases as the number who possess a particular power decreases, then the highest degree of responsibility could be expected from the executive when that office was in the hands of a single person. "Responsibility," Hamilton observed, "is of two kinds, to censure and to punishment." Censure is the "most important of the two, especially in an elective office," because it commonly means losing an election. Yet to hold an executive accountable in an election, the people must know who is responsible for good or ill in the administration. A plural executive tends to deprive the people of the "two greatest securities they can have for the faithful exercise of any delegated power: first, the restraints of public opinion, which lose their efficacy, as well on account of the division of the censure attendant on bad measures among a number, as on account of the uncertainty on whom it ought to fall; and secondly, the opportunity of discovering with facility and clearness the misconduct of the persons they trust."[20] The people do not know whom to blame when things go wrong. Worse, those who might fear blame fear it less because they are able to implicate others whom they can claim were at fault. Unity therefore preserves the "due dependence" necessary to republican safety because it enables the people to hold the executive accountable for the public welfare.

Another part of Hamilton's strategy for reconciling executive energy with republican safety was a substantial duration of office. Duration supports energy primarily through its impact on ambition: it gives those individuals who wish to undertake extraordinary tasks, the kind of statesmen who build great empires, the time to get the job done. Ambitious characters will always struggle to be first among their fellow citizens, but if they can be first for only a short period, their ambition may be unconnected to anything but being first. It may serve no useful purpose for the public; indeed, it might become positively pernicious. When such figures can be first for a prolonged period, however, their ambition can acquire a different character, the kind that relishes and undertakes responsibility for herculean projects for the public benefit. Hamilton clearly doubted that a four-year term was long enough to support those executives who meant to undertake such enterprises, but he was certain that the longer the term, the more the nation could draw on this kind of ambition as the foundation of firmness in the executive. "It is a general principle of human nature that a man will be interested in whatever he possesses in proportion to the firmness or precariousness of the tenure, by which he holds it; will be less attached to what he holds by a momentary or uncertain title; and of course will be willing to risk more for the sake of the one, than for the sake of the other."[21] To attract energetic statesmen capable of building America's republican empire, national office had to become a prize worthy of extraordinary political ambition.

Then, perhaps, the executive might become more responsible, or willing to "risk more" in the pursuit of fundamental national interests because he could hope for "lasting monuments" of popular gratitude. That hope might encourage anyone who possessed a "tolerable portion of fortitude" to risk the temporary displeasure of the people for the sake of their lasting approbation. The longer the tenure, the greater would be the opportunity to "make the community sensible to the propriety of the measures he might incline them to pursue." Though Hamilton was referring specifically to the veto in this passage, his meaning also has important strategic implications. An executive with a substantial duration might continue an unpopular but necessary war, or discontinue a popular but unnecessary or unjust war, or continue expensive preparations for war in the face of dangers not adequately understood by the people. He could take risks to preserve the republic from harm because there might be time for the fruits of his policies to show themselves and redeem him to the public. His firmness might decline as an election approached, but he might derive much moral "support from the opportunities" he had already taken advantage of in "establishing himself in the esteem and good will of his constituents." Even as an election approached, he might risk more because he had acquired the confidence of the people. This line of political credit could be a fund of political capital, which the president could save or invest according to the necessities and opportunities of the times.[22]

The impact of duration is felt primarily in the day-to-day administration of the government, in the innumerable matters of detail that must be managed with method and system over prolonged periods of time. As Harvey Flaumenhaft observes, the need to manage these details according to a systematic plan goes far to explain why the executive tends to become the focal point of government, even in republics. Although the term "administration" generally includes each branch of the whole government, in its "most usual and precise signification," Hamilton observed, it is usually confined to "executive details, and falls peculiarly within the province of the executive department." In daily practice, the executive *is* the government.[23] Though careful attention to detail would build trust in the executive, and loyalty to the new Republic, it would also build the American empire. Under the heading of executive administration, Hamilton included foreign negotiations, preparatory plans of public finance, the actual expenditure of funds, the organization of the army and the navy, and the direction of the operations of war. Although these are matters in which quickness can be extremely important, Hamilton stressed preparation and organization, that is, good staff work, in order to organize measures and events to suit a grand design. This is the work for which Hamilton claimed a numerous body serving for a brief period, like the Continental Congress, was inherently unfit. It is also the work that most concerned him during and after the Revolution and during the administration of George Washington. Such work does not attract public attention because it takes place behind the scenes, but it could accumulate, day by day, like compound interest, until the infant Republic became a powerful empire.[24]

Duration therefore favors energy by promoting stability, understood in this instance as the ability to maintain a constant purpose and steady pace. The longer the duration, the greater the security against a "ruinous mutability in the administration of the government." Every change of administration brings with it a change of men, and most changes of men involve changes of policy. This is not simply because new men sometimes have new ideas, but also because the new men are likely to be rivals of the old. "To reverse and undo what has been done by a predecessor is very often considered by a successor, as the best proof he can give of his own capacity and desert." Moreover, the successor is often "warranted" in assuming that his predecessor was dismissed because he was unpopular. The "less he resembles him the more he will recommend himself to the favor of his constituents."[25] He therefore seeks to build popularity, and perhaps even lasting monuments to himself, by tearing down the work and destroying the monuments of his predecessor. Change, however, is not the same as energy. Change appears to be energy because events and people are moving, but it is quite possible to spin one's wheels, to move in place, or even to move backward. A people whose administration is constantly changing is unlikely to move in any one direction for any considerable time. Indeed, the more the administration changes, the more it may remain the same and the less the nation will be likely to move with any degree of momentum and to build or maintain its empire.

Duration was therefore necessary not merely to stability, but to sustained movement or prolonged change over time, a prospect rendered more possible through reeligibility for office. When an executive has demonstrated his ability to produce energy rather than mere change, Hamilton argued that reeligibility enables the people "to prolong the utility of his talents and virtues, and secure to the government, the advantages of permanency in a wise system of administration." Reeligibility could provide an executive of monumental ambition the opportunity of "*obtaining* by *meriting*" the approval of his countrymen.[26] The indispensable tool of extraordinary political responsibility in the executive is the time to do extraordinary things. Precisely because empires are not built in a day, Americans could not reasonably expect to harness the ambition of empire builders unless they gave such figures the time to begin their arduous enterprises, prove their value before an election, and substantially complete them in another term or series of terms of office.

Surprisingly again, Hamilton once more turned the tables on the Anti-Federalists by arguing that duration was necessary to the due dependence of the executive in a republic. The fundamental assumption of representative democracy is that the people are capable of judging their representatives, including the executive. If they are not to be mere tools of slogans or sound bites, however, the people must judge by the visible and tangible results of the executive's administration. They can judge well only when the executive's plans reach fruition, which takes time. Adequate duration allows the "community the time and leisure to observe the tendency of his measures, and form an experimental estimate of his merits."[27] The people want energy rather than mere change. Yet to get energy, they have to wait and see where they are going. When they give the executive enough time to act effectively (and rope to hang himself), they give themselves enough time to judge him well.

Hamilton also considered reeligibility important to preserve the republican rule of law. A republic with a constitutional prohibition against harnessing the services of extraordinary individuals might sometimes have to choose between defeat or violating its own laws. It was a "fundamental maxim" of republican jealousy among the Spartans, for example, that no person should hold the post of admiral of their fleet twice. Nonetheless, after a severe defeat, the Spartans felt obliged to recall an indispensable man, Lysander, who had previously served well as admiral. To preserve the forms of "adherence to ancient institutions," they gave Lysander the real power of admiral under the title of vice-admiral. This ruse fooled no one. The necessities of war obliged the Spartans to violate their own constitution, a fact that illustrates that "nations pay little regard to rules and maxims calculated in their nature to run counter to the necessities of society."[28]

Ambition denied the means of acquiring power and fame by legitimate means often feels obliged to seek these goals illegitimately. "Would it promote the peace of the community, or the stability of the government," Hamilton asked, to have "half a dozen men" who had reached the pinnacle of their nation's honors "wandering among the people like discontented ghosts and sighing for a place which they were no longer destined to possess?" Suppose a man of "irregular ambition," a Sulla or a Marius, were in office. Would he not with "infinite reluctance yield to the necessity of taking his leave forever of a post, in which his passion for power and preeminence had acquired the force of habit"? If he were "fortunate or adroit enough," he might convince the people that it was a "very odious and unjustifiable restraint upon themselves" to "debar them of their right of giving a fresh proof of attachment to a favorite." In such a case, the demands of the "people, seconding the ambition of a thwarted favorite, might occasion greater danger to liberty" than could be imagined from the "perpetuation" of a man of such irregular ambition, who would serve his people well and legally, if only he were allowed to keep his post. Otherwise, the ambition that might take the responsibility to build a powerful but free republican empire could be corrupted by the laws. It might then seek to found a private empire on the ruins of the republic.[29]

As Hamilton understood the term, republican safety was the product of a due dependence and a due responsibility, and its significance depended on the meaning of the word "due." An executive who was completely independent of Congress or the people would no longer be accountable, but an executive who was completely dependent on the legislature might not act responsibly toward his office, the safety of the republic, or the welfare of the empire. An undue dependence might produce an irresponsible executive; an undue independence could be a threat to republican government. A duly responsible executive had to be duly dependent, but upon whom should the executive depend, and for what should the executive be responsible? The beginning of Hamilton's answer lies in his account of the executive's veto power.

Hamilton's principal fear was the tendency in "governments purely republican" for the "legislative authority to absorb every other." Contemporary scholars have sometimes worried about an imperial presidency; Hamilton was worried about an imperious Congress.[30] "The representatives of the people seem sometimes to fancy that they are the people themselves." Clothed with this majestic authority, they often "betray strong symptoms of impatience and disgust" toward opposition from any quarter as a "breach of their privilege and an outrage of their dignity." Whether in exercising a veto or simply in pursuing a policy unpopular with the legislature, the executive seems to forget his place as a servant of the people, or rather, of those who presume they are the people. In his wartime briefing to Duane, Hamilton complained of the "vanity" of Congress, which presumed it could handle all aspects of the war effort, including administration. By meddling in every administrative detail, it prevented an energetic administration of the war. Hamilton expected the same vanity to arise in Congress under the new Constitution, and this time it would become a threat to liberty as well. The legislature would seek an "imperious control" over other departments. Moreover, he believed congressmen would "always act with such momentum" that it would be difficult for any but the firmest public servants to resist them. In a republic, moral "momentum" tends to be on the side of the legislature, which makes energy, understood as firmness, extremely difficult for the executive.[31]

Although some might think that republican government requires a "servile compliancy" to the legislature, Hamilton insisted that independence was essential to prevent that branch from dominating each part of the government. The great problem was to establish actual independence in the executive. On paper, a qualified veto, requiring two-thirds of both houses of Congress for override, gave the executive a share in the legislative power. Indeed, it made the national government a tricameral institution. By giving the executive a share in legislative deliberations, tricameralism had the potential to raise the dignity of the executive, who did not have to be a mere servant of the legislature. He might be the member of an equal and coordinate branch of the government, like Locke's king in Parliament. Yet being like that king is more than a little problematic in a republic. To address the Anti-Federalists' fears that the executive would become a king, Hamilton borrowed some moral authority from the people in order to lend it to the president. As much because of the rhetorical necessities of the debate over ratifying the Constitution as by design, he thereby made the executive much stronger than the British king, who no longer dares to exercise a veto because he lacks the legitimacy arising from consent.

Because the American executive is elected, however indirectly, he does not represent a different social estate; instead he is "himself a servant of the people" who can lose his office if he violates his trust or fails to manage it responsibly. The executive is also the only representative chosen through the suffrages of all the people. The executive is therefore the only representative with the moral authority to speak or act in the name of the whole people when the people must speak and act as a whole. Precisely because his authority depends upon the people as a whole, he can be morally independent of Congress. He can lay at least as much claim as Congress to the republican principle of consent. In seeking to legitimize the veto power, Hamilton therefore discovered a new and important aspect of executive power in the American Republic. A due responsibility for the people's welfare requires the executive to be completely independent of Congress and completely dependent upon the people, through their electors, for the title to his office and the possession of his powers. Otherwise, he can have no moral authority to exercise his powers, that is, no real power at all.[32]

Just as Hamilton elevated the moral authority of the executive by making him the only representative of the people as a whole, he also denigrated the moral authority of Congress by distinguishing between Congress and the people. Congress is not the people. The people may "sometimes stand in opposition" to Congress; at other times, they may be "neutral" in a quarrel between Congress and the executive. "In either situation, it is certainly desirable that the executive should be in a situation to dare to act his own opinion with vigor and decision." After all, some executives have saved the people from the "very fatal consequences of their own mistakes," and the people have sometimes shown enduring "gratitude to the men, who had courage and magnanimity enough to serve them at their displeasure."[33] Under a Constitution that vests the executive with a veto, the people consent to the possible opposition of their representatives by the executive. Such opposition is therefore not a restraint upon the people. Instead, it is a manifestation of their authority and just as legitimate as a congressional override of the veto. As a result of his equal claim to represent the people, a daring and capable president can invoke this moral authority to use his other powers, even without consulting Congress and sometimes in defiance of it.

A clear explanation of Hamilton's intentions in this regard are found in his discussions of the pardoning power in *The Federalist* and still later during the Whiskey Rebellion. Although most of Hamilton's discussions of executive power focus on the ends of defense and law enforcement, his account of the pardoning power focuses on two other ends: subduing rebellions and checking assaults against liberty resulting from ambition, faction, and anarchy. Neither of these ends fits nicely under the theoretical rubric of executive power as it had been developed by Locke and Montesquieu. They focused primarily on the executive who arrests individuals and brings them to court, or on the executive who is a virtually unrestricted free agent in foreign policy. Consequently, neither of them offered much guidance to the executive faced with the danger of civil war. Hume, perhaps, came closest to saying what needed to be said: he proposed a "protector" to guard at least as much against civil as foreign war. Yet even Hume's protector was a far cry from Hamilton's executive. The protector was both too strong and too weak: too strong because, along with a council, chosen by the Senate, the protector had the power to rule by decree, like a Roman dictator, for up to six months; too weak because, as a plural executive, Hume's defanged Cromwell was unlikely to have the decisiveness necessary to react quickly and firmly to events.[34]

Given these difficulties, a case could be made that pardoning should be left to the legislature, not to the executive. Indeed, since "treason is a crime leveled at the immediate being of society, when the laws have once ascertained the guilt of the offender, there seems a fitness in referring the expediency of an act of mercy towards him to the judgment of the legislature." Yet there were important practical reasons against delegating this power to the legislature. Treason "might often be connected with seditions which embrace a large portion of the community." In the course of such seditions, one could expect to see at least some of the "representatives of the people tainted with the same spirit" as the rebels. The "secret sympathy" of friends of the condemned might then "bestow impunity where the terror of an example was necessary." On the other hand, if the sedition "inflamed the resentments of the major party," just the opposite might occur. The majority party might well be "obstinate and inexorable" in its desire for vengeance, when "policy demanded a conduct of forbearance and clemency" to end the revolt.[35]

For Hamilton, the pardoning power was designed to end revolts; the great question was which branch, Congress or the executive, was most fit to use this power effectively. As Machiavelli observed, it is almost always unwise to leave an opponent no alternative but to fight, for then necessity will encourage the spirit of resistance. He therefore advocated "promising pardon if [enemies] fear punishment" because pardons give enemies and traitors the hope of preserving their lives, and even of escaping punishment altogether, if they surrender. Like Machiavelli, Hamilton was well aware that in "seasons of insurrection and rebellion, there are often critical moments, when a well timed offer of pardon to the insurgents or rebels may restore the tranquillity of the commonwealth and which, if suffered to pass unimproved, it may be never possible afterwards to recall." A pardon to some rebels might even lead them to betray others and thus enable the government to overcome the rest by dividing them. Moreover, when charity toward all may be essential to bind up a nation's wounds, the "dilatory process" of the legislature might let slip a "golden opportunity" for putting down a rebellion. In contrast, "a single man of prudence and good sense" would be "better fitted, in delicate junctures, to balance the motives, which may plead for or against the remission of the punishment." As a representative of a whole nation, such an individual might rise above the extreme partisanship of its parts and then make a timely decision when the "loss of a week, a day, an hour" could be "fatal" to the future of the republic.[36]

Pardons suspend the operation of the law toward particular individuals. Especially when offered before conviction, they are in substantial tension with the republican principle of the rule of law. Theoretically, they lie somewhere between Machiavelli's dictatorship and Locke's prerogative. Like the former, they are a constitutional means to react quickly to events when the ordinary processes of law are unable to do so. Like the latter, they do not involve a broad power to rule by decree but instead are confined to particular instances. To avoid the danger of a Machiavellian dictator who ruled by decree or a Lockean executive who violated the law for the public benefit, it was best to have a lawful means by which the executive could act quickly to end a revolt and thereby restore the rule of law.

The Whiskey Rebellion in 1794 is a good example of Hamilton's effort to put this theory into practice. This insurrection in western Pennsylvania was directed against a federal excise on alcoholic spirits. Although excises were clearly authorized by the text of the Constitution, some Republican opponents of Hamilton's fiscal policies in Congress alleged that Hamilton, as secretary of the treasury, was using the excise as part of a monarchical and plutocratic conspiracy to oppress the settlers of the Western territories, who processed much of their grain into alcohol. Moreover, the so-called democratic-republican societies of the 1790s, which were modeled at least in part on the Jacobin clubs of revolutionary France, poured oil on the combustible passions of the westerners. Firebrands readily convinced the frontiersmen that excises were the favorite tax of tyrants, and thus, that tax evasion was synonymous with patriotism.[37]

Hamilton's and Washington's strategy during the event was aimed partly at the rebels and partly at public opinion. They believed they had to terrify the rebels without making them believe their only hope lay in resistance. This approach required them not only to generate a massive military force but also to promise pardons. And they had to defend the legitimacy of suppressing the rebellion before the rest of the nation. Thus they preferred to call out the militia, with its impeccable republican credentials, rather than use the small professional army, which was an object of popular mistrust. Contrary to Richard Kohn's claims, however, Hamilton did not relish the opportunity to employ force against the rebels; nor did he deliberately provoke the rebellion in some half-baked scheme to give the government an opportunity to display its authority by subduing it.[38] Instead, he saw a genuine crisis developing in Pennsylvania. Hamilton insisted that, in contrast to the previous three years when evasion had been declining, it was now clearly proper and indispensably necessary for an immediate resort to force because the evaders were openly defying the law in an organized fashion, and their resistance might spread elsewhere. It was also absurd for federal marshals, excise officers, and judges to oppose as many as 6,000 armed men (who had occupied and threatened to burn Pittsburgh) with nothing but subpoenas and law books. Fearing that insurgent strength might amount to as much as 7,000 men, Hamilton advised Washington to prepare for the worst and to call up a force of 9,000 infantry and 3,000 cavalry from the neighboring states. Although the state governors were loath to call out the militia, Washington staked his prestige on the event, and the popular response was enthusiastic. The militia then marched on Pennsylvania, towing federal judges along to ensure due process for those who were arrested. Most of the insurgents then vanished into the woods. Hamilton wrote Washington that 150 insurgents had been arrested, but there was no organized resistance. A general amnesty (pardon before trial) was proclaimed for all who took an oath of allegiance to the government. Not a single shot was fired, but twenty insurgents not covered by the amnesty were tried for treason, and two were convicted. Washington then pardoned both, and the rebellion was over.

Although Hamilton did not seek this test of the new government's authority, he recognized that a skillful response to the insurrection might well do a "great deal of good and add to the solidity of everything in this country" because it would inspire confidence in the strength of the new government. As Machiavelli observed, however, the key to inspiring respect for strength is to do so without producing hatred among ordinary citizens. From this point of view, the expedition to subdue the rebels could help the government only if it was perceived as a last resort, and only if subsequent punishment appeared to be employed in a spirit of justice and humanity.[39] Though decorum prevented Washington from defending his initiative in person, Hamilton paid enormous attention to public opinion during this crisis so that Washington's response would also be seen as the legitimate act of the representative of the whole nation.

In Hamilton's view at least, Washington's response was clearly not an effort to rest the authority of the government on force but to defend the republican principles of the rule of law and consent as the only practical alternatives to such a government. After the Whiskey Rebellion was over, for example, Hamilton told newspaper readers of resistance by a minority (amounting to one-sixtieth of the population) to "your authority," that is, the authority of the American people. This was not a contest of wills between a few individuals in government and a few others on the frontier of the empire; rather, it was between those who meant to "defeat the exercise of constitutional and necessary authorities" and the people themselves. "Ye," that is, the people at large, "cannot but remember that the government is YOUR OWN work—that those who administer it are but your temporary agents; that YOU are called upon not to support their power, BUT YOUR OWN POWER." Every "virtuous man, every good citizen, and especially EVERY TRUE REPUBLICAN" had to support putting down the rebellion or he would otherwise acquiesce in the destruction of republican government. The people had to be able to "discriminate the *true* from *pretended Republicans; your* friends from the friends of *faction.*" Even though a demagogue might "prate and babble republicanism," he was not a republican if he supported the "*will* of a part against the *will* of a whole, the *will* of a faction against the *will* of a nation." To such demagogues, the people needed to say that "in a full respect for the laws we discern the reality of our power," but in "the contempt of the laws we see the annihilation of our power." An "inviolable respect for the Constitution and Laws" was the "most sacred duty and greatest source of security in a republic." It was by this that the "rich and powerful" were restrained from assaults on the "common liberty." By this too, "in a still greater degree, caballers, intriguers, and demagogues" were prevented from "climbing on the shoulders of faction to tempting seats of usurpation and tyranny." The American public knew that if the Republic became incapable of a "GOVERNMENT OF LAWS," it would have to become a government of "FORCE, for mankind MUST HAVE GOVERNMENT OF ONE SORT OR ANOTHER." Only the most artful sophistry could understand this rebellion as an expression of the principles by which Americans had justified their independence. In the former case, Americans risked "civil war" rather than surrender their liberty to "foreign domination"; but in the latter case, Americans had to risk civil war rather than surrender their "sovereignty to the tyranny of faction." Yet Hamilton then observed that even this comparison was not quite true. "A civil war is a contest between two GREAT parts of the same empire," which was not the case in a quarrel between the nation and four sparsely populated counties of Pennsylvania. Americans would risk civil war only if the government failed to vindicate its authority by putting a stop to the rebellion before it spread. If demagogues continued to "fan the flame" of resistance, the republican principles of consent and the rule of law would be destroyed by those who misguidedly believed that they were fighting the Revolutionary War against the British Crown again.[40] Excessive vigilance, in other words, would kill the republican experiment in its infancy.

Contemporary political scientists often speak as if Americans have two presidents, a strong president in foreign policy, and a much weaker one in domestic policy.[41] Though we often attribute the weakness of the executive in domestic policy to "Madisonian pluralism," which establishes the president as but one of many players in a system of opposite and rival interests, the strength of the presidency in foreign policy is often said to have arisen from the presumed necessities or hysterical fears that led to the establishment of the so-called national security state during World War II and the cold war. No doubt, the pressures of many wars led many presidents in this century to assert powers they had not needed in the generally safer international environment of the nineteenth century. Yet it would be a mistake to explain the two presidencies simply or even primarily as a result of the great wars of our own age. They were built into the system from the beginning.

In theory, they arose from the tension between the executive and federative powers as Locke and Montesquieu described them. In practice, they arose from the tension between the competing visions of James Madison, the Republican leader of the House of Representatives, and Alexander Hamilton, the first secretary of the treasury, who often acted as if he were the prime minister of the Washington administration. Merely by virtue of their different leadership roles, each would have felt a substantial obligation to claim a preeminent role for his own branch of the new government. In this important way, ambition clearly was pitted against ambition at the beginning of the Republic. When one adds that Madison admitted to Washington before the Constitutional Convention that he had no clear idea of the future role of the executive in the Republic but that Hamilton had spent much of his life thinking about that role, it was perhaps inevitable the two would come into conflict.[42] Paradoxically, both of them seem to have won the battle. The weak domestic presidency is quite consistent with Madison's vision, and the strong foreign policy presidency owes even more to Hamilton.

Their conflict was foreshadowed in Hamilton's discussion of the treaty power in *The Federalist*. Hamilton had to defend the treaty powers of the executive and the Senate against the "trite" criticism that they mixed powers that some observers claimed belonged to the executive alone, and still others, solely to the legislature.[43] His discussion deserves attention because some apparent inconsistencies in his view of the treaty power arise from it. In *The Federalist*, he made the treaty power appear more legislative than he actually believed. He later spoke much more boldly by incorporating the treaty (federative) power into the executive.[44]

Although "several writers on the subject of government," such as Locke and Montesquieu, placed the treaty power "in the class of executive [read federative] authorities," Hamilton initially argued in *The Federalist* that this was an "arbitrary disposition" of that power. If one focused exclusively on the "operation" of the treaty power, it partook "more of the legislative than of the executive character, though it does not seem strictly to fall within the definition of either of them." Employing public strength to execute the laws or for the common defense seemed to "comprise all the functions of the chief magistrate." Consequently, making treaties did not seem to fall under the definition of executive power. Yet it did not follow that because the treaty power was not, strictly speaking, an executive matter, that it was simply another power of the legislature. "Its objects are CONTRACTS with foreign nations, which have the force of law, but derive it from the obligations of good faith." Treaties are "not rules prescribed by the sovereign to the subject," as is the case when a legislature makes laws, "but agreements between sovereign and sovereign." Hamilton therefore concluded that the treaty power seemed to form a "distinct department" that belonged "properly neither to the legislative nor to the executive."[45]

In *The Federalist*, Hamilton was far less concerned with defining who possessed the power of making treaties than with making the power effective and ensuring that the Republic would be safe under it. John Jay, Hamilton's other and often forgotten partner in the Publius troika, listed several qualities essential to the effective management of foreign negotiations, such as system, firmness, secrecy, and dispatch. Precisely because the executive was most likely to possess these qualities, Hamilton believed he was the "most fit agent" for conducting the nation's transactions with foreign nations.[46] Although it was unsafe for the Republic to entrust so important a power to one individual, excluding the executive from any role in negotiations would have forfeited the advantages of energy. Even if the Senate occasionally delegated negotiations to the executive, the mere "ministerial servant of the Senate could not be expected to enjoy the confidence and respect of foreign powers in the same degree with the constitutional representative of the nation; and of course would not be able to act with an equal degree of weight or efficacy." Yet because treaties are contracts, supported only by the obligations of good faith, the good faith of other nations would depend on two qualities not to be expected even from the Senate: discretion in matters requiring secrecy, and respect for the national government, when good faith must be supplemented or guaranteed by the swift or firm application of the public strength. The Senate, however, could act in one way that the executive could not. It could transform treaties into part of the Supreme Law of the Land, which the executive would then have to enforce and the courts to interpret. Indeed, it is precisely because of the "operation of treaties as laws" in America that Hamilton initially argued that the treaty power was more legislative than executive.[47]

A good example of Hamilton's effort to put this theory into practice is the debate over the Jay Treaty with Great Britain, in which he argued that treaties become law as soon as the Senate ratifies them. In principle, Hamilton asserted, the Constitution gave the executive and the Senate a "*plenipotentiary* authority" to make treaties. The term to "make treaties" was subject to no specified limitations and thus was a "*carte blanche*" for these two departments to make any agreements between the United States and other governments that seemed necessary or useful to the country. Hamilton believed there were only two exceptions to this authority; each was first explained by John Locke. The first was that a treaty could "not change the constitution" itself because "a delegated authority cannot rightfully transcend the constituting act unless so expressly authorized by the constituting power." No matter how much the executive and the Senate believed it was necessary to change with a changing world, they could not change the document designed to enable Americans to remain free. The second exception was "*natural.*" It applied to treaties because it applied to "every other delegated power" in "palpable and extreme cases" of "abuses of authority." "On natural principles, a Treaty which should manifestly betray or sacrifice interests of the state would be null." A possible example of such a nullity might be a treaty, exacted under coercion perhaps, that denied Americans the right to arm to deter or defeat an attack by a foreign power. Otherwise, Hamilton believed there were no limits on the power of the president and the Senate to make treaties.[48]

Nonetheless, some members of the House, and James Madison especially, argued that regulating commerce, appropriating money, declaring war to defend an ally, and any other powers vested in both houses of Congress were also exceptions to this plenipotentiary authority. Consequently, they argued that the treaty power is not plenipotentiary at all but subject to the deliberations of both houses. Hamilton observed that "two obvious considerations refute this doctrine."[49] First, the power to make treaties and the power to make laws are two quite different matters and operate by different means on different subjects. Laws operate only over a nation's own citizens and territory and over foreigners who visit the territory or extensions of the territory, such as embassies and ships at sea. Thus, laws can have "no obligatory action whatsoever upon a foreign nation or any person or thing within the jurisdiction of such a foreign nation." In contrast, treaties operate between nations to establish rules respecting their citizens and property. Law concerns the "will of a SUPERIOR that commands," but treaties concern "the consent of two independent parties that contract." Hence, a "treaty may effect what a law can" by binding independent sovereigns to bind their own citizens, but "a law cannot effect what a Treaty may" because it simply does not reach across borders. Hamilton therefore declared that "no two ideas are more distinct than that of *legislating*" for a nation and "*contracting*" between nations. The House of Representatives was authorized to legislate for Americans but not to make contracts between Americans and foreign states.[50]

The Constitution recognized this natural distinction between laws and treaties; it assigned the former to Congress (with the important exception of the executive's veto) but delegated the latter to the executive (with the important exception of the advice and consent of the Senate). Moreover, executive power as such was vested in the president and specifically included the power to make treaties. The agency of the Senate was "auxiliary" to this power. The executive was to make treaties, "while the force of law" was or was not to be "annexed to the results" by the Senate. It was therefore up to the executive to lead, and the Senate to follow or refuse to follow, by deliberating on the results of negotiations undertaken by the executive. Hamilton believed the constitutional distinction between laws and treaties agreed with the "distribution" of powers "commonly made by theoretical writers" who had understood the difference between legislation and foreign policy. Consistent with his arguments during the struggle to ratify the Constitution, he again wrote that "perhaps the power of Treaty from its peculiar nature ought to form a class by itself." Hamilton did not give this class of power a name at first, but on the next page he mentioned a "pactitious power," which was the "power of Treaty." Later, he simply called it by its Lockean name, the "federative" power. If this power was shared exclusively by the executive and the Senate, then the "legislative power of a nation may be restrained in its operation by the agreements of the Organ of its Federative power or power to contract" with other nations.[51]

When Hamilton decided to climb out on this limb, he once again relied on the moral authority that arises from consent. He asked his readers to remember that the "Nation is the CONSTITUENT; & that the executive within its sphere is no less the organ of its will than the Legislature." Because treaties are best made and enforced by the executive, the federative power was naturally a part of the executive; but because nothing can be law in a republic without the consent of the legislature, treaties could not become law until they had been ratified by the branch of the legislature most capable of deliberating wisely and responsibly on treaties. Hamilton then went so far as to argue that, once ratified, treaties not only were law but also overturned antecedent laws made by both houses that conflicted with them. At a minimum, they obliged the legislature to remove any conflict by amending the laws.[52]

Hamilton's invocation of the federative power in his discussion of the Jay Treaty in 1796 occurred long after his first great quarrel with Madison over Washington's Neutrality Proclamation in 1793, but it helps us understand Hamilton's practical-minded theory of the presidency in that far more famous debate. On the advice of Hamilton and Henry Knox, the secretary of war, Washington issued the proclamation, drafted by John Jay, in response to the outbreak of war between Great Britain and revolutionary France in 1793. Although the proclamation did not mention neutrality, its intention was to make clear to foreigners abroad and citizens at home that the national government meant to abide by international law for neutral nations. Since the United States had formed an alliance with France during the American Revolution, both foreigners and citizens might presume the United States was bound to fight with France against England. Hamilton and Washington therefore concluded that immediate action was necessary to preserve peace. Otherwise, England might attack the United States; or Americans, presuming they were or soon would be at war, might engage in filibustering expeditions or acts of privateering that could lead to war. Hamilton insisted the alliance was defensive only and did not apply to the current war, which had been begun by France. He thus offered a legal justification for remaining neutral. Washington's initiative shocked and angered Jefferson and Madison, who believed it was inconsistent with republican government. If the executive has a constitutional right to determine whether the nation is legally obliged to go to war on behalf of an ally, then one might say that the executive can also declare war. Jefferson and Madison feared that Washington had usurped a power that belonged to Congress alone and that was far too dangerous to be left to the discretion of one individual.

Although Hamilton's defense of the proclamation in his *Pacificus* essays made use of his skills as an advocate, it ought not to dismissed as a mere "legalistic" or "ad hoc" rationalization of the executive's conduct crafted for the occasion.[53] Hamilton regarded his arguments as his best published work and even called for including them in later editions *of The Federalist*.[54] His first line of defense for the proclamation worked by process of elimination. Under the Constitution, the legislature is not the organ of intercourse or official communication with foreign nations; nor is the legislature responsible to make treaties (the executive's job); nor is it assigned to interpret the nation's obligations under treaty (a function of the courts). The courts, however, are involved with treaties and international law only when presented with a specific legal case or controversy. They cannot anticipate those controversies in advance. If one presumes that proclaiming neutrality, which is an essential aspect of sovereignty, belongs to the United States as an independent nation, then the only branch left capable of exercising the power is the executive. This negative inference was also justified by the Constitution's positive grants of authority to the executive. This branch is designated as responsible for official communications between the United States and other nations; by default, it must interpret treaties in cases when the judiciary lacks jurisdiction; it is responsible for executing the laws of the nation, including treaties; and it is vested with command of the forces that might be involved in a war when the United States cannot remain neutral.[55]

The grapeshot in the old artilleryman's second barrage issued from the differences between the wording of Article 1 and Article 2 of the Constitution. Article 1 stated that the powers "herein granted" were vested in Congress, but Article 2 said the "executive power" was vested in the president of the United States. Article 1 was clearly a limited grant of authority; some legislative powers were retained by the people or the states. In contrast, Hamilton believed Article 2 was a complete grant of authority. Thus, the enumeration of specific executive powers in Article 2, such as pardoning, receiving ambassadors, and so on was not a complete list. Since Article 2 contains no "herein granted" qualification, the presumption is that every power in its nature executive belongs to this department. Which powers then are executive by nature?

Montesquieu's transformation of Locke's teaching supplies an important part of the answer. Montesquieu both clarified and confused Americans' understanding of the separation of powers by speaking of "the executive in respect to things dependent on the law of nations; and the executive in regard to matters that depend on the civil law." "The latter," he called the "judiciary power," with the important consequence that the executive was ministerial for law enforcement to the legislature and the courts. The former was the "executive power of the state," by which Montesquieu meant Locke's federative power. With it, the executive "makes peace or war, sends or receives embassies, establishes the public security, and provides against invasions."[56] This power was not ministerial but independent and discretionary. Unfortunately, however, by calling the federative power the executive power, Montesquieu allowed some observers to think the executive was merely ministerial. If so, assertions of discretionary power in foreign policy would then have to be understood as unconstitutional prerogative. Hamilton, however, stuck to Locke's original meaning but employed Montesquieu's terminology. He was not advocating unconstitutional prerogative; instead, he followed Montesquieu by collapsing the federative into the executive power.

Thus, for Hamilton, the only exceptions to the American president's executive-federative powers are those specifically stated in the text of the Constitution, such as the powers to declare war, grant letters of marque, and ratify treaties. The text of the Constitution specifically places the first two in Congress and obliges the executive to share the latter with the Senate. Yet since these exceptions are specifically stated, Hamilton believed they ought to be construed narrowly, lest a broad reading of them undermine the possibility of any flexibility in foreign policy. Congress, in fact, had recognized this principle of narrow construction of its share of the executive power in its own practice. After some debate, the power of the Senate to participate in executive administration was limited to advising and consenting to executive nominations exclusively and did not extend to their removal.[57]

Hamilton's final barrage on behalf of Washington's initiative rested on the executive's oath to take care that the laws are faithfully executed. The traditional federative power of declaring war had been transferred from the executive to Congress, but this did not exclude the executive from any share of deliberation or independent judgment in time of peace. Until Congress declares war (or another nation declares war on the United States), peace is the law of the land. It is therefore the "duty of the executive to preserve peace until war is declared." If the executive is to "take care" to enforce the law, however, he must be careful. Some element of discretion is necessary even to the executive's ministerial duties. He must deliberate upon the policies required to fulfill the law. If treaties that have become part of the law of the land do not require war, then it is the executive's duty to enforce peace by upholding the laws of neutrality.[58] This would justify an executive initiative in proclaiming neutrality, but significantly, Hamilton understood this duty as the kind that would support rather than violate the rule of law. The Neutrality Proclamation did not violate any law, nor did it enact a new law or otherwise transfer any part of the legislative power to the executive. It simply proclaimed a judgment of fact to the world: under existing circumstances the individual responsible for enforcing the law believed he had no obligation to wage war. He would therefore uphold the existing law of the land, the law of neutrality, as he was obliged to do by his oath.

It should be remembered that Washington might have reached a different conclusion. When Congress makes an alliance, it often promises to provide aid to an ally in the future without deliberating upon the matter. If the executive interprets a ratified treaty to require rendering aid to an ally, it would seem that Hamilton believed he could go to war without a congressional declaration of war. In such cases, the branch responsible for deliberating on treaties authorizes war in advance of actual hostilities. It has given the executive not only the right but also the legal obligation to wage war when a treaty requires it. For example, if in the 1980s the Soviet army had actually attacked the Federal Republic of Germany, the executive would have been under no obligation to wait for a declaration of war from Congress. By consenting to the NATO alliance, the Senate had already agreed to its consequences. The alliance would have had no credibility had not the consent of the Senate authorized the executive to employ his full powers as commander in chief in case of attack on an ally.

If only because of such authorization, Hamilton suggested that the executive's own right of deliberation could and even should influence the deliberations of Congress. For example, the executive, as the representative of the nation, had the right to receive foreign ambassadors. When other nations have undergone a revolution, however, receiving ambassadors is tantamount to diplomatic recognition. Had the United States' alliance with France been offensive as well as defensive, recognition would have proclaimed to the rest of the world that the United States believed itself obliged to go to war on behalf of its ally. Although only Congress had a right to declare war, the world might not have waited for it to do so. Some nations might have presumed the United States was at war and assumed the offensive. Thus, the executive, by recognizing another government, might establish an "antecedent state" that might lead to war or even place Americans under legal obligations to go to war. That antecedent state necessarily ought to weigh in deliberations of the legislature and "affect the proper or improper exercise of the Power of the legislature to declare war." In the case of diplomatic recognition of an ally undergoing a revolution, the war power was therefore not in Congress alone but a "*concurrent* authority" shared with the executive.[59]

This concurrency is probably what troubled Madison and Jefferson most about Hamilton's defense of the proclamation. It sounded like an invocation of prerogative to them, though in fact it was nothing of the sort. For Locke, the federative power (including the war power) had to be left primarily "*to* the *Prudence*" of the executive because he is most fit to adapt to the "variations of designs and interests" among foreign states. Hamilton's point was that an effective constitutional division of labor required the executive to maintain control of most of the federative power. Though the "Legislature can alone declare war, can alone actually transfer the nation from a state of Peace to a state of War," Hamilton argued that it "belongs to the 'Executive Power,' to do whatever else the laws of Nations cooperating with the Treaties of the Country enjoin, in the intercourse of the United States with foreign Powers."[60]

As even one of Madison's great admirers observes, his response as Helvidius to Hamilton's Pacificus was partly dismissive and partly ad hominem.[61] The notion that the powers to make treaties and war are essentially executive, Madison suggested, was an anachronistic legacy of the Dark Ages. In supporting this notion, Locke was "warped" by a patriotic regard for the British constitution. Montesquieu admired that constitution with a passion "bordering on idolatry." The only people who read Hamilton's defense of the Neutrality Proclamation with any degree of seriousness were "foreigners and degenerate citizens among us, who hate our republican government, and the French revolution." Then Madison either misunderstood Hamilton or attacked a straw man by portraying him as an advocate of prerogative. The power of making treaties and the power of declaring war were "*royal prerogatives in the British government.*" Accordingly, they were treated as "*executive prerogative by British commentators,*" and by people who treated the commentators seriously. Probably because he was certain that Hamilton was advocating prerogative, Madison made an important mistake that has misled scholars for two centuries. In *Helvidius* 4, he inserted the word "prerogative" in a quotation from Hamilton's *Pacificus* 1, thereby inducing generations to think that Hamilton himself meant to be understood as an advocate of prerogative, when in fact he was talking about the executive's federative powers.[62]

This confusion notwithstanding, Madison raised an important objection to Hamilton's efforts to unite the federative and executive powers. Hamilton asked whether it was prudent to confine the executive within such strict limits that he could not take the initiative to preserve the Republic from harm, but Madison asked whether it was prudent to allow the executive to take the initiative when his initiatives might lead to war. Madison believed that war is the "nurse of executive aggrandizement" and that the "executive is the department most distinguished by its propensity to war." Although Hamilton wrote under the pseudonym Pacificus to demonstrate his devotion to peace, his argument could be used to justify measures that might in some circumstances either lead directly to war or legally oblige Congress to declare war. Hamilton was characteristically defending the virtue of responsibility; Madison was practicing vigilance. Their great debate is the result of the different virtues favored by each of them at the time. Madison worried that if he gave Hamilton an inch, then some executive might later take a mile. Eventually, he feared, the entire power of Congress to decide whether and when to go to war might be absorbed by the executive. When one considers that Americans have been involved in many wars over the last 200 years but have had only five congressional declarations of war, Madison appears more than a little prescient. If the legislative check on the federative power were to have any lasting or significant meaning, he had to deny that the powers of war and treaty "are in their nature executive." Otherwise, he believed "no citizen could any longer guess at the character of the government under which he lives," and even the "most penetrating jurist" would be "unable to scan the scope of constructive prerogative." It therefore appeared safer for the Republic to adopt a simple, if not a simplistic, view of the separation of powers. Congress would make the laws; the executive would enforce them, and the federative power would be consigned to the dustbin of history. Though the executive might have some influence through his veto in domestic policy, in foreign policy he would become the mere agent of Congress. Otherwise, Madison feared, he could lead the Republic to war at any time.[63]

We can evaluate this great debate only by examining the dangers on both sides of the issue. Implicitly at least, Madison ultimately feared the American executive more than foreign governments. Both might be dangerous, but which was more dangerous? In the worst case, an executive rendered energetic through possession of most of the federative power might drag an unwilling nation into an unnecessary or unjust war. Yet without the federative power, he might also be unable to prevent unjust wars against the United States, or to defend against them after they had begun. Since the executive was elected, however indirectly, his dependence upon the people supplied some reasonable grounds to trust him. There was absolutely no reason to trust to the virtue of other nations to provide for American security, however. Indeed, Madison himself made this argument in *The Federalist:* "If a Federal Constitution could chain the ambition, or set bounds to the exertions of all other nations: then it might prudently chain the discretion of its own government, and set bounds to the exertions for its own safety."[64] Thus, the same Madisonian reasoning that called for an energetic Union for national defense pointed toward an energetic executive in foreign policy.

Moreover, a weak executive is no security against going to war. If only through inertia, a republic could easily drift into war because no enlightened statesman was able or willing to steer the ship of state. As Hamilton well knew, there have been almost "as many popular as royal wars," or wars provoked by the executive. "The cries of the nation and the importunities of their representatives have, upon various occasions, dragged their monarchs" and other executives "into war, or continued them in it contrary to their inclinations, and sometimes, contrary to the real interests of the state."[65] In such cases, executive energy is no less necessary to preserve peace than it is to wage war effectively. In this regard, the political contexts of Hamilton's *Pacificus* essays and his defense of the Jay Treaty are quite important. In both cases, he defended executive energy as a means to peace. Unfortunately, the president could not preserve peace or promote it after hostilities began without the energy that might sometimes lead to war or even prolong it, once it had begun. No course of interpretation was without risks, but the inducements to responsibility that Hamilton addressed in *The Federalist* inclined him to believe the executive was generally more likely to use this power well than to abuse it.

The greatest danger from Madison's strict construction of executive power was not the weakness that might lead to a war or an executive unable to conduct it effectively, however. Instead, it was the very prerogative Madison feared. As he had argued in *The Federalist,* "It is vain to oppose constitutional barriers to the impulse of self-preservation. It is worse than vain; because it plants in the Constitution itself necessary usurpations of power, every germ of which is a precedent of unnecessary and multiplied repetitions."[66] Like Madison, Hamilton believed it is in "the nature of war to increase the executive at the expense of the legislative authority." It is therefore in the nature of war to destroy strict interpretations of executive power. Far more than the abstract theories of Woodrow Wilson and Theodore Roosevelt, it has been the practical necessities of war that have led modern presidents to assert the federative powers Madison sought to banish from the Constitution. Because those powers have been abused more than once, it is impossible not to sympathize with Madison's fears. Yet as Hamilton consistently argued, the "possibility of abuse" of a necessary power is ultimately "no argument against the *thing*." One can only render the power as safe as its necessity permits through elections, the institutions of balanced government, and so on, and then hope for the best.[67]

Lance Banning is certainly right to stress Madison's fear that "'every power that can be deduced from'" Hamilton's synthesis of executive and federative powers "'will be deduced and exercised sooner or later by those who have an interest in so doing.'"[68] After 200 years, experience has proved Madison absolutely right. Whether by ordering the American navy to convoy British ships across the Atlantic before the United States' official entry into World War II or by ordering American troops into Korea without a congressional declaration of war under a United Nation's mandate, or by engaging in countless acts of brinkmanship during the cold war, recent American presidents have exploited the executive's federative powers as much as possible, and sometimes even more than Hamilton envisioned. Yet in the long run, which was preferable, to compel the executive to violate the law in order to preserve the Republic from harm, or so far as practicable, to provide the executive the means to fulfill this responsibility within the Constitution? Hamilton had no doubts:

> Wise politicians will be cautious about fettering the government with restrictions which cannot be observed; because they know that every breach of the fundamental laws, though dictated by necessity, impairs that sacred reverence which ought to be maintained in the breasts of rulers towards the constitution of a country, and forms a precedent for other breaches, where the same necessity does not exist at all, or is less urgent and palatable.[69]

Although American presidents may preach strict construction of their powers, strategic necessity often dictates otherwise. Responsibility then compels them to moderate their vigilance. Unfortunately, strict construction then leaves them no alternative but to invoke prerogative when extreme danger appears or great opportunity knocks, as Jefferson did in his defense of the Louisiana Purchase.[70] For the sake of preserving the constitutional rule of law, however, one often wishes presidents would not only act but also speak like Hamilton, who preferred for the president to act energetically within rather than outside the law. By showing that unity, duration, adequate support, and competent powers were necessary to a due dependence upon the people and a due responsibility for their welfare, he also showed that executive energy and republican safety are mutually dependent.

No republic can be safe without an energetic executive. In America at least, no executive can be truly energetic without the moral authority arising from the republican principle of consent. Though Hamilton did not complete the transformation of the executive into a branch of American government accepted as equally republican as Congress, he certainly began it. He made executive energy both constitutional and republican. He cannot receive all the credit for this accomplishment because it arose dialectically, from his responses to the fears, misgivings, arguments, and vigilance of his opponents. As a result of that dialectic, however, it is possible to speak boldly and without contradiction in asserting that Hamilton was both a constitutionalist and the most important Founder of the modern presidency.

7. National Security, Popular Sovereignty, and a Limited Constitution

Hamilton spent most of his career trying to reconcile the necessity of empire with the moral authority of consent, a problem that was perhaps most acute in his discussions of the federal courts and broad construction of the Constitution. The Rousseauian character (though not inspiration) of Hamilton's reconciliation has been suggested (see chapter 5). As sources of authority, American citizens collectively would be to the sovereign as the sovereign would be to individuals subject to its laws. As represented in the Constitution immediately and the people originally, authority would arise from consent, and effective government would thereby become legitimate as well.

The federal judiciary was an important part of Hamilton's vision of an American republican empire. Precedents for judicial review of unconstitutional legislation had existed for quite some time in both the United States and England, but it was unclear how this power could be legitimate when consent was presumed to be the only source of political authority. Though today it is common to portray the federal courts as the least republican components of American government, the necessity of legitimizing what we now call the review power in a republic compelled Hamilton to innovate by casting the courts as both defenders and agents of popular sovereignty. They would not only defend the consent of the people to the Constitution against usurpers in the legislature, but they would also act as agents of laws made by national majorities through their representatives. Though we today look to the federal courts especially to uphold clear or deduced limits to popular sovereignty, Hamilton usually cast the federal courts as indirect but quite significant instruments for establishing domestic tranquillity (avoiding civil war) and serving the common defense. By supplying an alternative to enforcing the law through an army, he also believed the courts might constitute an almost invisible but nonetheless important bulwark against militarism.

For the vigilant, the great problem with the role Hamilton assigned to the federal courts was that it seemed to make the national government the final judge of quarrels between itself and the states. If the courts accepted Hamilton's broad reading of the Constitution, the perhaps inevitable result might be that the national government would consolidate most political power unto itself. After examining why he thought judicial review was legitimate in a republic and the strategic functions he assigned to the courts, it may therefore prove useful to investigate the variety of limits that Hamilton himself set on the power of the national government.

In the *Phocion* letters, Hamilton had argued that a legislature that violated a constitution usurped the sovereignty of the people. Likewise, in *The Federalist*, he observed that "every act of a delegated authority, contrary to its commission, is void. No legislative act contrary to the constitution can be valid. To deny this would be to affirm that . . . the representatives of the people are superior to the people themselves; that men acting by virtue of powers may do not only what their powers do not authorize, but what they forbid."[1] Once again, however, the great question arose: Who was to judge whether a legislature or any other part of the government had usurped the authority of the people? No matter that the legislature had a right to judge its own powers in order to exercise them properly. Its judgment was not "conclusive upon the other departments," or else the separation of powers would exist on paper only. Then there would be no limits on the power of the legislature, which could disregard the Constitution at will. To avoid the danger of legislative usurpation, it was prudent to remove the final interpretation of the legislative power from Congress to some other body. The "courts were designed to be an intermediate body between the people and the legislature, in order, among other things, to keep the latter within the limits assigned to their authority." This did not mean the judiciary was superior to the legislature but that the "power of the people is superior to both." The same reasoning applied to both the executive and the state governments. Allowing the executive to be judge in his own cause might well lead to unlimited executive power; allowing the states this right was a recipe for anarchy, if not civil war.[2]

The judiciary was the safest branch with which to trust this power because it had no direct influence "over either the sword or the purse, and can take no active resolutions whatever. It may truly be said to have neither Force nor Will, but only judgment; and must ultimately depend upon the aid of the executive for the efficacy of its judgments." Hence, the judiciary was "beyond comparison the weakest of the three departments of power." Quoting Montesquieu, Hamilton observed that of the three great powers of government, the "'JUDICIARY is next to nothing.'"[3] Though vigilance dictated placing this authority where it was least likely to be abused, responsibility required placing it in the hands most likely to exercise it cautiously, after painstaking review of precedents. Together, vigilance and responsibility suggested the courts were best suited to exercise an authority that Hamilton considered both absolutely necessary and inherently dangerous.

Though Hamilton is famous for explaining why the courts might declare some acts of Congress unconstitutional, the common tendency to focus almost exclusively on this theme supplies a warped vision of his intentions for the judiciary. Most of the time he hoped the courts would be useful allies of Congress when it sought to assert its authority over the Union, but authority over which powers and for what purposes? In *Rutgers v. Waddington* Hamilton looked at judicial review as both a means to keep the peace with England and to secure minority rights at the end of the Revolutionary War. Similarly, in *The Federalist,* he observed that a "circumstance, which crowns the defects" of the Articles of Confederation, "was the want of a judiciary power" because "laws are a dead letter without courts to define their true meaning and operation." Hamilton was particularly concerned about treaties. If the lackluster enforcement of the Treaty of Paris were any evidence, the treaties of the United States under the Articles were subject to the "infractions of thirteen different legislatures" and as many different courts of final jurisdiction. Consequently, the "faith, the reputation, the peace of the whole union" were "continually at the mercy of the prejudices, the passions, and the interests of every member of which it is composed." He was at least as concerned with faction within the states as James Madison, but primarily because of its threat to an effective foreign policy. He doubted that foreign nations would either "respect or confide" in the government unless it was capable of upholding its treaties.[4] No less important to Hamilton was the potential for the courts to prevent war with foreign powers, civil war between the states, and war between the states and the national government. John Jay, the former secretary of foreign affairs for the Continental Congress (and quite significantly, the first chief justice of the Supreme Court), anticipated much of Hamilton's position in *The Federalist.* Indeed, a comparison of Jay's arguments at the beginning of *The Federalist* with Hamilton's at the end suggests that it would have been impossible to provide for the common defense and domestic tranquillity without judicial review.

Jay observed that war with foreign powers would arise from the "number and weight of causes, whether *real* or *pretended,* which *provoke* or *invite* them." Real causes, Jay suggested, would arise from acts of injustice committed by Americans that provoked other nations to defend themselves; pretended causes, from weaknesses that led foreign nations to believe they could get away with injustice toward Americans.[5] The just causes of war would consist of American violations of treaties or acts of direct violence by Americans against the subjects and property of other nations. As Frederick Marks reveals, these acts of injustice ranged from American violations of the Treaty of Paris to the various plans of western frontiersmen to seize New Orleans from Spain.[6] Jay reminded his readers that the United States already had treaties with six different nations, all but one of which were maritime powers able to menace the United States and its commerce. He also noted that the United States had an extensive commerce with Portugal, Spain, and England, and that Spain and England were on its borders. Moreover, in the West, a chief object of policy would be to form treaties with the Indians in order to prevent direct acts of violence from or against them. The danger of giving unjust offense was therefore quite serious. Americans had already done so by violating the treaty with England, which therefore had a right to renew war against the United States at a time and place of its own choosing. Further, "several instances of Indian hostilities" had been "provoked by the improper conduct of individual States" that were "either unable or unwilling to punish offenses" by their own citizens. Failure to punish these offenses had "given occasion to the slaughter of many innocent" Indians. Those who survived then became inveterate foes of the white man.[7]

There is no evidence that Jay was sanguine about the capacity of the federal government to prevent such slaughter in all cases. Yet he did suggest that the general odds in favor of preventing American injustices (and therefore war) were stronger under "one National government" than under the Articles of Confederation. Jay submitted that "treaties and articles of treaties, as well as the laws of nations," would "always be expounded in one sense, and executed in the same manner." Instead of being interpreted by a "variety of different courts and judges" influenced by "different local laws and interests," treaties would be "under the jurisdiction and judgment of courts appointed by, and responsible only to one national government."[8] A uniform interpretation, of course, is not the same as a fair one, but Jay presumed the federal courts would believe themselves responsible for the peace and safety of the whole nation. Hence, they would be less likely to misinterpret or disregard treaties deliberately in order to serve the interests and ambitions of particular states. Moreover, a variety of interpretations risked that foreign nations would presume that some states were upholding treaties while others were not. One state, then, through an errant interpretation, could provoke a war with a foreign nation for which the rest of the United States would be held responsible. Even if foreign nations responded only against states that they believed were guilty of injustice, the Union was responsible for protecting each state. Since the Union had this obligation, Jay presumed it should also have the means of preventing one state from provoking a war for which all would be held responsible and in which all would have to fight.

Jay, of course, did not think the federal courts would or could undertake the responsibility to prevent war by themselves. As Nathan Tarcov has noted, Jay anticipated much of James Madison's argument in *Federalist* 10 but applied it to war and foreign policy instead. Under the new Constitution, he suggested, Congress was likely to be less prone to faction than the state governments, because the odds favored a greater diversity and superior quality of representation in Congress than was likely in the state legislatures. Controlling factious majorities dangerous to the rights of other nations and unconcerned with the common good of the whole Union was therefore as important to national security as it was to the stability and dignity of republican government itself. Yet Jay went a step further than Madison. Because the national government was likely to be less subject to local interests and passions than the states, Jay observed that it would be more likely to possess the will to "punish the aggressors" when Americans were in the wrong.[9] The will and ability to punish would go a long way toward deterring aggression by Americans acting privately in filibustering expeditions or collectively through the states. It might also help American diplomats avoid war when such violence occurred. They could promise that the suspects would be prosecuted and assure other nations of a probability of conviction. There would then be no need for foreign countries to punish Americans when their government was in the process of doing so itself. Even if the accused were not convicted, the period between bringing the first charges and the end of trial would give diplomats their most treasured weapon: the time for passions to cool and for reasonable negotiators to cut a deal.

Although Jay paid careful attention to the just causes of war, he was not blind to the realities of the international competition for power. He also recognized that "acknowledgments, explanations, and compensations are often accepted as satisfactory from a strong united nation, which would be rejected as unsatisfactory if offered by a State or Confederacy of little consideration or power." He then told a story about the tiny city-state of Genoa. In 1685, Genoa had offended Louis XIV of France and then tried to appease him. The haughty Sun King demanded that the Genoans send their doge, or chief magistrate, accompanied by four of their senators to France to beg his pardon. The Genoans were obliged to submit to this humiliation for the sake of peace. Jay then asked whether Louis could have "demanded, or have received the like humiliation from Spain, or Britain, or any other *powerful* nation." As Tarcov suggests, the moral of Jay's story appears to be that if a nation wants to avoid choosing between war and national humiliation, it should not commit or allow its citizens to commit injustices toward other nations. Yet it must not count on its own justice to keep it out of trouble. No nation will ever be so virtuous that it will always act justly. It is therefore prudent to become the kind of nation that can get away with injustice (while, of course, conscientiously making restitution for injustice when it occurs).[10]

If Americans could not count on their own justice, still less could they count on the justice of foreign powers. Jay was well aware that all nations invoke justice when they go to war. They cannot all be right. Some must therefore pretend to have justice on their side but commit injustice because they think they can get away with it. Thus, it was wise to establish "*such a situation* as instead of *inviting* war will tend to repress and discourage it." That situation would consist in "the best possible state of defense, and necessarily depends on the Government, the arms, and the resources of the country."[11] Or rather, to use terminology more familiar in our time, Jay insisted that a credible deterrent depended upon a well-constructed union, based on a new Constitution, which would enable the national government to draw on the resources and employ the arms of the country with vigor.

Establishing the authority to prevent Americans either from provoking wars by their injustice or inviting them by their weakness was Hamilton's fundamental concern in his account of the six objects of federal jurisdiction in *Federalist* 80. The first and most general object was over all laws of the United States, "passed in pursuance of their just and constitutional powers of legislation." If the laws were not to be dead letters, there ought "always to be a constitutional method of giving efficacy to constitutional provisions." This method "must be either a direct negative on the state laws or an authority in the federal courts, to over-rule such as might be in manifest contravention of the articles of union." Hamilton could not imagine a "third course." The Federal Convention had found the second alternative preferable to the veto plans first advocated by both Hamilton and Madison. Judicial review was "most agreeable to the states" that might well have perceived a national veto in the hands of Congress (Madison's plan) or nationally appointed state governors (Hamilton's plan) as too reminiscent of the British Empire for American tastes. Nonetheless, the "horrid picture" of the "dissensions and private wars which distracted and desolated Germany" demonstrated to Hamilton the utility of the "IMPERIAL CHAMBER," or final court of appeal established by Maximillian "for appeasing the disorders and establishing the tranquillity of the empire." If Americans meant to maintain peace within their own far-flung empire, Hamilton saw no alternative to establishing a similar chamber.[12]

The second object of national jurisdiction was over all cases "which concern the execution of the provisions expressly contained in the articles of union." This was similar to the first object of giving efficacy to the laws, but like Jay before him, Hamilton stressed the importance of uniformity—not for its own sake but for the sake of peace. "Thirteen independent courts of final jurisdiction over the same causes, arising under the same laws, is a hydra of government, from which nothing but contradiction and confusion can proceed." It would certainly undermine the "fair interpretation and execution of our treaties" and might also disrupt "the harmony between the individual states." In contrast, one national court of final appeal, substantially independent of local passions, interests, and prejudices, would do a much better job of preventing foreign and civil war by "frustrating the effects of partial laws, in any one [state] injurious to the rights" of citizens of other states or other nations. "To avoid the confusion which would unavoidably result from the contradictory decisions of a number of independent judicatories," Hamilton observed, "all nations have found it necessary to establish one court paramount to the rest—possessing a general superintendence, and authorized to settle and declare, in the last resort, an uniform rule of civil justice."[13]

Significantly, Hamilton defended this general superintendence as the only practical alternative to militarism. "Between a government of laws, administered by an independent judiciary, or a despotism supported by an army, there was no medium. If we relinquish one," Hamilton wrote after repeal of the first Judiciary Act, "we must submit to the other." Or, as he is said to have spoken in a more sanguinary manner, "if the *laws* are not suffered to control the passions of individuals, through the organs of an extended, firm, and independent judiciary, the bayonet must." Without such courts, the Union would "crumble to pieces in a few, very few years," or the nation would "become the prey of a usurper, and sink into the calm of a military despotism." As usual, Hamilton sought to counter the critics of the courts by giving a republican twist to his defense of them. Those who "truly value our republican government," he declared, had to support the independence and broad jurisdiction of the federal courts, or they would unintentionally contribute to an elevation of the military over the civil authorities. They would thereby destroy the liberty they sought to defend.[14]

The third object of jurisdiction, "controversies between the nation and its members or citizens," simply extended the reasoning of the second. If it was unsafe to allow the states to be judges in their own cause, it was even less safe and "contrary to reason, to precedent, and to decorum" to allow individuals to be judges in their own cause (or what could amount to the same thing, to have the states judge between them and the federal government). The fourth object went to the heart of the matter. It comprised all cases that "involve the PEACE of the CONFEDERACY, whether they relate to the intercourse between the United States and foreign nations, or to that between the states themselves." The logical conclusion of Jay's arguments at the beginning of The Federalist was Hamilton's at the end. Hamilton observed that

> the peace of the WHOLE ought not to be left to the disposal of a part. The union will undoubtedly be answerable to foreign powers for the conduct of its members. And the responsibility for an injury ought ever to be accompanied by the faculty for preventing it. As the denial or perversion of justice by the sentences of the courts, as well as in any other manner, is with reason classed among the just causes of war, it will follow that the judiciary ought to have cognizance in all cases in which the citizens of other countries are involved.

The last two objects of national jurisdiction, admiralty and maritime law as well as cases where the state courts might not be impartial, have been anticipated. The former clearly concerns the dangers of foreign war in cases of captures on the high seas, and more indirectly, in the complex regulations of international commerce. The latter just as clearly concerns the danger of civil war insofar as the "claims of land grants of different states, founded upon adverse pretensions to boundary" might furnish an immediate cause of quarrel between them.[15]

Standard accounts of American foreign and national security policy have little if anything to say about the judiciary. For both principled and prudential reasons, this weak sibling usually treats the issues of national security as political questions, which Congress and the president must settle between themselves and the electorate must ultimately judge at the polls.

As a result, American national security policy is usually understood as the effect of two different sets of constraints, or variables: perceptions of threats from abroad, and the clash of institutions, opinions, and interests at home that commonly go under the name of "Madisonian pluralism."[16] If the objects of jurisdiction in Hamilton's account of the judiciary are any evidence, however, this conventional approach is in no way sufficient to account for the Founders' understanding of national security under the Constitution. For Hamilton at least, the courts were absolutely essential to prevent civil war, to preserve peace by upholding treaties, and to establish the authority of the national government to raise troops and money for war. Because the only practical alternative to the rule of force is the rule of law, Hamilton also regarded the courts as essential to avoid militarism. We today can generally ignore their indirect but significant influence on the American Republic's capacity to wage war effectively and remain free at the same time because they have been enormously successful at performing the functions that Hamilton first assigned to them. They are the almost invisible hands that make it possible for American national security policy to be both coherent and effective.

According to Clinton Rossiter, Hamilton virtually "invented" a new Constitution in the 1790s.[17] Because he was more concerned with unleashing than restraining national power, he came close to establishing by legal construction what he had failed to obtain at the Federal Convention: congressional authority to make all laws whatsoever for the safety and welfare of the Union. In practice, though not always in theory, the federal courts have largely accepted Hamilton's broad reading of the Constitution. When the enumerated powers of Congress are read in light of both the ends of the Preamble and the necessary and proper clause, there seems to be no limit to what Congress can do, apart from the constitutionally specified or judicially mandated exceptions to its authority that go under the name of heightened scrutiny. One must therefore once again wonder whether Rossiter and other scholars who stress Hamilton's influence on the modern Constitution have unintentionally damaged his reputation as a faithful servant of the limited Constitution of 1787. Did Hamilton sacrifice the Founders' Constitution to popular sovereignty and the presumed necessities of modern war? If he did invent a new Constitution, can his innovation be justified on constitutional grounds? Or were his critics right? Was his broad construction mere usurpation? What limits remain in his understanding of constitutional government?

The first limit consisted of powers specifically forbidden to the national government. "The complete independence of the courts of justice," Hamilton observed, is "peculiarly essential in a limited constitution." As he first used this term, however, it applied to a constitution with "certain specified exceptions to the legislative authority; such for instance that it shall pass no bills of attainder, no *ex post facto* laws, and the like." A limited constitution recognizes the sovereign right of the people to govern themselves but also sets bounds to their power by specifying exceptions to it. When Hamilton wrote this, the Constitution had no Bill of Rights, however. He also feared that further exceptions to national authority might go too far and deprive it of essential energy (for example, by prohibiting standing armies in time of peace). So far as possible, he opposed amendments to limit the powers of the national government. Hence, it is impossible to avoid the conclusion that Hamilton's original vision of the federal courts as the "bulwarks of a limited constitution against legislative encroachments" was quite limited indeed.[18]

Generally, Hamilton wanted the courts to be bulwarks of popular sovereignty. As he made clear in his defense of the constitutionality of the first Bank of the United States, popular sovereignty is different from and bigger than national or state sovereignty. Or rather, popular sovereignty includes both national and state sovereignty. In the United States, all sovereign power belongs to the people, but they entrust their sovereignty to different governments—sometimes delegating a portion completely to the national government, sometimes to the states, and sometimes giving both concurrent authority over the same objects. Everywhere, however, "every power vested in a Government is in its nature *sovereign*, and includes by force of the *term*, a right to employ all the *means* requisite, and fairly *applicable* to the *ends* of such power; and which are not precluded by restrictions & exceptions in the constitution, or not immoral, or not contrary to the essential ends of political society."[19]

Although many scholars have suggested that Hamilton accepted a Hobbesian understanding of sovereignty as simply unlimited, this passage reminds us of the important Lockean distinction between arbitrary and absolute power. Even Locke, with whom Hamilton has much more in common than Hobbes, granted the necessity of absolute power in time of war. The difference between the philosopher of Malmesbury and the friend of Shaftesbury is that the latter insisted that even absolute power could not be employed arbitrarily, that is, contrary to the ends of civil society. Like Locke, Hamilton supported absolute power, but only in the sense of unlimited means for the national government to fulfill the ends specified in the Constitution and to serve the common defense especially. Granted, this approach is quite a slippery slope, but it does have the advantage of balancing the actions a government might have to take in time of war against those it ought never to, even in time of war.[20] The powers precluded in Hamilton's understanding of a limited constitution are those which it is improper for the government to exercise, either because they are specifically forbidden or because no legitimate government has a right to them; the means included are those necessary to the ends of any delegated power.

Necessary, however, did not mean "*absolutely* or *indispensably*" necessary. Once again, Hamilton sought to outmaneuver his critics. Far from maintaining the authority of a limited constitution, he suggested that a strict construction of implied powers would pave the way for prerogative. It would "make the criterion of the exercise of any implied power a *case of extreme necessity;* which is rather a rule to justify the overleaping of the bounds of constitutional authority, than to govern the ordinary exercise of it." To avoid both national weakness and prerogative, "necessary" had to mean "*needful, requisite, incidental, useful, or conducive to*" obtaining an end of a specific constitutional power. Anticipating John Marshall's conclusion in *McCulloch v. Maryland,* Hamilton therefore observed that "if the end be clearly comprehended within any of the specified powers, & if the measure have an obvious relation to that end, and is not forbidden by any particular provision of the constitution, it may safely be deemed to come within the compass of the national authority."[21]

Nonetheless, Hamilton's broad construction was not meant to justify unlimited discretion in the national legislature, for "no government has a right to *do merely what it pleases.*" Hamilton actually added two new elements to his understanding of a limited constitution in his defense of the Bank: no clearly immoral laws (perhaps like those in New York at the end of the Revolution for the sake of vengeance against suspected Tories) and no laws inconsistent with the ends of civil society (such, perhaps, as laws denying the right to property). It is not clear whether Hamilton believed these elements were judicially enforceable limits, however. The former risked judicial usurpation of the legislative power by making abstract justice rather than constitutionality the standard for overturning laws. The latter might well be the basis for exercising the right of revolution. Though this limit could lead to reflection on natural rights, it might not be safe or wise to leave it to judges to interpret it. If they understood it too narrowly, American liberty would be abridged; if they understood it too broadly, they might become the sources of revolutionary change.

Hamilton insisted his doctrine of broad construction did "not affirm that the National government is sovereign in all respects, but that it is sovereign to a certain extent: that is, the extent of its specified powers." Yet if an act of Congress did not "abridge a preexisting right of any state, or of any individual," there was a "strong presumption in favor of its constitutionality; & slighter relations to any declared object of the constitution may be permitted to turn the scale." It did not matter if an act of the national legislature altered the laws of the states. "If the government of the United States can do no act, which amounts to an alteration of a State law, all its powers are nugatory. For almost every new law is an alteration, in some way or other of an old *law*, either *common*, or *statute*."[22] Indeed, if the pretext of interference with the laws of a particular state were allowed, then a minority would have a veto over the acts of a national majority, acting by virtue of its constitutional powers. The republican principle of consent as the foundation of national laws would then lie in ruins.

This view did not mean the states would have no means to check the national government. Their senators were appointed by their legislatures. They could be counted on to speak up perhaps even more than they should on behalf of their states' rights and interests, and so too could their representatives. Yet precisely because national laws would apply to individuals, the states would lose the right, or rather, the de facto power (through noncompliance), to veto laws made by national majorities. Hamilton thus anticipated later, and often successful, efforts in American history to trump partisans of states' rights with the republican principle of majority rule. Ironically, perhaps the only way he could make national authority effective was to make the Constitution much more republican than he is given credit for and therefore less federal as well.

By far the most important elements in Hamilton's understanding of a limited constitution, however, were the procedures for making law and exercising power in the new Republic. As he often observed, the great safeguard of liberty in the Constitution is its structure.[23] Because all power may be abused, these procedural limits often seem unsatisfactory, but because they allowed Congress and the executive to exercise a high degree of flexibility in time of war or near-war, they were perhaps the only constitutional limits compatible with the potentially unlimited character of modern war.

Especially if the national courts had greater independence than the state courts, Hamilton believed the former could make a significant procedural contribution to a limited constitution by separating the power of judging from making and executing law. Above all, due process of law must mean a chance for the accused to have his day in court; otherwise, he has no security for his rights. Lack of due process had been Hamilton's fundamental objection to the New York legislature's persecution of suspected Tories at the end of the Revolution. By usurping the judicial power, the legislature denied the accused an opportunity for an independent determination of guilt or innocence. Due process requires independent judges to guard both

> the constitution and the rights of individuals from those ill humors which the arts of designing men, or the influence of particular conjunctures, sometimes disseminate among the people themselves, and which, though they speedily give place to better information and more deliberate reflection, have a tendency in the mean time to occasion dangerous innovations in the government and serious oppressions of the minor party in the community.[24]

If only because the courts would not wish to see their own power transferred to another department, they would have strong motives to prevent these dangerous innovations. Precisely because the people are sovereign, however, Hamilton chose his words carefully. He did not suggest that the courts could crusade for justice, but he did suggest that they could limit the impact of unjust laws.

This additional element in Hamilton's understanding of a limited constitution arises more from the prudence than from the authority of courts. They might play an important role in "mitigating the severity and confining the influence" of "unjust and partial laws" dangerous to the "private rights of particular classes of citizens" arising from the "occasional ill humors in the society." Significantly, Hamilton did not say the courts could overturn such laws. When faced with laws that they believed were unjust but constitutional, the courts would still have a duty to uphold them. Yet they could also interpret them in such a way as to render them much less dangerous. A good example is Hamilton's effort to convince the *Rutgers* court that the laws of war had been incorporated with the common law by the New York Constitution. Since the New York legislature had not said it meant to abolish the laws of war, the court was in a position, if it dared, to assert that the legislature had not intended to do so and was still bound by them. In such cases, the courts might "moderate the mischiefs" of the legislature but not necessarily confront it head-on. Even if limited to such a role, they could "operate as a check upon the legislative body in passing" such laws. When legislators perceived "the obstacles to the success of an iniquitous intention" that were to be expected from the "scruples of the courts," the legislators would "in a manner" be "compelled by the very motives of the injustice they meditate, to qualify the attempt." Although such a check provided only a marginal advantage for the rights of the minority, Hamilton believed this was a circumstance

> calculated to have more influence upon the character of our governments, than but few are aware of. The benefits of the integrity and moderation of the judiciary have already been felt in more states than one; and though they may have displeased those whose sinister expectations they may have disappointed, they must have commanded the esteem and applause of all the virtuous and disinterested.[25]

For the vigilant, these limits on the authority of the national government were not enough. Among the Anti-Federalists, Brutus and the Federal Farmer anticipated most of Hamilton's critics in his time and our own. They observed, first, that without a bill of rights the Constitution seemed to have no moral compass, and second, that judicial review would make the national government judge in its own cause, an effect they found no more palatable than leaving any other part of the government as judge of its own powers. In demanding a bill of rights, the Federal Farmer observed that "if a nation means its systems, religious or political, shall have duration, it ought to recognize the leading principles of them in every family book."[26] Hamilton focused on procedures for making national power both effective and safe; the Federal Farmer stressed writing the substantive principles of the Revolution in the hearts of ordinary citizens. Yet the animating spirit of the Anti-Federalists' demand for a bill of rights was vigilance, the ambiguous virtue or vice that Hamilton feared would make it impossible to write the Union in the hearts of American citizens. In *Federalist* 84, he therefore put the best face he could on the Federal Convention's decision to frame a Constitution without a bill of rights, but not because he believed there were or ought to be no such limits. Rather, he suspected the Anti-Federalists would propose the wrong kind of limits, which would prevent the national government from performing its most necessary responsibilities. At the time, an effective national government seemed more important than prohibitions that might prevent it from abusing its powers. In the long term, however, it was much harder to dismiss the vigilance a bill of rights was meant to inculcate. At some point, the national government would inevitably abuse its authority; and then, the Federal Farmer, other Anti-Federalists, and Thomas Jefferson had a significant point: it is not enough to have procedures for preventing abuses of power. As Jefferson observed to James Madison, the people must "have principles furnished them whereon to found their opposition" or else they would not be able to discern when such abuses occurred or to act effectively to restore the government to its first principles.[27]

Like many who came after him, Brutus was not sure the federal judiciary was the least dangerous branch of the government. He must also have inflicted a painful wound on Hamilton by questioning whether "the world ever saw, in any period of it, a court of justice invested with such immense powers" as the Supreme Court, "and yet placed in a situation so little responsible." Hamilton and his allies were being accused of irresponsibility, which the experience of the Revolution led them to regard as a cardinal sin. To be sure, Brutus did not use this term the same way as Hamilton. As Herbert Storing suggests, Brutus meant accountability or responsiveness; Hamilton meant dedication to the public good.[28] Brutus was surely right that an independent court could become as arbitrary as any other branch of government. Yet Hamilton was all too aware that excessive responsiveness to public opinion could lead to no less arbitrary judicial decisions. So there the different versions of responsibility came to rest, like irreconcilable Kantian antinomies, with one side understanding responsibility as a result of popular vigilance and the other seeing it as a necessary corrective to the excesses that sometimes arise from vigilance.

Though muted in 1787, those antinomies exploded in 1791 in Hamilton's debate with Jefferson and Madison over the constitutionality of a national bank. The virulence of Madison's denunciation of his former partner as Publius has puzzled many scholars in this century. Yet according to Lance Banning, Hamilton and James Madison were like two ships passing in the night in 1787: they appeared to be identical nationalists as Publius because they covered much the same ground, but they were actually moving in radically different directions while they collaborated on *The Federalist.* Indeed, because he believes Madison was always much less a nationalist than Hamilton and more a strict constructionist in his youth than commonly believed, Banning implies that even in *The Federalist,* Madison and Hamilton were almost defending two different constitutions. Madison defended the constitution of a compound republic with clear divisions between state and national authority, but Hamilton supported the constitution of a republican empire that Madison later came to fear would make such divisions impossible. In reality, Banning suggests, Madison was much closer to the Anti-Federalists than to Hamilton and might even have refused to sign the Constitution had he understood the uses (abuses) Hamilton had in mind. To calm the Anti-Federalists in Virginia in 1788, Madison had insisted that under his constitution, the government could make no laws that were not fairly deducible from some enumerated power. The bill to establish a national bank was the first great test of this doctrine and the good faith of those who established it. As an eighteenth-century man of honor, Madison could not abide selling his constitution one way in 1788 and then radically reinterpreting it in 1791. The Federal Convention had debated and specifically rejected a national power of incorporation, and therefore, in the view of both Jefferson and Madison, the bill to incorporate the Bank of the United States was as unconstitutional as it was hypocritical. The bank bill would set a precedent that would eventually destroy the doctrine of enumerated powers, as indeed the doctrine of implied powers has done over time. As the prescient Madison observed, "To borrow money is made the *end* and the accumulation of capitals implied as the *means.* The accumulation of capitals is then the *end* and a bank implied as a *means.* The bank is then the end and a charter of incorporation, a monopoly, capital punishment, etc. implied as the *means.*" The problem with this mode of reasoning, he observed, is that "a chain may be formed which will reach every object of legislation, every object within the whole compass of political economy." In practice, then, there would be no limit to the authority of the national government.[29]

At the core of this critique was the status not merely of a compound republic but probably also of the spirit of liberty, which a compound republic helps to preserve. Jean Yarbrough has made a powerful case that the most important Founders, save Thomas Jefferson, significantly undervalued the contribution of state and local government to preserving the Republic by preserving the spirit of citizens who take an active part in public affairs. For Publius, she suggests, the goal was less to include than to exclude the people from participation, except of course through elections and the debates that precede them. Lance Banning suggests this sort of critique applies much more to Hamilton than to Madison. Given Madison's general suspicion of independent wills in government, Banning is probably right. One therefore cannot avoid this disturbing question: If Hamilton's virtue of responsibility necessarily requires broad construction, does it not also risk what Paul Rahe has referred to as an "enlightened despotism" of an ambitious few over a lethargic many?[30]

Obviously, the answer is yes; but in fairness, one must also consider Tocqueville's distinction between a central government, with complete sovereignty over national objectives, and a centralized administration, which manages every detail of public life at both the national and the local level. The United States, Tocqueville observed, was fortunate to have the former; France was cursed with the latter. "For my part," the Frenchman observed,

"I cannot conceive that a nation can live, much less prosper, without a high degree of centralization of government. But I think that administrative centralization only serves to enervate the peoples that submit to it, because it constantly tends to diminish their civic spirit."[31] Like Tocqueville, Hamilton supported a strong central government, not an omnipotent and omnipresent central administration. As revealed by the ends he ascribed to the national government (war, foreign policy, finance, and commerce), he did not support unlimited but effective government, with the degree of its actual power depending upon circumstances and the variety of possible threats from foreign or civil war especially. Unlike more recent nationalists, he had no intention of the national government's interfering with the traditional police powers of the states over health, safety, welfare, and morals, except when the states' exercise of those powers constituted an obstacle to national responsibilities. Unfortunately, however, it is much easier to maintain the distinction between these spheres of authority in theory than in practice. Especially in time of war, it is also much easier and perhaps sometimes even necessary for a central government to fulfill its responsibilities by centralizing the administration of almost every aspect of governance. And once it starts, it becomes extremely hard to stop.[32]

For Tocqueville, the driving force behind the soft despotism of the modern administrative state was the love of equality, to which he opposed the love of liberty.[33] Precisely because Hamilton shared his critics' goal, to secure liberty rather than to promote equality, his broad construction was still far more limited than that which has arisen in the twentieth century. In Hamilton's view, the greatest danger to the civic spirit cherished by Tocqueville was not a responsible (and therefore, in his view, significantly independent) central government, however broadly its powers are defined, but war on American territory. If Americans were mortals too, they would panic in a crisis and lose their constitutional equilibrium. They would be more than willing to sacrifice even their most fundamental liberties when their safety appeared to be at stake, as in fact they have been whenever war has pressed hard upon them.[34] Perhaps the most important reason Americans have preserved much of their spirit of liberty is that they have usually felt safe from foreign and civil war. Safety has given them the leisure to practice vigilance. This was not merely the result of geographical good fortune but also of the foresight to exploit it. To the extent that Hamilton's broad construction of national power made it possible to build a powerful American empire, he was at least as responsible as any other Founder for preserving the spirit of liberty in America because he helped to establish the secure conditions required for that spirit to survive and flourish.

There may be no alternative to Hamilton's broad construction of national power in time of war, but strict construction might still be better for peace, when Tocquevillian administrative decentralization would seem to be de rigueur. If so, we might comfort ourselves with the hope of being broad constructionists in war and strict constructionists in peace, but experience suggests that this would be a vain effort to avoid the harsher truths of modern warfare. As was evident throughout the cold war, the speed and scale of modern wars sometimes require nations to be armed to the teeth even in time of peace. Broad construction therefore seems as necessary in peace as it is in war. Yet there are also different kinds of peace. Some are long and durable; others, little different from temporary truces between adversaries determined to go on the offensive whenever they have an opportunity to do so. With the end of the cold war, with few clearly identifiable threats to American national security, it is possible that the former sort of peace is more likely than the latter. If so, one suspects that, like Thomas Jefferson and James Madison, even Hamilton would speak in favor of a much more modest and frugal national government. Yet because the degree and variety of threats to American national security is not fixed, and may change rapidly, one also suspects that such talk would be a matter of prudent policy rather than of constitutional principle for Hamilton, who refused to deny his country any weapon, strategy, or means that might someday be necessary to the common defense. In this respect, he was much more an advocate of limited government than of a limited constitution.

Or rather, Hamilton was much less an advocate of national than of popular sovereignty. As David Epstein reveals, even James Madison admitted that the appropriate divisions between state and national power, not to mention between the institutions of national government, do not exist by nature. Instead, they are conventions constructed by fallible human beings with limited powers of understanding and expression. Necessarily, then, they are not susceptible to precise definition.[35] For Hamilton perhaps even more than Madison, free government was not an exact science with absolutely certain rules. Instead, it was a calculated risk that ultimately depended on the prudence and character of the people themselves. Hence the balance between state and national authorities neither was nor ever could be immutable; instead, it was dependent on time and circumstances, including and perhaps especially the degree and variety of threats from abroad. Hence, too, the appropriate balance was much less a constitutional than a political question to be decided by the ballot.

Until the end of the Civil War at least, Hamilton was probably right that the states were more dangerous than useful to a durable Union, but even he recognized and stressed one residual advantage of Madison's compound republic within his republican empire. It allowed the people to adjust the balance of power within the Union according to the necessities of their times through state and national elections. As an advocate of popular rather than national sovereignty, Hamilton did not think this balance would or even could be established by the courts. Instead, he suggested that

> the people, without exaggeration, may be said to be entirely masters of their own fate. Power being always the rival of power; the General Government will at all times stand ready to check the usurpations of the state governments; and these will have the same disposition toward the General Government. The people, by throwing themselves into either scale, will infallibly make it predominate.[36]

In the Founding era, Hamilton generally wanted the people to side with the national government, but different times might require more vigilance among the people than responsibility in their government, and vice versa. John Locke's revolutionary claim that the people shall be judge is surely the most important conclusion of modern liberal-republicanism.[37] It was not only the fundamental premise of Hamilton's republican empire but also his best hope for American liberty in a warlike world that would require far more innovation than most of his contemporaries imagined.

Part Three

STATESMAN

8. Commercial Republicanism

Hamilton, by most accounts, was a mercantilist with little but contempt for the most humane hope of the Enlightenment, that commercial republics would be more peaceful, at least toward each other. His goal, it seems, was not to make the United States different from the quarrelsome and warlike states of Europe but to make it exactly like them, and the sooner the better. As usual, the conventional opinion contains a good deal of truth, but not enough to get to the heart of the matter. Although Hamilton doubted that either commerce or republican government would suffice to preserve peace within the Union and with other nations, he was not a Hobbesian who assumed that relations between sovereign nations were and simply had to be a state of war. Although there is no reason to think he would ever have sacrificed American independence for free trade, he feared that trade wars would issue in shooting wars. In a world dominated by mercantilist empires, however, he also feared that practicing free trade unilaterally would leave the United States poor, weak, and dependent upon them. He drew on so many sources (David Hume, Jacques Necker, Vattel, Adam Smith, Sir James Steuart, Malachy Postlethwayt, William Pitt, and so on) that it is impossible to call him a follower of any major economic thinker. Consequently, his political economy is best understood as a prudential synthesis of different approaches to promoting peace through both free trade and national strength.[1]

Increasing national wealth and power were not ends in themselves for Hamilton, however. Even or especially when he served as secretary of the treasury, his larger object was not growth for the sake of growth but to foster American political independence by establishing the foundations of greater economic independence. He also believed the protocapitalist economy he sought to establish would have two major advantages for liberty in America. First, it would supply greater opportunities for individuals to develop their faculties and thereby encourage an independent spirit of enterprise. Second, Hamilton's system was deliberately intended to avoid the danger that the nation's army might have to rob citizens to support itself in time of war. Though this objective is commonly ignored in accounts of his political economy, he himself suggested it was the greatest advantage of his system. It was a vital part of his strategy to enable the United States to become a great power without falling victim to militarism.

Hamilton's system was denounced by critics throughout the land as the harbinger of the corrupt politics Americans associated with the British court. In conventional terms, according to the language of the country persuasion, the denunciations made substantial sense. As he intended, the first secretary of the treasury did link monied men to the cause of the national government, but he also encouraged a good deal of feverish speculation. Some of the capital created may well have been diverted from more productive pursuits as a result; and initially at least, the few who got in quick on the game made a financial killing. Not least, the increase in executive power through the influence of the treasury secretary looked like corruption, understood as the ability of the executive to coordinate powers that are separated in the Constitution.[2]

Yet what looks like vice to the vigilant often appears to be virtue to the responsible, and there are usually reasonable grounds for dispute. This is not to relativize the meaning of virtue but simply to acknowledge that, in politics at least, virtue is not an "it," but a "they." "It" is not one but many qualities that are not necessarily compatible. The wheels of American government do not turn without some effort to unite what James Madison had split asunder in theory in *Federalist* 10 and 51. By assuming the responsibility to form a governing coalition, Hamilton unintentionally became a founder of the American party system. By establishing credit, he moved toward realizing his ambition to render the United States both fit for war and safe for liberty. By revealing the conditions under which commercial republican theory might work in America, he also helped to make civil war less likely. Insofar as he considered civil war most likely to result in the elevation of the military above the civil authorities, even his critique of commercial republican theory can be considered part of his strategy to establish public strength while discouraging militarism.

Hamilton called the theory that commerce and republican government lead to peace a "deceitful dream" that rested on a merely speculative hope of universal enlightenment and moral regeneration: on "the happy empire of perfect wisdom and perfect virtue." Yet his critique ought not to be overstated. It is best understood as an explanation of why even a union of commercial republics could not prevent civil war without the power to regulate commerce. Hamilton, of course, was not the only Founder to recognize the necessity of this power. If Madison was ultimately less sanguine about the advantages and more fearful of the costs of commercial society, he nonetheless made the power to regulate commerce a central element of his proposals for constitutional reform and of his foreign policy vision as well.[3] Since the theory of liberal democratic peace has received considerable attention in the latter half of the twentieth century, it may therefore prove useful for understanding this theory's strengths and weaknesses to investigate why some individuals supported it in Hamilton's time, and why Hamilton critiqued it in *Federalist* 6.[4]

No one knows who Hamilton's opponent was when he launched his critique.[5] He might have believed the theory was shared widely enough to deserve to be a general target. One Anti-Federalist, however, Agrippa (James Winthrop) of Massachusetts did write a good deal about the pacific tendencies of commercial republics. His argument reveals that the Anti-Federalists were a diverse group. Although Winthrop wrote under a classical pseudonym, he had little but contempt for ancient practice. Though some Anti-Federalists stressed the need for virtue, with an often implicit agrarian foundation, Agrippa was much closer to modern libertarians who hope the invisible hand can overcome almost all political problems, including those of domestic tranquillity and the common defense. Agrippa was not responding to Hamilton or he (directly) to Agrippa, but examining their different positions can supply us with a rough sense of how Hamilton might respond to libertarians and other doctrinaire free traders today.

According to Agrippa, the Greek and Roman republics believed that "war was the employment most becoming freemen." Largely because their citizens were too busy waging war to do much else, they also required slavery to sustain themselves. "Agriculture, arts, and most domestic employment were committed chiefly to slaves." Among the ancients, Agrippa preferred Carthage, "the great commercial republic of antiquity," because Carthage "retained her freedom longer than Rome, and was never disturbed by sedition during the long period of her duration." For Agrippa, Carthage was proof that the

> spirit of commerce was the great bond of union among citizens. This furnishes employment for their activity, supplies their natural wants, defends the rights of property, and by producing reciprocal dependencies, renders the whole system harmonious and energetic. Our great object therefore ought to be to encourage this spirit. If we examine the present state of the world we shall find that most of the business is done in the freest states, and that industry decreases in proportion to the rigor of government.[6]

Agrippa believed there could be a substitute for public strength. "This is commerce. All the states have local advantages, and in considerable degree separate interests. They are, therefore, in a situation to supply each other's wants. . . . The most friendly intercourse may therefore be established between them. A diversity of produce, wants, and interests produces commerce, and commerce, where there is a common, equal, and moderate authority to preside, produces friendship." Significantly, Agrippa maintained that his argument applied to settlers in the West, too. It offered the possibility of a new, almost Jeffersonian empire of liberty, which would not be despotic because its government would not be energetic. "Here, then, we have a bond of union which applies to all the parts of the empire, and would continue to operate if the empire included all of America." If commerce could substitute for the public strength that had held great empires together in the past, Americans could have domestic peace without any coercion from the center.[7]

Though he did not cite Montesquieu, Agrippa sometimes sounded like the gentle French philosopher. According to Montesquieu, the "spirit of monarchy is war and enlargement of dominion; peace and moderation are the spirit of a republic." Yet Montesquieu deliberately contradicted himself when he wrote this. The spirit of the Roman republic was the spirit of spiritedness and aimed solely at "increase of dominion." The contradiction can be explained only by noting that, for Montesquieu, "peace is the natural effect of trade," and the ancient republics supposedly knew very little of trade. Commerce makes nations "reciprocally dependent" on their trading partners. They want, or ought to want, their trading partners to prosper so they can prosper through them. Commerce renders men's "manners" more agreeable as well. To get ahead, they must get along, and consequently, commercial nations are "less savage than formerly." As usual, something was lost during this historical transformation. Or rather, Montesquieu predicted what might be lost. Both the generous spirit of aristocratic liberality and the compassionate spirit of Christian charity might suffer from the harsh spirit of "exact justice" required to balance a merchant's books; so too might whole-hearted dedication to a republic. Nonetheless, Montesquieu hinted strongly that the gains outweighed the sacrifices. If commercial nations also became republics and the generally peaceful interests, sentiments, and principles of the people were represented in the government, then the spirit of modern commercial republics would generally be peaceful as well. Hence Montesquieu concluded that

we begin to be cured of Machiavellianism, and recover from it every day. More moderation has become necessary in the councils of princes. What would formerly have been called a masterstroke in politics would be now, independent of the honor it might occasion, the greatest imprudence. Happy it is for men that they are in a situation in which, though their passions prompt them to be wicked, it is, nevertheless, to their interest to be humane and virtuous.[8]

Hamilton's critique of this theory rests on his understanding of the causes of war, which was as old as Thucydides and is as recent as yesterday. He anticipated much contemporary research in international relations by working at three different levels of analysis: the impact of an anarchic world system on competition between sovereign states, the impact of different forms of political and economic organization at different stages of human history, and the impact of individual statesmen. Hamilton placed special stress on the passions of human nature in anarchic state systems. Such passions have "a general and almost constant operation upon collective bodies of society. Of this description are the love of power or the desire of preeminence and dominion—the jealousy of power or the desire of equality and safety." From this point of view, the problem with the kind of commercial republicanism preached by Agrippa was that it abstracted from the obvious fact that some American states would be stronger than others and tempted to use their power whenever they had a chance. As Hamilton wrote to James Duane during the Revolution, "A little time hence, some of the states will be powerful empires, and we are so remote from other nations that we shall have all the leisure and opportunity we can wish to cut each others' throats." He implied that the love of power would lead some states to seek hegemony and the jealousy of power would lead others to balance against those they believed were seeking hegemony. In turn, the mutual efforts of states to seek and balance power would produce "security dilemmas" that would eventually lead to war.[9]

The second class of causes of war concerned relations between particular kinds of societies at a particular moment, such as Sparta and Athens, Carthage and Rome, or England and France in the eighteenth century. These relations have a "more circumscribed, though an equally operative influence, within their spheres" because they give a particular form to the love and jealousy of power. One such form consists of the "rivalships and competitions of commerce between commercial nations." This form was most prevalent in Hamilton's time, but we ought not to forget that Hamilton knew it was time-bound. The theoretical question was whether it had to lead to war for the rest of time; the immediate, practical question, whether it would result in war in America in Hamilton's time.

At the end of the Revolutionary War, Hamilton had few doubts about the practical question. The Confederation was a powder keg waiting for a match to explode it. In 1783 he wrote Gov. George Clinton that the "fisheries, the fur trade, navigation of the lakes and Mississippi—the Western territory—the islands of the West Indies with respect to traffic, in short the passions of human nature" would be "abundant sources of contention and hostility" among the states. Independent of such considerations as territorial disputes and the apportionment of the national debt, Hamilton later argued in *The Federalist* that "the competitions of commerce" would inevitably be "a fruitful source of contention" among the states. Some states, such as New York, were favored by immense safe harbors. New York would "neither be able nor willing to forego" the advantage of laying heavy duties on goods destined for other states. "Would Connecticut or New Jersey long submit to be taxed by New York for her exclusive benefit?" Under the existing Confederation, Hamilton was certain that the "opportunities, which some States would have of rendering others tributary to them, by commercial regulations, would be impatiently submitted to by the tributary states."[10]

Jealousy and ambition could lead to the disintegration of the Union, as it had to virtually all other confederations. Then, "Each State, or separate confederacy, would pursue a system of commercial policy peculiar to itself. This would occasion distinctions, preferences, and exclusions, which would beget discontent." Each state, in other words, would become a tiny mercantilist power unto itself.

> We should be ready to denominate injuries those things which were in reality the justifiable acts of independent sovereignties consulting a distinct interest. The spirit of enterprise, which characterizes the commercial part of America, has left no occasion of displaying itself unimproved. It is not at all probable that this unbridled spirit would pay much respect to those regulations of trade, by which particular States might endeavor to secure exclusive benefits to their own citizens. The infractions of these regulations on one side, the efforts to prevent and repel them on the other, would naturally lead to outrages, and these to reprisals and wars.[11]

In sum, trade wars would lead to shooting wars, but two corollaries follow from Hamilton's embryonic philosophy of history: first, the precondition of peace within the American Union was free trade among the states; second, free trade might be equally necessary to peace between the United States and the rest of the world. The logic of Hamilton's analysis pointed away from mercantilism toward free trade, so far as that was possible under the circumstances of his time.

The third class of causes of war consisted of those that "take their origin entirely in private passions, in the attachments, enmities, interests, hopes and fears of leading individuals in the communities of which they are members." This class affects both monarchies and republics. Whether the "favorites of a king or of a people," some public figures have waged war for merely private reasons, ranging from Pericles' love of a prostitute to Cardinal Wolsey's ambition to wear the pope's hat to Madame de Maintenon's hatred of the Huguenots. Commercial republics, Hamilton implied, would be no more able to predict or control such individuals than would other states. Therefore, they would be just as likely to go to war, even with each other. Or would they? Would not the institutions of balanced government and representation serve as some kind of brake on wars of ambition? Insofar as Hamilton considered these institutions the most important developments in modern political science, did they not also have relevance to foreign policy?[12]

Perhaps they did, but just to be safe, Hamilton insisted that we test commercial republican theory in light of the experience of history. Among the ancients, Sparta, Athens, Rome, and Carthage were republics, and Athens and Carthage were commercial republics. Sparta, however, was "little better than a well-regulated camp; and Rome was never sated of carnage and conquest." If merely being a republic like Sparta and Rome was not sufficient to make a nation peaceful, then one might perhaps follow Montesquieu and suggest that commerce was necessary to turn republics from war to peace. Yet Carthage was a commercial republic, and (contrary to Agrippa's view of its peaceful inclinations) was also the "aggressor in the very war that ended in her destruction." The Athens recorded by Thucydides was one of the most warlike regimes in ancient history. Indeed, modern republics seemed even more warlike. "Venice in latter times figured more than once in wars of ambition." Holland, another commercial republic, had "furious contests with England for the dominion of the sea" and was an implacable foe of Louis XIV. In England, where the people composed one branch of the most dominant part of the government and where commerce had been "for ages the predominant pursuit," commerce seemed to produce nothing but war. "Few nations," Hamilton remarked, "have been more frequently engaged in war." Though American republicans often wished to blame the British monarchy for England's wars, English practice did not always conform to American theory: "The wars in which that kingdom has been engaged, have in numerous instances proceeded from the people."

Hamilton paid particular attention to the most modern wars of the eighteenth century, which grew "in large measure out of commercial considerations." The love and jealousy of power became the "desire of supplanting and the fear of being supplanted" in trade. The "culpable desire of sharing in the commerce of other nations, without their consent" was the source of the most rapacious imperialism.[13] Worse, it led those empires to war with each other over the monopoly of colonial trade. Hamilton therefore had legitimate reasons to suggest that commerce had not yet made nations more peaceful.

Nonetheless, the wars of Hamilton's time clearly did have a "circumscribed" character that he barely addressed in his critique. Neither France nor England was a republic. Their examples were hardly apt for disproving the commercial republican thesis. Because the most modern wars were between mercantilist empires, their behavior was also ill-suited to test commercial republican theory, which depended on free trade. The wars of those empires actually supported that theory, and Hamilton knew it. During the Revolutionary War, for example, in the context of discussing Hume's arguments for free trade, Hamilton referred to England's mercantilist policies as "productive of so many wars."[14] Most of the republics he mentioned lacked all but a few of the improvements in political science that he stressed three essays later in *Federalist* 9. Despite Hamilton's sound and fury in *Federalist* 6, his critique signified little for testing commercial republican theory. There was not enough relevant experience to determine whether it was true.

Hamilton's critique must be interpreted politically, given the necessity of defending a union at least as energetic as the one proposed by the Convention. To the extent that a popular prejudice, mixing truth with error, might have prevented ratification of the Constitution, he apparently felt obliged to undermine that prejudice in a manner that not only showed the limits of the theory but also seemed to dismiss it as simply utopian. During the debate over Vermont, however, he observed that the spirit of modern commercial republics was more peaceful than the spirit of the ancient republics, and in his view, morally preferable. Later on in *The Federalist*, he undermined his critique of commercial republicanism by observing that "the industrious habits of the people of the present day, absorbed in the pursuits of gain, and devoted to the improvements of agriculture and commerce are incompatible with the condition of a nation of soldiers, which was the true condition" of the republics of antiquity. Certainly the militia, in which the majority would serve, "would not long, if at all, submit to be dragged from their occupations and families to perform the most disagreeable duty in times of profound peace." Hamilton's immediate point was that Americans needed professional and reasonably well-paid soldiers because no one else in a modern commercial republic has the time or the inclination to spend on the "disagreeable duty" that accompanies military service in time of peace. That insight has much larger implications, however. If modern commercial republican peoples love work and family so much that military service is disagreeable to them even in peacetime, then their aversion ought usually to be even greater in time of war, when terror is added to the tedium and uncomfortable discipline that always accompanies military service.

To be sure, there would always be exceptions to this rule. They might even be most prevalent at the birth of the Republic. Then, the touchy subjects of national honor and independence would perhaps have greater force than when the Republic was mature and confident of its place among nations. In all times, the young especially are more willing to welcome war as an opportunity to test themselves, and even modernity cannot eliminate that force of human nature. In a commercial republic, the old sometimes welcome war as a relief from the boredom of getting and spending, but Walter Mitty fantasies are just that: fantasies.

As Hamilton discovered during the Revolutionary War, the *rage militaire* would usually be fleeting in America. The percentage of Americans willing to serve their country with either their wallets or their persons would generally be quite low. Not without reason, they believed they had better things to do. On balance, then, they would be more averse to war than willing to engage in it. A representative democracy that reflected those sentiments would generally be averse to war as well. This would be even more true if one realized that the people and their representatives would reason, feel, and act with mixed motives. Not only a selfish desire to avoid disagreeable duty, but a genuine dedication to universal rights, including the rights of other nations, would generally (but not always) incline them to view war as Hamilton suggested it ought to be understood in his debate with Samuel Seabury. They would not see it in Clausewitzian terms as an instrument of policy but as the failure of policy. They would usually regard it as an unfortunate necessity to be employed only after all other diplomatic instruments, from diplomacy to economic sanctions, had clearly failed.[15]

As Samuel P. Huntington suggests in his account of American "business pacifism" in the early twentieth century, capitalism does not necessarily lead to imperialism and therefore to war. Sometimes quite the opposite results, for example, the isolationist sentiments of leading business figures in America in the 1930s, including and perhaps most especially those of the probusiness editors of the *Chicago Tribune*.[16] Long before those sentiments came to dominate American politics, Hamilton understood the character of his people remarkably well. They might often be too pacific for their own good. That premise might well be considered the major strategic foundation of his contribution to *The Federalist*: Americans would need to prepare for war, constitutionally, militarily, and economically, before it was too late to do so. That premise was the basis of Hamilton's various proposals for a rapidly expandable peacetime military establishment. It was no less important in his defense of the power of Congress to declare war and raise money and troops by simple majorities. It was implicit in his defense of the six-year term to the Senate, so that it could take a strategic view of the necessities of the American empire. It may well have been at the core of his defense of an energetic executive to prepare for future necessities while capitalizing on current opportunities in foreign policy. To be sure, precisely because in modern republics the people judge, republics would be likely to go to war when the people were angry or fearful enough to demand it (remember the Maine, and so on), but the general balance of passions among Americans and in their representatives would favor peace more than war. Alexis de Tocqueville later made essentially the same argument about modern democratic nations:

> The ever-increasing number of men of property devoted to peace, the growth of personal property which war devours, mildness of mores, gentleness of heart, that inclination to pity which equality inspires, that cold and calculating spirit which leaves little room for sensitivity to the poetic and violent emotions of war time—all of these causes act to damp down warlike fever.[17]

If the foregoing account is correct, the real target of Hamilton's critique was not Agrippa's premise but the overly complacent conclusion he drew from it: that there was no need for an energetic government to preserve the Union, especially not for one with the power to regulate commerce. Economic interdependence might be necessary to secure peace in the modern world, but Hamilton did not believe it was sufficient. Interdependence breeds competition as well as cooperation. It had long been an axiom in politics that vicinity or nearness of situation "constitutes nations natural enemies." The conventional remedy for natural animosity was free trade, which Hamilton endorsed wholeheartedly when it was possible to practice it reciprocally. As he observed in defending freer trade with British Canada during debate over the Jay Treaty in 1795:

It is almost always mutually beneficial for bordering territories to have free and friendly intercourse with each other. This relates not only to the advantages of an interchange of commodities for the supply of mutual wants, and to those of the reciprocal reaction of industry connected with that interchange, but also to those of avoiding jealousy, collision, and contest, of preserving friendship and harmony. . . . Perhaps it may be safely affirmed that freedom of intercourse, or violent hatred and enmity, is the alternative in every case of contiguity of territory.[18]

The logical conclusion of Hamilton's critique was that there would be no peace at home or abroad without the power to regulate commerce.[19] With such a power, the United States could become one enormous free trade zone. Then economic interdependence could strengthen the bonds of Union and make militarism less likely by minimizing the dangers of civil war. Because other Federalists shared Hamilton's belief that the power to regulate commerce was necessary for a free and peaceful union of commercial republics, his argument in *Federalist* 6 is quite within the mainstream; but that is the fundamental point. Hamilton was not nearly as much of a Hobbesian realist as is often asserted. He did sound like Hobbes when Hobbes sounded like Thucydides and others who stressed competition between states, but he was also aware that states had histories and characters that changed over time. He knew that commerce had begun to change the behavior of states. Though it had not changed human nature, it had changed the ways in which states related to each other. In his time, it made mercantilist states warlike; but under the right conditions, it might go a long way to promote peace. Yet unless other states began to practice free trade, war would continue to result from their commercial policies. The mercantilist empires of Hamilton's time were unlikely to make many important concessions until the United States negotiated from a position of strength. In the 1790s, he therefore emphasized generating the economic independence necessary to genuine political independence, but he also left open a door to peace through free trade.

In 1789 the continental debt consisted of approximately $52 million in securities of various kinds, with $11.7 million owed to foreign creditors and the balance owed to domestic ones. The states owed approximately $25 million. The value of continental securities had fluctuated significantly after the war, but in 1789 they could usually be purchased at about twenty-five cents on the dollar. State securities were in even worse shape, at ten cents on the dollar. Creditors in the North owned most of the debt, so any effectual provision for paying it would benefit them more than those in the South. At the same time, approximately 75 percent of American trade was with England. The overwhelming majority of American exports to that country were unrefined agricultural products; the majority of American imports of manufactured goods came back from there. Still worse, within two years, 90 percent of American tariff revenues arose from import taxes on British goods and 80 percent of all federal revenue was pledged to fund American debts.[20] As in many Third-World states today, such severe economic dependence cracked the hard shell of the state and called American political independence into question. The structure of debt ownership also made it highly likely that quarrels over how to pay the debt would become sectional. True political independence required an economic revolution to establish economic independence from England and to avoid a civil war in the process. When should such a revolution start, how should it be accomplished, and what did Americans need to do in the meantime?

Hamilton's answer lay in his three great reports as secretary of the treasury in the Washington administration: first, his *Report Relative to the Provision of the Public Debt* in January 1790; second, his *Report on the Further Provision Necessary for Establishing Public Credit* in December 1790; and third, his *Report on the Subject of Manufactures* in December 1791. Because of his synthetic mind, he wrote so much and drew on so many diverse sources that even today it is not easy to tell how all the components fit together. Late in his career, however, after he resigned from the Treasury in January 1795, Hamilton wrote his *Defense of the Funding System*. As always when reading a statesman's memoirs, however short they may be, one needs to be aware of the possibility of bias, but the *Defense* also supplies a much-needed outline of the main features of Hamilton's system. When considered along with his reports, it can enable us to grasp the essence of his economic policies, which were always subordinate to his political objective of making his country fit for war while keeping it safe for liberty.

Hamilton's system rested on seven policies. First, the new government would assume the responsibility for the debts of both the states and the Confederation left over from the war. Second, the new government would fund securities on those debts at par. Third, the federal government would pay the foreign debt exactly as contracted but modify payments on the domestic debt to make them more manageable. Fourth, the national government would not discriminate between the original holders of the debt and those who later bought securities after they had depreciated. Fifth, to give immediate relief to anxious creditors, the government would give first priority to paying off interest past due. Sixth, the government would borrow abroad to pay off the total debt at a lower interest rate and fund payment on the new debt through duties on imports. Seventh, though it is often forgotten, he believed it would be best to establish the rule that every proposal for a new government debt be accompanied by some method of retiring it. Despite all that has been written about the system, Hamilton believed it to be this simple.[21]

Before attempting to defend each one of these policies, Hamilton explained the necessity of compromise in formulating his plan. His prelude was a short disquisition on republican statesmanship, which he believed required the executive's energetic leadership of Congress. The compromise was not simply among at least five different opinions about the most just and expedient way to provide for the debt but also between the "intrinsic goodness" of his preferred funding system and the "probability of success" in getting any system through a Congress divided among these different groups. One group argued for paying the national debt only and leaving the states to fend for themselves; a second (led by James Madison) supported paying the national debt only but discriminating between original and subsequent holders of it; a third opinion was in favor of paying the national debt but arbitrarily changing the rate of interest; a fourth called for paying the national debt, assuming the debts of the states, and paying both exactly as promised; and a fifth group called for paying both the state and the national debts but arbitrarily changing the interest rate again. Though all parties wished to pay the debt, Hamilton feared that some plans, such as those calling for discrimination, came close to de facto default. As a matter of national honor, they could not be accepted on any terms. He suggested that the second and fifth groups had the largest number of partisans. Rather than defend the best solution, which he did not identify in his defense (but is probably represented most closely by the plan of the fourth group), he focused on the best practicable solution at the time.[22]

Perhaps the most important reason for the adoption of his first report was that Hamilton changed tactics. He did not hold out for the best plan, or call for something utopian under the circumstances, as he had in his letter to Duane in 1780 and his speech of 18 June 1787 at the Federal Convention. With some reluctance, he granted that to have insisted on the best plan would only have increased the odds of adopting a bad one. The parties were divided not simply by different opinions about justice and expediency but also by different "interests and passions." These divisions made it doubtful he would ever get his view of an intrinsically good plan put into law. Had he held out for that plan, nothing would have been passed. He would have sacrificed confidence in the Washington administration and the new government before he had had any chance to demonstrate his skill and consolidate support for his system. Though clearly acknowledging the diversity of interests and opinions produced by the extended republic that Madison celebrated in *Federalist* 10, he also pointed to the most problematic feature of Madison's strategy for controlling majority faction. It risked producing such diversity that the "public deliberations left without any rallying point" would have been "apt to be distracted between jarring, incoherent, and indigested projects." Congress might well either have done "nothing" when there was little time to wait or have decided on "something manifestly contrary to the public interest." There was no guarantee that compromises between different interest groups would add up to service to the public good. To supply the necessary leadership from the executive, Hamilton had to begin with a plan that would probably be passed or risk never being able to lead again.[23]

Though time was ripe for some action, the moment could have been squandered. Many creditors had supported the Constitution because they had hoped Congress would do something to pay the debt. They would lose confidence in the government if it delayed so much that it appeared as feeble as the Continental Congress. Failure to provide for the debt would strike them as a "severe blow to the security of property." Since such security was one of the fundamental goals of the Revolution, creditors might consider the new government either incapable or unwilling to fulfill the ends of civil society. They might then invoke their right to alter or abolish the government. The "possible subversion of the Government" even before it had started to operate suggested there was no time to develop a perfectly good plan. Not only Hamilton, then, but the government itself had to act immediately, lest it forfeit its legitimacy in the eyes of those people who had supported the new Constitution most ardently. Although Hamilton seized a moment that might never come again, he stressed that accommodation ought not to sacrifice "any essential principle. This is never justifiable. But with the restriction of not sacrificing principle," he asked, "was it not right and advisable so to shape the course as to secure the best prospect of effecting the greatest possible good?"[24]

Hamilton then turned to the policy of assuming the debts of the states. Like the national debt, state debts resulted from paying for the Revolutionary War. Each state contributed to the common good of independence, but not in equal amounts. Since each benefited equally from independence, it was only just that individual citizens should pay for it as equally as possible. Yet an exact formula to equalize the contributions of each state was impossible. Therefore, it was best to pursue a policy most likely to lead to the greatest degree of justice. Since the debt would be funded by the impost, it would be a voluntary tax that consumers imposed on themselves. In most cases, the poor would not feel it at all, but those with means would contribute to paying for the common good according both to their means and their desires. Hamilton believed that though admittedly imperfect, this form of collective responsibility for the collective debt of the nation was reasonably equitable. It had the additional advantage of appearing so, which might consolidate public opinion behind it.[25]

Assuming the states' debts as soon as possible was also good policy for preserving the harmony of the Union. By reducing the states' need to raise revenue, assumption made it less likely that the states and the national government would compete for the same sources of revenue. It therefore reduced the most likely cause for quarrel between them. Hamilton considered quarrels over limited sources of revenue the "Gordian Knot" of the Constitution. With the national government assuming the state debts before major quarrels began, he believed he had cut that knot and made civil war less likely. Most important, he knew most expenses of the new government in the future would come from new wars. Who could say how long it would be before Americans were compelled once more to "defend [their] independence against some one of the great competitors still in the theater?" The potentially infinite costs of such wars required the new government to be able, when necessary, and as soon as possible, to "command all our resources." Without assumption, competition between the states and the national government for funds to pay their debts would have exhausted all possible sources of revenue, leaving nothing available for current or future expenses. For Hamilton, it sufficed to justify assumption to say that it opened up sources of revenue for the national government in emergencies and wars that otherwise would never have been available.[26]

It was so important to assume the states' debts quickly that Hamilton was willing to forego an examination of the records of their existing accounts with the federal government. During the war, the states often spent money to support the army, for which they had a right to be compensated by Congress. In theory, no state would gain or lose from assumption because the final settling of accounts would debit some if the national government assumed too much and credit others if it assumed too little. Yet partly because of wartime emergencies, the records for these expenditures were sloppy, to say the least. Since this invited fraud, and each state wished to claim as much for itself as possible while jealously guarding against paying too much to others, it might have taken years to settle the accounts. Quarrels over the accounts could even have led to civil war. It was therefore best to allow some states to engage in possibly fraudulent billing, initially, in order to preserve the principle that everyone should pay for the independence that benefited everyone. This, after all, was the magnanimous spirit underlying assumption, and it was quite strong at the beginning of the first Congress. Yet Hamilton feared it could not last and ought not to be thrown away by encouraging the states to quarrel over their accounts with the federal government.[27]

Without assumption, it was likely that many citizens would move from high- to low-tax states, which generally meant moving west. If too many Americans moved west before they were united by habit, interest, and affection, however, their inclination to remain within the Union might decline so much that they would secede, as many in Kentucky, for example, talked of doing. It was important to act quickly before Americans moved west so rapidly that the Union collapsed. There was also no way to assume state debts without establishing internal federal taxes. To ensure the government could tax in the future, Hamilton wanted to set the precedent immediately. It was best to introduce taxes, which are always unpopular, quite early, while there was still time to do so, that is, while the Washington administration was still popular.[28] The necessity of preserving the Union led Hamilton to make an important concession, and then to take it back. He did wish to unite creditors in support of the government, but he also said this motive counted least to him. His most important goals were energy and simplicity in finance, avoidance of conflicting systems of state and national finance (with their accompanying risk of civil war), and giving the new government complete command of the nation's resources in case of war with foreign powers.[29]

Hamilton's second task was to defend funding at par. His fundamental practical problem was to reduce payments on the national debt without diminishing the faith of creditors—a responsibility that was both complicated by assumption (which made the national debt bigger) and facilitated by it (because it removed the states from competition with the federal government for revenue). Since Congress had virtually no money when the funding system began, he asked for two new foreign loans to pay off the old debt abroad and to capitalize payments on the debt at home. Payments on the new debt would be reduced because the new loans would have a lower rate of interest. If Congress then promised to pay that interest in the form of annuities to the debt holders, it could both honor and fund the debt. Once again, timing was crucial to Hamilton's plan. If Congress funded the debt quickly, it would raise the value of securities at home and also minimize the danger of foreign manipulation of the debt. Yet Hamilton was well aware that Americans desperately needed foreign capital to jump-start their commerce. He did not wish to prevent foreign investors from purchasing American securities. So long as foreigners bought them at stable prices, they would help rather than hurt national credit. The sooner they did so, the better.[30]

Indeed, the point of the funding scheme was not to get Americans out of debt, though that was largely desirable whenever it was possible, but to help their government manage it. Effective management included using the debt to spur economic growth. As Forrest McDonald has observed, Hamilton understood that the debt could become a substitute for money in a nation severely short of investment capital. Because new securities issued by the government could be traded and would possess the confidence of investors, they would do the same work as money. They would in fact be transformed into money. By monetizing the debt, Hamilton not only stabilized but also substantially increased the nation's money supply; thus a nation still recovering from a long and costly war would have the capital required to become prosperous again and grow quite strong in the process.[31]

Effective management required the ability to borrow at a reasonable rate of interest, both at home, where there was little capital, and abroad, where there was much more. Within one year of the enactment of the funding system, the United States was able to borrow on terms competitive with the oldest independent states in Europe. Paradoxical as it may sound, Hamilton recognized that the ability to borrow in time of need, even from foreign creditors, would be a sure sign that Americans were on the road to national independence. The fundamental proposition underlying the funding system was that the new government would have to borrow in the future to face unanticipated dangers and unexpected opportunities, such as Napoleon's offer to sell Louisiana to Jefferson. Although the price was far beyond the immediate means of Jefferson's administration, it was not beyond the credit-worthiness that it had inherited through Hamilton's previous efforts to fund the debt.[32]

Hamilton also proposed a sinking fund, to be paid for through revenues from the post office. Long before, England had developed a sinking fund for its debt, but its many wars had made it impossible to reduce it. This did not matter; confidence in England's ability to pay its debt gave the British the soundest credit in the world. Though revenues from the post office would have only a marginal impact on the principal, they would also establish the opinion that the debt would be paid off when it was convenient for the government to do so. Opinion is the soul of credit. The necessity of establishing a good credit rating suggests that Hamilton was mildly disingenuous in his *Defense.* Yes, he did think it was a good idea to require all proposals for new borrowing to be accompanied by plans for retiring the debt, and yes, he did mean to retire the debt, eventually, when it was convenient to do so. But he was ultimately less concerned with retiring it than with producing confidence in the government's ability to retire it. Thus, a properly funded debt might prove extremely useful, though Hamilton never said it would be intrinsically good. He was well aware that governments, like individuals, sometimes borrow beyond their means. He was not proposing the massive deficit spending that many people think caused a fiscal crisis in the United States in recent decades. He simply wished to establish the investor confidence required to make such spending possible when there was no alternative to it, as is often the case in war.[33]

There were also important and competing matters of justice and law at stake in funding the debt at par. If the new government did not provide for interest on the debt, it would violate the Constitution, which required giving full faith and credit to the debts of the Confederation. Failure to honor this promise would violate the first principle of the social compact. There could be "no middle ground" between government by force and government that secured rights. Since the national government simply could not pay off its creditors at once, it had no choice but to fund the interest either exactly as promised or in a manner that most creditors would find highly agreeable, such as through annuities. Failure to pay the creditors the interest on their securities would be to defraud them and, Hamilton implied, to convert the government into a despotism. Hamilton thus conflated honor and liberal principle, but he also made honor expedient and therefore good policy. Future credit required an opinion that the new government would honor its past promises. Honoring the nation's debts was therefore both desirable in itself and the best policy for the present and future.[34]

Because many Americans blamed England's many wars on its funding system (rather than its funding system on its many wars), Hamilton had to confront the objection that funding made wars easier, apparently less expensive, and therefore more likely. In theory at least, the complaint made a good deal of sense. A funded debt allowed the British people to pay a professional army and navy to fight their wars. Since most Englishmen did not have to perform this disagreeable duty themselves, England's many wars had few immediate costs, financially or personally, for its people. As a result, perhaps, the popular check on British imperialism was quite weak. Both for partisan purposes, to remind Americans of the resemblance of Hamilton's system to the wicked practices of the British court party, and to strengthen the popular check on ambition, James Madison countered with his view on the theory of republican peace. For Madison no less than for Jefferson, the earth belonged to the living, who had responsibilities to the future. If each generation bore the full costs of the wars of its time, the interests of the many would counteract the ambitions of the few, and peace would become more likely. Yet England's wars were at least partly due to England's enemies. It was not merely imprudent but also irresponsible to the people whom governments are supposed to protect, to deny elected, popularly accountable representatives the means to wage a successful defensive war for fear that they might wage offensive wars. Besides, Hamilton observed, other European nations were as frequently at war as England. They too had heavy debts, but without the support of the funding system that enabled Britannia to rule the waves. In truth, it was not funding systems but human passions that caused war. The appropriate cure was to control the passions, not the means of self-defense.[35]

Hamilton conceded that his system was not without risks, both moral and political. Great wealth could lead to great power, which could then lead to sentiments of superiority, pride, ambition, and insolence. "These lead directly to War and consequently to all the calamities and expenses which march in the train of War." Commerce and republican government might incline Americans to peace, but even they could not avoid the temptations of great power. When credit and industrial development made even a commercial republic much stronger than its neighbors, the probable result would not be peace but rapacity, as in fact it was for much of the expansionist period in American history. By begetting opulence, a funding system also risked luxury, extravagance, dissipation, effeminacy, "disorders in moral and political systems," and the convulsions and revolutions that seemed to lead to the overthrow of nations and empires. Material progress was therefore not identical to moral or political progress and might sometimes result in the opposite. Hence, even Hamilton regarded commercial society as a mixed blessing. It seemed to be the "portion of man assigned to him by the eternal allotment of Providence that every good he enjoys, shall be alloyed with ills, that every source of his bliss shall be a source of his affliction—except Virtue, the only unmixed good which is permitted to our temporal Condition."[36]

After making this concession, however, Hamilton let loose with an extended barrage, which is most revealing about his ultimate objectives as secretary of the treasury. Great wealth and a good credit rating might tempt Americans to exercise their power unjustly, but those assets could also deter others from acting unjustly toward America. From this point of view, his position was the same as always: the danger of abuse was ultimately no argument against a truly necessary power. What did the ills produced by commerce and credit count compared to combining national security with individual liberty?

> The very objection to funding systems makes their panegyric—"*they facilitate credit*. . . . They enable [government] in great and dangerous emergencies to obtain readily and copiously the surplus of money of which it stands in need for its defense, safety, and the preservation or advancement of its interests.—They enable it to do this too without crushing the people beneath the weight of intolerable taxes, without taking from industry the resources necessary for its vigorous prosecution, without emptying all the property of individuals into the public lap, without subverting the foundations of liberal social order. . . . Indeed War in the modern system of it offers but two options—Credit or the devastation of private property. . . . Tis the signal merit of a vigorous system of national credit that it enables a government to support war without violating property, destroying industry, or interfering unreasonably with individual enjoyments.[37]

To Hamilton at least, the choice was clear: funding, even with the evils it might produce, or militarism, understood as the result of forcing citizens to supply the military at bayonet point. If E. J. Ferguson is correct that perhaps half the cost of the Revolutionary War was "paid" for through military impressment of private property, Hamilton's point cannot be dismissed as a statesman's after-the-fact rationalization of his policies. He was self-consciously seeking to prevent the greatest threat to private rights that had occurred in the war in which he took a most active part. Because the costs of war may be unlimited, they may well exceed the taxing power of the state. When this happens, as it has increasingly in the last 200 years, governments must have an almost unlimited capacity to borrow or face the consequences: either they must surrender because they are bankrupt, or they must become military despotisms, struggling to the bitter end to provide for the common defense by violating the rights of property at home. The wonder is not that Hamilton half-anticipated the possibility of modern unlimited war (though that is amazing enough) but that he found a way to support it that was still compatible with securing the rights of citizens. His strategy for combining public strength with individual security confirms that the "premiere state-builder in an age of state-builders" undertook this responsibility because of his liberal principles, not in spite of them. If Hamilton had a heroic conception of the state, it was largely because the kind of state he had in mind would not sacrifice the rights of its people to its strategic necessities.[38]

Hamilton then digressed, for a moment, from his defense of his funding system to supply his understanding of a statesman. He distinguished between a "true politician" (before that term was debased to cover any political actor) and a "political empyric." It is not clear why he chose to make this distinction at this point in the argument. Perhaps he was responding to those who feared the benefits of the system were distributed too unequally. Perhaps he was thinking of others who preferred the public good to be pursued without any admixture of selfish interest. To the latter he seemed to be saying that, however laudable their motives might be, their expectations were far too high, especially in the world of finance. The true politician must take human nature as he finds it, a compound of good and evil passions. He does not try to bend human nature from its natural direction; nor does he reject good plans even if they have some disadvantages and inequalities. He seeks to make men happy according to their natural bent, partly because it is utopian to go against their grain and partly because it would be despotic to do so. The political empyric, on the other hand, is either unrealistic in his opposition to the selfishness and pride of human nature (a tendency that lends itself to despotism); or he is full of empty, demagogic criticisms but lacking practical alternatives.[39]

In short, individuals who criticized the funding system had to propose a better one. As Hamilton argued in *The Federalist,* a true Founder, including a Founder of national credit, does not confine his view to the present period but looks "forward to remote futurity." He does not base his proposals merely on a "calculation of existing exigencies; but upon a combination of these, with the probable exigencies of ages, according to the natural and tried course of human affairs." Critics therefore could not avoid facing the much larger moral-strategic problem Hamilton's system was designed to address. They had to show that their alternatives would be at least as good, especially for combining the strength necessary for war with the individual security required for freedom.[40]

Perhaps more than any other criticism, Hamilton resented charges that his funding system increased the debt and allowed speculators to picnic at the public trough. He had not made the debt. It was a legacy of the Revolutionary War, and it existed long before he came to office. In 1787 the disproportion between the government's enormous obligations and its ability to pay them was so great that virtually no one thought it was possible to balance them. Hamilton did so not only by decreasing current obligations but also, and far more important, by monetizing the debt. When the debt substituted for money, it spurred investment and led to a substantial economic boom. In turn, the new wealth created by funding the old debt was available for taxation, which could help retire the old principal, if the government's necessities allowed it to do so. A case could therefore be made that Hamilton actually made it easier for his successors to retire much of the debt, as Thomas Jefferson and Albert Gallatin later sought to do during their watch. The price of the funding system was a credit bubble that burst and almost ruined Hamilton's plan. Yet the overall tendency of the system was to stabilize securities and thus to make the wildest speculation less likely. Sensible men know that speculation of some sort is inseparable from the spirit of freedom and commerce, even necessary to it. Like Madison's famous cure for faction, the cure for imprudent speculation had to arise from the disease, and it usually did.[41]

Nonetheless, one might argue that it was simply unfair to treat speculators the same as the original holders. Speculators bought up securities on the cheap in the hope that their value would rise when the debt was funded. In contrast, the original holders were sometimes old soldiers who had accepted the securities as a substitute for their pay. As their market value depreciated, the original holders, who were arguably the most loyal citizens, often sold them and could thus claim they did not receive the full value of the securities. Hamilton's response has already been anticipated. The distinction between a free and an arbitrary government is that the former fulfills its contracts and the latter does not. The government promised to pay whoever owned the debt. Cases of extreme necessity, when the survival of the whole depended upon the sacrifice of a part, might constitute an exception even to that fundamental principle of free government, but neither the convenience of the government nor sympathy to the original holders nor populist prejudice against investors would suffice to violate the contract.[42]

Hamilton, unfortunately, was faced with a problem that Aristotle at least considered the most intractable in political science: the necessity of reconciling incommensurable claims of justice. In this case, at least three claims were important: justice understood as the common good, justice understood as fulfilling contracts, and justice understood as giving each individual his due, with the recognition that some had contributed more to American independence than others. It deserves notice that many people, and probably most who originally had owned the securities, were not veterans, though James Madison, among others, often invoked their plight to justify discrimination.[43] The original holders were usually merchants and farmers who had contracted to supply the army, or worse, had been compelled to accept government paper when their property was impressed. Those who contracted freely knew they were taking a risk. Discrimination was therefore not especially relevant for them. Besides, so many of the securities had changed hands so many times that Hamilton believed it would have been difficult, though perhaps not impossible, to discriminate between presumably virtuous original holders and possibly vicious speculators.[44] Discrimination might even have punished the wrong people. Was someone who bought a security from someone else in the middle of the Revolution or even long after it guilty of a crime? Did it matter when someone bought a security from someone else? What would be the appropriate threshold of patriotism? 1776? 1780? 1783? 1789? To the extent the buyer helped support the market value of the security, he had actually helped the government and the cause of independence and ought not to be punished for it. Above all, Hamilton believed there was something ungenerous about discrimination. As he observed from the beginning of his defense, there were so many competing claims of justice at stake that even a Solomon might find it impossible to reconcile them. If the aggregate tendency of the plan was to favor the general prosperity of the Republic and of each member of it, Americans needed to think of the future.

Hence, it is grossly misleading to suggest Hamilton was more concerned with developing a strong state than with the welfare of the people who constituted it.[45] After all, his republican empire depended upon attaching citizens to the new government by affection, which would have been impossible if it did not improve the daily lives of most Americans. Moreover, he was always at least as concerned with the will as with the means to fight, and thus with nation as well as state building. In his view, nothing had undermined morale in America during the Revolutionary War more than the army's recourse to impressment, which also shocked his humanity. During the war, he carried out impressment orders from Washington and gave many others himself but always with great reluctance. In one case, he received an order from Washington to confiscate all the unsold shoes in Philadelphia to equip the army. In another, he ordered an officer to impress all the horses in that city, "except" those that were "the property of the poor needy persons, whose livelihoods depend upon them" and others who needed the horses to flee the city before the British occupied it. In still another case, he intervened on behalf of a farmer whose hay was about to be impressed, with the result that his cattle and his family "must starve." So far as possible, without seeming to give in to partiality, he instructed an officer to "spare" the farmer and thereby "have the pleasure of doing an act of humanity." As a responsible officer, he granted that the "necessities of the army must ultimately" outweigh all other considerations. Taking the farmer's hay and cattle then would have been unavoidable, but he begged that his property be "the last to be devoured." The supposedly heartless state builder and ruthless militarist declared that this would "give him a chance to escape," either because the army would move on or by allowing him time to hide his cattle and feed his family.[46]

For Hamilton, one of the most problematic features of discrimination was that it risked alienating creditors, thereby making it much harder for the government to secure future loans. Hamilton was compelled to think about doing justice to the past, the present, and the future. America's future depended on doing justice to present holders, which was impossible if he allowed discrimination in favor of the original holders.[47] If he could not do enough for the past, it was largely because he felt a responsibility to ensure that the American military never again had to support itself by stealing from ordinary citizens.

Hamilton's unfinished *Defense of the Funding System* ends with his critique of discrimination, so it is perhaps best to consider the roles of the Bank of the United States and his *Report on the Subject of Manufactures* in his system. His explanation of the Bank did little more than extend his arguments for establishing one during the Revolutionary War and for monetizing the debt in his defense of the funding system. The Bank was a means to increase the total sum of capital in the nation by making up for its lack of specie. It was originally capitalized at $10 million, with $2 million of its stock owned by the government and $8 million by investors (who were allowed to purchase up to three-fourths of the stock with government securities). Public utility, Hamilton maintained, was the primary object of banks. For the sake of responsible management, however, he meant this in quite a limited sense. Although the bank was useful to facilitate administration of the nation's finances, especially in time of war, it was not meant primarily to finance wars or other government activity, at least not directly. Instead, it would help supply the capital necessary to establish genuine political independence by funding the investment required for economic independence. For this reason, and to produce confidence in the Bank, he insisted that private investors run it rather than the government itself.[48]

Hamilton's *Report on the Subject of Manufactures* has more than a little of the futuristic, almost utopian character of his letter to Duane in 1780. It reads much more like the product of some whiz kid at a think tank such as the Rand Corporation than the bland position papers usually written by committees of government bureaucrats today. He was probably asking for too much, too fast, given the existing domestic climate, in which many people saw no good reason to imitate England's rise to great power and more than a few resented any scheme that suggested special breaks for monied investors. Yet it was also utopian to think Americans could compete with great powers without developing their own manufacturing base. Because national security is the fundamental national interest, Hamilton believed he had to try to sponsor manufactures, even if the effort was likely to fail, as in fact it did when Congress tabled most of Hamilton's plan.[49]

The third *Report* needs to be understood in the context of a larger quarrel over how the economic foundations of American political independence were to be established. For Hamilton's leading critics, Thomas Jefferson and James Madison, the answer seemed to be clear. Americans needed to open up foreign markets to their trade while simultaneously reducing their dependence on England for manufactured goods. As Hamilton himself suggested in *Federalist* 11, the new Constitution seemed to offer the perfect means to do so. With the power to regulate commerce, Congress could impose discriminatory tariffs on the goods of other nations that excluded American ships and goods from their ports. In theory, discrimination could apply to any nation, but since England was the major trading partner of the United States, in practice it was meant to be applied against the British especially. Jefferson and Madison thought such tariffs would work because they believed the United States could negotiate from a position of strength. On the first day of the first federal Congress (8 April 1789), for example, Madison observed that the Constitution had been brought about, in part, by a desire to vindicate American independence and honor. It was time to make the Europeans pay Americans "that respect that they have neglected on account of our former imbecility." Like Hamilton in *Federalist* 11, he wanted to teach the Europeans a lesson, that Americans had the "power to extend or withhold advantages as their conduct shall deserve." He also seemed to see no danger in treating the Europeans, and England especially, as they apparently deserved. As Madison later wrote, "America had nothing to fear from Great Britain." England was a nation of shopkeepers, but the United States was still mainly a nation of farmers: "The farmer can live without the shopkeeper better than the shopkeeper without the farmer." If discrimination led to reprisals from England, there was no need to worry. In a trade war, British interests could be "wounded almost mortally, while ours are invulnerable." England, after all, depended on the United States, or so Madison thought, for vital raw materials, but American imports from the empire were "either superfluities or poisons."[50]

Where Madison saw strength, Hamilton saw vulnerability. Three-fourths of American trade was with the British Empire, but only one-sixth of British trade was with the United States. Hence, Americans had much more to lose than the British from a trade war. It was also by no means clear that

British imports were mere superfluities and poisons, or would be regarded as such by Americans if they were denied them.[51] Most important, discrimination seemed likely to ruin his funding system. For Hamilton, political independence depended on credit that depended on tariffs that depended on England. From at least the time his funding system was enacted, he saw no practical alternative to peace and growing trade with England, and he was probably right. Unfortunately, peace was made less likely by a domestic climate in which England still stood for all things evil. Times had changed in the international arena. The Revolutionary War was over, but as even Merrill D. Peterson suggests, for many Americans, and Jefferson and Madison especially, England "was still the enemy." Ironically, Americans needed England, temporarily, in order to become independent of it, but this paradox was not of the sort that most Americans of the emerging Republican persuasion were able to comprehend or willing to accept.[52]

Although in *Federalist* 11 Hamilton did suggest that commercial discrimination might open some foreign markets at some unspecified future time, he did not think mere ratification of the Constitution was sufficient to force concessions from any country. Although Madison in 1789 sounded a good deal like Hamilton before the Revolution, Hamilton's quarrel with Samuel Seabury in 1774 and 1775 must have convinced him that economic coercion was unlikely to have much impact on John Bull. In conversations with England's confidential minister in the United States, Maj. George Beckwith, Hamilton also frankly admitted the obvious, that the United States was an agricultural nation and would remain so for quite a long time. In this position, he did not ask for much more from the British than he thought them likely to concede. Though he hoped for a broad commercial treaty opening up all England's markets, he focused on partial concessions in British trade policy, and especially on freer trade with the British West Indies. Commercial leaders in America informed Hamilton that a discriminatory tariff would be "productive of a war of commerce." Beckwith also told Hamilton that discrimination would be unlikely to produce commercial friendship with England because Prime Minister William Pitt and his cabinet planned to "hold their Nation high, in the opinion of the world." Thus, Hamilton concluded, commercial discrimination would not accomplish much besides annoying the proudest and most dangerous power of the age.[53]

Because France was the other great trading nation of the era, the practical consequence of Jefferson's and Madison's efforts to reduce American dependence on England was that they often favored it as much as Hamilton favored England. Though the United States had a commercial agreement with France, favoring it risked provoking England, which was much more capable of doing the United States harm, militarily and economically. At a time when his relations with the secretary of state were still cordial, Hamilton therefore warned Thomas Jefferson in 1791 not to pay too high a price for the friendship of France. He rejected Jefferson's advice to exempt French vessels from a duty on shipping tonnage as exceedingly ill-timed. Precisely because funding the national debt depended on tariff revenues, any exemptions from the impost had to be overwhelmingly necessary and could not be accepted unless the secretary of state proposed an alternative source of revenue. If Jefferson wished to deal out broad favors to French trade, Hamilton concluded, he ought to request "*immediate reciprocity*" from France. Otherwise, he would merely undercut American shipping, the funding system, and in Hamilton's view, American long-term independence without receiving any substantial advantage in return.[54]

In his correspondence with Jefferson, Hamilton also made a bold statement that calls into question his reputation as a mercantilist: "My commercial system depends very much on giving a free course to Trade, and cultivating good humor with all the world." He was reluctant to take any risk that might lead to a "commercial war with any power." Such wars were not only full of "mutual inconvenience and injury" but also produced "dispositions tending to a worse kind of warfare. Exemptions & preferences which are not the effect of Treaty are apt to be regarded by those who do not partake in them as proofs of an unfriendly temper towards them." Hamilton put this theory into practice in his defense of the Jay Treaty in 1794. Although he was far from satisfied with it, he defended it for promoting peace, in part because it permitted somewhat freer trade with the British Empire. The treaty allowed, or created no obstacles to prevent, the movement of Indians freely across the border (which was probably impossible to stop anyway). It also allowed citizens of both countries to trade with them for furs. Though only a minor concession from the British, England nonetheless "departed from her system of Colonial monopoly and exclusion." The concession was a Trojan horse for more: "every relaxation" in England's mercantilist practices paved the way for "other and further relaxations" that would make the balance of trade more symmetrical by making trade more free.[55]

Unfortunately, those relaxations in British policy were slow and grudging. Hamilton was no quisling for the British, but for most of the 1790s he saw no alternative to swallowing some national pride, temporarily, for the sake of greater independence later. The Virginians, on the other hand, were not animated merely by hatred of England, but they found American dependence so humiliating that they could not tolerate it. Yet until Americans had much greater economic and military clout, Hamilton was probably right in believing that discrimination would do more harm than good and could even provoke a war. This position suggests that Hamilton did not support domestic manufacturing out of any principled commitment to mercantilism but because the mercantilist powers felt no need for reciprocal free trade with the United States. That being the case, the best strategy for national independence seemed to be encouraging manufactures so that the United States could compete with the Europeans on their own terms. Ironically, the precondition of the Virginians' strategy of commercial discrimination was the success of Hamilton's program in America.[56]

The *Report on the Subject of Manufactures* was a response to a request from the House of Representatives, perhaps planted by Hamilton's friends, for a plan "for the encouragement and promotion of such manufactories as will tend to render the United States independent of other nations for essential, particularly for military supplies." This element, "for military supplies," is often forgotten, but it is extremely important. Hamilton was an emphatically political kind of economist. Economic policy was clearly subordinate to foreign and defense policy throughout the report. Hamilton admitted that from the standpoint of prosperity, a system of free trade might well be the best policy for all nations. They could then concentrate on their comparative advantages to sell high and buy cheap. Yet to practice free trade when other nations do not is chimerical. It is to risk becoming the "victim of the existing system" and to remain dependent on others within it. At the beginning of the industrial revolution, Hamilton refused to sacrifice national security to a principle practiced by no other nation in the world at the time. In making this exception, he was completely consistent with another nuanced, synthetic mind, Adam Smith, the foremost advocate of free trade in the eighteenth century. Even Smith admitted that defense was more important than opulence. Therefore, protecting strategic industries, such as the merchant marine, through the British Navigation Acts, had to be an exception to reliance on the invisible hand. In Hamilton's view, this exception would clearly be larger and more important for an infant nation with no strategic industries of its own.[57]

Moreover, Hamilton detected an error in the doctrine that trade would naturally regulate itself. Opinion, that is, confidence, is not merely the soul of credit. It is also the determinative passion of investors who lend their credit and confidence to new industries. Risky manufacturing enterprises, especially new ones, would not develop, or develop as quickly as might be necessary from a strategic point of view, unless investors had confidence that they would make a profit. Fulfilling the spirit of Smith's system therefore required establishing investor confidence. Smith meant, among other things, to break the tyranny practiced not only by monopolists within nations but also by great and powerful nations over weak ones. At the birth of the Republic, Hamilton could see only one result from rigidly practicing free trade in all circumstances. America would remain a primarily agricultural country dominated by the great commercial nations of Europe. Sometimes Smith's exceptions were more important than his rules.[58]

Though long on thought, the *Report* is extremely short on policy guidance. Although Hamilton worked hard to support the failed private Society for the Encouragement of Useful Manufacturing (SEUM), he did not in practice do much to encourage manufactures through direct government intervention. Thus, he had little to say about tariffs in his third *Report*. They existed primarily for raising revenue for the funding system, which might unravel if tariffs were used to price foreign goods out of American markets. With a free trade zone within the United States, the capital created by funding was far more important to the success of manufacturing in America than any measure Hamilton recommended in the third *Report*.[59] His preferred alternatives to an exclusionary tariff were bounties to encourage new industries rather than (as protectionists today sometimes wish) to support old, declining ones. To avoid the well-known Smithian danger that some industries would use protection to establish monopolies, he also suggested that bounties expire after ten years. He seems to have understood them on the model of patents; they were investments in the future. If a few individuals benefited disproportionately from them for ten years, the nation as a whole would benefit so much that the advantage outweighed the cost.

Equally useful, he observed, might be a deliberate effort to encourage "brain drain" by offering premiums to reward immigrants with particular skills. The centrality of strategic considerations in the report is revealed by Hamilton's observation that "manufactories of all the weapons of war" should be government-owned and -operated. It is also confirmed by the specific industries that Hamilton wished to encourage. They were primarily heavy industries, such as mining coal and saltpeter, smelting iron, growing hemp, and so on. Though often the weak industries of our time, they were the most important for military power in the nineteenth century. The former soldier reminded Congress of the "extreme embarrassments" encountered during the "late War, from an incapacity of supplying themselves." That incapacity had to be "changed by timely and vigorous exertion. To effect this change as fast as shall be prudent, merits all the attention and all the

Zeal of our Public Councils; 'tis the next great work to be accomplished."
Otherwise, Hamilton implied, the next war might be much less successful
than the last one.[60]

Did the domestic costs of Hamilton's system outweigh its strategic advantages? For Hamilton, and Jefferson too, the answer depended
primarily on the likely impact of commercial society on human liberty,
Jefferson fearing for its survival and Hamilton hoping fervently for its increase. Jefferson sometimes seemed to think the passage from an independent agrarian to a commercial republic would be a banishment from Eden,
but Hamilton suggested just the opposite: it would be a release from
Pharaoh's Egypt that would bring Americans into the Promised Land. How
could they reach such diametrically opposite conclusions? Which one was
right? Could they both be right? How can we know?

Part of the answer has already been suggested: Hamilton treated sound
credit as the only practicable alternative to defeat or military despotism in
time of war. As a student of Hume, Hamilton also recognized that modern
commercial republics were capable of infinitely more social energy than
merely agrarian republics. Hume and Hamilton also recognized that the
durable agrarian republics of antiquity were dependent upon slavery (to free
citizens to train and fight in time of war). So neither wished to preserve a
way of life that he found incompatible with the freedom and humanity he
hoped for in the modern era. For Hamilton, the division of labor, the introduction of machinery, the employment of otherwise idle individuals, and the
encouragement of immigration also had the potential to produce greater
opportunity for individual achievement than a merely agricultural society
had. As he learned from Hume again, such opportunity was essential to
encourage a spirit of industry, enterprise, and personal autonomy. "It is a
just observation, that minds of the strongest and most active powers for their
proper objects fall below mediocrity and labor without effect, if confined
to uncongenial pursuits. And it is thence to be inferred, that the results of
human exertion may be immensely increased by diversifying its objects."
This observation could be developed into a powerful and by no means
merely Marxist critique of the very division of labor required for commercial society to exist. Even Adam Smith foresaw that men, women, and children who did nothing but put heads on pins might quickly be reduced to a
subhuman status. Hamilton is famous for noting the opportunity for employment that manufacturing offered to women and children, that is, for
failing to anticipate the many threats that early industrialization posed to

human development and the family especially. Yet on balance, he seemed to think the division of labor actually increased the odds that most human beings would fulfill their natural potential. When laborers can vote with their feet, the variety of pursuits in a commercial republic enables them to make more of their talents and ambitions. In his youth, Hamilton wrote of a right not merely to property but also to beatify our lives, to try to do something splendid with our existence. He blessed commercial society because it could arouse men from the idleness, boredom, and misery that often results from work unsuited to their capacities and tastes. "When all the different kinds of industry obtain in a community, each individual can find his proper element, and call into activity the whole vigor of his nature. . . . The community is benefited by the services of its respective members, in the manner, in which each can serve it best." As a result, both the public and each individual stood to gain from increasing specialization in occupations.[61]

In contrast, Jefferson believed that when farmers and husbandmen own their own land, agricultural life is better for human freedom, and Madison made quite similar arguments himself. In theory at least, the economic independence of farmers makes them politically independent, and therefore less corruptible. They are less likely to sell their liberty for bread and circuses than the mobs of big cities who depend on customers and other patrons to survive and flourish. Hence, for Jefferson, they were the "chosen people of God." At this point, Jefferson's empire of liberty and Madison's compound republic seem to merge into one. Preserving the edenic liberty of Americans required remaining an agricultural nation as long as possible, and the vast expanses of the frontier made this possible for quite some time. Especially when strict construction was enlisted on the side of agrarianism, the corruption they feared from commerce, credit, and manufacturing might be postponed for so long that perhaps other, enduring characteristics of Americans would be strong enough if not to resist, then at least to temper it significantly.[62]

Although some scholars suggest that the quarrel between Jefferson and Hamilton was a continuation of a quarrel between the apparently classical republicanism of Machiavelli and liberal modernity, a case could be made that Jefferson and Hamilton actually seized on two different strands of modern Machiavellianism. For Machiavelli, the greatest threat to liberty was a landed aristocracy with enormous wealth and private armies. As in many Latin American countries today, this combination of military and economic power enables a landed aristocracy to make ordinary citizens dependent upon its members. To found a republic where a landed aristocracy exists, Machiavelli observed, one must "wipe it out." With this terrifying advice, he inaugurated a true political revolution, which took many different forms among different thinkers in different countries in the modern world. In Jefferson's case, Machiavelli's advice led to proposals for forbidding primogeniture and entail. These were not the only ways of destroying the power of a landed aristocracy, however, and Machiavelli knew it. He had enormous respect for the Venetian commercial republic, which had done "wonderful things" with its sea power in his time and also kept its liberty far longer than Machiavelli's Florence. Its gentlemen, or aristocrats, were so only in name because their power was based on "movable" property. The opportunity to acquire such property was available to all and allowed merit to rise from obscurity. The heroes of Machiavelli's writings are almost always what we today would call entrepreneurial, self-made men, that is, individuals who rely on their own arms and virtue. Perhaps fundamentally, the modern spirit of enterprise celebrated by Hamilton (and Madison too, in *Federalist* 14, for example) is the spirit of Machiavelli, the champion of new modes and orders, such as the American *novus ordo seclorum*. For Machiavelli, a simple agrarian society could prevent corruption, such as the dependence of Roman citizens when they left the land for the city, but he was more than aware that commercial society could encourage independence, too. Davy Crockett symbolizes the self-reliant spirit of Machiavellian heroism in America, but so too does Horatio Alger.[63]

Like a contemporary supply-side economist, Machiavelli observed that a true prince should "show himself a lover of the virtues," especially those connected with industry. A true prince "should inspire his citizens to follow their pursuits quietly, in trade and agriculture and in every other pursuit of men, so that one person does not fear to adorn his possessions lest they be taken away from him, and another to open up a trade for fear of new taxes." Picking up where Machiavelli left off, Locke suggested that the "Prince who shall be so wise and godlike as by established laws of liberty to secure protection and encouragement to the honest industry of Mankind against the oppression of power and narrowness of party will quickly be too hard for his neighbors. But this bye the bye." Locke did not return to this Machiavellian insight, but Hume ascribed enormous significance to it as a source of both public strength and individual security. Where "luxury nourishes commerce and industry," Hume observed, "the peasants by a proper cultivation of the land, become rich and independent; while tradesmen and merchants acquire a share of property, and draw authority and consideration to the middling rank of men, who are the best and surest guardians of liberty." "Mr. Hume," Adam Smith would later remark, was the "only writer" in his time who had "taken notice" of this remarkable historical development. The "inhabitants of the country, who had lived in almost a continual state of war with their neighbors, and of servile dependency upon their superiors" became safer and freer by moving to the cities, getting jobs, and engaging in trade. Hamilton was equally aware of this phenomenon. Until his time at least, the growth of political liberty went hand in hand with the growth of commercial society. "As commerce enlarged, . . . the people began to feel their weight and consequence; they grew tired of their oppressions; united their strength with that of the prince; and threw off the yoke of the aristocracy."[64]

Strictly speaking, Smith's model of the rise and revolt of the bourgeoisie does not fit well in America. Outside of Hamilton's state of New York, where great manorial estates did in fact exist, there was not much of a rentier class in America. Yet in a spirited as well as a spiritual sense, Smith's model, with its Machiavellian origins, applies quite well because it was about human mobility based on movable property. Is the life of a farmer good for liberty? Yes, if all he wants or has is the potential to be a farmer. Then staying put (or perhaps worse, in one's place) is fine. Is the life of an artisan or the chief executive officer of a modern corporation good for liberty? Yes, if he wants or has the potential to be something other than a farmer or any other trade practiced by his parents. Then a bustling commercial society may enable him to move from his accustomed way of life to something he considers more worthwhile, as it enabled not only Hamilton but also Ben Franklin and many others to do in Hamilton's time. To be sure, Jefferson also encouraged mobility, but generally he was thinking of individuals moving west, where they could establish themselves on the land. Both for better and for worse, his vision was not nearly as rootless as Hamilton's. Indeed, roots were his solution to the ills he feared from commercial society. Hamilton had no local roots and could easily become a nationalist (devoted to an idea) as a result. In contrast, Jefferson's roots in Virginia were so deep that, on occasion, he would play with the idea of secession to protect his state. Because roots give citizens a stake in their local communities, they encourage Jefferson's hope for ever-vigilant citizens. Because motion cuts those roots, it animates Hamilton's hope for a national identity, a new kind of public-spiritedness, based on affection for a government that secures the freedom to keep on moving.[65]

If the quarrel between Jefferson and Hamilton ultimately amounts to rootedness versus motion, Hamilton was once again the historical victor, but perhaps at a significant price. As a commercial people, Americans today are always in motion. They are freer to change their lives by changing their occupations than any other people in history. Is this motion good for us? That is hard to say. Sometimes, it seems, nothing makes Americans more unhappy than their restless pursuit of happiness. Because even Hamilton recognized that commercial society is a mixed blessing, one hesitates to say that his political economy was superior to Jefferson's from a merely domestic point of view. As Jefferson himself reluctantly came to admit, however, his agrarianism was a recipe for national weakness and military defeat in the modern world.[66] If so, even the most ardent Jeffersonians might have to accept Hamilton's commercial republican empire, not as a positive good but as a necessary evil.

9. The Gathering Storm

The hard core of the thesis that Hamilton was the "personification of American militarism" in the Founding era rests on his policies as inspector general of the army under Pres. John Adams during the Quasi-War against France from 1798 to 1800. Especially after the British defeated the French navy in the Battle of the Nile in August 1798 and following the formation of the second coalition against France in December, the odds of a French invasion of the United States appeared to many observers in Hamilton's time as remote to nonexistent. As a result, even today, many scholars find it hard to see a legitimate strategic rationale for what Stanley Elkins and Eric McKitrick refer to as Hamilton's "grim commitment to a permanent army" during this war.[1] Militarism therefore seems to be the most plausible explanation for Hamilton's efforts to expand the army despite growing opposition to it from both Republicans and President Adams.

Four propositions are usually introduced to support the thesis. First, Hamilton is often said to have been a military adventurer ambitious to use an expanded army to win glory by seizing New Orleans, the Floridas, and perhaps regions even further south. Second, it is frequently suggested that his principal purpose in expanding the army was not to address the danger of foreign invasion but to intimidate the Republican opposition at home. Third, he and other Federalists supposedly feared anarchy and a leveling spirit so much that they became obsessed with building up the army merely for the sake of the ordered hierarchy it symbolized to them. Last, it has even been suggested that Hamilton hoped to become an independent will in American politics, the J. Edgar Hoover of his time, so to speak, by establishing himself as permanent commander of the army. From this nonelected position of substantial influence, he might then have stood like a colossus over the United States for decades to come. If these propositions are true, they lend substantial weight to the venerable and bipartisan judgment of Thomas Jefferson and John Adams: Hamilton was an American Caesar, Cromwell, and Napoleon rolled into one. If so, Richard Kohn was surely right to conclude that Hamilton was the "most dangerous" man in America during the Founding era.[2]

Or was he? The militarist thesis depends on so many wild allegations that it is impossible to test it without paying careful attention both to the foreign policy context of Hamilton's remarks, as we shall do here, and the domestic policy context (see chapter 10). In evaluating that thesis, however, we should bear in mind that attitudes that scholars bring to their understanding of Hamilton before the Quasi-War largely determine how they will understand his activity during this crisis. If they follow Kohn in assuming that Hamilton was predisposed to settle political disputes at home and abroad by "force alone," then a half-dozen ambiguous remarks he made during the war could be interpreted as evidence of the activation of his latent militaristic tendencies. Yet we underestimate Hamilton's ambition if we reduce him to a military adventurer. As a liberal-republican, his goal was to accomplish the unprecedented, to found the world's first empire resting on consent. During debates over ratifying the Constitution, he did not shrink from discussing the possible necessity of suppressing a civil war by force, but so far as possible, he meant to build a nation by means of affection rather than fear. His constitutional and economic policies were designed not merely to enable his country to become a great power but also to do so without violating the rights of ordinary citizens or other nations.

From this different point of view, Hamilton appears to have been as far ahead of his time as a strategist as he was as a political economist. His contemporaries generally viewed the Quasi-War as an isolated, limited conflict in the West Indies; he saw it as part of a world war that was also the beginning of the modern age of unlimited war. Although a good number of Americans in the 1790s believed the greatest threat to American independence and liberty arose from England, not France, Hamilton understood France in much the same way that Americans later came to view Germany during World War II. He saw France as an opportunistic and (let us not forget) a militaristic state driven by a mixture of nationalism, ideology, and lust for conquest. As a result, when Hamilton began to talk about preparedness, deterrence, credibility, foreign aid, covert operations, and preemption to address the danger from France, he often sounded more like American statesmen during the cold war than a conventional American Whig. In truth, he was a hybrid, but the more he sought to prepare his country for the new age of warfare, the more likely he was to produce a reaction among his vigilant adversaries. Hamilton was emphatically not a militarist, but under the circumstances, he was doomed to be misconstrued as one. He is best understood as an American Churchill warning of a gathering storm about to vent its fury on the Western Hemisphere. To explain why, it is fundamentally important to begin with his assessment of the strategic situation of the United States in 1790.

A t the beginning of the Washington administration, the United States had no navy. The army consisted of 700 poorly paid and ill-supplied troops. These facts compelled Hamilton to balance two different strategic objectives imposed by time. First, he had to keep the United States out of war with any major power for as long as possible, so that his embryo of a great empire could develop its latent strength; second, he had to develop American power while there was still time to do so, that is, before the United States went to war with a major power. Militarism connotes a warmongering, jingoistic disposition. For most of the 1790s, however, Hamilton sought peace, so far as he believed that goal was compatible with American sovereignty and national honor.[3] In one near diplomatic crisis (the Nootka Sound affair in 1790) and two genuine crises (the outbreak of war between England and France in 1793 and the initiation of British attacks on American shipping in 1794), Hamilton did his best to avoid war with both countries. So far as possible, he hoped to maintain strict neutrality during the great war in Europe, but neutrality did not mean impartiality.

The problem for all neutral countries is that their very neutrality may offend one or more of the parties engaged in a war. The neutrals may wish to offend none of the parties, but sometimes they have to choose between them. If Americans had to choose, Hamilton's sense of the national interest made him anxious to preserve peace with England more than any other country. Although it is quite common to say Hamilton's tilt toward England in the 1790s was prompted by a desire to save his funding system, this important half-truth can be dangerously misleading.[4] There could be no turning back; once Congress adopted Hamilton's funding system, it became the American funding system. Everyone knew that in the short run the American funding system entailed substantial dependence on England for tariff revenue. Once it was established, it became a matter of national honor to uphold it. Without it, a financial collapse was virtually inevitable and perhaps even the disintegration of the Union as well. Without the funding system, the United States would have been as weak in the next war as it had been in the Revolutionary War. Until the United States was no longer dependent on England, peace with that country simply was a fundamental national interest, if not the most important foreign policy objective of the 1790s.

Serving this national interest was difficult because of American treaty obligations to France, and also because of American sympathy for its cause. Since the United States had become a legal ally of France during the Revolution and was partly in debt to it for American independence, most Americans felt a high degree of affection for the French. Because the Declaration of the Rights of Man seemed to be modeled on the Declaration of Independence, Americans also tended to think their own Revolution was responsible for the French Revolution. Americans seemed to have almost parental wishes for the success of that foreign revolution, and Hamilton was typical in that regard. As events in Europe unfolded, however, he grew increasingly worried about both the strategic and the moral significance of the French Revolution. In response to the Prussian-Austrian alliance of February 1792, France declared war on these countries the following April. After five months of severe defeats, the French inaugurated the modern age of nations in arms. Even if Gouverneur Morris exaggerated when he told Hamilton that the French had raised 600,000 troops, the mass armies it began to field during this war were unprecedented. They turned the tide for France when 18,000 citizen-soldiers achieved the first great French victory in the battle of Valmy in September. In January 1793, Louis XVI was beheaded. A month later, France declared war on Spain, England, and the Netherlands. Because this declaration of war drew in the leading maritime powers of the age, the war in Europe thereby became a world war.

Since France was at war with the United States' two most powerful neighbors, President Washington called on his cabinet to discuss American policy. At the same time, the new minister from France, Citizen Edmond Genet, arrived in America at Charleston. Genet assumed that the United States would cooperate with the French out of gratitude for its aid during the American Revolution, the Franco-American alliance, and their apparently shared political principles. His assumption was not entirely misplaced. Because all the monarchies of Europe were arrayed against France, many Americans believed it was fighting the cause of the United States on the Continent. Because this sentiment was commonly linked to deep hostility toward England, Hamilton feared it could lead to a dangerous war at the wrong time with the wrong enemy. He therefore wrote thirteen questions for Washington to distribute to the cabinet about the implications of receiving Genet. His answers to Washington's (that is, his own) questions raised a number of moral, legal, and strategic issues that grew in importance as the war progressed.[5]

So far as and as soon as possible, Hamilton wanted to be released from the Franco-American alliance, but unfortunately, it was supposed to last in perpetuity. Sooner or later, the marriage of convenience of 1778 would become an albatross, and it happened sooner than anyone could have imagined. In 1793 Hamilton predicted that France would lose the war. He also feared it would drag Americans into a war on the losing side against both

England and Spain, which had been forced into an alliance when France declared war on them. Fortunately, however, the Franco-American alliance was merely for defensive purposes. Since France had begun the war, it was the offensive party under international law, and the United States therefore had no legal obligation to supply any military aid to it. Yet Hamilton also agreed with Thomas Jefferson that treaties bind nations, not simply governments. Hence, even for Hamilton, the revolution in France was not sufficient cause for suspending or renouncing the alliance. With the support of the legal writings of Grotius and Vattel, however, Hamilton was able to demonstrate that international law allowed allies to suspend or renounce a treaty if it became dangerous to their fundamental interests. Though the French had a right to revolt against their established government, neither international law nor liberal principle gave them a right to involve the United States in their wars unequivocally or without condition. If the character of their revolution was such that they would unite the great powers against them, they had no right to ask the United States to commit suicide with them. Moreover, if the French monarchy were restored (as Hamilton predicted it would be), it would undoubtedly look unkindly on the United States for any aid supplied to French republicans. Hamilton therefore considered the treaty dangerous enough to justify suspension, at least until the situation was more stable.

The secretary of state disagreed with Hamilton's interpretation of this principle, but not with the principle itself. Jefferson granted that extreme danger might justify suspending or renouncing the treaty, but he did not think war with England and Spain was imminent. Besides, as Attorney General Edmund Randolph observed, suspending the treaty to avoid war with England and Spain contained the risk of provoking a war with France. Unknown to Hamilton, a month before Genet's visit, Jefferson had also instructed Gouverneur Morris, the American envoy in Paris, to make the United States the first nation to recognize the French republic. Hence, recognition was a moot question for the secretary of state, who preferred to set a price on American neutrality in the hope of bargaining for trading concessions from the warring powers, from England especially. On this occasion, Jefferson won most of the cabinet debate. He was able to convince Washington that suspending the treaty was precipitous and to accept Citizen Genet as the legitimate representative of the French government. Hamilton, however, convinced Washington that American principles allowed, and prudence required, neutrality in the war. The result was Washington's Neutrality Proclamation. To satisfy Jefferson, the proclamation did not contain the word "neutral." It merely proclaimed Washington's opinion that the

United States was not at war or bound to go to war and would therefore abide by the law of nations for neutral states.[6]

To many Republicans, the proclamation seemed the height of ingratitude to France, if not a sacrifice of revolutionary principle. In his *Americanus* and *Pacificus* essays, however, Hamilton insisted that the debt of American independence was to the French king, not to the new republic in France. Indeed, the more Republicans justified the French Revolution as necessary to overthrow a despotic king and corrupt aristocracy, the more French aid to America during the Revolutionary War had to be seen as an act of an unaccountable government, not of the French people. Besides, the French monarchy supported the United States during the American Revolution not out of love for its principles but out of hatred for England and a desire to weaken it. This fact did not lead Hamilton to practice realpolitik but to suggest that "the rule of morality was not exactly the same between nations as between individuals."

Hamilton reasoned from Lockean rather than Hobbesian or Machiavellian premises to explain why the national interest ought to come first. He deduced his virtue of responsibility from the modern liberal-republican premise that governments are but trustees of their people. This premise made self-interested state behavior, within the confines of good faith and international law, a fundamental duty of nations. Their governments, Hamilton argued, are responsible for not only the present but also for generations unborn. Just as individual self-preservation is the first premise of civil society, so too, Hamilton observed, is it "the first duty of a nation." Responsible statesmen, he insisted, could not, "consistently with their trust, follow the suggestions of kindness or humanity towards others, to the prejudice of their constituents." A nation should hazard any risks, Hamilton declared, to "vindicate its own rights, to defend its own honor," but neither principle nor prudence required taking unnecessary risks on behalf of France. Though some observers suggested the proclamation was precipitous—because none of the warring powers had attacked the United States yet—Hamilton believed those powers might have assumed the Franco-American treaty secured Americans as active belligerents on the side of France. Washington therefore had a responsibility to let the other maritime powers, and the American people, know that the United States did not consider itself a belligerent at that time.[7]

In contrast, for Madison and Jefferson, the Neutrality Proclamation was called for neither by duty nor interest. To them and many other Republicans, it seemed to be a desertion of the rights of man, if not the beginning of a league with England against France. Some opponents even feared it as the harbinger of worse events. As Stanley Elkins and Eric McKitrick observe, Jefferson especially was "obsessed" with the notion that Hamilton was the leader of a monarchical conspiracy in the United States. He and his allies were partial to France in no small part because they feared for the future of the republic in America. For the Virginians, enthusiasm for the French Revolution therefore became a litmus test of fidelity to the Revolution in America. Accordingly, individuals who failed to support the republic abroad were suspect of being disloyal to the republic at home. To preserve domestic vigilance, the Virginians felt obliged to encourage sympathy toward France and suspicion of England. Thus, said Madison in the *Helvidius* essays, the only people who supported the proclamation were British sympathizers infected by British, that is, monarchical principles. Moreover, both Jefferson and Madison tended to understand the national interest differently from Hamilton. They too wanted neutrality. Yet the emerging Republican leaders feared what might happen to the United States if the coalition of monarchies arrayed against France were able to defeat it. Would the United States be next? They did not know. Nor did they wish to find out by seeing the French republic defeated and overthrown. In that worst case, the United States might stand alone against an alliance determined to stamp out republicanism once and for all.[8]

As Lance Banning observes, the Jeffersonians were blind for years to both the Terror in France and subsequent French schemes for establishing a "universal empire." In January 1794, for example, Jefferson did not want to hear of the September massacres in France. In a flush of enthusiasm in a letter to William Short, the newly appointed American minister at The Hague, the secretary of state even exonerated the French for the Terror, which had begun in fall 1793 and eventually cost 20,000 heads.[9] In contrast, the Terror struck Hamilton as an act of barbarism and the beginning of a bloody tyranny. As he later wrote to Lafayette, the Terror "cured" him of his previous enthusiasm for the French Revolution. He regarded Robespierre and Marat as assassins who had inflicted a grave wound on the cause of ordered liberty. When Americans erected mock guillotines in their city squares, he also wondered whether they had begun to catch the French disease of revolutionary fanaticism. Almost foreseeing the rise of Napoleon, he worried that the most likely outcome of the French Revolution would be a militaristic regime. "After wading through seas of blood in a furious and sanguinary civil war," he predicted that "France may find herself at length the slave of some victorious Scylla or Marius or Caesar." Hamilton was also aware that the Girondist party in France, of which Genet was a member, saw no reason not to spread their revolution by armed force.

Robespierre even referred to the French as armed missionaries. When the French announced that they would treat as enemies all peoples who maintained their loyalty to their established kings, Hamilton began to associate their revolution with a religious crusade. He viewed French fanaticism as a violent attack on the sovereignty of nations and a threat to the principle of consent, that is, the right of each people to choose its own form of government, including a monarchy. After France annexed conquered territory in the Netherlands, Hamilton also began to view France (in the language of contemporary international relations) as a rising hegemon. It was a threat to the European balance of power, which had to be contained. If France lost, Hamilton was skeptical that the United States would be next to suffer the wrath of European monarchies. However, Americans would be safe only so long as other powers did not associate their Republic with the excesses of the republic in France. If the great powers of Europe saw the United States as an accomplice in French crimes, he feared his country might pay a severe price for standing too firmly by an ally no longer worthy of allegiance.[10]

The quarrel over the French Revolution in America, then, was emphatically not between champions of republican government and proponents of monarchies. Instead, it was about whether the French republic stood for the same principles as the American one or embodied their antithesis. By the end of 1793 Hamilton was predisposed to think of France as the archenemy of free government everywhere. Nonetheless, he erred in assuming the French government acted according to a coherent plan. The new republic was too distracted by internal factions for coherent strategic planning either to occur or to endure. Still, the French government was extraordinarily opportunistic, not least of all in the United States. The most notorious example of incoherent French opportunism, of course, is Citizen Genet. On the one hand, he wanted the United States to supply France, especially with food. This objective required the United States to remain neutral. On the other hand, he wanted to wage war against England and Spain from the United States, which would inevitably compromise American neutrality in their eyes. As events soon proved, both courses posed severe risks for the United States, yet Hamilton found the latter more alarming.[11]

Genet's plans were apparently far more ambitious than even Hamilton imagined. Before England entered the war, Genet had asked his government for forty-five ships-of-the-line to attack Spanish possessions in the West Indies and to wage war against Mexico. Shortly after arriving in the United States, he also issued commissions in a French-sponsored *Armée du Mississippi* and an *Armée des Floridas*. According to some reports, he induced as many as 16,000 Americans to volunteer to attack St. Augustine. Genet also sought to purchase the services of George Rogers Clark to lead an attack on New Orleans. The only significant obstacle to his plans was lack of money. Though Genet hoped advance payment from the Treasury on American debts to France would fund these operations and purchases of supplies, Hamilton refused to give him one penny ahead of schedule. Genet did not need money to start a war, however. He brought hundreds of commissions with him from France for American privateers. After landing in Charleston, he issued some of them to Americans to attack British ships even before Washington had received him. Some eighty ships were captured by American-based privateers, some even in American waters. They were then sold as prizes to fund Genet's projects. As Hamilton later observed, Genet came to America "with neutrality on his lips and war in his heart." Had Washington not forbidden American citizens to serve either as privateers or in filibustering expeditions on behalf of France, Genet's activities might well have provoked England and Spain to declare war on the United States. Genet also helped found the Democratic Club in Philadelphia, which came to be seen as the headquarters of Girondist missionary republicanism in America. Enormous popular sympathy for France apparently made him presume he could defy the U.S. government. He encouraged an American privateering ship, the *Little Sarah,* to leave American waters against Washington's orders. When Genet threatened to appeal over the head of Washington to the American people to justify this defiance, even Jefferson was convinced that the Frenchman had no respect for American sovereignty.[12]

Though Hamilton desperately wanted peace with England to give the Union time to consolidate its strength, the unfolding world war made it extremely difficult to remain at peace. The mission of the British navy was not only to keep open England's sea lines of communication with its empire but also to starve the French and otherwise weaken them economically by denying them supplies by sea from any country, including the United States. In early 1793 England had proclaimed a blockade of France. In November of that year, the British government issued Orders-in-Council allowing the Royal Navy to capture any neutral ships carrying French property in the French West Indies, which France had previously opened to trade for neutral vessels. As American ships hurried to the French West Indies to take advantage of the opportunity supplied by France, they thereby fell into the British trap. The Orders-in-Council were kept secret long enough for the Royal Navy to seize between 250 and 300 American ships (no one is certain of the exact number). While British naval captains grew rich from this legalized form of piracy, the British also needed sailors to man their fleet.

Since many British sailors were impressed to serve in the Royal Navy, they often had no reason to be loyal to it. They frequently jumped ship to serve on American merchant vessels, which offered higher wages without the risk of combat. As the naval war progressed, British naval officers increasingly began to impress suspected British sailors on American ships and were none too careful in discriminating between American and British citizens. In this crisis, even Hamilton believed war with England was justified, and almost certain.[13]

The U.S. government had four options during this crisis. One was to do nothing, but at the risk of inspiring the wrath of the electorate, which viewed the seizures as an insult to American honor as an independent nation and as significant violations of American neutral rights. Another option was to employ economic sanctions at the risk of destroying the funding system and perhaps even provoking a full-scale war (if Americans sequestered debts they were required to repay British creditors under the Treaty of Paris, for example). Though Hamilton campaigned successfully against sequestration, Congress did impose a temporary embargo on American trade with England in 1794. Another option was to declare war. Yet this policy added the risk of severe military defeat to the economic devastation (and potential disintegration of the Union) that Hamilton believed a war was likely to produce. Last, the government could arm while seeking to negotiate a settlement of all the major grievances between the United States and England.[14]

Hamilton advocated the last policy because it seemed least dangerous and most likely to work, but only if Americans did not demand more than they had the means to secure from England. Partly as a result of this crisis (but mainly for protection against Algerian pirates), Congress ordered the construction of six frigates. Since the United States was unable to compete with the British at sea at the time, however, Hamilton did not think it could secure much from England while it was at war for its survival. He also viewed sanctions as an ultimatum to England, which was both too proud and too resentful of American independence to succumb to threats from the upstart Republic in North America. To Republicans who hoped sanctions could substitute for military power in this quarrel, Hamilton responded, "Tis as great an error for a nation to overrate as to underrate itself. Presumption is as great a fault as timidity. Tis our error to overrate ourselves and to underrate Great Britain. We forget how little we can annoy and how much we can be annoyed. Tis enough for us, situated as we are, to resolve to vindicate our honor and our rights to the last extremity." Because initiating a "great conflict" was "utterly unsuited to our condition, to our strength, and to our resources," provoking a war through sanctions had to be avoided at almost any cost. Arming while negotiating seemed to have the dual advantage of strengthening the weak hand of American diplomats while producing some means to resist England, if negotiations failed to bring about satisfactory terms of peace. And if they failed, Hamilton hoped their failure would unite public opinion for determined resistance to England.

Republicans, however, tended to oppose arming, from traditional fears of standing armies, as well as worries that paying for an army and navy would increase the debt. In turn, they feared the debt would increase the power of creditors whom they often suggested were part of Hamilton's supposed plot to anglicize and monarchize the American system of government. Far more than fear of war, then, fear that arming for war would destabilize the Republic appears to have been behind what Lance Banning calls the Republicans' "ultimately disastrous" support for economic sanctions as an alternative to military preparedness in the 1800s. Though they hated England, they seemed to have feared both Hamilton and military preparations more than the combined military threat from England, France, and Spain.[15]

In spring 1794, news that the British had repealed the Orders-in-Council gave Hamilton hope that war might be avoided. He beseeched Washington to make use of the window of opportunity opened by the repeal. He also helped draft diplomatic instructions for John Jay, the minister Washington sent to negotiate with England in summer 1794. The eventual result was the Jay Treaty, officially known as the Treaty of Amity and Commerce Between the United States and Great Britain. The treaty lived up to Hamilton's low expectations. It was so unpopular that Hamilton was stoned by a mob in New York City when he stood up to defend it. The British did not agree to compensate Americans for slaves they took with them when they evacuated the United States in 1783 (an issue Hamilton was unwilling to quarrel about); nor did they agree to stop impressing American seamen. The British gained most-favored-nation status under American tariff laws, but their ports still remained largely closed to American trade. Jay also agreed to forbid the French to use American territory as a base for privateers. The humiliating Article 17 allowed the British to seize French property on American ships. This American departure from the principle in the Franco-American treaty that free ships made free goods guaranteed that the British would consider themselves within their rights to stop American shipping to French ports whenever it was convenient to do so. In return, the British agreed to evacuate American posts in the Northwest. That was no significant gain, however, because they had been obliged to evacuate the Northwest under the Treaty of Paris since 1783. Some British ports in India were opened temporarily to American shipping, and American ships gained limited trading rights in the British West Indies. In addition, a variety of commissions were established to arbitrate disputes over Americans' debts to British creditors and to compensate Americans for cargoes and ships captured by England. The silver lining was that American exports to England increased by over 300 percent between 1795 and 1800. Sadly, however, the treaty, which barely passed the Senate, was more of a truce than the beginning of a durable peace. Because it did not remove the most important causes of conflict between the United States and England, it was highly probable that they would eventually come to blows again to settle their disputes.[16]

Hamilton supported the treaty less because of what Americans gained from England than for what they avoided. The Jay Treaty prevented a protracted war at a time when the United States could not afford war with any major power. It bought time for the world war to end and for Americans to prepare for war if it did not. Though it was humiliating to settle for so little, Hamilton insisted that "true honor is a rational thing" (a view one wishes he had practiced as much in his private life as in his public policies). True honor did not require the United States to sacrifice its fundamental national interest in peace with England. If the British did not acknowledge American maritime rights, neither did Americans surrender them. They came out of the negotiations with as much honor as possible under the humiliating circumstances of national impotence. Since Americans had not complied with all the provisions of the Treaty of Paris, Hamilton also suggested that they ought not to be too self-righteous in their quarrel with England. Neither England nor the United States were guiltless. True policy was not to sacrifice the national interest to a quarrel in which both sides were partly at fault. "True policy was to defer to a state of manhood a struggle to which infancy is ill-adapted."[17]

Although Republicans often portrayed the Jay Treaty as an alliance with England and a betrayal of France, even the French foreign minister, Charles Talleyrand, acknowledged that it did not provoke war with France, which had many other reasons to initiate hostilities against the United States. In fact, the French had been attacking American shipping intermittently since 1793. In May 1796 the War Department informed Gen. Arthur St. Clair that French agents were encouraging secession among frontiersmen in the West. When the Directory heard of the Jay Treaty, it considered declaring war on the United States; but the American envoy, James Monroe, apparently convinced it to wait until the presidential election of 1796, which Monroe suggested the Republicans might win. Nonetheless, it was possible for the French to have the fruits of war without declaring it. Instead of provoking the French, the Jay Treaty seems to have convinced its members that they had little or nothing to lose from an undeclared war on American ships bound for British ports. In the naval war with England, the Directory's paramount object was to deny it supplies from its empire and neutral countries, including the United States. By mid-1796, the French had seized over 300 U.S. ships, but for fear of driving Americans even closer to England, the Directory refrained from stating the fact that France was at war with the United States.

The Directory apparently hoped that attacking U.S. shipping would persuade Americans to support Republicans in the election of 1796, who would then repeal the Jay Treaty. The latest French minister, Pierre Auguste Adet, even wrote essays for the Republican press a month before the November election with the objective of swaying votes to the Republican side. Since John Adams, not Jefferson, won the presidential election, this plan to influence the election may well have backfired. It also confirmed Hamilton's suspicions of France and made him fear a larger war. In January 1797 he therefore called for the same strategy he had advocated before the Jay Treaty. The United States needed to arm while negotiating, with the hope that negotiations would produce peace and that arming would make American negotiators more credible. He proposed sending James Madison, Charles Pinckney, and George Cabot as envoys to France. Clearly, Hamilton did not want war at this time. By the end of 1796, the first coalition against France seemed to be falling apart. There was no reason to enter the war when it was at the peak of its power. Hamilton also knew that pro-French parties in Europe had sometimes constituted a fifth column aiding French victories and feared they might do so in the United States. He recognized that war with France might well aggravate sectional divisions among Americans, the South supporting France and the North supporting England. He also doubted that the American people would support a war unless the failure of negotiations demonstrated there was no other alternative.[18]

For these reasons, perhaps, the lame-duck President Washington sent Charles Cotesworth Pinckney to treat with the Directory. He arrived in Paris in summer 1796, but the Directory refused to negotiate with him unless he first satisfied all outstanding French grievances against the United States. Hamilton learned of this diplomatic snub in spring 1797, as John Adams was assuming the presidency, but even then he did not give up on negotiations. From retirement in New York City, he proposed sending a new delegation to France. He wanted some leading Republicans included, preferably Jefferson or Madison, or both, in order to convince the French and the American public that the government intended peace, if it could be acquired on honorable terms. He wanted Federalists to serve as well in order to ensure the Republicans did not concede too much to France. He recommended that the envoys be authorized to offer France trading terms equal to those offered England under the Jay Treaty. Consistent with the advice that he formulated when he drafted Washington's Farewell Address, he recommended that the envoys do everything possible to liquidate the Franco-American alliance, so that in the future, Americans would have greater diplomatic flexibility. At the time, John Adams supported essentially the same negotiating and party policy, though his cabinet and other Federalists did not. The latter feared disgrace if another mission were rejected; or perhaps worse, from their point of view, they worried that Jefferson or Madison might take credit if a new mission succeeded. Hamilton, however, took great care to observe that neither national pride nor a party spirit should allow the government to drift toward war. The Virginians, he told other members of his party, would be unwilling to sacrifice a vital national interest out of partisan support for France. Hamilton insisted it would be political folly for the Federalists to allow themselves to be seen as the war party and the Republicans the party of peace. Besides, if even the Republican leaders failed to secure peace, public opinion would be better prepared for war. Apart from the considerable partisan advantage of getting the Republican leaders out of the country, placing the onus of failed negotiations on them is most probably why Hamilton was anxious to send the Virginians. The likely prospects of failure may also explain why they displayed no desire to participate in the proposed mission.[19]

On 2 March 1797 the Directory declared that it would abrogate the principle that free ships made free goods in the Franco-American alliance. As a result, American ships would be in an intolerable position. They risked being seized by England if they carried French goods and by France if they carried British goods. The Directory also announced that any American citizens serving on British ships, even those who claimed to have been impressed, were liable to be hanged if captured. French privateers then captured hundreds of American ships in the West Indies; they soon began to attack American ships along the Atlantic coast as well. Ominously, John Quincy Adams, the president's son, wrote his father from Paris of rumored French schemes to seize Louisiana from Spain. On 16 May 1997 the new president prepared a message for Congress calling for arming in earnest while still attempting to negotiate with France. Vigilant Republicans then responded by accusing the Federalists of seeking to provoke a war with France. Predictably, they complained that by this means the Federalists would establish a permanent army, increase taxes and debt, and generally promote their alleged conspiracy to establish the corrupt British system in the United States.

To demonstrate his desire for peace, Adams sent another delegation, consisting of John Marshall and Elbridge Gerry, to join Pinckney in negotiating with the Directory. The new members reached Paris in October 1797, with instructions to seek compensation for American shipping losses, to end the Franco-American alliance, and to allow France the same commercial privileges granted England under the Jay Treaty. After prolonged stalling, Talleyrand approached the Americans through his envoys, who were code-named X, Y, and Z in American diplomatic dispatches. The envoys shocked the American negotiators by demanding an apology for remarks Adams had made about France in his speech to Congress, a large loan to France, and a bribe for Talleyrand and the Directory before the French would begin negotiations. Talleyrand dismissed the United States as no more worthy of military consideration than tiny Genoa. His envoys even threatened America with the fate of Venice, which had been overrun by France, if they failed to promise the loan. Marshall and Pinckney refused to negotiate on these terms and returned to the United States, though Gerry stayed in Paris, apparently to keep open communication with the French government. Though his threats were alarming, Talleyrand probably did not wish open war with the United States then or at any other time during the crisis. Instead, his goal seems to have been to force the envoys to renounce the Jay Treaty under the threat of war. If they refused, the wily Frenchman apparently hoped to cast the blame on the envoys, with the hope of continuing lucrative privateering in the West Indies and aiding more sympathetic Republicans in the United States, who could blame the war on the Jay Treaty. Talleyrand, in other words, had turned the undeclared war into a test of American will. Federalists could either renounce the Jay Treaty or wage a war with France, one that would have at least two fronts: the Gulf of Mexico and American public opinion.[20]

In January 1798, while awaiting news from the American envoys, Adams sought the advice of his cabinet, which consisted of holdovers from the Washington administration. It was also as divided as the rest of the nation about how to deal with France. For fear of expense, taxes, credit, and the influence of monied men, Republicans opposed fortifying harbors; for fear of provoking a wider war and the militarism they believed it would produce, they also opposed sending American warships to sea. If only because a war was likely to increase the power of the Federalists, Jefferson, the vice-president, was deeply opposed to declaring it or otherwise escalating the conflict. In contrast, the secretary of state, Timothy Pickering, a hot-tempered

New Englander who hated all Jacobins, believed a declaration of war was in order and even contemplated an alliance with England. Though Hamilton communicated regularly from retirement in New York City with the Adams cabinet, only the secretary of war, James McHenry, regularly followed his advice. To preserve American diplomatic flexibility, McHenry restated Hamilton's opinion to the cabinet by opposing a declaration of war and urging the government to begin arming seriously. At this stage of the conflict, then, Hamilton was clearly a moderating influence on the cabinet. He was still hoping negotiations would avoid a full-scale war.[21]

On 4 March 1798 Adams received John Marshall's report on the XYZ affair. His original reaction was to draft a message asking Congress to declare war, but upon further reflection, he decided not to send it. That same month, the Directory announced that any American ship carrying any goods produced in the British Empire was liable to seizure. It also closed French ports to American ships trading with England. Adams then renewed his call to arms, a move that led vigilant Republicans in Congress to demand to see the dispatches about the XYZ affair. Adams sprang the trap on 2 April 1798 by releasing the documents, which were subsequently published to ensure broad public support for military preparedness. The French demands were so humiliating that they angered most Americans enough to support a significant military buildup, with the taxes and borrowing that it necessarily entailed.

After the release of the XYZ dispatches, Hamilton, along with many other Federalists, came to regard negotiations as both disgraceful and fruitless. Though Hamilton still opposed a declaration of war, the Federalists in Congress were just a few votes short of a majority in favor of it. Congress nonetheless severed trade with France and suspended the alliance of 1778. For fear of subversion by immigrants sympathetic to France, the naturalization period was extended from five to fourteen years. Military preparations then consumed the attention of Congress for the rest of the summer, and the Republicans were terrified.

Partly to calm them, Washington was persuaded to command the army. As McDonald observes, the president erroneously believed that Hamilton had worked in private to swing Federalist electors to support Pinckney over Adams in the election of 1796. He was therefore deeply opposed to having Hamilton serve in his administration. Nonetheless, Washington insisted that Hamilton be made inspector general and second in command, and Adams reluctantly accepted the suggestion. Washington had no intention of taking command of the army unless there was an immediate threat of battle with French land forces, so Hamilton and McHenry assumed most of the responsibility for organizing a new American army almost from scratch. In this crisis, Hamilton believed energy was wisdom. Through friends in Congress, he had several bills introduced to increase the army and expand the navy during summer 1798. Though unpaid for seven months and still deeply involved in his legal practice, Hamilton then undertook his military responsibilities with the same enormous drive he had applied to his previous work in the Treasury.[22]

Contemporary intelligence analysts, who have no crystal balls, commonly examine threats from abroad in light of the perceived intentions and capabilities of other states. If the former are warlike, but the latter insubstantial, analysts tend to discount threats, at least in the short term. If perceived capabilities are formidable, however, the guessing game becomes more complicated. An ally with a demonstrated record of loyalty might be presumed no serious threat, but the more dubious the record and the more significant the perceived capabilities, the more analysts start to take threats seriously. When warlike intentions are combined with enormous capabilities, their worries increase proportionately. The analysts do not always agree about either the intentions or the capabilities of the countries they study. As time goes by, however, they sometimes learn lessons from experience. After the Gulf War, for example, it is difficult not to conclude that American intelligence exaggerated Soviet conventional military capabilities. Stunning victories against a Soviet-equipped Iraqi army must make more than a few contemporary intelligence officers blush at their former naiveté. As a military crisis unfolds, however, no one can be certain, and that is the fundamental point. Just as there is a Clausewitzian fog of war, in which generals must make decisions with incomplete and sometimes distorted information, so too is there a fog of politics, in which statesmen must do the same. Before attributing illegitimate motives to any of the major figures in the United States during the Quasi-War, we should therefore try to grasp how they understood French intentions and capabilities. Bearing in mind that they were only human, how did Hamilton, Adams, and the Republicans see the threat? What different kinds of strategies did they develop to face it? Were their strategies rational responses to the threat as they understood it?

These questions suggest two different ways of testing the militarist interpretation of Hamilton during the Quasi-War, an objective and a subjective one. Objectively speaking, we could conclude that the threat from France was serious, or not. If the former, we do not need to concoct ulterior motives for Hamilton's strategic planning. If the objective threat was not serious, we might be led to wonder about his motives. Yet it is quite conceivable, indeed highly probable, that his quarrels with Adams and the Republicans during the Quasi-War arose from honest differences of opinion about the nature, direction, and extent of the French threat. Since such honest quarrels happened frequently during the cold war, when threat assessment was just emerging as a field of political science, we have every reason to think they might have happened from 1798 to 1800, when there was no science and no enormous intelligence establishment to evaluate the threat. If we recognize that the highly charged political climate of the 1790s created an atmosphere of suspicion that was bound to be increased by virtually any efforts to raise an army, it seems highly plausible that the militarist interpretation of Hamilton is rooted more in others' perception of him than in his policies during the crisis. That Hamilton produced such fears in his contemporaries suggests some disturbing quality about him, but it may also suggest tendencies no less problematic about them. Hamilton never came close to developing the rhetoric—much less the democratic manners—that would have made Adams and the Republicans trust him. Yet if traditional fears of standing armies were as deep-rooted as recent historians have suggested, perhaps he never had a serious chance of doing so.[23] Adams and the Republicans, however, may well have lost touch with strategic reality because of their fears for the Republic at home, not to mention their desires to be elected or reelected to public office.

Indeed, even if Hamilton was wrong about the threat, we might learn one lesson of enduring significance about war and free government from this crisis. Little is more common in free governments in time of war than for different parties to perceive the nature and degree of danger in significantly different ways. When doves see little or no threat, they often suspect the worst from hawks who do. A necessary debate about strategy, which ought to precede any military action, can then quickly devolve into an unnecessary crisis in civil-military relations, which are a two-way street. Not only must the military be kept subordinate to the civil authorities, but it must also be able to communicate effectively with the elected civilian leadership. Nothing like this two-way communication happened during the Quasi-War, however. Hamilton explained different elements of his strategy during the Quasi-War on several occasions to members of Adams's cabinet and other Federalist leaders. Yet on perhaps only one occasion did he have an opportunity to explain his strategy to the president. After all, the president did not like him and put up with him only because Washington refused to serve without him. By the time Hamilton and Adams actually sat down to speak to each other, the president was so disposed to suspect the worst from Hamilton that he was determined to do the opposite of almost any action Hamilton advised. Consequently, there was a true crisis in civil-military relations during the Quasi-War, but not because Hamilton was a militarist. Instead, it was because Hamilton and the president had radically different views of the French threat and how to confront it. Adams was also much closer to the Republicans than to Hamilton in his suspicion of standing armies; hence, even regular strategy sessions might not have prevented them from misunderstanding each other. Yet the general absence of such sessions made it almost inevitable that the president and his inspector general would eventually quarrel bitterly.[24]

For Adams, the Quasi-War was exactly what the name given it by later historians implies: a half war not to be taken too seriously. It was a limited naval action confined primarily to the Atlantic coast and the West Indies. Because most historians accept this characterization of the war, Adams has often been praised as a measured and responsible war president. Under the vigorous leadership of Benjamin Stoddart, the first secretary of the navy, American merchantmen were allowed to arm themselves. The navy had twenty-two ships at sea by December 1798, a rapid mobilization rate that put Hamilton's fledgling army to shame. The navy quickly cleared the Atlantic seaboard of French privateers and deterred French attacks on American vessels in the West Indies. By 1800 the French had lost eighty-four vessels, and the American navy was earning respect abroad. Perhaps for this reason Adams was never enthusiastic about increasing the size of the American army. Because he assumed the West Indies were the strategic center of gravity in this war, an army seemed increasingly unnecessary, if not irrelevant.

Though Adams was an ardent navy man, he never seems to have believed there was a serious land threat to the United States from France. "Where is it possible for her to get ships to send thirty thousand men here?" he asked. "We are double the number we were in 1775. We have four times the military skill, and we have eight times the munitions of war. What would thirty thousand men do here?" Hamilton's consistent efforts to increase the army therefore appeared ever more suspicious to Adams. The president was also greatly annoyed that Washington had forced him to accept Hamilton as second in command of the army. He increasingly came to suspect that a military officer was running the administration behind his back through sometimes-sympathetic members of his cabinet. For Adams, then, the inspector general was an implicit threat to civilian control of the military. That Hamilton also spoke of offensive operations in the South must have confirmed Adams's worst fears. In his view, Hamilton was raising an increasingly unpopular army because he was ambitious to win glory for himself through the war. As his wife Abigail wrote, Hamilton seemed to be on the road to becoming an American Bonaparte.[25]

Hamilton saw the Quasi-War in radically different terms from Adams, however. In 1798 he too hoped to keep the war limited and advocated strict rules of engagement to prevent it from escalating. Thus, for example, he opposed allowing American ships to attack French shipping, issuing letters of marque for American privateers, and imposing an embargo unless France declared war. Yet he did not rest his strategy on hope alone. In the worst case, the Quasi-War would not remain a limited naval action because it was part of a world war, which virtually all contemporary military historians now agree was the beginning of the modern age of unlimited war. Between 1792, when the world war began, and 1815, when peace was established, more soldiers and sailors fought over greater expanses of land and sea for novel ideological and nationalistic objectives than in any previous time in human history. Eighteenth-century generals had husbanded their armies and waged complicated battles of maneuver to avoid excessive casualties, but the French and their greatest general, Napoleon, sought decisive battles that produced casualties on a massive scale. For the French this was not a serious problem; indeed, it was a positive advantage, at least until the disaster in Russia in 1812. The political revolution in France gave the most populous country in Western Europe a seemingly inexhaustible supply of manpower. After suffering heavy casualties in any campaign, the French could raise a new citizen-army for another. Then, the more traditional and significantly smaller professional armies of the rest of Europe would have to face the French juggernaut again. Perhaps no one in 1798 could have grasped the full character of the military revolution that arose from the political and economic revolutions of the end of the eighteenth century, but Hegel's owl of Minerva does not always fly at dusk. Hamilton clearly thought about this revolution's strategic, moral, and political significance in great detail. Indeed, as second in command of the army, it would have been irresponsible for him not to have thought about it in his time. He knew that the war had many theaters, ranging from Europe to Egypt to India to the Atlantic and potentially even to North and South America. In the face of the unprecedented expansion of military capabilities and political objectives produced by the French Revolution, Hamilton was deeply worried.[26]

Neither Adams nor the Republicans shared his anxieties, however. Republicans still feared England more than France, so much so in fact that many hoped that France would defeat England. In 1795 Jefferson even expressed a wish to drink tea in London with French generals. The Republicans suspected the French threat was a mere bogey to justify a standing army. The appointment of Hamilton as inspector general no doubt confirmed their worst fears, which were from threats at home rather than from abroad. The French attacks on American shipping were worrisome but could readily be blamed on the Jay Treaty, which seemed unnecessarily provocative toward France. Adams probably had no better estimation of French intentions than Hamilton, but he simply did not think they had the capability to do much in the Western Hemisphere. In contrast to the Republicans, Hamilton believed French intentions were warlike; unlike his president, he also believed they were capable of doing enormous harm to the United States.[27]

Despite the absence of coherent planning in France, Hamilton had good reason to suspect French intentions. In 1789 the French Assembly had debated whether to reacquire Louisiana. In March 1796 Adet sent the French general, Victor Collet, on a ten-month survey of the Mississippi and Ohio territories. He also encouraged frontiersmen to secede but was so indiscreet that eventually he was followed by American agents. Moreover, Adet urged his government to acquire the Mississippi Basin all the way to the Alleghenies, to fortify the mountain passes, and to block American expansion in the process. Then he sought to intervene in the election of 1796 by writing for Republican papers. When combined with the missionary style of French warfare and the terrorism within France itself, such machinations were not a mere continuation of eighteenth-century imperialism. For Hamilton, they were a complete break with the somewhat civilized character of limited war as he had experienced it during the Revolutionary War.[28]

Hamilton viewed France as many Frenchmen viewed their republic, as a new Rome. Yet he did not see the new Rome as a recovery of the best in the republics of antiquity; rather, the revolutionary republic was "aping ancient Rome, except in her virtues." Hamilton suggested that the French strategy was the same as that of Rome in employing its allies against Carthage. Under the appealing banner of the rights of man, it would first use its friends to subdue its most powerful enemies and then seek to dominate its friends. For Hamilton, the French effort to make Rome rise from the dead had therefore produced a Frankenstein that mixed the worst of both ancient and modern politics. Hamilton did not have the vocabulary to describe what he saw in France, where he believed nationalism and revolutionary ardor had produced a paradoxical atheistic religion. Nonetheless, he recognized a deep kinship between the spirit of "religious persecution" and the spirit of political persecution that we commonly explain as the result of ideological fanaticism.

When worship of the new Goddess of Reason replaced worship of the older, gentler Lamb of God in France, Hamilton believed the moral restraints that Christianity often imposed on war and despotism had begun to disintegrate. Though he usually refrained from mixing politics and religion in any direct manner, he began to display enormous respect for the "venerable pillars that support the edifice of civilized society." "The politician who loves liberty," he observed, "knows that morality overthrown (and morality must fall with religion), the terrors of despotism alone can curb the impetuous passions of man." The French crusade against Christianity was not merely an effort to overthrow the traditional social order. For Hamilton, it was also an attack on one of the most important restraints on the militaristic spirit that he identified with antiquity. When the French "renounce[d] Christianity," Hamilton observed, they imitated the "same spirit of dominion which governed the ancient Romans," who believed they had "a right to be masters of the World and to treat the rest of Mankind as their vassals." Modern war then resumed the "hideous and savage form which it wore in ages of Roman and Gothic violence." "Like the prophets of Mecca," he asserted, "the tyrants of France" hypocritically carried the Rights of Man as their Alkoran while proselytizing with the sword. This was what we today would call Orwellian doublespeak: words become the opposite of what they mean. Forcing conquered peoples to accept French notions of government (while demanding tribute from the conquered at the same time) was not freedom. It was tyranny. If indiscretion was Hamilton's great vice, candor was also one of his virtues. The French republic was the "most despotic government the world had ever seen." "If there be anything solid in virtue," Hamilton declared, a time would come when it would be considered a "disgrace" for any true partisan of the rights of man to have defended the revolution in France in its later stages.[29] Why? Because if Americans were afraid of militarism, understood as an intention to govern by force alone, then they only had to open their eyes and look at France.

French military capabilities shocked the world. In spring 1798 Hamilton believed the nation in arms was at the apex of its power; its enemies were in decline. Napoleon had beaten the Austrians in Italy, which was under French control. Russia was equivocal about fighting France. Prussia was probably out of the war. England appeared to be bankrupt and ready to sue for peace. The Royal Navy was rife with mutiny. Hamilton was also aware of rumors of a French cross-channel invasion of England. If it succeeded or if France dictated terms to an exhausted England, Americans might then have been forced to fight alone at a time when France would have had huge armies to redeploy. Once France gained control of Spain, it was reasonable to assume the French would also seek control of the Spanish empire in the Western Hemisphere, including New Orleans and the Floridas. If the Spanish wanted genuine independence, ceding Louisiana and the Floridas to France was undoubtedly one of the best ways they could get it. Frenchmen highly sympathetic to France populated New Orleans. They might therefore welcome a French army, if it managed to cross the Atlantic. All American trade in the West had to go through the Gulf of Mexico, which had a number of possible choke points, including New Orleans and the Floridas. If the French got to New Orleans or merely to the Floridas, the Gulf of Mexico, the true geopolitical center of gravity in this war, would then be dominated by the most formidable military power of the late eighteenth century.[30]

Many Federalists regarded France as unbeatable, which helps explain why Hamilton did not initially rule out appeasing them. At the beginning of the crisis, he suggested that it might be best to seek a separate peace with France, thus perhaps turning its attention elsewhere. Yet French diplomatic credibility was at a nadir because French ambitions seemed unlimited. There was no reason to believe a country that had invaded as many countries and broken as many treaties as France had would keep its agreements with Americans. Hamilton was always averse to relying on other countries, especially former and potential enemies, to do for Americans what he believed they ought to do for themselves. He did not wish to rely on the British navy or any other foreign military forces to provide for American security. "Standing in the midst of falling empires," Hamilton concluded, it was best to "avoid being overwhelmed by their ruin." It was best, he argued throughout the war, to develop a substantial navy and prepare for invasion by land. In this respect at least, Hamilton was more like Machiavelli than any of the Founders. He believed Americans had no choice but to rely on their own arms and virtue rather than on fortune and the arms of others.[31]

Surprisingly, Hamilton did little to prepare for a French invasion of the United States. Apart from calls for improving harbor defenses and increased readiness in the local militias, he paid little attention to his country's Atlantic coast, which suggests that he was no more afraid of a French invasion in that theater than Adams. Hamilton devoted most of his attention to his country's southern flank, but why? One has only to look at a map and remember that the French had in fact displayed aggressive intentions in that region. Hamilton apparently feared the French might concentrate their forces where the United States was weakest. If either victory over England or peace in Europe enabled the French to cross the Atlantic, its armies might easily land unopposed in the Floridas, New Orleans, Mexico, or elsewhere in Latin America. French control of the Gulf of Mexico could possibly amount to de facto control of the United States. The ability to turn the trade spigot off and on might have given the French the power to control American foreign policy, or worse, to determine whether the United States would remain united. By encouraging secessionist movements in the West, for example, they could have contained the rising American empire and reestablished their own empire on the North American continent.[32]

Of course, none of this happened; rather, none of it turned out exactly as Hamilton feared at exactly the time and place he feared, although it could have. As inspector general, Hamilton was responsible for preparing for the worst, so we should try to assume his perspective. His attitude toward military preparedness was the same as his attitude toward constitutional government. Just as constitutions ought not to be framed only for existing exigencies but also for the future, according to the probable necessities of any government, so too ought military strategies take into account not only current but also possible threats. However improbable some threats might be, the potentially most dangerous are often no less deserving of attention than the most immediate ones. They might even deserve more attention. Probably more because of the gravity than the probability of the threat to America's southern flank, Hamilton came to the same conclusion in 1798 that he had reached in 1780 in his letter to Duane. Americans needed to develop not only the tangible capabilities to wage a protracted war with France but also the perhaps even more strategically important intangible will to fight it "in the last ditch."[33]

Though Hamilton did not rule out appeasement, he generally supported deterrence because he believed the French would see American concessions as a sign of weakness. As Gilbert Lycan has observed, Hamilton believed France had little chance of defeating a united America. He even compared Republicans in 1798 to Tories in 1775, that is, to defeatists who would sap the will required to preserve American independence. If the French succeeded at intimidating Americans, as the XYZ envoys and Adet had clearly intended, he feared they would win the battle for public opinion in America, and thus, the war for the Gulf of Mexico as well. Sounding like an American Churchill, Hamilton therefore began to warn that the immediate danger in this war was not a loss of shipping but a French "conquest over the American mind." Thus the busy inspector general often spent as much time writing for the newspapers as he did mobilizing the army. Young and weak nations had to avoid war whenever possible, but to "capitulate with oppression," he observed, "is in any nation that has power of resistance as foolish as it is contemptible. The honor of a nation is its life. Deliberately to abandon it is to commit an act of political suicide. . . . The Nation which can prefer disgrace to danger is prepared for a Master." And worse, Hamilton suggested, it even "deserves one."[34]

Since Hamilton had encouraged Americans to swallow their pride during the debate over the Jay Treaty, his emphasis on national honor during the Quasi-War may seem incongruous. Indeed, there is something comic about both the Federalists' and the Republicans' appeals to national honor throughout the 1790s. The Republicans invoked it to increase Americans' determination to resist England but downplayed it in discussions of American relations with France, and the Federalists did just the opposite.[35] Were these appeals merely partisan maneuvering? Can Hamilton's call to honor during the Quasi-War be justified? Yes, if one takes into account that he believed Americans would usually be too pacific rather than too warlike. If the Quasi-War required proving they could not be intimidated, it was best to appeal to national pride to fortify the determination to defend American rights and interests.

Besides, Hamilton did think that honor was a rational quality, and therefore worthy of a measure of respect by those who wish to respect themselves. It was an intangible national interest that was neither to be dismissed nor exaggerated as an object of national policy.[36] When little could be done to defend American rights and honor as an independent nation, as Hamilton believed was true in his defense of the Jay Treaty, the rational response was to cut the best deal under the circumstances while refusing to surrender the principle at stake. In the Quasi-War, however, Hamilton believed the fate of Americans truly was in their own hands. They could wait until the French arrived in the Gulf. Then they would have to choose between suffering the consequences of French control there or making a determined effort to eject French veterans, possibly commanded by Napoleon himself, after they had already consolidated their foothold.[37]

Americans might also prepare for the worst. They could prevent French control of the Gulf but only by establishing American control of that theater. For this end, they would require a much bigger army and navy than most of them had contemplated at the beginning of the war. Then, perhaps, the French might be deterred from attacking the Gulf, or even better, persuaded to negotiate with Americans on honorable terms. In this respect, Hamilton anticipated much twentieth-century strategic thinking. Deterrence theory did not begin in the twentieth century, though of course nuclear weapons made the need to establish a credible deterrent ever more urgent. In turn, credibility is no less necessary for diplomacy than it is for military deterrence. Credibility is commonly understood as a product of intangible will and the tangible means at a state's disposal.[38] Just as it takes national will to mobilize national means, so too is the willingness to develop the military instrument of state power one of the best indicators of the national will to use those means. If Americans convinced the French they meant to fight on land as well as sea, deterrence would reinforce diplomacy by making them think they could not intimidate Americans.

Though the XYZ affair helped develop national will, the means to demonstrate it were sorely lacking and called American credibility into question. The six forty-four-gun frigates Congress had authorized in 1794 were not complete. Since it can take years to build warships, Hamilton believed it was essential to complete the frigates, to begin constructing twenty sloops, and to arm American merchant ships as soon as possible. Probably for reasons other than Hamilton's arguments, Adams and Stoddart followed these policies with great success in the limited naval war in the West Indies. Nonetheless, their tiny navy was insufficient to deal with a full-scale French attack in the Gulf of Mexico. Hamilton therefore made a startling suggestion. As early as 1797, he proposed an early version of the lend-lease policy established between the United States and England before World War II; but in this case, England would lend, and the United States would lease. He suggested it was best to buy or borrow two ships-of-the-line and three frigates from England. As the crisis intensified, Hamilton consistently raised the number. Maybe the British could lend ten ships-of-the-line, or twenty, or as many as they could spare. After all, a fundamental source of conflict between England and the United States was that the former needed to field far more ships than it had sailors to man. Since Americans did not have enough ships for their many sailors, this policy would have both mitigated the quarrel over impressment and increased the total force required to fight the French at sea.[39]

Of necessity, lend-lease would have led to a temporary, quasi alliance with England. As John C. Miller notes, the British actually supplied Americans with cannon, ammunition, and naval stores. A century and a half before World War II, they convoyed American ships in the Atlantic and allowed the American navy access to the Caribbean. To some observers, this unofficial cooperation might appear to be a departure from Washington's advice in the Farewell Address. Yet as Gilbert Lycan notes, Hamilton wrote the paragraph addressing alliances in Washington's Farewell Address. Hamilton did not write the address dogmatically; nor did he and Washington intend it to be thus interpreted. Following Hamilton's advice, Washington warned Americans to avoid permanent alliances, like the one with France, but conceded that "temporary" alliances would sometimes be prudent according to the fluctuations of the European balance of power.

Though the idea of no alliances of any kind quickly became an American dogma that lasted until World War I, Hamilton had deliberately built exceptions into the rule in order to allow for a significant degree of strategic flexibility.[40]

The mere existence of a quasi alliance had the potential to make American deterrence and diplomacy more credible. It might suffice to bring the Quasi-War to an end, and then the United States and England could shift for themselves again. Hamilton insisted on avoiding a formal alliance with England, however, since the United States was far too valuable to allow any other country to control it. If England could survive, it would not allow North America to be dominated by France. If England could not survive, a formal alliance would not help Americans and might even hurt them. If the United States were bound by treaty to England, it might go down with it. A formal alliance would also limit Americans' ability to seek a separate peace. Perhaps, then, only an informal alliance, a coalition in fact, would combine the necessary strength to deter or defeat a French attack with the credibility required to negotiate successfully with France.[41]

On the land front, Hamilton proposed a total force of 50,000 men, with 20,000 regulars and 30,000 reserves in various stages of readiness in July 1798. By the end of summer, Congress had authorized a four-tiered force. The first consisted of 3,000 troops (the so-called Old or Western Army). For fear of Indian attacks, however, this component could not be redeployed from its frontier garrisons to deal with the French. The second component consisted of 12,000 other regulars in another army, called the Additional or New Army, which was designed to be deployed against the French. The third consisted of 10,000 reserves for the Provisional Army, to be mobilized in case of invasion or a declaration of war. Congress also authorized President Adams to call up the fourth component, subject to the same limitation, which consisted of up to 80,000 militiamen. In theory, and very much to Hamilton's liking, the Additional Army would consist of twelve regiments of infantry and six regiments of dragoons (mounted infantry). In theory, it would have both the mobility and the professionalism to engage in a land battle with a European army. Hamilton always wanted to have on hand enough noncommissioned officers to train as many as 50,000 men. In theory, then, this army, in which the chief job of the professionals was to teach citizens how to be soldiers, would be capable of rapid and significant expansion.

Practice turned out to be significantly different from theory, however. The Additional Army was the only component to enlist and train new soldiers. Largely because all fighting was confined to the sea, Hamilton found it extremely difficult to recruit as well as to supply and train the army. The army was also much bigger than President Adams wanted. Though he did not try to stop it, he did delay the appointment of midlevel officers. Moreover, Washington, McHenry, and Hamilton took painstaking care in the selection of officers. They wanted the army to represent the nation and therefore spent months screening candidates so that all sections would be represented. Washington and McHenry also made loyalty to the government their first priority. Though Hamilton was not indifferent to that priority, he also insisted on appointing some Republicans to win their loyalty. He even supported Aaron Burr's officer candidacy, which is hardly the sort of conduct one would expect from a militarist who meant to use the army to intimidate his political adversaries. From his experience during the Revolutionary War, Hamilton was aware that military service had turned citizens from various states into national patriots. Likewise, during the Quasi-War, he hoped that the army would unite Americans, not through force but through the affection that comradeship breeds. He wanted Republicans appointed as officers since he believed military service could have a "very assimilating influence" on them. Because of these considerations, months passed with few results. Even at its peak, the Additional Army never amounted to much more than half its authorized strength of 12,000 officers and men. For the sake of accommodating different sections, its troops were spread out in New England, the Middle States, and the South, with a small band also in Kentucky. This dispersed force might scare individuals who saw standing armies as harbingers of tyranny, but it could hardly intimidate a professional army, much less engage in sustained operations against the legions of Napoleon. The army was also deployed where it was least needed, far from the threat, and was therefore useless for the offensive operations Hamilton soon came to advocate.

Both the dispersal and the lilliputian size of the army must always be borne in mind in considering the proposition that it was raised to intimidate domestic opposition. In *The Federalist,* Hamilton wrote several essays belaboring one fundamental point: it was absurd to think an army many times the size of the one he proposed in 1798 could maintain the semblance of authority in a nation as large and decentralized as the United States. The mere effort to do so, he insisted, would inspire such enormous, dispersed, but organized opposition by the state governments that it would condemn itself to ruin. Significantly, while Hamilton struggled to organize the army, Rufus King, the American minister in London, wrote him that delays in raising the army caused many observers in Europe to doubt that Americans had the will to defend themselves. As Republicans worried that the army was too big to be safe, Hamilton worried that it would be too small, untrained, and disorganized to reinforce American diplomacy or to be effective in the field.[42]

The rate of mobilization was slow in part because there was virtually no logistical support system for the army; it was also extremely difficult to command and control forces dispersed throughout the United States. These urgent problems drove Hamilton almost to distraction. They eventually led him to anticipate another modern conclusion first reached by the Prussians after their defeat by Napoleon in the battle of Jena in 1806. Rapid mobilization required Americans to develop the embryo of a general staff system. They also had to establish a military academy. Experienced officers were hard to find; those who were available were often far too old to be effective. Looking to the future, Hamilton insisted that a military academy ought to become a permanent fixture, if not even the foundation of the American military establishment. In 1799 Washington made the same proposal in his final letter to Hamilton before he died. Hamilton also proposed a million-dollar fund for secret services, a good deal of money at the end of the eighteenth century. With such money, perhaps some daring brains might compensate for the lack of American brawn in a variety of covert operations.[43]

Supposing these forces actually developed as Hamilton envisioned them; what then did he intend to do with them? Perhaps for fear of tipping his hand, Hamilton wrote extremely little about his plans. Before assuming the worst, however, we should remember that militarism and strategy are not the same. The former is a character trait that republics need to discourage as much as possible; the latter is a mode of thought required even in republics. Hamilton's fundamental objection to Adams's conduct of the war is that he seemed to have no strategy. "It is a pity," Hamilton wrote to James McHenry, "that the administration has no general plan," at least not for the theaters of most concern to him. "If the chief is too desultory, his ministers ought to be more united and steady." To Rufus King, Hamilton also observed that there was a major difference between energy in the imagination and execution in detail. He also implied that Adams lacked the capacity for the latter.[44] These criticisms of the commander in chief were not entirely fair, however. The president felt no urgency about the army and could spend much of his time at home in Braintree rather than at the capital, because he believed he only had to manage a naval war. Hamilton felt great urgency because he believed it essential to be prepared for a major land war as well.

Hamilton's first objective apparently was to prevent France or any other foreign empire from controlling Louisiana and the Floridas. Washington expressed great fear that the French would seek control of Louisiana.

Adams's secretary of state, Timothy Pickering, fearing that Spain would cede Louisiana to France, asked Hamilton to develop a plan to forestall a French occupation of New Orleans. Hamilton himself regarded Louisiana as "essential to the unity of our empire" and the "permanency of the Union." To be sure, after the Battle of the Nile in August 1798, the immediate danger from France began to dissipate, but Hamilton took that fact as an argument for energy rather than for procrastination. He frequently expressed hopes for Anglo-American cooperation in an expedition to New Orleans, the British blockading the city by sea and the Americans descending the Mississippi to attack from the north. Though he did not say so, he may have wished to take advantage of French weakness before they recovered their strength. In Hamilton's view, the best defense was a good offense. To prevent foreign control of the Gulf of Mexico America had to establish control of New Orleans and the Floridas as soon as possible. Washington, with whom Hamilton was in constant communication (and whom no one dares to call a militarist) raised no objections. If war was declared by either France, Spain, or the United States, he called for prosecuting Hamilton's strategy like "lightning."

Both for political and constitutional reasons, however, Hamilton never suggested a descent on these territories unless France, or its new ally, Spain, declared war on the United States, or vice versa. Rather, he assumed that if France declared war, so too would Spain, and then offensive operations would acquire popular support. Without a graver threat than the immediate naval conflict, an offensive against France and Spain was unlikely to receive the full support of the American people, and Hamilton knew it. Nothing less than a declaration of war would suffice to supply the national will required to legitimize and sustain offensive operations. In May 1798 he therefore insisted that the mitigated state of the Quasi-War required Adams to seek a declaration of war from Congress if the president believed it necessary to escalate from mere defense of American shipping to open attacks on French shipping and possessions. Then in January 1799 Hamilton suggested that Adams issue France an ultimatum. It had to agree to begin negotiations by 1 August 1799, or the United States would declare war on France. On the one hand, the ultimatum was designed to enhance American credibility at the bargaining table by displaying the will to fight; on the other, it was designed to prepare public opinion for offensive operations. It was also a test of French intentions. Fearing that they would seize New Orleans and the Floridas, he wanted the French to show their cards. If they refused to negotiate, Hamilton meant to deny them control of the Gulf of

Mexico and thus of the United States by keeping New Orleans and the Floridas out of their hands.[45]

One cannot understate the risks involved in Hamilton's southern strategy. An expedition to New Orleans would have been the most complicated logistical enterprise in American military history thus far. Washington trusted Hamilton with the sword of America because he had well-grounded faith in Hamilton's administrative skills and believed the charges of an American Caesar to be sheer nonsense. Virtually every scholar agrees that no one else in the United States understood how to organize a massive project according to a grand design better than Hamilton. The 3,000 infantry and artillery support troops Hamilton wanted for the expedition to New Orleans required a large number of boats, a vast and reliable chain of supply, and both rapid and reliable communications between the West and the East. Even these forces might not have been enough, however. The standard rule of thumb for offensive military operations is that the attacker needs a three-to-one advantage over the defender. Hamilton had reason to believe the Spanish had 1,000 infantrymen and 500 chasseurs in New Orleans. Thus, the expedition required a minimum of 4,500 American troops to have reasonable prospects of success. General James Wilkinson, the American commander in the West, told Hamilton the expedition needed 6,000 men and a river navy. Partly because both Adams and Congress were growing cooler to the army in 1799 and 1800, however, neither the boats nor the supplies were available in sufficient quantities even for Hamilton's tiny force, and communications were dismally slow. If anything went wrong during the expedition, the troops would have to fight their way back through Spanish troops and Indians from the Mississippi Delta to Georgia. General Wilkinson was also rumored to be a Spanish agent. Because he supplied Hamilton with valuable intelligence, and Hamilton (perhaps naively) hoped command would attach the general more to the United States than to Spain, Hamilton was willing to work with him. Nonetheless, there was an enormous danger that Wilkinson would either reveal American plans to the Spanish or betray the army to them. Even assuming glory was Hamilton's only or principal motive for this expedition, there was clearly no glory in being the commander of the greatest military disaster in American history. If only because of these serious risks, Hamilton's (and we ought not to forget, Washington's) plans for an expedition to New Orleans never transpired. Since he knew more about the disorganization of the army than anyone else in the United States, Hamilton was deeply aware that Americans simply lacked the means for such operations.[46]

Hamilton's second objective was to weaken France in the larger world war while enhancing American security in the Western Hemisphere. Toward this end, he made some tentative proposals for cooperating with both the British navy and Latin American revolutionaries to promote independence in Spanish colonies and perhaps even seize them for the duration of the war. He never said these strategies ought to be carried out, but he did suggest that Americans "squint" at Latin America, meaning to look hard at the relation of this theater to the larger war. Hamilton believed the French attacked American shipping in part because they were bankrupt and desperately in need of both money and supplies. "If a universal empire is still to be the pursuit of France," Hamilton asked, "what can tend to defeat the purpose better than to detach Latin America from Spain, which is the only channel through which she receives the riches of *Mexico* and *Peru*?"[47]

Would the French seek control of Spain's colonies? Hamilton could not know for sure, but the most aggressive general in American history prior to George Patton generally acted under the assumption that opposing generals thought as he did. They would take the initiative to exploit their enemy's most vulnerable weaknesses and obtain the maximum advantage in the process. This was probably a mistake, for no state or military organization ever approximates that degree of efficiency or rationality in the pursuit of its objectives. A thousand obstacles, ranging from partisan domestic politics to logistics to quarrels among generals always slow down, complicate, moderate, distort, and sometimes even destroy the best-laid strategies. Hamilton's assumption was nonetheless a good axiom. As Clausewitz observed, the longer a way lasts, the more it leads to polarity, in which the actions and reactions of opposing sides push them ever more toward absolute or total war, when pure strategic logic often acquires ever greater power. The danger of preparing for the worst is that one may unintentionally bring it about, but the danger of not being prepared for it is that it might happen. Hamilton saw in French behavior a desire to expand without limit. Apparently it was only a matter of time before France turned from the East to the West. It thus seemed best for the United States to act while there was still time.

The only theater of the world war in which the United States had even a slim chance of making an impact was the Western Hemisphere. Hamilton never explained why he wanted the million-dollar secret service fund, but in all probability he hoped to give covert aid to revolutionaries in Latin America. In June 1798, as Congress began to authorize expanding the army, he wondered whether the United States ought to make the "independence" of French colonies a principal war aim. He also had some secret communications with a professional revolutionary, Francisco Miranda, who requested American support for revolutions to gain the independence of French and Spanish colonies throughout the Western Hemisphere. The British had similar communications with him. Partly as a result, Hamilton proposed that a British navy and an American army, which he would command, wage unspecified operations in Latin America. Yet he specifically disavowed a militaristic intention toward these colonies. He wrote that England and the United States should issue a "joint guarantee" of the colonies' independence under "*moderate*" governments. He was willing to demand (and allow the British to demand) only "equal privileges" in trade from the colonies if they won their independence. He probably wanted the American army to do the footwork because he feared that once the colonies were occupied, the British would not leave. Given the logistical difficulties he faced in planning the New Orleans expedition, however, he must have been aware that an extended occupation of the colonies was impracticable, especially if American forces met resistance from their inhabitants. As Stanley Elkins and Eric McKitrick observe, Hamilton was extremely cautious in his dealings with Miranda, making no promises without the permission of the president. In any event, Adams would have been extremely reluctant to authorize any offensive operations likely to increase Hamilton's fame, which could easily have come at his own expense. As Lycan observes, Hamilton's son, James Hamilton, wrote that his father sometimes expressed a desire to be the "great liberator" of Latin America. To the extent that Hamilton expected to earn glory from the expedition, it was for being a liberator who enabled subjugated peoples to govern themselves freely, not a conqueror, like Bonaparte, who imposed his will by force alone.[48]

Although James Hamilton had partisan reasons for casting his father as an American liberator, his understanding of the general's ambition is consistent with Hamilton's own observations about imperialism. In the Vermont debate in 1787, for example, Hamilton warned that the costs of occupation in wars of empire often exceed the costs of conquest. It was hard enough persuading Americans to support preparedness; if their forces met resistance, the costs of pacification in Latin America would probably be too great to win the support of the American people. Moreover, in the Vermont debate, Hamilton suggested that Americans had legitimate reasons not to support wars against other peoples indisposed to live under U.S. authority or wars that established government based on force alone. It would certainly illbecome Americans to oppose France for violating the right of European nations to live under their own laws and then to play that role in Latin America.

Hamilton's objective was to use Latin American independence to support American independence. It was best to get the European empires out of the Western Hemisphere, which was the long-term implication of Hamilton's argument in *Federalist* 11. Prudence demanded aiming at an "ascendant" in the Western Hemisphere, but principle required opposition to imperialism, to the "force" and the "fraud" by which the Europeans had come to dominate the globe. American ascendancy did not require imperialism, however. It was sufficient to acquire New Orleans and the Floridas and then to encourage Latin American independence movements to destroy the European empires in the Western Hemisphere. Hamilton had no illusions about Latin America, most of which he probably believed was incapable of republican government. Yet there is no evidence he believed such incapacity gave Americans or any other people a right to govern them without their consent.[49] Indeed, the evidence points in the other direction. The sooner Latin Americans achieved their independence, the safer the United States would become and the more its principles would begin to inform the New World.

We therefore need a new way of understanding Hamilton during the Quasi-War that synthesizes the many different strands of his thought, from the most realistic to the most romantic. We must do justice to his realistic assumption that force ruled the relations between the New World and the Old World and at the same time to his principled hope that consent would eventually govern in the New World. We might begin with a design for a Seal of the United States that he sketched near the end of Washington's second term, in words obviously meant for the purposes that we call propaganda today. Yet such symbols are necessary in war, and perhaps especially in the wars of modern republics. They are often more powerful in proportion to their capacity to define the essence of the time to an entire people. Though Hamilton never made his design public, it certainly captures his grasp of the essence of the war with France, and perhaps of his country at its best. The seal was to be a globe depicting Europe and a part of Africa, America, and the Atlantic Ocean. A Colossus representing the French Directory had one foot in Europe and another extending partly across the Atlantic toward the United States. The Colossus had a quintuple crown and a broken iron scepter in its right hand. It also wore a pileus, or cap of liberty, but significantly the cap was on backward, suggesting that the Directory had twisted its original cause, or never understood it. A snake had wrapped itself around the staff of the scepter, as if it were in the act of strangling a label on which was written, "Rights of Man." In the New World was Pallas Athena, the patron goddess of Athenian democracy, representing the

"Genius [or spirit] of America." She bore a "firm and composed countenance" and an "attitude of defiance." With a gold breastplate, a shield in
one hand, and a spear in the other, she was capable of both offense and
defense.

For Hamilton, the genius of the New World was or ought to be different
from the genius of the Old World. So far as possible, he meant to unite his
country (and apparently even the Western Hemisphere) through consent
and affection rather than fear. Instead of the customary terrifying Medusa's
head, Athena's shield was therefore engraved with the "scales of Justice" and
her helmet encircled with olive wreaths. She also wore a radiated crown of
glory, or halo, as a sign of providential interposition on behalf of the United
States in its quarrel with the Jacobins. The allegory was meant to show that
"though loving peace," the genius of America was "yet guided by Wisdom,
or an enlightened sense of her own rights and interests." She was determined
to exert her "valor, in breaking the scepter of the Tyrant," but could do so
only through a firm union; thus Athena stood on fifteen columns representing the American states. In a postscript, Hamilton suggested it would
improve the allegory to "represent the Ocean in a Tempest & Neptune striking with his Trident the projected leg of the Colossus." Yet he also wondered
if the addition of multipolar ambiguity would render the allegory too "complicated" to be readily comprehended in America, where the people prefer
to understand all conflict in Manichean terms, as pure good versus pure evil.
The addition of Neptune would call for a degree of moral and strategic
thoughtfulness that Hamilton was unsure the American people possessed.
It implied that sometimes Americans might have to cooperate with a less
dangerous tyrant, such as England, in order to deter or defeat a more dangerous one, like France in the 1790s.[50]

With this design, Hamilton was at his most poetic. Although it would take
a century and a half before his poetry could capture the hearts of his countrymen, his vision of his country's role in the world seems as recent as yesterday. His vision also helps explain his third and probably most important
objective as inspector general. We see hints of it in the numerous letters he
wrote about the army and navy during the crisis. A military academy, a
general staff system, the capacity to mobilize quickly, an ocean-going navy,
plans to seize the initiative, clandestine operations—these are features that
the American military takes for granted today, but no one could do so during the Quasi-War. Hamilton's revolutionary writings are a testament to
his hatred of the disorganization he believed was responsible for numerous
casualties and several humiliating defeats he had seen as a soldier in his
youth. They also reveal his determination to prevent such casualties and

defeats from occurring again. As the wheel of fortune turned during the Quasi-War, who could say which nations would win? How long would Americans rely on the Royal Navy to protect them? Was it safe to rely on England to provide the shield of America? Why leave Spain in possession of New Orleans and the Floridas, when its possessions in North America were vulnerable to attack by either England or France? Why, indeed, when France dominated Spain?

These questions explain the "grim determination" that Elkins and McKitrick ascribe to Hamilton's efforts to preserve and expand his tiny army. Americans could not afford to rest their security on the fortunes of the war in Europe. Nor could they rely on the goodwill of an ally that had proved itself a mortal as well as a moral enemy of free government everywhere. Thus, even though the immediate threat declined after 1798, Hamilton considered it "ridiculous to raise troops and immediately thereafter disband them." Sooner or later (and Hamilton feared sooner), it was highly likely that Americans would be involved in a land war with one or more of the great European empires in the Western Hemisphere. Thus Hamilton's army was not raised merely to provide against attack from France and Spain. For example, in June 1798, when popular anger at France was at its peak, repeated British attacks led Hamilton to suggest that the United States ought to declare war on both England and France, though it would involve fighting against two nations at war with each other. In time, however, Hamilton believed one or the other would court American friendship.[51] The better prepared Americans were, the more likely the friendship would be solid and durable and the less likely they would be pawns of the great powers. Yet, as amply demonstrated by Hamilton's difficulties in raising troops, the recruiting, organizing, training, and strategic planning for an army capable of competing with European armies on their own terms would take decades to become effective. Having already established the power of the purse in the Washington administration, Hamilton's third objective was therefore to establish the power of the sword as quickly and permanently as possible. The geopolitical situation at the end of the eighteenth century was so volatile that Americans could rely only on their own forces. If Hamilton enabled them to do so, he could then regard his life's work, the founding of a republican empire, substantially complete. This was a worthy objective, but it would also destroy Hamilton, his army, and his party as he sought to pursue it.

10. Shipwreck

It was perhaps inevitable that Hamilton, as the most romantic of the Founders, would end his story as a tragic figure. That term ought not to be used loosely, however. Tragedy originated as a religious celebration in honor of Dionysius, the Greek god of wine and sexual desire. As the god most concerned with the passions that lead us to forget the limits of our minds and bodies, he might also have been called the god of madness. The end of Hamilton's story is therefore better explained through the classical than the modern science of politics. The latter's assumption of progress implies the reconciliation of all contradictions and thus the end of tragedy. The former's doubts about progress imply that tragedy will always be with us. It also suggests that the experience of tragedy is the beginning of political education.

Aristotle, for example, concluded his *Politics* with an extensive discussion of the role of tragedy in educating citizens in the polis. He was especially concerned with the essentially religious passions, designated as "enthusiasm" in the Founding era. The poets have their own ends in writing tragedies, but for Aristotle, the purpose of tragedy was to purge the spectators of enthusiastic passions likely to lead to immoderate judgments, such as pity and fear. Since the original spectators of a tragedy were also citizens, its political role was to detoxify the system, so to speak. It was to induce greater sobriety among the members of the audience so that they could deliberate more dispassionately when they reconvened to discuss their political affairs.[1]

Aristotle's discussion of tragedy is important for evaluating the various interpretations of the Founding era as a classical moment in American political thought. If Gordon Wood is correct in calling the republicanism of the American Revolution "secularized Puritanism," then little could be less classical in the Aristotelian sense than the various forms in which American Puritanism manifests itself. To be sure, Aristotle did speak of virtue as the purpose of political life, but if one rests with that abstract premise, then anyone who ever talked about virtue becomes a classical republican. For Aristotle, the political problem was much less the absence of virtue from politics than the partisanship that different claims to rule, based on different virtues or contributions to the common good, produced within the city. Quite frequently, the problem was that partisans of one virtue came to think it was the only virtue, the political problem we find built into Sophocles' *Antigone*. Antigone treated piety and loyalty to her family as the only relevant virtues; but Creon, who had forbidden the burial of one of her brothers for instigating a civil war, stressed the preservation of his city above all else. Both Antigone and Creon seem to get drunk on their virtues and become exceedingly self-righteous as a result.

No people spoke more about moderation than the ancient Greeks, and few practiced it less. In addition to mundane causes of faction, such as the greed of the few and the many, quarrels between partisans of different but partly legitimate claims to rule often polarized the ancient cities. Those quarrels helped produce the oscillations between tyranny and anarchy that both Hamilton and Madison deplored in the ancient republics. Perhaps fundamentally, Aristotle's mixed regime was designed to prevent such drunkenness from infecting entire cities. To make this possible, however, the different parts of the city, that is, the spectators of a tragedy, had to come to terms with the limits of their own virtues. The political moderation Aristotle hoped for from a mixed regime therefore required a philosophical critique of self-righteousness. Since philosophy is the province of a few, that was impossible for an entire city. The next best hope was the experience of tragedy, which pulls us apart by making us both sympathize with and be horrified by the fate of its protagonists.[2]

The great quarrel between Hamilton and Jefferson, which eventually evolved into a quarrel with John Adams, does not appear to owe much to classical political thought. It was a modern phenomenon arising from the tension between the different modern virtues of vigilance and responsibility. Yet the lines between the Reformation and the Enlightenment are so blurry at times that one might easily call modern liberal republicanism a form of secularized Puritanism, which has frequently mutated into religious schisms between different apostles of liberty. Moreover, precisely because the quarrels produced during the Quasi-War were between partisans of different virtues, who became ever more self-righteous as the quarrels intensified, the ancients' tragic understanding of politics may be the best antidote to the enthusiasm that increasingly began to infect the writings of Republicans and Federalists in the 1790s. No people ever talked more about establishing the rule of reason over passion than the Founders, yet few of them came to terms with the enormous extent to which their moral passions were out of control. The self-righteousness of the partisans might tempt us to follow Shakespeare's Mercutio in casting a plague on both their

houses, but to do so would be an injustice. If we can see their quarrel as a tragedy, we might acquire some of the freedom from moralism that Aristotle
apparently hoped the experience of tragedy might produce in the ancient city.

Both for Aristotle and for Sophocles tragedy was not mere fable. Its implications about our nature, our limits, and our pride, which lead us to reach
too far, made it much more universal in significance than history. Because
tragedy could reveal the essence of political problems much more clearly
than a mere chronicle of events, Aristotle treated poetry as more philosophical than is history.[3] It is unclear why Aristotle ended the *Politics* with his
account of tragedy, but he may have believed it could remind us that the
immoderate pursuit of any virtue is indeed a vice. In the spirit of Aristotle
and Sophocles, then, perhaps the best way to shift from a view of Hamilton
as a historical figure to a more philosophic understanding of his strengths
and weaknesses as a statesman is to investigate the unique personal qualities and circumstances that made him tragic.

Hamilton's closest counterpart in antiquity is one of the few Plutarchian
figures he never mentioned, Coriolanus. Comparing Hamilton to this deeply
flawed Roman is dangerous, especially in our time, when many productions
of Shakespeare's play cast Coriolanus in jackboots and a brown shirt. To
avoid misleading implications, then, we should be aware that Hamilton
rejected much that Coriolanus came to represent in the West. For example,
in Shakespeare's version of Roman history as it occurs in three plays,
Coriolanus, Julius Caesar, and *Antony and Cleopatra,* Augustus is the natural culmination of Caesar's ambition, which is revealed in starkest form in
the character of Coriolanus. To demonstrate his own worth, Coriolanus
must triumph over all worthy adversaries, which means he must be constantly at war—even with his city. When Coriolanus betrays Rome, he also
foreshadows the greater betrayals of Caesar and Augustus, when they not
only lead their armies against Romans but conquer them as well. Their common desire to be first, and to be recognized as such, inevitably sets Rome
on the road to war abroad and tyranny at home.[4]

Hamilton's quarrel with Samuel Seabury in 1774 reveals his contempt for
this dimension of Rome, which he correctly saw as the source of ancient
militarism. Nonetheless, Coriolanus and Hamilton do share a common trait.
The love of honor produced enormous energy in both the Roman and the
American. Each could fly into a rage when he failed to get what he believed
were his just deserts; thus, each was extraordinarily indiscreet. Each let his
heart rule his words. Largely because of their indiscretions, even their closest friends turned against them. They were not merely banished from politics; they had also banished themselves.[5]

How did this happen to Hamilton, or, in the paradoxical manner of the ancient tragedians, how did Hamilton bring it on himself? More generally, what does his tragedy reveal about the unique problems of military men who serve free governments? How does Hamilton's fate prefigure the problems that other American generals, such as Douglas MacArthur and George Patton, have faced in time of war? The best answers lie in the domestic crisis in the United States produced by the Quasi-War. There was no responsible alternative to the significant military buildup Hamilton advocated (see chapter 9), so he had to risk the domestic backlash it would perhaps inevitably produce. Nonetheless, Hamilton made that backlash much worse than it might have been. More than a few Republicans feared that the Federalists' objective in raising the army was to attack them. Some of the former even accused the latter of seeking to establish a military dictatorship. Although John Adams did not, partly to defend his honor and partly because he did suspect the worst of Hamilton, Adams and his descendants often cast him in the role of a potential dictator and military adventurer.[6] When coupled with suggestions that Hamilton was the leader of a British faction in America, these unjust charges took a severe toll on him. When he struck back to defend his honor, the American Coriolanus sent himself into a political wilderness from which he never returned.

Act 1 of this tragedy begins on 31 May 1798, in the immediate aftermath of the publication of the XYZ papers. President Adams received an "address" from the militia of New Jersey supporting his then vigorous policy of mobilizing the nation for war. Adams responded with an address of his own to the militia, or rather, with a threat to the opposition, which struck Hamilton as "intemperate & revolutionary." Largely because Americans were remarkably united in the first moments of the crisis, Adams boasted that the "greatest nation may menace [the United States] at its pleasure" but not expect victory in the contest. Adams then added that "degraded and deluded characters may tremble, lest they should be condemned to the severest punishment an American can suffer—that of being conveyed in safety within the lines of an invading enemy." At a moment when he enjoyed near universal popularity, Adams suggested he might banish members of the opposition, who were citizens. Hamilton wrote to Oliver Wolcott, Adams's secretary of the treasury, that to this point he had "much liked" Adams's efforts to face the French with vigor. Nonetheless, there were "limits which must not be passed." From his "knowledge of the ardor of the President's mind & this specimen of the effect of that ardor," Hamilton began to fear that "he may run into indiscretion." Hamilton worried that Adams would do great "harm to the Government, to the cause & to himself." Confidentially to Wolcott, Hamilton observed that "some hint" of his intemperance should be given to Adams, "for we must make no mistakes."[7]

Neither Adams nor Hamilton was responsible for what eventually became the Alien and Sedition Acts.[8] These were products of the Federalist-controlled Congress, but Hamilton clearly recognized that Adams and other Federalists were indulging self-righteous tendencies that might get out of control, and eventually they did. Congress did confine banishment, the classic republican cure for faction, to resident aliens, and Hamilton had no objections to deporting aliens who could be proven dangerous to the Republic. Yet he was consistently afraid that the same angry spirit that had led Whigs to persecute suspected Tories at the end of the American Revolution might manifest itself in similar acts by the Federalists during the Quasi-War. Thus, for example, he requested detailed information from Timothy Pickering, in order to learn the policy of the executive if the measure that eventually became the Act Concerning Aliens were to pass in Congress, as it later did on 27 June 1798. This act gave the president the power to deport aliens suspected of being dangerous to the peace and safety of Americans without benefit of trial. An Act Concerning Enemy Aliens, which followed on 6 July, gave the executive, upon a declaration of war, the authority to apprehend, restrain, secure, and remove unnaturalized alien males above the age of fourteen. Hamilton wanted far more moderate measures. "Let us not be cruel or violent," he cautioned the secretary of state. He insisted on exceptions for foreign merchants protected by treaties, aliens who might be subject to punishment in their own countries if sent away, and immigrants whose behavior had been unexceptionable. Hamilton feared that arbitrary power would be transferred to the executive because the Alien Acts left the determination of guilt or innocence to the executive alone. The acts united executive and judicial powers and thus denied the accused the security required for genuine civil liberty. The amendments Hamilton proposed would have given aliens an opportunity to appeal to the courts, and thus have restored substantial security to civil liberty.[9]

Hamilton's objections to the Alien Acts are an important footnote in American civil-military relations. Sometimes, it is the civilians in Congress, not the generals, who constitute the most serious threat to liberty in a republic. There are times when the generals should imitate Hamilton's example and speak up before the civilians do incalculable damage to themselves and the Constitution. To prevent such damage, Hamilton was even more adamant in protesting against a bill in the Senate "to define more

particularly, the crime of treason, and to punish the crime of sedition."
Section 1 of the bill stated that France and the United States were enemies.
It also said that "any person or persons owing allegiance to the United States,
who shall adhere to the aforesaid enemies of the United States, giving aid
and comfort," could be punished with death under a different statute.
After seeing the Senate version of the bill, Hamilton wrote to Wolcott that
it contained provisions that on a "cursory view seem to me highly exceptionable & such as more than anything else may endanger civil war. . . . If
we make no false step," he told Wolcott, "we shall be essentially united;
but if we push things to an extreme we shall then give to faction body &
solidity." Although some scholars have claimed that a prudent desire to
avoid strengthening the opposition and causing a civil war was his only
objection to the bill, this is clearly not true. He did not wish to see the bill
"hurried through" because it was "highly exceptionable" in itself. "Let us
not establish a tyranny," Hamilton told Wolcott. "Energy is a very different
thing from violence."[10]

The effort to define treason more specifically (or vaguely?) than under
the Constitution failed to pass, but an amended version of the bill, without
the death penalty, passed the House by a 44 to 41 vote on 14 July, with most
of the Republican South deeply opposed to it. The "Act for the punishment
of certain crimes against the United States" has since been known as the
Sedition Act. Section 2 prohibited false, scandalous, and malicious speech
and writings against Congress or the executive with the intent to defame
them, bring them into contempt or disrepute, excite hatred against the
government by the people, or stir up sedition in the United States. The
wording of the act is important. Its purpose was to criminalize seditious
libel, that is, false attacks on public officials with the intention of inspiring contempt for the laws, if not resistance to them. Yet there was also a
grave risk that it would be used simply to silence opposition to the Adams
administration.

To guard against that danger, section 3 of the act contained two securities for the rights of the accused that Hamilton considered extremely important and essential to make the act constitutional. First, in contrast to the
common law, which did not allow truth as a defense in seditious libel, the
Sedition Act did allow it. If opponents of the Adams administration could
prove that he and his cabinet intended to establish a monarchy, for example,
then this standard would enable them to be acquitted; if not, they would be
convicted of seditious libel in the law courts and demagoguery in the court
of public opinion. Second, juries were allowed to determine the law as well
as the facts of cases brought under the act. In principle at least, Hamilton

believed these provisions could supply substantial security against the danger of kangaroo courts in which prosecutors and judges would have decided the guilt of the accused before the trial. In practice, the Alien Acts were never enforced, but the Sedition Act was enforced by Federalist judges with a partisan vengeance. Federalist prosecutors issued fifteen indictments under the act, and ten resulted in conviction, sometimes on trumped-up charges. The three most prominent Republican propagandists (Thomas Cooper, James Thompson Callander, and William Duane) were convicted, with the ironic result that the Sedition Act helped bring about what it sought to prevent. It produced martyrs for the Republican cause, whose proponents then became ever more angry, organized, and self-righteous.[11]

At perhaps no time during the 1790s was Jefferson's virtue of vigilance more relevant or effective than during this crisis. To mobilize opposition to the Alien and Sedition Acts, Jefferson wrote the *Kentucky Resolutions* in 1798 and Madison his *Report on the Virginia Resolutions* in 1800. Together, they developed the constitutional doctrines of nullification and interposition. Jefferson's *Kentucky Resolutions* are not a defense of free speech; instead, they are the classic statements of strict construction of the Constitution. The Constitution, he observed, established a government of enumerated powers. What was not delegated to the federal government was left to the people or the states. On this principle, the federal government had usurped the states' right to regulate speech, for the "states retain the right of judging how far the licentiousness of speech and the press may be abridged without lessening their useful freedom." The Alien Acts, Jefferson observed, violated the guarantees of due process of law and jury trial in the Fifth and Sixth Amendments of the Bill of Rights. He then asserted that "whenever the General Government assumes undelegated powers," or worse, violates strict constitutional prohibitions, "its acts are unauthoritative, void, and of no force."[12]

No one disputed that unconstitutional acts were void. The great issue again was clear: Who should judge when laws are unconstitutional? For Jefferson, the partisan behavior of the courts confirmed that it was unsafe for the federal government to be the "final judge of the extent of the powers delegated to itself, since that would have made its discretion, and not the Constitution, the measure of its powers." In Jefferson's view, since there was no common judge between the states and the federal government, each state had an "equal right to judge for itself, as well of infractions as of the mode and measure of redress." The discretion of the state legislatures was not limited to protest. It included "nullification" of an act as a "rightful remedy." Practically speaking, however, it would have been difficult and perhaps impossible for one or two states to resist the rest. For nullification to be effective, Jefferson understood that it would require organized, determined resistance, beginning with "committees of correspondence," the predecessors of the Continental Congress before the American Revolution. Republicans thereby joined Federalists in succumbing to hysteria, albeit of a radically different kind. In the fright of the moment, some Republicans, such as John Taylor of Caroline, considered secession. Jefferson, however, suggested that they should merely organize vigilant opposition and trust that the people would side with them in the next election. Consequently, many scholars view the *Kentucky Resolutions* as quite innocuous, as nothing more than the party platform of the Republicans, who meant to appeal to the ballot rather than to the sword.[13]

The Republicans' opponents neither knew nor believed this, however. For Hamilton and many Federalists, the *Virginia* and *Kentucky Resolutions* suggested an invitation for the states to set in motion the series of events that ultimately had led to war between the United States and Great Britain in 1776. Hamilton suspected that the most extreme Republicans were willing to employ "physical force," and Jefferson himself gave him good reason to think so. Unless these acts, and the entire course of Federalism in the 1790s, were "arrested at the threshold," Jefferson observed, they would and should "necessarily drive these states into revolution and blood." Jefferson's public words thus seemed radically different from his private advice; they sounded like a call to arms. Indeed, they probably were, as a last resort. If this issue could not be settled through an election, Jefferson's words indicated that he at least believed the matter was serious enough to be worth fighting about. For this reason, perhaps, Jefferson chose to keep his authorship of the *Kentucky Resolutions* secret until 1821. Had it been known that the vice-president of the United States risked civil war in these resolutions, his reputation as a responsible statesman would undoubtedly have been questioned.[14]

In one respect, however, Jefferson and Hamilton were closer to each other than either was to Madison. Though Jefferson and Hamilton disagreed about whether the national government had the authority to prosecute seditious libels, both agreed that laws against such libel were legitimate means to make free speech responsible. In contrast to both of them, Madison adhered to a much more absolute understanding of free speech. He feared that efforts to prosecute seditious libel would undermine the accountability of the government. Like Jefferson, however, Madison saw the states, or more accurately, the peoples of the states, as parties to the social compact. When the

courts sanctioned usurpation, as he believed they did in enforcing the Sedition Act, the different peoples of the United States had a right to judge the
courts through their representatives within the states. He substituted the
milder phrase, "interposition of the parties [the peoples of the states] in
their sovereign capacity," for Jefferson's "nullification." He also deliberately waffled by leaving it unclear whether interposition meant nullification or was merely a peaceful way to protest laws deemed unconstitutional
by one or more states. He also left it unclear when or how interposition was
to take effect. Was the decision of one legislature enough to justify it? Did
it require a majority? Did it require a constitutional convention? No one
knows. His ambiguity reveals a strong desire to avoid a civil war, but the
ultimate implication from his report was the same as Jefferson's. On "occasions deeply and essentially affecting the vital principles of their system,"
Madison argued, the states had the right to judge the constitutionality of national laws and to take such measures as seemed necessary and proper to them
to uphold the Constitution as they understood it. He walked a delicate line
between loyalty and disloyalty to the Union, but he too was aware that effective interposition of the states might ultimately require them to use force.[15]

In principle at least, Madison and Jefferson could find ample support for
their positions in the Declaration of Independence. Because a long train of
abuses revealed there was no peaceful way to resolve the American quarrel
with England, Congress had asserted the revolutionary right to settle it
through force. Since the current Congress, the executive, and the judiciary
were in the hands of the Federalists, the only peaceful alternative left for the
Republicans was to appeal to the state legislatures to declare the Alien and
Sedition Acts unconstitutional. If that alternative failed, however, the logical implication was that it would be 1776 again in America. The only resort
left would be the one suggested by Jefferson, "revolution and blood."

Thus, the polarization of the parties was following the script of Sophocles'
Antigone. Each side was pushing the other to extremes it would usually have
preferred to avoid. Several years before, Hamilton had recognized this potential in party politics. One side, he observed, appeared to

> believe there is a serious plot [led by Hamilton] to overturn the state
> governments and establish monarchy.... The other side firmly believes
> there is a serious plot [led by Jefferson] to overturn the General govern-
> ment and elevate the separate powers of the states upon its ruins. Both
> sides may be equally wrong and their mutual jealousies may be materi-
> ally the causes of the appearances which disturb the other, and sharpen
> them against each other.[16]

This view largely explains why both Hamilton and Washington implied Americans could have too much of a good thing in Washington's Farewell Address. The pluralism suggested by Madison in *Federalist* 10 made a good deal of sense, but not if party conflict brought the nation to the brink of civil war. In this case, the imprudence of the Federalists in passing the Alien and Sedition Acts was matched by the imprudence of Republicans who spoke of nullification and interposition as means to oppose them.

Few scholars doubt that Jefferson and Madison opened a Pandora's box that would not be closed until 1865.[17] The great question is whether it was necessary to do so. In 1776 Jefferson asserted that the ultimate right of revolution ought not to be threatened for light and transient causes and certainly not before all peaceful appeals have been exhausted. However grievous one might deem them, the Alien and Sedition Acts did not represent the kind of threat Americans had faced in 1776. Boston was not under military occupation. Legislatures had not been suspended. Americans were not being threatened with transportation across the sea to be tried in British courts. No foreign legislative power claimed a right to make whatever laws it wanted without the consent of Americans. Violence by established authorities and their opponents had not yet broken out. Most important, the Alien and Sedition Acts did not amount to a settled "design" of tyranny. At best, they were an effort to avoid a revolution (and almost caused one); at worst, they were misguided acts of passion. In response, the Virginians both risked a civil war in the immediate crisis and set an extremely dangerous precedent. Perhaps despite their best intentions, they lent moral authority to John C. Calhoun's later arguments for nullification, but the South Carolinian was not the only southerner to take his bearings from the most extreme statements of Jefferson and Madison. Rightly or wrongly, Jefferson Davis believed he was the legitimate heir of the Republican principles of 1798. When "in the judgment of the sovereign states" the Constitution has been "perverted from the purposes for which it is ordained" and ceases to answer them, then, the Confederate president announced, "a peaceful appeal by the ballot box" in the state governments gave those sovereign states the right to declare that "the Government created by the compact should cease to exist." It gave them a right to secede from the Union.[18]

Jefferson's talk of "revolution and blood" struck Hamilton and many other Federalists as the height of political irresponsibility. It led them to fear for the Union, as sacred to them as the Bill of Rights was to Jefferson and Madison. For the Federalists, the great question was whether the United

States would become a nation. For Hamilton especially, the Union was as important to durable liberty as the Bill of Rights, perhaps more so. Because the Constitution had been ratified by state conventions, there is good reason to think that Madison was right to treat it as a compact between separate peoples in different states. Yet because its first three words could be taken to imply that the Constitution received its authority from one united people, there is good reason to think that Hamilton was right, too. For Hamilton at least, the Constitution was meant to transform many peoples into one, which was impossible if state legislatures could nullify any act of the Union they deemed unconstitutional. In more moderate times, each side could make an uncomfortable peace with the paradoxical notion of a nation of states, but by the end of 1798, such moderation became increasingly difficult to sustain. In desperation, the vigilant pitted jealousy of power against love of the Union. Consequently, Hamilton feared the struggle would destroy the emotional bond that constituted Americans as a people.

The *Virginia Resolutions,* Hamilton wrote to the Federalist leader Theodore Sedgwick, were "a very serious business, which will call for all the wisdom and firmness of the government." To close the Pandora's box, he told Sedgwick that the Federalists' first object had to be to "secure the opinion of the people." Within a year of their publication, the *Virginia* and *Kentucky Resolutions* were condemned by the northern state legislatures, and most said the courts must decide the constitutional questions that gave rise to them. The rest of the South remained prudently silent. If the federal government played its cards carefully, Hamilton believed it might also confine supporters of the resolutions to the partisans of Madison and Jefferson in Kentucky and Virginia, where a sizable minority (led by John Marshall) had opposed the resolutions in the legislature. Securing public opinion required referring the resolutions to a special committee of Congress, which Hamilton believed should report quickly on the tendency of the doctrines to "destroy the Constitution of the United States." The committee should treat them as part of a "regular conspiracy to overturn the government." Though this conclusion was false, since Jefferson and Madison meant to save the Constitution as they understood it, it nonetheless recognized the tragic potential of the resolutions to destroy what they meant to save.

Hamilton then suggested that the committee should point out that the resolutions had the "inevitable effect and probably the intention" of encouraging a "hostile foreign power to decline accommodation and proceed to hostility." There is no reason to believe Jefferson and Madison meant to encourage the French to keep fighting, but France would have been delighted to see America involved in a civil war at this time. For Hamilton, a civil war while still fighting the French would be a disaster, with one part of the Union sympathizing with and influenced by France and another sympathizing with and influenced by England. This was the Trojan horse of foreign influence that he (and Madison) had often warned against. He therefore believed the government had not only to "defend itself, but must attack and arraign its enemies" in the court of public opinion, and even in the courts of law.[19]

To divide the opposition as much as possible, Hamilton suggested that the congressional committee distinguish between the people of Virginia and their legislature and even between the legislators who had voted for the resolutions and their leaders. The committee might go a step further by combining conciliation with firmness. "On a recent though hasty" reading of the Alien Acts, Hamilton had concluded that they were "deficient in precautions against abuse and for the security of citizens. This," he added firmly, "should not be." It is not clear what to make of his words. Since the Alien Acts did not apply to citizens, perhaps the overworked general was thinking of the Sedition Act when he wrote them. More probably, he believed that aliens had to have the same protection of judicial process as citizens and therefore could not be deported without benefit of trial. Whatever the case, Hamilton did not think the committee could undo the mischief begun by his party. The committee could admit "no cause for repeal of the laws" without setting a precedent that would justify nullification and interposition. "If however on examination modifications consistent with the general design of the laws, but instituting better guards" could be devised in private, then the committee could add motives of policy to those of principle for amending the acts. It was unwise to leave opponents no recourse but to submit or fight. If word spread that the Federalists were disposed to compromise, amendments could form a "bridge for those who may incline to retreat over" them. "Concessions of this kind adroitly made may have a good rather than a bad effect."[20]

Measures to support the army had to "proceed with activity," first because the United States was still at war with France, and second because the army might be necessary to subdue potential rebels at home. This time, however, Hamilton would not rely on the militia. Drunken and disorganized bootleggers could be checked by the militia during the Whiskey Rebellion, but "whenever the experiment shall be made to subdue a refractory & powerful state by Militia, the event will shame the advocates of their sufficiency. In the expedition against the Western Insurgents," the inspector general remarked, "I trembled every moment lest a great part of the Militia should take it into their heads to return home rather than go forward." He hoped his plan of combining firmness with conciliation would "give time" for the fervor of the moment to subside and for reason to resume the reins. By "dividing" the government's enemies, it might then "triumph with ease"; but against a large, powerful, and stubborn state, the federal government could not count on an easy victory.

In the worst case, a "clever," that is, a skillful, professionally led, and well-disciplined force would have to be "drawn towards Virginia for which there is an obvious pretext" and the Virginians put to the "test of resistance." As even Richard Kohn acknowledges, Hamilton "wished to move troops toward Virginia not to jail or overturn the Republicans in that state, but to threaten the opposition, parade the government's power, and to nip a civil war in the bud as the Washington administration had done in Western Pennsylvania in 1794." As Stanley Elkins and Eric McKitrick observe, we should also distinguish between what Hamilton and other Federalists said in moments of fear and anger, when their understanding of the Constitution and the Union seemed to be in danger, and what Kohn calls a militaristic predisposition to use force to settle disputes. It was also unlikely that Washington could have been persuaded to lead a force against his own state unless there was overwhelming evidence that it was preparing to fight. If such evidence existed, however, there is no doubt that Hamilton would have acted to preserve the Union.[21]

During a minor tax revolt in a few counties in Pennsylvania, for example, Hamilton had advised James McHenry to avoid magnifying a riot into an insurrection. Whenever the government appeared in arms, it was best to appear like Hercules and to inspire respect by the display of strength. Nonetheless, it is important to distinguish between how Hamilton meant to address open rebellion and how he meant to address a vague threat of it. There is no evidence that he meant to use force unless Virginia used it first. Yet it was logical to infer that the "hostile declarations" of the Virginians would be "followed up" by an actual preparation of the means of supporting them by force. Indeed, on the basis of perhaps false intelligence that confirmed his worst suspicions, Hamilton believed the Virginians were in fact arming for war. Work proceeded in earnest on the Richmond Armory. Though most Virginians said it was not directed against the federal government, a few men, such as William Branch Giles and John Randolph, said it was. In this circumstance, Hamilton believed it would have been an "unpardonable mistake" for those who possessed "all the constitutional powers" not to "surround the constitution with new ramparts and to disconcert the schemes of its enemies."

From Hamilton's point of view, it would have been irresponsible to avoid nipping rebellion in the bud. It therefore seems likely that he would have wished to move the army toward Virginia as soon as there was reason to think it was in arms. The problem, of course, is that any effort to check rebellion in its infancy might well have encouraged it. Significantly, Hamilton never again proposed moving the army toward Virginia, suggesting that, after more reasoned consideration, he came to view the measure as more provocative than necessary. It was much better to prevent a civil war than to aggravate its potential causes. The goal, then, was to end this cycle of action-reaction extremism by divising new means to reconcile the partisans while of course being prepared for the worst case if a peaceful settlement proved impossible.[22]

Ever the man with a plan, Hamilton advocated four different steps to avoid but also to prepare for a constitutional nightmare. As usual, the steps blended a good deal of realism with utopianism. They deserve special attention because they are inconsistent with the disposition to rely on "force alone" to establish authority, which Kohn treats as the essence of militarism. By seizing on only one of five of the effectual sources of authority in Hamilton's thought, Kohn has made the common mistake of treating a part of Hamilton's vision for the whole. On 18 June 1787 Hamilton spelled out these sources: ambition, interest, influence, habit, and force had to be on the side of the national government if it were to have any chance to compete with the empires of the states. Even in the most indiscreet speech of his political career, he never suggested that it was possible to rely on force alone, much less that it was desirable to do so. His arguments in *The Federalist* in favor of extending the authority of the national government to individuals are also a painstaking effort to explain to the people precisely what was necessary to prevent American quarrels from being settled by force alone. In his most thoughtful and romantic moments, he also suggested that the perception of the government as an act of choice rather than as force would be the essential emotional bond of American national identity and a source of enormous national pride. He returned to that theme in 1796 by writing it into Washington's Farewell Address.[23] Hamilton's plan to prevent a civil war was therefore a return to the first principles of his essentially Machiavellian psychology of empire: combine fear with love to produce loyalty; but if one is compelled to rely on fear, then take great care to avoid producing hatred for the authority one seeks to establish. Otherwise, one risks destroying it in the effort to save it.

One anecdote sometimes speaks volumes. Desertion became a serious problem for the Additional Army, when enlistees discovered that most soldiering consists of waiting and drilling. The standard way of dealing with deserters at the time was to execute them. Hamilton nonetheless advised

James McHenry to spare the life of a deserter because the temper of America was opposed to frequent capital punishments. Cruelty, he suggested, inspires disgust and hatred and is therefore less favorable to authority than an excess of leniency. McHenry therefore had to exercise "caution not to render our military system odious by giving it the appearance of being too sanguinary." One deserter had been executed already, which was enough to set the appropriate example. Inevitably, others would desert in the future, so it was better to save the most extreme punishment for later, when it would refresh fear without producing unnecessary hatred. In the meantime, it was best to concentrate on the chief bonds of union in any army, the pride that comes from its discipline and the comradeship that arises from shared suffering in a common cause. Force and fear clearly played a significant role in Hamilton's advice, as they do in the advice of anyone who has ever thought seriously about governing. Most striking in Hamilton's advice, however, is the combination of passions on which he relied, his sense of the temper of his country, and his efforts to calibrate a response that was both effective and as humane as the necessity of preserving military discipline required. "It is the true policy of the government," Hamilton observed, "to maintain an attitude which shall express a reluctance to strike together with a firm determination to do it whenever it shall be essential."[24]

Hamilton's plan to avoid a civil war while preparing for it followed the same pattern. The first step consisted of measures to "extend the influence and promote the popularity of the government." Extending its influence included extending the federal judicial system to the lowest possible level in the states. Fearing the "indisposition of the local magistrates," Hamilton aimed to establish district courts, with their own federal judges and justices of the peace, in each of the states in order to guarantee the "energetic execution of the laws." In contrast, building popular affection for the government required demonstrating the positive advantages of energy. This objective led Hamilton to anticipate the Whigs of the 1830s. He advocated an immense program of road building, or internal improvements, which he believed would be a "measure universally popular. None," he declared, "can be more so."

This effort to produce affection was designed to help the Federalists as well as to preserve the Union. To retain their control of the government, the Federalists needed to win at the polls. Since they had made themselves unpopular, they also needed new ideas. Hamilton's party did not accept his proposals, but they were a blueprint for political survival based on changing with the changing needs of the Union. Internal improvements could promote commerce and thus help retain Federalist control over the votes of the commercial sector of society. Hamilton did not intend merely to defend old territory, however. He meant to attack the Republicans on their own turf by going after their strongest source of support, the agrarian vote. A society to promote "new inventions, discoveries, and improvements in Agriculture and the Arts" would not only be "productive of general advantage," but would also "speak powerfully to the feelings and interests of those classes of men to whom the benefits derived from the Government have been heretofore the least manifest." Hamilton did not say so, but road building would also tie the parts of the empire together, enable the army to move quickly in a crisis, encourage the mutual dependence of its parts, and thereby attach the interest of citizens, especially frontiersmen in the West, to the survival of the Union.[25]

The second step consisted of provisions for "augmenting the means and consolidating the strength of the Government." These provisions consisted largely of finding ways to raise extra money through indirect taxes and of efforts to keep the army and navy at their current level for at least five years. The third step consisted of arrangements for "enlarging and confirming the legal Powers of the Government" and included extending the law that had enabled Washington to call out the militia to suppress unlawful combinations and insurrections during the Whiskey Rebellion. These arrangements also included a constitutional amendment to allow the national government to build interstate canals. Broad construction was fairly secure whenever the Convention had not rejected a specific power that might otherwise be implied from an enumerated power, but since that body had debated and rejected the power to build canals, an amendment seemed necessary to remove all doubts about its legitimacy. Since canals could possibly have been justified under the necessary and proper clause of the Constitution, Hamilton's willingness to support such an amendment testifies to his sense of danger. To the extent the *Virginia* and *Kentucky Resolutions* constituted an attack on broad construction, the amendment was essential to defuse the current controversy. Moreover, canals could promote affection for the national government by giving the public another display of the advantages of national energy. For the sake of consolidating the Union by affection, then, Hamilton was willing to risk a constitutional precedent that would undermine the broad construction he considered essential to national strength.[26]

For the sake of the Union, Hamilton also engaged in some remarkable daydreaming. "Happy would it be if a clause were added to the constitution" which allowed Congress, upon application of 100,000 persons in a state, to erect them into a separate state. Without doubt, Hamilton had his mind on the dangers posed by Virginia and Kentucky. "The subdivision of the great states," he observed, "was indispensable to the security of the general government and with it of the Union. Great States will always feel a rivalship with the common head, will often be disposed to machinate against it, and in certain situations will be able to do it with decisive effect." Hamilton's third strategy, then, was not to divide and conquer by force, like Caesar, but to divide the states in order not to have to conquer them. It was therefore an alternative to Caesarism, but like Madison's strategy in *Federalist* 10, it was also based on the same principle. The best way to control faction was to divide it.

Hamilton did not think this policy was a threat to republican government, whose cause was not identical to the survival of large and powerful states. In Hamilton's view, the existence of such states was the primary threat to a durable union and the liberty it was established to protect. So far as dividing large states might prevent a civil war, it would help ensure the survival of America's republican empire. Moreover, consent would be required to effect the subdivision of the states, and the states would remain republics; only their size would change. Like his speech of 18 June 1787, however, Hamilton's suggestion was "merely thrown out for consideration." Even he was aware that it would be "inexpedient & even dangerous" to propose an amendment of this kind in the current crisis, when it was obvious the amendment was aimed at Virginia especially. Nonetheless, a strong case could be made that Hamilton was right. Eventually, Americans had to choose between the survival of the Union and the survival of one of its largest and most powerful states. It was impossible to defeat the rebels in the American Civil War without destroying the power of Virginia. In part, that task required keeping the supercommonwealth divided into two states. Ironically, it was James Madison at the Federal Convention who first proposed subdividing the large states as the appropriate defense against a union dominated by them.[27]

The last step in Hamilton's plan concerned laws for "punishing incendiary and seditious practices." The leading Federalists—Washington, Hamilton, Adams, Jay, and numerous lesser lights—were branded as enemies of the Republic in the Republican press. If people believed the charges, the inevitable result would be that they would lose confidence in the government and perhaps even resist its laws. Thus, Hamilton wanted all writings that were personally libel in common law to be cognizable in the U.S. courts if they were directed against any officer of the national government. Preserving "confidence" in the officers of the government by "protecting their reputations from malicious and unfounded slanders" was essential to enable them "to fulfill the ends of their appointment." It was therefore "both constitutional and politic" to place their reputations within the jurisdiction of the federal courts. They certainly "ought not to be left to the cold and reluctant protection of the state courts," which were "always temporizing" and "sometimes disaffected."[28]

Hamilton's remarks were ambiguous. They led James Morton Smith to suggest a dilemma in interpreting them: either Hamilton "meant exactly what he said—that all writings which at common law were libels should be regarded as seditious if leveled against federal officials," or he meant that the Sedition Act should be expanded to include all common law libels directed against any federal officer whatsoever. In the first case, truth would not be a defense, and the Sedition Act would then be deprived of its major innovation in favor of the rights of the accused. In the second case, truth could remain as a defense but then we would have to conclude that "Hamilton was in favor of protecting the reputations of all federal officers from political criticism by enacting an even tougher Sedition Act than that of 1798. Moreover, any new law modeled after this suggestion would have protected Hamilton from Republican criticism of his administration of the army."[29]

Smith's first alternative does not withstand careful scrutiny. Hamilton coupled "unfounded" with "malicious" when he spoke of protecting federal officials from slanders. If Hamilton meant what he said, he did not mean to abandon the new standard of truth as a defense against seditious libel. During a gubernatorial race in New York in 1801, he conflated his own proposal to Jonathan Dayton with the Sedition Act, but he did so in a manner that clarifies his intentions. He observed that "the most essential object" of the Sedition Act "was to declare the Courts of the United States competent to the cognizance of those slanders against the principal officials and departments of the federal Government, which at common law are punishable as libels; with the liberal and important mitigation of allowing the truth of an accusation to be given in exoneration of the accuser."[30] This explanation perhaps is why Hamilton was not as troubled by the Sedition Act as by the Alien Acts. In principle at least, the former increased security for the accused; the latter denied the accused any security at all.

Smith's second alternative, that Hamilton meant to expand the Sedition Act to include common law libels, must therefore be the true one; but precisely because truth would be a defense, the inference that Smith draws from that alternative is unjustified. The statute would change the common law. Any federal official whatsoever would indeed be protected from slander in the conduct of his duty, but only insofar as the charges leveled against the official were false. Neither Hamilton nor anyone else in the administration would have been immune from criticism, but critics would have to be able to prove their accusations or go to jail if convicted for lying, not only about individual officials but to the American people as a whole.

Smith's book, a classic in American civil liberties, first appeared in 1956, at the height of the McCarthy era. Smith shows enormous sympathy for those people prosecuted by the government in the crisis over the Alien and Sedition Acts. Yet he shows no sympathy for the individuals in government who were slandered by the Republicans. This lack of sympathy makes little sense if we remember that many, perhaps even most of those persecuted in the McCarthy era suffered from slander and innuendo (blacklists) rather than from government prosecution. Indeed, fear of being slandered by McCarthy led many individuals, including those in the highest offices in the land, to be more than reluctant to challenge him. McCarthy's slanders thus intimidated others' free speech, especially from those who might have criticized him. Apart from inattention to Hamilton's words, the principal fault in Smith's reading of the crisis produced by the Alien and Sedition Acts is that he does not take into account the possibility that slander and libel can have a chilling effect on political opposition. Though this is an old-fashioned view, it is not without its thoughtful advocates, including Thucydides and Machiavelli, who suggested that slander may be most dangerous to free speech in time of war. Hamilton himself suggested that fears of being slandered increasingly deterred leading Federalists from seeking public office, with grave consequences for the future of party conflict in America. If only the naive and the undistinguished chose to serve or run as Federalists, it was merely a matter of time before they would become so ineffective and demoralized that they could no longer compete in the system.[31]

Slander was not confined to the Republicans' arsenal, however. Federalist newspapers, including some influenced by Hamilton, gave as well as they got throughout the 1790s. They slandered Jefferson as much as his allies slandered Hamilton. In the increasingly apocalyptic Federalist press, Jefferson was cast as a wild-eyed atheist and a rabid Jacobin with blood dripping from his mouth. As Miller observes, no Federalist ever suggested enforcing the Sedition Act to protect the reputation of the vice-president. Nonetheless, Jefferson emerged from this nasty morass with much more of his reputation intact than Hamilton, possibly because, unlike Hamilton, he did not waste his time trying to refute every slur on his honor. Hamilton wrote long hours into the night trying to save his fame, but the sage of Monticello prudently demurred from tactics that might have lent credence to slander by appearing to take it seriously. Before he became president and long before there was a White House rose garden, Jefferson adopted what we today call a "rose garden" political strategy for the election of 1800. Though he wrote volumes to friends and allies, he wrote almost nothing for the public papers. He commonly refused to respond to his critics, a task that he left to others. He thereby appeared to be above the fray that he helped to inspire.[32]

It is not clear whether Republican editors knew it, but this difference in political tactics, arising from significant differences in character (Jefferson generally preferring to avoid direct conflict and Hamilton seemingly leading with his chin), was a godsend to their cause. Jefferson appeared presidential precisely because he did not seem political. In contrast, Hamilton sometimes appeared far less statesmanlike because he could never shrug off slurs as a necessary and inevitable consequence of political partisanship. Among the slanders Hamilton suffered was the partisan-inspired charge that he had used federal funds for private speculation as secretary of the treasury. This led to the remarkable spectacle of Hamilton's confessing to the private vice of adultery to save his public honor as a statesman. After a lengthy congressional investigation, the Republicans could pin on Hamilton only some creative accounting by which he temporarily used money from one federal account to serve the needs of another. Despite the evidence in Madison's own handwriting (which Jefferson must have seen) that Hamilton said he meant to go only as far "as republican principles will permit" to strengthen the national government, he was never able to confound the persistent accusations that he actually meant to establish a monarchy at the Federal Convention. Jefferson, who consistently treated Hamilton as the head of a monarchical conspiracy, encouraged those accusations in every possible way.

In response, Hamilton could say only that

> a very small number of men indeed may entertain theories less republican than those of Mr. Jefferson & Mr. Madison; but I am persuaded there is not a Man among them who would not regard as both criminal & visionary any attempt to subvert the republican system of the Country. Most of these men rather fear that it may not justify itself by its fruits, than feel a predilection for a different form; and their fears are not diminished by the factions and fanatical politics

encouraged by the Republican press. In notes Jefferson himself took to record a conversation with Hamilton, the latter was quite blunt in explaining his own ambivalence toward the republican experiment. He feared the Republic would not be energetic or stable enough. If it failed, then something more elevated might have to be tried. Yet he also said the experiment was more successful than he had originally expected and was susceptible to even greater improvement. All such improvements, he said, "ought to be tried before we give up the republican form altogether for that mind must be really depraved which would not prefer the equality of political rights which is the foundation of pure republicanism, if it can be obtained consistently with order." Yet Hamilton also hated saints, especially self-appointed political ones. Not surprisingly, as early as 1792 and for the rest of his public career, he complained bitterly against the self-righteous spirit that led his adversaries to stigmatize mere disputes over policy as signs of infidelity to the Republic. He realized that

> a certain party considered themselves the sole and rightful censors of the Republic; and every attempt to bestow praise or blame not originating from them, as an usurpation of their prerogative, every stricture on their immaculate band as a breach of their privilege. They appear to think themselves authorized to deal out anathemas, without measure, or mercy, against all who dare to swerve from their standard of political orthodoxy, which are to be borne without retaliation or murmur. And if any system of either shows itself, they are sure to raise the dismal cry of persecution; themselves the first to avail, and the first to complain. But what is not permitted to men who have so clearly established a title, little less than divine, to a monopoly of all the patriotic virtues![33]

As John C. Miller has observed, in Hamilton's view the "favorite device of these assassins of character . . . was the Big Lie." Quoting Hamilton, Miller then observes that

> "it is a maxim deeply engrafted in that dark system, that no character, however upright, is a match for constantly reiterated attacks, however false. . . . Every calumny makes some proselytes, and even retains some; since justification seldom circulates as rapidly or as widely as slander. . . . The public mind fatigued at length with the calumnies which eternally assail it . . . is apt at the end to sit down with the opinion that a person so often accused cannot be entirely innocent."[34]

This is the fundamental principle of what we today call negative political advertising. Where there is so much ugly smoke, the public is led to believe there must be an evil fire. In the face of the big lie, there are only two serious options. Statesmen can ignore it, as Jefferson usually did, or they can attack it, as Hamilton almost always did. Each tactic has its risks, but for attack to have any chance of being effective, it has to be measured, stated in the right time in the right way to the right people. By 1800, however, this approach grew increasingly more difficult for Hamilton, who resented deeply Republican insinuations that he was a Caesar (and therefore, that they were the party of Cato and Brutus).[35] It was bad enough that he had to sustain such charges from his worst enemies. When John Adams chose to lend his authority to the prevailing slanders against the inspector general, Hamilton decided to defend his reputation by destroying that of the president.

T wo common answers account for the feud between Adams and Hamilton that helped split their party during the election of 1800: Adams came to see Hamilton as a militarist, who had to be stopped at all costs; and the leading Federalists saw Adams as erratic and indecisive. In the first explanation, Adams appears as a traditional Whig more representative of the country persuasion's fears of standing armies than as a modernizing Federalist of the more courtlike persuasion of Hamilton. In the second, Adams seems jealous, vindictive, and unstable. Thus, for example, Theodore Sedgwick wrote Hamilton of Adams's "odd brooding" about fatalistically submitting to the general's raising an army. He feared that taxes and the army would render him and the Federalists unpopular. He also complained of a conspiracy in his own cabinet, none of whose members were especially fond of him, to rob him of his power and elevate the military over the civil authorities. To supply balance to policy as he understood it, Adams unbalanced his party, which regarded his efforts to seek peace with France as both disgraceful and dangerous.[36] Neither of these views is incompatible with the other. The more the Hamiltonian wing of the party stressed firmness, the more Adams might convince himself he was opposing militarism; the more quickly and decisively he moved to stamp it out, however, the more other members of his party would regard his approach as unbalanced. Though helpful for explaining the dynamic of the feud, neither of these views gets to its source. Neither says much about Adams's and Hamilton's different perceptions of the French threat and the appropriate means to confront it. If we grant each of them their assumptions, then their suspicions of each other appear quite reasonable.

Rather than impute illegitimate motives to either man, in the traditional fashion of their descendants and most ardent partisans, it seems both more fair and accurate to think about how their different understandings of themselves at their best contributed to their misunderstandings of each other. In this case, classical history may be more important for understanding them than modern philosophy. Equality, rights, consent, and revolution—these modern principles were as self-evident to them as they were to Jefferson. Yet the roles American statesmen would play as they sought to establish their new order of the ages were not. The most illustrious models of republican statesmanship lay in the writings of the ancient historians, whose heroes were objects of envy and emulation for Americans, and perhaps to none more than Adams and Hamilton, who were both desirous of great fame. If an American Plutarch ever chose to write their stories, they therefore meant to play their parts well.

In the Quasi-War, Hamilton cast himself as an American Demosthenes, warning of danger from a new Macedonia. Indeed, one of his favorite passages from antiquity was from Demosthenes. "As a general marches at the head of his troops," said the Athenian, "so too ought wise politicians, if I dare use the expression, to march at the head of events; insomuch as they ought not to wait the *event* to know the measures to take, but the measures they have taken ought to produce the *event*." This maxim could be regarded as the essence of Hamilton's conception of responsible statesmanship: the effort to carve out room for choice by means of reflection, based on anticipation of future danger and opportunity. Next to the passage from Demosthenes, Hamilton copied another from Longinus: "Where attack him it will be said? Ah Athenians, war, war itself will discover you his weak sides if you seek them." Hamilton then added his own estimation of these precepts of ancient military wisdom: "sublimely simple."[37] To shape events rather than to see his country shaped by fortune and the arms of other countries during the Quasi-War, Hamilton developed an aggressive strategy that not only prepared for the worst but also sought to derive maximum advantage from the vulnerability of the South, and of New Orleans especially. Perhaps inevitably, however, this aggressive strategy was likely to be understood as militaristic by observers who saw no immediate need to act with energy. It led not only Jefferson but also Adams to see Hamilton in a radically different role from the one he envisioned for himself; it also led them to cast themselves in more conventional republican roles. If Hamilton was an American Caesar, Adams had no choice but to play an American Cato.

According to Elkins and McKitrick, Adams began to think of peace almost immediately after Washington forced him to accept Hamilton as inspector general. Other Federalists, however, doubted that a stable peace with France was possible. They also feared that a peace mission would undermine the army by producing a false sense that the war was over. When Adams began to receive hints from Talleyrand in fall 1798 that the Directory was willing to negotiate a peace, his cabinet opposed sending a new mission to France, fearing that the government would be humiliated again. Nonetheless, Adams hinted in a message to Congress on 8 December that he might send a new envoy to France if he were treated with respect. That same month, his cabinet proposed a new general officer position, general of the army, which outraged Adams, who saw it as an effort to limit his power. Not surprisingly, he was completely unwilling to work with Francisco Miranda or otherwise to support Hamilton's southern strategy.

Quite rightly, as events turned out, Adams feared the taxes that were required to support the army would render the Federalists unpopular. He also saw the *Virginia* and *Kentucky Resolutions* as a deep wound to the Union. The pressure from Hamilton and other Federalists to maintain the army after the Battle of the Nile seemed more than likely to aggravate this wound and to doom the Federalists at the polls. On 18 February 1799, Adams therefore struck out with a policy calculated to "damage extremists" within his party and end the war as well. Without consulting his cabinet, which he mistrusted and despised, he nominated William Vans Murray as the new envoy to France. This abrupt move stunned other Federalists, who did think Adams was erratic, suspected that negotiations were a French trick, worried about the impact of a new mission on national resolve, and wondered whether Adams was sacrificing national honor and security in a bid to improve his prospects for reelection. Quite erroneously, both Washington and Hamilton feared that Adams would involve the United States in the world war on the side of France. When Washington died in December 1799, Hamilton also worried that there would be no one left to control Adams (and Adams as well as leading Republicans apparently feared the reverse, that no one would be able to control Hamilton). In mid-1799, however, prospects of some kind of agreement looked promising to Adams. Napoleon was stranded in Egypt, and the French had been defeated in Italy. From Adams's point of view, it was therefore a good time for the French to consolidate and for the Americans to seek a bargain. He must therefore have been overjoyed when news arrived in September that the French would receive the new envoy. Since Republicans consistently accused the Federalists of warmongering to maintain their power (a tactic designed, in part, to help them win at the polls), negotiations allowed Adams to remove that stigma from his administration. Not coincidentally, it also allowed him to put on the toga of Cato.[38]

In October, Hamilton met Adams by coincidence in Trenton and asked him to suspend the mission. Hamilton's pleas appear to have been based on two assumptions: that the Directory would soon fall (as it did a month later) and that rumors of peace would lead England to attack American commerce (which happened within months of Murray's appointment). As Forrest McDonald suggests, Hamilton apparently feared French diplomacy almost as much as French arms. Rather than negotiate openly with France, Hamilton later advised John Marshall that he thought it best for Adams to proclaim the de facto end of the war. To do so, he suggested, would gain the fruits of peace without negotiations (which might produce a false sense of security among Americans). The Franco-American alliance of 1778 was certainly nullified by French attacks on American shipping, but Hamilton feared that France would demand to be released from obligations to compensate Americans for lost shipping in exchange for a formal renunciation of the alliance. He also worried that the French peace offensive was another effort to manipulate American elections. That Congress had suspended further enlistments in the army in December struck him as strategically absurd. He regarded the American buildup, and the resolve it had shown, as one of the chief reasons the French were willing to negotiate; to give it up was therefore to remove the principal cause of their desire for peace. In his view, proclaiming the de facto end of the war and abrogation of the alliance would give Americans as much as they were likely to achieve through negotiations, without the illusion that the international crisis was over. The inspector general insisted that the United States could not rely on treaties for its security, especially not with France. Americans still needed to be prepared for war.

Gilbert Lycan and John Miller suggest that Hamilton came very close to understanding French diplomatic intentions. According to them, undermining American resolve was probably Talleyrand's essential purpose. He was determined to acquire Louisiana, by purchase if necessary, and did not want any interference from the United States. Negotiations thereby became a means to achieve at the bargaining table what he had failed to win by arms. If Lycan and Miller are correct, Talleyrand largely succeeded. The combined effects of the confinement of the war to the Caribbean, French defeats, and renewed hopes for peace made measures that seemed like prudent policy in 1798 look like hysteria in 1799. With no French to fight in the United States, few citizens volunteered to join the army. Officers began to refuse their commissions; they had better things to do than parade soldiers for a war that seemed as distant as France itself. Pending the outcome of negotiations in Paris, Congress reduced the Additional Army to 4,000 soldiers in February 1800. By spring of that year, most Americans assumed the war was over.[39]

With Washington dead, the army becoming ever more unpopular, deep suspicions of everyone around him, and a strong determination to save his presidency, Adams decided to fire the most Hamiltonian members of his cabinet, Timothy Pickering and James McHenry, in May 1800. Perhaps to shore up the southern vote, they were replaced by Virginians, John Marshall as secretary of state and Samuel Dexter as secretary of war.[40] In the view of many Federalists, as well as of Hamilton, Adams had thereby compounded strategic folly with personal vindictiveness. In the heat of firing Pickering and McHenry, Adams not only suggested that these men were mere tools of Hamilton, but he also asserted that Hamilton was a bastard and the leader of a "British faction" in the United States. Hamilton could not deny the facts of his birth, though they hardly seemed relevant to great issues of state. He was nonetheless incensed by Adams's charge that he was leading a British faction, which seemed to call into question Hamilton's loyalty to his country.[41]

This was not the sort of remark Hamilton was likely to take lightly. In 1779, for example, he had challenged William Gordon to a duel for asserting that Hamilton was an American Cromwell who had said it was time for the army to rise up and get rid of Congress. That Hamilton was willing to risk his life to defend his honor against this kind of allegation reminds us of his own opposition to militarism. Nonetheless, he must have said something to have inspired the comment. He apparently never understood that the kinds of arguments he made in his letter to James Duane in 1780, for example, alarmed the more conventional Whigs, who often feared American armies more than foreign enemies. Moreover, Hamilton had been involved in other affairs of honor. All told, he participated in eleven of them, either as a second or as a potential combatant, including a near duel with a future president, James Monroe.[42] Though only the last affair, with Aaron Burr, issued in an actual duel, the habitual pattern in Hamilton's behavior deserves attention. He believed his intentions were honorable and yet had a habit of giving others the impression that they were not. Consequently, his honor was frequently questioned, and he believed he was compelled to defend it.

At this point, Hamilton's quarrel with Adams takes on the character of a Renaissance revenge tragedy. In August 1800 Hamilton sent Adams a terse note asking him to explain his comment about Hamilton's leadership of a British faction. Since such notes were customary preludes to duels, one must wonder about Hamilton's intentions when he sent it. Did he mean to challenge the president to a duel? The idea was insane. For precisely that reason, Hamilton was left with precious few means of vindicating his name. When he received no reply from the president, he sent Adams a letter complaining of his "base, wicked and cruel calumny." He also suggested that the president was sacrificing the reputation of a loyal servant of the Republic to "electioneering purposes." This act of disrespect bordered on insubordination from the inspector general and ought not to have been tolerated by Adams, even though he had inspired and largely deserved it. Hamilton should have resigned or Adams have demanded his resignation. Instead, the latter remained silent, which led the former to fire off a pamphlet-length *Letter from Alexander Hamilton, Concerning the Public Conduct and Character of John Adams, Esq., President of the United States.*[43] Written 24 October, just weeks before the November presidential election, it was a thinly disguised effort to shift the votes of Federalist electors from Adams to Charles Cotesworth Pinckney. Though advised by other leaders of his party not to circulate the letter, and certainly not to put his name to it, Hamilton spent forty-nine printed pages attacking the sitting president and leader of his party as vain, jealous, vindictive, impractical, and capricious. He spent the last three pages defending his own name against Adams's accusation that he was the leader of a British faction. Strangely, he concluded by calling on Federalist electors to give equal votes to Pinckney and Adams, apparently believing this suggestion would protect him from the charge that he had divided his party during the election. Though supposedly meant to be confidential, the letter eventually found its way into the newspapers. Republicans were delighted at the spectacle of their two worst enemies feuding at a time when unity was essential to preserve their control of the government.[44]

It is difficult to understand why Hamilton believed this letter would serve a useful purpose for his party. In truth, it was a cry of pain—an act of defiance against a president who seemed both foolish and cruel to Hamilton. In private, however, before he released the letter, he suggested that Adams was such a terrible president that it was best to support Pinckney, even at the risk of dividing the party and seeing Jefferson elected. Indeed, Hamilton suggested that it was preferable for the Federalists for Jefferson to be elected: "Under Adams as under Jefferson," Hamilton observed, "the government will sink. The party in the hands of whose chief it shall sink will sink with it and the advantages will all be on the side of its adversaries." If the Federalists in New England and the Middle States supported Adams and Pinckney equally, but Pinckney's supporters in South Carolina refused to support Adams, then Hamilton believed either Pinckney or Jefferson would become president. In the first case, Hamilton would have had his personal choice as president; in the latter, he would have prevented his party from assuming the responsibility for a bad government. Strangely, Hamilton seemed to think it was better to unite the party through hatred of Jefferson than to see it divided through hatred of Adams. Thus, even if Jefferson won in 1800, his election might improve the Federalists' chances in the 1804 presidential election.[45]

These speculations were not the only signs that Hamilton's partisanship was getting the better of his judgment. As Elkins and McKitrick reveal, exactly how Americans would select presidential electors was in considerable flux at the time. Some states had their legislatures pick electors, and others had them chosen by citizens in their districts. There was a good deal of maneuvering to extract the maximum partisan advantage from the different processes. In theory, there was nothing odd about Hamilton's notorious suggestion to John Jay, the governor of New York, that the Federalist-controlled legislature allow the electors to be selected in their districts rather than by the state legislature, as had been the previous practice in New York. As Hamilton emphasized to Jay, such a move was both "*legal* and *constitutional.*" Yet the proposal was also designed to prevent an incoming Republican legislature from picking the electors. As Jay suggested when he received Hamilton's proposal, it appeared to be governed too much by the spirit of party. Hamilton's maneuvering was not duplicitous, however. The legislature would have had to vote publicly to change the selection method, and he was certain this would provoke a bitter partisan fight. He granted that the suggestion violated decorum, if nothing else, because it would have changed the electoral rules in the middle of the game, but he insisted the Federalists would go down in defeat if they stuck to the high road while their opponents did not.

This rationalization of a policy, which he admitted he would not have advocated in other circumstances clearly reveals the extent to which all sides in this dispute were guided by faith in their own rectitude. Despite the moderation Hamilton had shown in opposing the Alien and Sedition Acts and in reacting to the *Virginia* and *Kentucky Resolutions,* he too was getting drunk on his party's cause. Jay was much more sober. Changing the rules in the middle of the game was going too far.[46]

Nonetheless, Hamilton played the electoral college game as well as anyone in the country. He had sought to sway the votes of electors to ensure that Washington rather than Adams would win the first two presidential elections and to prevent Jefferson from winning the presidential election of 1796. In light of his apparent success through 1796, Hamilton's scheme in 1800, though admittedly bizarre, was not simply crazy. As he had predicted, most of New England voted for Adams and Pinckney, but South Carolina's votes went to Jefferson and Burr. Had South Carolina supported Pinckney, the scheme would have worked. Instead, Jefferson and Burr tied in the Electoral College with seventy-three votes each; Adams received sixty-five and Pinckney sixty-four.[47]

In 1800 the kingmaker lost, and he lost his party's confidence as well. It is unclear whether Hamilton's critique of Adams had any decisive influence on the presidential election, however. The result may well have been a foregone conclusion by the time the letter was published. Many attribute the Federalists' defeat to other causes such as high taxes, Adams's confusing shifts in policy, and the galvanizing force of the Alien and Sedition Acts on the Republicans. Nonetheless, the letter could have made a difference, and that was enough for most leading Federalists to come to doubt Hamilton's judgment and loyalty as a party leader. Even the most ordinary party hack knows that actual control of the presidency is almost always preferable to the mere possibility of future control under presumably more favorable circumstances. When the election was thrown into the House, Hamilton's efforts to sway Federalists to support Jefferson over Burr revealed the absurdity of preferring Jefferson even to Adams. Hamilton observed that Jefferson would probably temporize when faced with the responsibility of governing. From previous experience, Hamilton also argued that Jefferson would be a much firmer supporter of energy in the executive in practice than he was in principle.[48] If so, there was no good reason to think that Jefferson's administration would necessarily fail or prove itself immediately unpopular; indeed there was every reason to fear it would succeed, especially if the Republicans gained control of Congress, as in fact they did in 1800. By risking the election of Jefferson in 1800, Hamilton made a riverboat gamble on an assumption that he himself had to admit was not necessarily true. Insofar as his letter may have helped Jefferson, he may also have given his greatest adversary time to consolidate power while denying his own party the most effectual means of resisting the Republicans.

In the absence of a rational political motive for Hamilton's public critique of Adams, many of its readers thought it was written for vainglory. As Fisher Ames politely but firmly scolded Hamilton, in "political affairs few act so much from respect for truth as for stage effect." Ames then quoted a passage from Alexander Pope's *An Essay on Man* that suggested that the appearance created by the letter contained more than a little truth. "In the sphere of politics," he observed, "'All would be gods and rush into the skies.'" Though the quotation was inaccurate, Ames must have presumed Hamilton knew the poem well enough to catch his drift:

> In pride, in reasoning pride, our error lies;
> All quit their sphere and rush into the skies!
> Pride still aiming at the blessed abodes,
> Men would be angels, angels would be gods.
> Aspiring to be gods if angels fell,
> Aspiring to be angels men rebel.[49]

George Cabot wrote Hamilton that his letter was not only untimely and imprudent but also perceived as a sign of a fundamental flaw in his character. He was accused by "respectable men of Egotism" and of the "same vanity" that he had claimed was a "dangerous quality & great weakness in Mr. Adams." Cabot also knew how to misquote Pope with skill. He asserted as "a fact" another line from Pope's *Essay*. The "'truths would you teach or save a sinking land, all shun, none aid you & few will understand.'"[50] The message from Hamilton's friends and allies was clear. His pen was out of control because his pride had no limits.

Hamilton's sword, however, was not out of control. In the months prior to the election and his critique of Adams, the inspector general was required to demobilize the army. Jefferson feared that Hamilton would launch a coup d'etat rather than do so. He carried out the order from the elected civilian leadership, however, just as he had carried out the other orders he had received. As a last stab at his opponents, however, Hamilton asked McHenry to set up a camp of instruction for the army. With at least four professors to teach much-needed technical skills in engineering and artillery fire, and with the best officers and NCOs selected to keep the dwindling army in professional form, he hoped it would be a "perfect substitute for a military academy." With his inauguration pending, Jefferson then rode in from Monticello to destroy what Richard Kohn calls the Hamiltonian "cancer" on the Republic.[51]

In truth, however, there was no such cancer. It existed in the minds of Jefferson and Adams, among many others, but certainly not in Hamilton's practice. If the successful transfer of power from one party to another is one of the great lessons all republics must learn about civil-military relations, Hamilton, his army, and his party graduated from the school of hard knocks summa cum laude. As the new Republican administration moved in, Hamilton retired to practice law, rally the faithful as best he could, and contemplate writing his Baconian treatise on government. He still had some allies and some influence, but he never again had a significant impact on national policy. Thus, unlike Churchill, whose years in the wilderness preceded his finest hour, Hamilton found himself unable to make a substantial impact on the greatest war of his time. Like one of those "discontented ghosts" he had described in *The Federalist,* he could do little more than sigh for a place he was "destined never more to possess."[52]

Perhaps the ancient philosophers were partial to tragedy primarily because the tragedians shared a common goal, self-knowledge. This is most exemplified in Oedipus, who was blind to (and blinded by) his pride long before he blinded his own eyes. Hamilton's friends saw blindness in him long before he saw it in himself, but in a moment of tragic recognition even he admitted that his pride had made him indiscreet on more than one occasion. In a letter to his son, James Hamilton, just a few days before his death, he wrote a short treatise on discretion. Jonathan Swift, Hamilton wrote, called discretion an "Aldermanly virtue," that is, a low, mundane form of prudence that enables individuals and even statesmen to pass through the world without either giving or taking much offense. Given his great and estimable qualities, Hamilton continued, Swift possessed little discretion himself and thus "was disposed to turn it into derision. But his own experience should have taught him, that if not a splendid, it is at least a very useful virtue, and ought on that account to be cultivated and cherished." This admission becomes even more poignant when one realizes that Hamilton's son Philip had been killed a year before in a duel arising from the young man's indiscreet efforts to defend his father's honor. Hamilton must have wanted to see at least one of his sons survive the bitter quarrels of New York City politics in the first decade of the 1800s. He objected that Swift's view of discretion was "extremely dangerous." Such contempt for prudent speech "ought not to be hazarded even in jest, from [its] tendency to mislead the young and inexperienced." Then, sounding more like Polonius, he added that a "prudent silence will sometimes be taken for wisdom, and a sentence or two cautiously thrown in will sometimes gain the palm of knowledge."[53]

Hamilton's duel with Burr needs to be interpreted in light of this treatise. It suggests that the duel was the denouement rather than the climax of Hamilton's career. Were not the pseudonymous letters Hamilton wrote to defend his honor an extension of the dueling mentality into the newspapers? Eventually, a statesman with that mentality was bound to generate more enemies than friends in political life. And thus did Hamilton become an outcast from national politics. Sooner or later, he was also bound to encounter a rival who would prefer to settle their disputes on a more conventional field of honor. For many years, Hamilton had written numerous letters denouncing Burr. They were meant to be widely distributed and therefore could not have escaped Burr's notice. He warned that Burr was an "embryo-Caesar," an idolizer of Bonaparte, a debtor, a voluptuary, and a political opportunist without honor, principle, or any love of fame. Rightly or wrongly, he regarded Burr as the most dangerous man in America. Precisely because Hamilton saw Burr as many of his contemporaries saw him, his confrontation with the vice-president becomes even more poignant. Hamilton declared that he felt a "religious duty" to oppose Burr, apparently for the same reason that Adams, Jefferson, and others felt such a duty to oppose Hamilton. Ironically, then, Hamilton did to Burr what Adams had done to him. He called into question his loyalty to the United States. Given Burr's later trial for treason in the Jefferson administration, there is ample reason to suspect that Hamilton had divined Burr's character. Since he had successfully opposed Burr's bids to become president in 1800 and governor of New York in 1804, it was also likely that Burr blamed him for his own political misfortunes.[54]

Hamilton went further than he believed delicacy allowed to avoid a duel, but he also refused to give in to Burr's ultimatum that he disavow any accusations that might have implied that Burr's character was "despicable." Given his earlier candor, to have granted Burr a complete disavowal would have been an absolute disgrace for Hamilton. He disavowed any words that might have called into question Burr's private character as a gentleman, but he refused to retract any he had said about Burr as a politician. In several notes and letters, he asserted that he could no longer be politically useful if he caved in to Burr's demand, which required him to treat their long political opposition as a complete lie. He also pledged not to fire at Burr, because, he wrote, it was incompatible with his religion to kill in private combat. Nor did he wish to violate the laws against dueling. He was therefore trapped in a dilemma from which he believed no gentleman or successful politician of his time could escape. In his world, it was dishonorable not to accept Burr's challenge if he refused to disavow his charges, but it was equally dishonorable to try to kill him. Thus he believed he could do only what he had advised his son to do before he was killed. He had to stand his ground and then fire in the air. Had he done less, he would have been unworthy of his own son's death; had he done more, he would have been guilty of murder. To avoid even the accidental death of Burr, he is reported to have refused to set the hair trigger on his pistol. Although Burr's seconds insisted that Hamilton actually shot at him, Hamilton's seconds claimed that he did not try to do so but that his pistol went off when he was wounded. Hamilton did not believe it had been fired, however. He even warned one of his seconds that it was still loaded as he was evacuated from the field at

Weehawken. As McDonald observes, the *code duello* did not require either Burr or Hamilton to try to kill each other. Quite commonly, each participant in a duel proved his manhood, if not his honor, by facing the shot of his adversary, who deliberately sought not to kill him and hoped not to be killed in return. Killing Hamilton was Burr's choice.[55]

No matter how much one might sympathize with Hamilton's dilemma, or admire his courage, his treatise on discretion reveals that he accepted the blame for putting himself in a position in which he had to choose between risking death or dishonor. Before he died, he admitted that he might have expressed his opposition to Burr in a manner far less dangerous to himself. As if he were telling his son the story of his life, the worried father observed that a man, like himself, "well informed but indiscreet and unreserved will not uncommonly talk himself out of all consideration and weight. . . . The greatest abilities are sometimes thrown into the shade by this defect or are prevented from obtaining the success to which they are entitled." Those who cannot overcome this vice, "are apt to make and have numerous enemies" and become involved in great "difficulties and dangers." Hamilton therefore wanted his son to take Homer, not Swift, as his model. "Discretion is the MENTOR which ought to accompany every young Telemachos in his journey through life." Hamilton did not recommend that his son should follow the example of Benjamin Franklin, by disguising his pride as humility. The point was not to be loved or idolized but to survive, and to be worthy of surviving, by developing a solid character as a man of sober judgment. How might military men avoid the fates of Coriolanus, and of Hamilton himself? Hamilton's implicit answer to his son was to be more like George Washington. Though taking care "not to assume a character artificial, disguised, and covert," Hamilton advised his son to study or methodically to attempt in his "discourses and actions to be circumspect and discreet."[56] One can only conjecture whether James Hamilton took his father's parting words to heart, but he survived to care for his bereaved mother and later to write a multivolume biography of his father.

Epilogue:
Vigilance and Responsibility
Reconsidered

In Book 6 of the *Peloponnesian War*, Thucydides reports a debate in Syracuse between Hermocrates, the leader of the oligarchic faction, and Athenagoras, the leader of the democratic faction. Hermocrates warns the Syracusans that the Athenians are determined to conquer all of Sicily. He knows the Athenians have sent several reconnaissance expeditions to seek out allies among its constantly warring cities. To be sure, Sicily is separated from Athens by a large expanse of water, but the Athenians have already proved themselves daring beyond all measure. Not many years before, they had sent their navy to conquer Egypt, and they almost succeeded. As the Peloponnesian War spreads throughout Hellas, the Athenians have become adept at exploiting democratic factions within the Greek cities in order to divide them and weaken their will to resist. Hermocrates fears this will happen in Syracuse. In response, Athenagoras takes the view that the Athenians have no intention of overextending their empire by attacking Sicily. He accuses Hermocrates of whipping up war hysteria merely in order to give his oligarchic party control of the Syracusan army. With such control, he fears, Hermocrates would overthrow the democracy and rule by force alone. At the end of the debate, an elder citizen of Syracuse stands up and pleads for moderation. It is not fitting, he says, for the partisans to slander each other thus when the fate of their city is at stake.

As it turns out, Hemocrates was right: the Athenians did come, and in large numbers. The Syracusans were so unprepared that they almost lost the war. Consequently, students of this great war commonly have enormous admiration for Hermocrates. Athenagoras has gone down in history as a demagogue, although there was absolutely no necessity for his ill-repute. Hermocrates may have intended to use the war to increase his party's power, in which case the suspicions of Athenagoras seem quite reasonable. Indeed, just a few years later, an oligarchy overthrew the Athenian democracy, justifying itself by asserting it was more capable of managing Athens' war with Sparta. This claim turned out to be largely true, but the oligarchs were so determined to keep their power that they later conspired to open the Piraeus, or port of Athens, to the Spartans, whom they hoped would protect them from democrats in Athens. To preserve their power, they betrayed their city.

Thucydides' study of war and free government was meant to be a legacy for all time.[1] If we extrapolate from a historical case study, which Thucydides did not hesitate to suggest might have universal significance, we can say that the quarrel between the vigilant and the responsible is rooted in the nature of democratic politics. The quarrel also tends to become most intense in time of war. There is good reason to suspect that some individuals may rely on war fever in order to preserve and increase their power. There is equally good reason to suspect that others, in order to preserve or gain power for themselves, will accuse even the most responsible statesmen of exaggerating threats from abroad in order to rule by force at home. It is also completely possible for the vigilant and the responsible to be animated by the most upright intentions. They may suspect the worst of each other because they perceive threats differently and have developed distinct strategies for confronting them. This tragedy of mutual misperception, each side pushing the other to ever greater extremes, seems most likely to occur in the founding of a republic, when it is most fragile and fears for its durability are most acute.

Quite unintentionally, the leading Founders staged this sort of tragedy during the Quasi-War. The Federalists were no less loyal than the Republicans to the new Constitution's efforts to replace the government by "accident and force" with a new kind of political order, rooted in "reflection and choice," but they feared France and disunion more than England and military power. As one of the leaders of the most hawkish wing of the Federalists, Hamilton feared French intentions much more than the Republicans did and at least as much as Adams. Yet because Adams did not share Hamilton's perception of French capabilities, it is fair to say that the president and his inspector general were waging two completely different kinds of wars, a limited eighteenth-century naval war in Adams's case and a modern world war in Hamilton's. The more Hamilton struggled to prepare his country for the new age of warfare, the more he sowed the seeds of his own destruction by pushing Adams in the direction of the most vigilant Republicans.

The Founders remained generally moderate until 1798, but faith in one's virtue often blurs judgment. One by one, the leading actors in the drama, Adams, Jefferson, Madison, and Hamilton, not to mention numerous minor players, grew drunk on their own rectitude. The extreme charges during the polarization of the parties and within the Federalist party then led Hamilton to make an enormous error in judgment. Though the provocations from his president were serious, he overreacted in defense of his honor. He thereby contributed to the downfall of the Federalists in 1800 and significantly limited his chances of exercising great political influence again. From this perspective, Hamilton was responsible for his own tragedy, because it resulted partly from his indiscretions, and yet not responsible for it, because his more conventional contemporaries did not understand the true character of the war in which their country was engaged.

Was Hamilton right about the danger from France? If Adams's decision to send William Vans Murray to Paris truly succeeded in ending the struggle with France, there is reason to suspect he was not. Indeed, in later years, Adams referred to this decision as the most disinterested act of his life. Lest the judgment of history fail to take his service into account, however, he also asked that the inscription on his grave read, "Here lies John Adams, who took upon himself the responsibility for peace with France in the year 1800." Since the Quasi-War never became a land war in the United States, historians have generally accepted Adams's version of the story. As his term came to an end in spring 1801, Adams did achieve a peace treaty with France. Although it provided no compensation to the United States, the alliance with France was officially terminated. In effect, Adams bought his way out of the 1778 alliance by surrendering American claims for compensation. The war ended and so too did the domestic convulsions it had produced in the United States. Hence, John Miller, John Bassett, Richard Kohn, and a host of other scholars suggest that Adams succeeded in stamping out the militarism that they associate with the Hamiltonian wing of the Federalist party.[2]

Yet there is good evidence to support Hamilton's suspicions that negotiations with France had lulled Adams and most Americans into a false sense of security. Especially under Napoleon, the real danger of militarism in the Founding era came from France. As Hamilton reminded Americans after the election of 1800, France was not a figment of the ideological imagination. It was a "real despotism garnished and defended by five hundred thousand men in disciplined array." Although Americans have traditionally looked at negotiations as an alternative to both war and arming for war, diplomacy is sometimes the continuation of war by other means. As Forrest McDonald observes, the same day that Napoleon agreed to end the war with the United States, he also acquired Louisiana and the Floridas by secret agreement with Spain. The United States was thereby removed from the list of combatants against France while the French achieved their objectives in

North America without having to fight for them. Would John Adams have concluded peace with France had he known of this secret agreement? Probably not. He might have asked Congress to declare war against France; Hamilton's dogs of war would probably have been unleashed against New Orleans; and then no one would have raised the ugly cry of militarism.

As Henry Adams suggested in his account of the retrocession of Louisiana, Napoleon and Talleyrand deceived his illustrious ancestor. In spring 1802, when the retrocession became public knowledge, Hamilton took it as substantial vindication of his strategy during the Quasi-War. Writing under the pseudonym Pericles in various essays in the *New York Evening Post*, he continued to insist that New Orleans was too important to be controlled by France or any other foreign power. As one option, he considered negotiations to acquire the mouth of the Mississippi, but he also suggested that the danger to the United States was dire enough to justify seizing and occupying Louisiana before French troops arrived. After all, if Napoleon meant to hold his newly acquired North American empire, he had to occupy it. The Corsican then raised not one but two armies to be sent to the Western Hemisphere. This was Hamilton's worst-case scenario, yet bad luck for the French quickly became good luck for the United States. The French generals had orders to occupy New Orleans (and then do what?), but one army was frozen in port in Holland and the other was waylaid to suppress a slave revolt in Haiti, where it quickly found itself in a quagmire. All told, 20,000 French soldiers, that is, more than three times as many soldiers as Hamilton raised in 1800, died in Haiti. As Hamilton observed, the courage of rebellious slaves and the persistence of malaria-carrying mosquitoes in Haiti did more for American security than the army and navy that the Republicans began to dismantle during their watch. Jefferson and his country then had a true stroke of luck. Because Napoleon needed hard cash for other projects, he offered American negotiators a deal no responsible statesman could have refused: he would sell all of Louisiana. By setting his constitutional scruples aside when he accepted the offer, Jefferson effected the greatest American diplomatic coup of the nineteenth century.[3]

Far more than is commonly acknowledged, then, chance has determined how we have come to understand the Founders during the world war from 1793 to 1815. Had even one of Napoleon's armies occupied New Orleans, we perhaps might think of Hamilton as an American Hermocrates. Or we might think of him as an American Demosthenes or a Pericles (names he chose for himself) rather than as an American Caesar, Cromwell, or Napoleon, the appellations he received from his adversaries. In truth, the name he deserves is ambiguous. In his handling of the Quasi-War he is best understood as an American Churchill, because he warned against the new and terrifying militarism from across the sea. In his relations with Adams and the Republicans, however, he was most like Coriolanus, because ultimately he could control neither his temper nor his tongue. Nevertheless, Napoleon's acquisition of Louisiana suggests that Hamilton's southern strategy was a reasonable response to a serious threat that could have brought lasting and severe damage to the Union. Since doubts about the seriousness of the threat are the major reason for the development of the militarist interpretation of Hamilton and his party, we should reconsider the propositions commonly advanced to support that thesis.

Like all parties, the Federalists had their share of hotheads and cranks. Hamilton himself believed that Timothy Pickering, for example, was easily one of them.[4] Hence, it is child's play to couple some angry statements by Federalists with suspicious ones by Republicans to create the specter of militarism in the Founding era. Such sensationalism does not get to the core of the matter, however. Instead of reading the great quarrel between the Federalists and the Republicans as a morality play, we should follow the example set by the bigger hearts and broader minds of the ancient tragedians, who understood that many of the bitterest political quarrels are rooted in opposing kinds of virtues. That some Federalist zealots may have wished to build up the army in case of subversion is undoubtedly true, but they honestly believed they were defending the Constitution against fanatics who would replace it with a system more French, and in their view, genuinely despotic. Few scholars doubt that these Federalists overreacted in their response to their opponents, but hasty decisions produced by anger, fear, and faith in one's own virtue do not constitute evidence of a militaristic predisposition to settle disputes by force alone.

The most striking feature of Hamilton's writings about the army is their focus on military strategy, organization, and logistics, that is, the responsibilities given him by George Washington and James McHenry. Hamilton never mentioned a desire to become permanent commander of the army, nor did he ever praise the army as a symbol or instrument of social control. Though there is absolutely no textual evidence of these two traits in Hamilton to support a militarist interpretation of him, there is abundant evidence to call into question a third feature, that Hamilton's overarching purpose was to use the army to intimidate his opponents. "Let us not establish a tyranny," Hamilton wrote; "energy is very different from violence." He therefore sought to moderate his party as it passed the Alien and Sedition Acts. His calibrated response to the threat of "revolution and blood" in the *Kentucky Resolutions* was designed to unite Americans through affection so far as possible, with force as the last resort and only if rebellion broke out.

The last component of the militarist thesis, that Hamilton meant to conduct offensive operations in the South, is undoubtedly true, but his stillborn strategy would have served both American interests and principles. If we try to understand the strategy in the larger context of Hamilton's view of the strategic situation of the United States, it emerges as part of his general plan to secure American independence by expelling the Europeans from the Western Hemisphere. Because he hoped to cast himself in the role of the liberator of Latin America during the Quasi-War, Hamilton is best understood as the great romantic of the Founding era. In the age of Bonaparte, he meant to be an anti-Bonaparte but with the same speed, energy, organization, and breadth of strategic vision. Ironically, and perhaps even inevitably, though his rivals perceived his many similarities to Napoleon (from whose talents Hamilton found it painful to detract), they overlooked his profound objections to the Corsican, whose megalomania led him to govern by force alone throughout Europe. The Republicans then overreacted in a manner that often made a bad strategic situation worse.

As one commentator has suggested, the election of 1800 brought the country party of vigilance to power in the United States. If that party's basic assumptions were that power was a "monster" and that governing was "wrong," however, it would be a mistake to interpret its moral animus as a rejection of modernity in the name of a system that we incautiously label classical politics.[5] Indeed, the practice of the ancients was essentially militaristic. As Hamilton recognized, the strategic situation of the ancient republics left them little alternative to turning their citizens into lifelong soldiers, who supported themselves by enslaving the majority of their populations, as in Sparta, or by conquering the world, as did Macedon and Rome.[6] Insofar as all the major Founders rejected these practices, the ancients represented a system they believed Americans should avoid, not one they should emulate. The common good is a dominant theme in classical political science, but the ancients have no monopoly on it. It also plays a significant role in modern liberal-republicanism, in which the security of individual rights is the common good of each citizen. Insofar as Jefferson made such security the goal of politics in the Declaration of Independence, for example, we ought to take him at his word. His quarrel with Hamilton did not arise from whether the United States should make securing rights the core of the American common good, but from how to do so in a world with no shortage of actual and potential threats to their common goal.

In reading Aristotle's *Politics,* among other works of classical political philosophers, those who wonder about the Founders' debts to the ancients need to go beyond his initial discussion of virtue as the goal of the city. They must also pay attention to the conclusion of his work, which is about tragedy, and the political enthusiasms that often produce it. If it is true that the Founders' republicanism was a secularized Puritanism, then this species of enthusiasm is foreign to the moderate spirit of classical political science as Aristotle understood it. Precisely because Puritanism, whether secular or not, lends itself to self-righteousness, it encourages the same moralistic immoderation among political partisans that Aristotle and the ancient tragedians meant to purge. That the leading Founders during the Quasi-War, save perhaps the ever-sober Washington, fell too much in love with their own virtues suggests the enduring value of the ancient science of politics, but more as a corrective to American moralism than as a source of it.

Most important, the vigilance we associate with the Jeffersonians is one of the major themes of the Enlightenment. As Paul Rahe has suggested, it arose from the politics of suspicion inaugurated by Machiavelli, but it quickly evolved into distrust of all authority and therefore into a clarion call for moral, intellectual, and political self-reliance. Hence, philosophers such as Descartes and Bacon sought to found a new science, a new way of interpreting the world, built on suspicion of any assumption we cannot prove and demonstrate for ourselves. Such suspicion is with us today, and has grown stronger with time, for it is now the animating spirit of modern science itself. That spirit had consequences for political science as well. Following Descartes, such political theorists as Hobbes and Locke, for example, sought to deduce a science of politics from axioms, such as the laws of nature, which they hoped would be as certain as the axioms of geometry. Still others, such as Hume and even Burke, radicalized the philosophy of suspicion even more, by insisting we take our bearings from experience and history rather than from abstract principles. Others, like Kant, went to the opposite extreme and became inhumanly dogmatic as a result. Still, even Kant gave voice to the Machiavellian spirit of the age when he defined the Enlightenment as man's emergence from his self-imposed immaturity, that is, the result of a manly struggle to replace the rule of coercion and tradition with the rule of independent human reason.[7] What could be more Jeffersonian than Kant's definition of the Enlightenment and the progress it was meant to produce? From this point of view, Jeffersonian vigilance, however immediately rooted it may be in the conventions of the English country party, is an emphatically modern phenomenon. As a result, it is difficult not to conclude that, in 1800, one party of modernity replaced another at the helm of state. Thereafter, American politics slowly began to settle down into its quintessential modern form, largely arising from the original quarrel between the virtues of Hamilton and Jefferson.

The quarrel contained some surprising ironies. After 1800 Hamilton and Jefferson slowly and reluctantly switched roles. The New Yorker became more vigilant; the Virginian, more responsible. In 1802 Jefferson signed into law a bill establishing an American military academy. He also recognized that nothing was more important to American security than preventing any foreign power from controlling the Gulf of Mexico. Before Napoleon sold Louisiana, Jefferson was even willing to make an alliance with England in order to defeat the French in the South. Through negotiations, covert operations, and even American-sponsored separatist movements, Jefferson and his secretary of state, James Madison, also sought American control of the Floridas. Madison obtained West Florida (now southern Mississippi and Alabama) between 1810 and 1813; James Monroe acquired East Florida in 1819. In 1805 Madison even negotiated with Francisco Miranda, the same Latin American revolutionary who had negotiated with Hamilton, and for precisely the same end: to sponsor independence movements in Latin America. With the important exception of developing effective fighting forces, then, the Republicans practiced the same policies that Hamilton had merely proposed, and they largely succeeded. By the end of the War of 1812, Jefferson and Madison had learned the hard way, at the cost of several humiliating military defeats, that Hamilton generally had been right, at least from a strategic point of view. An ocean-going navy, a standing army at least as large as the one Hamilton proposed in 1798, the encouragement of manufactures, even a bank to mobilize capital quickly in time of war—those policies that had seemed instruments of corruption in the hands of Hamilton now seemed the essence of prudent statesmanship. As a result, some observers noted wryly even in Hamilton's time, they had out-Hamiltoned Hamilton. The responsibility of office left them no choice.[8]

Likewise, Hamilton saw no alternative than to try to out-Jefferson Jefferson. Hamilton was sometimes unsure about what to do with himself and his demoralized party after the election of 1800. Though he sometimes seemed to give up in despair, he also recognized that the Federalists had been beaten partly because they had not yet organized themselves into a genuine political party. He therefore tried to steal some pages from the Republicans' political strategy and even to add a few of his own. Under the new banner of a Christian Constitutional Society, for example, he sought to mold the Federalists into an effective political opposition, complete with a party patronage system, several party newspapers, a party platform, dues-paying members, chapters in each state, and a national directing council. He meant to form a coalition between this society and the revolutionary veterans in the Society of the Cincinnati, of which he had been elected president. The two groups most likely to be offended and worried by the Republicans, the pious and the nationalists, would then seek to revive the battle with a new and better rhetorical strategy. They would claim to stand for the mild reign of rational liberty (and who can be against that?) while portraying their adversaries as fanatical Jacobins, who supported the opposite. The new party would pursue both the agrarian and the immigrant vote by promoting internal improvements and programs for the relief and education of new arrivals to the United States. Before Tammany Hall existed, then, Hamilton had developed a comprehensive vision of political machines as the best means for parties to win at the polls in the nineteenth century.

Hamilton had too many strikes against him in his own party for this plan to develop much support, however. Jefferson's successes in his first term also made it impossible for Hamilton and other Federalists to do much but lie in wait for an opportunity. Yet that fact alone reveals just how much the structure of politics after 1800 required Hamilton to practice vigilance. Like all opposition leaders, he had to be on the lookout for mistakes among those in power and then make the best use of them. The repeal of the Judiciary Act seemed to offer a chance for the new party to enlist supporters under the old-time religion of worship of the Constitution. He began to praise vigilance as the most important virtue in a republic. To keep the sacred fire of liberty burning, Hamilton even suggested that the state legislatures should follow the example set by Jefferson and Madison when they wrote the *Virginia* and *Kentucky Resolutions*. There was to be no talk of nullification or interposition, but they might nonetheless protest by asserting that the repeal was unconstitutional.[9]

In 1804, partly in order to embarrass Jefferson and partly to vindicate the honor of the Federalists, Hamilton moved even further in the direction of vigilance. He defended a Federalist newspaper editor against the charge of libeling President Jefferson. He defended free speech, based on the Sedition Act's standard of truth as a defense, as the foundation of effective opposition to tyranny. Sounding exactly like a vigilant Republican in 1798 (and himself in 1774), Hamilton observed that to "watch the progress" of efforts to enslave the people "is the office of a free press. To give us alarm and put us on guard against the encroachments of power. This, then, is a right of the utmost importance, one for which, instead of yielding it up, we ought rather to spill our blood." Admitting truth as a defense was not "dangerous to government," certainly not to any government that deserved to be called free. Without truth as a defense, Hamilton told the court, "you must forever remain ignorant of what your rulers do. I never can think this ought to be; I never did think truth was a crime. . . . My soul has ever abhorred the thought that a free man may not speak the truth." "Never," the so-called personification of American militarism observed, "can tyranny be introduced into this country by force of arms. . . . It is only by abuse of the forms of justice that we can be enslaved." Not the "few thousand of miserable, pitiful" soldiers he had once commanded, but the "pretense of adhering to all the forms of law" while "breaking down the substance of our liberties" was the great danger to public and private liberty in America.[10]

Though it took some time—in some cases more than 100 years—and his adversaries never acknowledged it publicly, Hamilton won all the fundamental debates about American national security policy. Broad construction of the Constitution and executive power; judicial review; a credit-based, manufacturing economy; military academies; an ocean-going navy; a rapidly expandable army in time of peace; and a national spirit rooted in Americans' devotion to both Union and liberty are now cornerstones of our common defense. Despite (and frequently even because of) these developments, Americans are still free, in large part for reasons Hamilton himself had explained. If the most likely source of a militarized state in North America was frequent war on American territory, then it was of prime importance to keep war at a distance, through an indissoluble Union on the one hand and rapid development of American power on the other. It is unthinkable that the United States could have triumphed in the world wars of this century and the cold war without having become the nation Hamilton wanted it to be, a republican empire. In this respect, Hamilton's design for a Seal of the United States was truly prophetic. More than anyone of his time, he envisioned and set in process the chain of events that would enable the United States to lead the free world against twentieth-century regimes far more militaristic and dangerous to the rights of man than revolutionary France.

Yet Hamilton's call for the Federalists to practice vigilance reveals that their adversaries' fears cannot be dismissed. Both the Anti-Federalists and the Republicans foresaw some of the long-term consequences of Hamilton's system. The great danger from his program was not a military despotism but the modern administrative state, perhaps first foreseen by Tocqueville, which saps the spirit of free citizens by assuming the responsibility for running all aspects of government (see chapter 7). Hamilton never advocated such a state, but it is extremely difficult for a necessary central government not to become a dangerously centralized, overreaching administration. To avoid that danger, Jefferson's stress on a bill of rights, local government, and above all, vigilance seems the best antidote. Yet if the price of Jefferson's virtue was irresponsible weakness at home and abroad, then neither is it sufficient as a foundation of free government.

A final irony is that organized party conflict, which none of the Founders envisioned or desired, eventually emerged as a means to unite the virtues of Hamilton and Jefferson. After 200 years, U.S. parties have switched roles so many times that no one today would call one the party of vigilance and the other the party of responsibility. Instead, the party system perpetuates the quarrel between the virtues of Jefferson and Hamilton by compelling the opposition to practice vigilance and the party in power to become more responsible. Similar phenomena occur in most Western democracies. As a result, those democracies and the United States seem to have achieved some of the stability that Machiavelli tried to build into his new modes and orders, his vision of a new and more successful Rome. Machiavelli opposed responsible patricians to vigilant plebs, or more properly, honor-lovers to security-lovers; we oppose different parties, but the end result is not radically different. In order to govern, the party in power has no choice but to act as Hamilton did in 1790. It must unite what Madison split asunder in *Federalist* 10 and 51. In contrast, the party in opposition must struggle just as hard to decentralize authority, in order to avoid being led in what it perceives as the wrong direction. However temporarily, one party marches under the banner of *e pluribus unum;* the other, under the flag of *ex uno plura.*

From this point of view, a complete victory of Jeffersonian vigilance over Hamiltonian responsibility, or vice versa, would be an American tragedy. Yet American history generally has been an ongoing drama because party politics perpetuates the quarrel between Hamilton and Jefferson. Although almost all candidates for office praise Jeffersonian vigilance, those in power often feel compelled to practice Hamiltonian responsibility. Moralists may be outraged by such hypocrisy; cynics are more likely to see it as the homage that vice pays to virtue. Neither view is accurate or fair, however. Recognizing that different times and circumstances require different kinds of virtues is a sign of political maturity. Whenever party leaders assume vigilance in opposition and responsibility in power as the standards of their politics, they recreate the original dialogue between the virtues that almost destroyed the Republic in its youth but that ultimately transformed Hamilton's personal tragedy into an American triumph.

Abbreviations

AF	Stanley Elkins and Eric McKitrick, *The Age of Federalism* (Oxford: Oxford University Press, 1993).
AH	Forrest McDonald, *Alexander Hamilton: A Biography* (New York: Norton, 1979).
AHAFP	Gilbert Lycan, *Alexander Hamilton and American Foreign Policy* (Norman: University of Oklahoma Press, 1970).
AHC	Clinton Rossiter, *Alexander Hamilton and the Constitution* (New York: Harcourt, Brace, and World, 1964).
AHIRG	Gerald Stourzh, *Alexander Hamilton and the Idea of Republican Government* (Stanford: Stanford University Press, 1970).
"AHMP"	Richard Loss, "Alexander Hamilton and the Modern Presidency: Continuity or Discontinuity?" *Presidential Studies Quarterly* 12 (1982): 6–25.
AHR	*American Historical Review*
AP	Forrest McDonald, *The American Presidency: An Intellectual History* (Lawrence: University Press of Kansas, 1994).
APSR	*American Political Science Review*
BNP	Jack N. Rakove, *The Beginnings of National Politics: An Interpretive History of the Continental Congress* (Baltimore: Johns Hopkins University Press, 1979).
CC	Edmund Cody Burnett, *The Continental Congress* (New York: Macmillan, 1941).
Creation	Gordon S. Wood, *Creation of the American Republic, 1776–1787* (Chapel Hill: University of North Carolina Press, 1969).
CSP	J. C. Vile, *Constitutionalism and the Separation of Powers* (Oxford: Clarendon Press, 1967).
DA	Alexis de Tocqueville, *Democracy in America*, trans. George Lawrence, 2 vols. (New York: Harper and Row, 1969).
Duane	Hamilton to James Duane, 3 September 1780, in Hamilton's *Papers*.
ER	Harvey Flaumenhaft, *The Effective Republic: Administration and Constitution in the Thought of Alexander Hamilton* (Durham, NC: Duke University Press, 1992).
ES	Richard H. Kohn, *Eagle and the Sword: The Federalists and the Origins of the American Military Establishment, 1783–1802* (New York: Free Press, 1975).
Essays	David Hume, *Essays, Moral, Political and Literary* (Indianapolis: Liberty Press, 1985).

F	Alexander Hamilton, James Madison, and John Jay, *The Federalist,* ed. Jacob E. Cooke (Middletown, CT: Wesleyan University Press, 1961).
Fame	Trevour Colbourn, ed., *Fame and the Founding Fathers: Essays by Douglass Adair* (New York: Norton, 1974).
FE	John C. Miller, *The Federalist Era, 1789–1801* (New York: Harper, 1963).
FF	James Morton Smith, *Freedom's Fetters: The Alien and Sedition Acts and American Civil Liberties* (Ithaca, NY: Cornell University Press, 1956).
FR	Alexander Hamilton, *The Farmer Refuted,* in Hamilton's *Papers.*
FS	John S. Bassett, *The Federalist System* (New York: Cooper Square Publishers, 1906).
FV	Alexander Hamilton, *A Full Vindication,* in Hamilton's *Papers.*
"GND"	Isaac Kramnick, "The 'Great National Discussion': The Discourse of Politics in 1787," *WMQ* 3d ser. 45 (1988): 3–31.
IOAR	Bernard Bailyn, *Ideological Origins of the American Revolution* (Cambridge: Harvard University Press, 1967).
IT	Frederick W. Marks III, *Independence on Trial, Foreign Policy and the Making of the Constitution* (Wilmington, DE: Scholarly Resources, 1973).
JAH	*Journal of American History*
JHI	*Journal of the History of Ideas*
JOP	*Journal of Politics*
JP	Lance Banning, *The Jeffersonian Persuasion: Evolution of a Party Ideology* (Ithaca, NY: Cornell University Press, 1978).
LA	Jerome Huyler, *Locke in America: The Moral Philosophy of the Founding Era* (Lawrence: University Press of Kansas, 1995).
LEFL	Nathan Tarcov, *Locke's Education for Liberty* (Chicago: University of Chicago Press, 1984).
LNY	Alexander Clarence Flick, *Loyalism in New York During the American Revolution* (New York: Arno Press, 1969).
LPAH	Julius Goebel, *The Law Practice of Alexander Hamilton,* 4 vols. (New York: Columbia University Press, 1964).
LWJM	William C. Rives and Philip R. Fendall, eds., *The Letters and Other Writings of James Madison,* 4 vols. (Philadelphia: J. P. Lippincott, 1865).
LWP	Richard H. Cox, *Locke on War and Peace* (Oxford: Clarendon Press, 1961).
MF	Marvin Meyers, ed., *The Mind of the Founder: Sources of the Political Thought of James Madison* (Waltham, MA: Brandeis University Press, 1981).
MM	J. G. A. Pocock, *The Machiavellian Moment: Florentine Political Thought and the Atlantic Republican Tradition* (Princeton: Princeton University Press, 1975).
NRNR	Michael P. Zuckert, *Natural Rights and the New Republicanism* (Princeton: Princeton University Press, 1994).
P	Harold G. Syrett and Jacob E. Cooke, eds., *The Papers of Alexander Hamilton* (New York: Columbia University Press, 1961).

PGW	Forrest McDonald, *The Presidency of George Washington* (Lawrence: University Press of Kansas, 1974).
PJ	Merrill D. Peterson, ed., *The Portable Jefferson* (New York: Viking, 1985).
PJM	*The Papers of James Madison,* ed. Robert A. Rutland et al. (New York: Columbia University Press, 1977).
PP	E. James Ferguson, *The Power of the Purse* (Chapel Hill: University of North Carolina Press, 1961).
"PPFP"	Nathan Tarcov, "Principle and Prudence in Foreign Policy: The Founders' View," *Public Interest* 76 (1984): 45–60.
PSQ	*Political Science Quarterly*
PTF	David Epstein, *The Political Theory of the Federalist* (Chicago: University of Chicago Press, 1984).
PTJ	Forrest McDonald, *The Presidency of Thomas Jefferson* (Lawrence: University Press of Kansas, 1976).
"RAFP"	Drew McCoy, "Republicanism and American Foreign Policy: James Madison and the Political Economy of Commercial Discrimination, 1780–1794," *WMQ* 3d ser. (1979): 633–46.
RAM	Paul Rahe, *Republics, Ancient and Modern,* 3 vols. (Chapel Hill: University of North Carolina Press, 1994).
Records	Max Farrand, ed., *The Records of the Federal Convention of 1787,* 4 vols. (New Haven: Yale University Press, 1966).
RMPE	Alexander Hamilton, *Report on a Military Peace Establishment,* in Hamilton's *Papers.*
ROP	*Review of Politics*
RPW	Charles Royster, *A Revolutionary People at War: The Continental Army and American Character, 1775–1783* (New York: Norton, 1979).
SF	Lance Banning, *The Sacred Fire of Liberty* (Ithaca, NY: Cornell University Press, 1995).
SL	Charles Secondat Montesquieu, *The Spirit of the Laws,* trans. Thomas Nugent (New York: Hafner, 1949).
SMR	Thomas Pangle, *The Spirit of Modern Republicanism: The Moral Vision of the American Founders and the Philosophy of John Locke* (Chicago: University of Chicago Press, 1988).
SR	Charles Kesler et al., *Saving the Revolution* (New York: Free Press, 1987).
SS	Samuel P. Huntington, *The Soldier and the State: The Theory and Practice of Civil Military Relations* (Cambridge: Harvard University Press, 1957).
ST	John Locke, *Second Treatise of Government,* in *Two Treatises of Government,* ed. Peter J. Laslett (Cambridge: Cambridge University Press, 1991).
TP	Harvey C. Mansfield Jr., *Taming the Prince: The Ambivalence of Modern Executive Power* (New York: Free Press, 1991).
TR	Ralph Lerner, *The Thinking Revolutionary; Principle and Practice in the New Republic* (Ithaca, NY: Cornell University Press, 1987).

VC   Samuel Seabury, *A View of the Controversy*, in *Annals of America* (Chicago: Encyclopedia Britannica, 1968), 2: 289–95.

What   Herbert J. Storing, *What the Anti-Federalists Were For!* (Chicago: University of Chicago Press, 1984).

WMQ   *William and Mary Quarterly*

WP   Bruce Russett and Harvey Starr, *World Politics: The Menu for Choice* (New York: W. H. Freeman and Company, 1992).

WTJ   *The Writings of Thomas Jefferson*, ed. Paul Leicester Ford (Washington, DC: Thomas Jefferson Association of the United States, 1905).

Notes

1. HAMILTON'S PLACE IN AMERICAN POLITICAL THOUGHT

1. Hamilton to Edward Stevens, 11 November 1769, in the *Papers of Alexander Hamilton*, ed. Harold G. Syrett and Jacob E. Cooke, 26 vols. (New York: Columbia University Press, 1961), 1: 581. Hereafter, all citations from Hamilton's *Papers* will be listed as P 1: 581, and so on, the first number designating the volume and the second the page. Likewise, all citations from *The Federalist* will be from Jacob E. Cooke's edition (Middletown, CT: Wesleyan University Press, 1961) and listed as F 1: 3, F 10: 59, and so on, the first number referring to the essay and the second to the page. Spelling, capitalization, and punctuation have been modernized whenever doing so has done no injustice to the original.

2. *The Stand* 3, 7 April 1798, P 21: 404. See also Broadus Mitchell, *Alexander Hamilton: The Revolutionary Years* (New York: Thomas Y. Crowell, 1970), and Forrest McDonald, *Alexander Hamilton: A Biography* (New York: W. W. Norton, 1982) (hereafter *AH*).

3. *New York Evening Post*, 17 July 1804, P 25: 322–29. See also Mitchell, *Hamilton*, 343, and McDonald, *AH*, 316.

4. McDonald, *AH*, 316; Clinton Rossiter, *Alexander Hamilton and the Constitution* (New York: Harcourt, Brace, and World, 1964) (hereafter *AHC*); Gilbert Lycan, *Alexander Hamilton and American Foreign Policy* (Norman: University of Oklahoma Press, 1970) (hereafter *AHAFP*); Gerald Stourzh, *Alexander Hamilton and the Idea of Republican Government* (Stanford: Stanford University Press, 1970) (hereafter *AHIRG*); Harvey Flaumenhaft, *The Effective Republic: Administration and Constitution in the Thought of Alexander Hamilton* (Durham, NC: Duke University Press, 1992) (hereafter *ER*); Morton J. Frisch, *Alexander Hamilton and the Political Order* (Lanham, MD: University Press of America, 1991); Edward Meade Earle, "Adam Smith, Alexander Hamilton, and Friedrich List: The Economic Foundations of Military Power," in *Makers of Modern Strategy from Machiavelli to the Nuclear Age*, ed. Peter Paret (Princeton: Princeton University Press, 1986), 217–61; Mitchell, *Hamilton*, 193; and John C. Miller, *Alexander Hamilton: Portrait in Paradox* (New York: Harper, 1959), xi.

5. See Richard H. Kohn, *The Eagle and the Sword: The Federalists and the Origins of the American Military Establishment, 1783–1802* (New York: Free Press, 1975), 194–95, 225–29, 253, 266, 272–73, 282, 285–86, 409 n.12 (hereafter *ES*). By militarism,

Kohn means an exaltation of the martial virtues, a disposition to employ force to govern at home, and a taste for military adventures abroad. Yet he also suggests that for the Founders militarism meant something different from the model we are accustomed to expect from the history of Prussia and Germany. For the Founders, he claims, militarism was virtually identical with support for a standing army (282). Thus, by definition, anyone who supported such an army was a militarist; those who supported it most ardently were extreme, that is, Hamiltonian militarists. If so, Kohn hardly needed a book to prove his thesis, which he seems to have assumed from the beginning.

6. Isaac Kramnick, "The 'Great National Discussion': The Discourse of Politics in 1787," *William and Mary Quarterly (WMQ)* 45, 3d ser. (1988): 3–32 (hereafter "GND"). Kramnick's various essays addressing these idioms have been collected in *Republicanism and Bourgeois Radicalism: Political Ideology in Late Eighteenth-Century England and America* (Ithaca, NY: Cornell University Press, 1990).

7. Milestones in the development of this school of thought are Carl L. Becker's *The Declaration of Independence: A Study in the History of Ideas* (New York: Vintage Books, 1922); Louis Hartz's *The Liberal Tradition in America* (New York: Harcourt Brace Jovanovich, 1955); and Martin Diamond's "Democracy and *The Federalist:* A Reconsideration of the Framers' Intent," *American Political Science Review (APSR)* 53 (1959): 52–68. The best recent work in the spirit of Diamond's interpretation is Thomas L. Pangle's *The Spirit of Modern Republicanism: The Moral Vision of the American Founders and the Philosophy of John Locke* (Chicago: University of Chicago Press, 1988) (hereafter *SMR*). In *Capitalism and the New Social Order: The Republican Vision of the 1790s* (Albany: New York State University Press, 1984), Joyce Appleby celebrates the progressive spirit of the liberal individualism that she sees in Thomas Jefferson especially.

8. Gordon S. Wood established much of the new orthodoxy in *The Creation of the American Republic, 1776–1787* (Chapel Hill: University of North Carolina Press, 1969) (hereafter *Creation*). He argues that Americans began as classical republicans who believed political liberty depended upon sacrificing individual interests to the common good in 1776 but emerged as modern liberals who sought to preserve civil liberty and the power of entrenched elites by pitting interests against each other in 1787. In *The Machiavellian Moment: Florentine Political Thought and the Atlantic Republican Tradition* (Princeton: Princeton University Press, 1975) (hereafter *MM*), J. G. A. Pocock traces the language of civic-humanist republicanism, with an emphasis on political participation, the life of the *zoon politikon,* from Aristotle through Machiavelli and English opposition thinkers to Thomas Jefferson and perhaps even beyond. In *The Jeffersonian Persuasion* (Ithaca, NY: Cornell University Press, 1978) (hereafter *JP*) and *The Elusive Republic: Political Economy in Jeffersonian America* (Chapel Hill: University of North Carolina Press, 1980), Lance Banning and Drew McCoy suggest that this classical strain of American political thought endured until at least the War of 1812. The last ten years have witnessed significant qualifications among republican revisionists, however. See Pocock, "Between Gog and

Magog: The Republican Thesis and Ideologia Americana," *Journal of the History of Ideas (JHI)* 48 (1987): 325–46; Wood, "Ideology and the Origins of Liberal America," *WMQ* 44 (1987): 634; and Banning's three essays, "Jeffersonian Ideology Revisited: Liberal and Classical Ideas in the New American Republic," *WMQ* 43 (1986): 3–19, "Some Second Thoughts on Virtue and the Course of Revolutionary Thinking," in *Conceptual Change and the Constitution,* ed. Terrence Ball and J. G. A. Pocock (Lawrence: University Press of Kansas, 1988), 198–200, 203, and "The Republican Interpretation: Retrospect and Prospect," in *The Republican Synthesis Revisited: Essays in Honor of George Athan Billias,* ed. Milton Klein, Richard D. Brown, and John B. Hench (Worcester, MA: American Antiquarian Society, 1992), 93–94, 98.

9. See, for example, Max Weber, *The Protestant Ethic and the Spirit of Capitalism* (New York: Scribner, 1958); Edmund S. Morgan, "The Puritan Ethic and the American Revolution," *WMQ* 24, 3d ser. (1967): 3–43; James T. Kloppenburg, "The Virtues of Liberalism: Christianity, Republicanism, and Ethics in Early American Political Discourses," *Journal of American History (JAH)* 74 (1987): 9–33; Joshua Foa Dienstag, "Serving God and Mammon: The Lockean Sympathy in Early American Political Thought," *APSR* 90 (1996): 497–511; and Quentin Skinner, *The Foundations of Modern Thought,* 2 vols. (Cambridge: Cambridge University Press, 1978), 2: 239. In contrast to those scholars who harmonize liberal capitalism and Protestantism, Barry Alan Shain explores the communitarian elements of early American Protestantism in *The Myth of American Individualism: The Protestant Origins of American Political Thought* (Princeton: Princeton University Press, 1994). Paradoxically, both sides may be right. See Alexis de Tocqueville, *Democracy in America,* trans. George Lawrence, 2 vols. (New York: Harper and Row, 1969), 1: 43–47, 288 (hereafter *DA*).

10. See, for example, John Fiske, *The Critical Period in American History* (Boston: Riverside Press, 1989); Russell F. Weigley, *Towards an American Army: Military Thought from Washington to Marshall* (New York: Columbia University Press, 1962); Samuel P. Huntington, *The Soldier and the State: The Theory and Practice of Civil Military Relations* (Cambridge: Harvard University Press, 1957) (hereafter *SS*); Frederick W. Marks III, *Independence on Trial: Foreign Affairs and the Making of the Constitution* (Wilmington, DE: Scholarly Resources, 1973) (hereafter *IT*); Charles Howard McIlwain's *Constitutionalism: Ancient and Modern* (Ithaca, NY: Cornell University Press, 1947), 5–33; Janet A. Rieseman, "Money, Credit, and Federalist Political Economy," in *Beyond Confederation: The Origins of the Constitution and American National Identity,* ed. Richard Beeman, Stephen Botein, and Edward C. Carter III (Chapel Hill: University of North Carolina Press, 1987); E. James Ferguson, *The Power of the Purse* (Chapel Hill: University of North Carolina Press, 1961) (hereafter *PP*), and "Political Economy, Public Liberty, and the Formation of the Constitution," *WMQ* 40, 3d ser. (1983): 389–412; P. G. M. Dickson, *The Financial Revolution in England: A Study in the Development of Public Credit* (New York: St. Martin's Press, 1967); E. Wayne Carp's *To Starve an Army at Pleasure: Continental Army Administration and American Political Culture, 1775–83* (Chapel Hill: Univer-

sity of North Carolina Press, 1984); Jack N. Rakove, *The Beginnings of National Politics: An Interpretive History of the Continental Congress* (Baltimore: Johns Hopkins University Press, 1979) (hereafter *BNP*); and Stanley Elkin and Eric McKitrick's now classic "The Founding Fathers: Young Men of the Revolution," *Political Science Quarterly (PSQ)* 76 (1961): 181–216.

11. Kramnick, "GND," 3.

12. Bernard Bailyn, "Central Themes of the American Revolution," in *Essays on the American Revolution,* ed. Stephen Kurtz and James L. Hutson (Chapel Hill: University of North Carolina Press, 1973), 7–10.

13. Wood, "Ideology and the Origins of Liberal America," 634.

14. Kramnick, "GND," 3. For the Founders' multilingualism, see Forrest McDonald, "The Intellectual World of the Founding Fathers," in *Requiem: Variations on Eighteenth Century Themes,* Forrest McDonald and Ellen Shapiro McDonald (Lawrence: University Press of Kansas, 1988), 9, and Forrest McDonald's *Novus Ordo Seclorum: The Intellectual Origins of the Constitution* (Lawrence: University Press of Kansas, 1985), 224.

15. Similar problems arise when scholars of American foreign policy try to understand statesmen like Hamilton and Jefferson as realists or idealists. These abstractions allow for consistency among scholars, but few statesmen fit these categories well, if at all. For a useful critique of thus categorizing the Founders, see Nathan Tarcov, "Principle and Prudence in Foreign Policy: The Founders' Perspective," *Public Interest* 76 (1984): 45–60 (hereafter "PPFP").

16. See Hamilton's *Report on the Subject of Manufactures,* 5 December 1791, P 10: 235; and *Examination* 16, 19 March 1802, P 25: 567.

17. For this approach to political theory and practice, I am much indebted to Ralph Lerner, *The Thinking Revolutionary: Principle and Practice in the New Republic* (Ithaca, NY: Cornell University Press, 1987), ix, 6, 11 (hereafter *TR*), and Tarcov, "PPFP."

18. See F 1: 6; William Kent, *Memoirs and Letters of James Kent* (Boston, 1898), 327–28; Flaumenhaft, *ER,* 10, 270 n.17; and Hamilton's preface to the first edition of *The Federalist,* ed. J. and A. McClean (New York, 1788), 1: iii–iv. The preface was last published in the edition of Paul Leicester Ford (New York: Henry Holt, 1898). In *The Political Theory of the Federalist* (Chicago: University of Chicago Press, 1984), ix (hereafter *PTF*), David Epstein cites the preface as some justification for considering the Founders' best-known collection of partisan essays also as a work of political theory.

19. Hamilton to James A. Bayard, 16 January 1801, P 25: 321.

20. See *The Farmer Refuted* (hereafter *FR*), 23 February 1775, P 1: 122. For Hamilton's enormous debt to these theorists, begin with Flaumenhaft, *ER,* 34–35, 41–42, 49, 55–56, 71–72, 160, 190, 215, 266, 272 n.10, 273 n.13, 275 n.27, 280 n.12, 281–82 n.24, 288–89 n.16, 293 n.18.

21. F 1: 5–6. Kramnick therefore errs when he asserts that "Hamilton was less interested in the liberal state than the heroic state" ("GND," 26). To the extent

Hamilton did make a hero of the United States, it was because the Union represented liberal principles in a hostile, illiberal world. For further reflection on this issue, contrast Hamilton's *Design for a Seal of the United States* (May, 1795, P 20: 208–9) with Pericles' vision of heroic Athens in his Funeral Oration, in Thucydides' *Peloponnesian War*, trans. Thomas Hobbes, ed. David Grene (8 bks.) (Chicago: University of Chicago Press, 1989), 2. 43. 112.

22. See Bernard Bailyn, *Ideological Origins of the American Revolution* (Cambridge: Harvard University Press, 1967), ix (hereafter *IOAR*), and Wood, *Creation,* 37, 135–55.

23. Jefferson's Draft of the *Kentucky Resolutions,* October 1798, in *The Writings of Thomas Jefferson,* ed. Paul Leicester Ford (Washington, DC: Thomas Jefferson Association of the United States, 1905), 7: 304 (hereafter *WTJ*).

24. See Paul Rahe's *Republics, Ancient and Modern,* 3 vols. (Chapel Hill: University of North Carolina Press, 1994), 3: 156–59, 176–77 (hereafter *RAM*).

25. Hamilton to James Duane, 3 September 1780, P 2: 401–4; and F 1: 5.

26. See *The Federalist Concordance,* ed. Thomas S. Engeman, Edward J. Erler, and Thomas B. Hofeller (Chicago: University of Chicago Press, 1980), 470; Hamilton to Duane, 3 September 1780, P 2; F 23: 146–49; and Stourzh, *AHIRG,* 180–89. In recent years, *Federalist* 63 has commonly been attributed to Madison, though Forrest McDonald is surely right that the concern for national character in that essay was more characteristic of Hamilton than of Madison. See Edward Gaylord Bourne, "The Authorship of the Federalist," *American Historical Review (AHR)* (April 1897) 2:443–60; Douglass Adair, "The Authorship of the Disputed Federalist Papers," *WMQ* (April and July 1944) 1:97–122, 235–64; and McDonald, *AH,* 387–88.

27. See Jefferson to George Washington, 9 September 1792, in *The Portable Jefferson,* ed. Merrill D. Peterson (New York: Viking, 1985), 455–64 (hereafter *PJ*).

28. Editors' suggestion in *To Form a More Perfect Union: The Critical Ideas of the Constitution,* ed. Herman Belz, Ronald Hoffman, and Peter J. Albert (Charlottesville: University Press of Virginia, 1992), xi. Much of the contemporary controversy over the liberal or republican character of the Founding arises from significantly different interpretations of Machiavelli and his influence. Some scholars, such as J. G. A. Pocock and Felix Raab, *The English Face of Machiavelli* (Toronto: University of Toronto Press, 1964), insist that the republicanism of Machiavelli and his heirs in seventeenth- and eighteenth-century England constituted a genuinely classical alternative to Lockean liberalism. Others, such as Harvey C. Mansfield Jr., *Taming the Prince: The Ambivalence of Modern Executive Power* (New York: Free Press, 1989) (hereafter *TP*), and *Machiavelli's Virtue* (Chicago: University of Chicago Press, 1996), have stressed Machiavelli's influence on early modern liberal thought from Hobbes through Locke and Montesquieu to *The Federalist.* In contrast, in "Republicanism Reconsidered: Some Thoughts on the Foundation and Preservation of the American Republic," *Review of Politics (ROP)* 41 (1979): 61–95, Jean Yarbrough argues that Machiavelli, Harrington, Montesquieu, and Trenchard and Gordon developed a "neoclassical" strand of modern thought. In her view, civic virtue became a means to serve liberal ends (securing life, liberty, and property) rather than a classical end

in itself. Whereas Mansfield generally ignores English opposition thinkers (except-ing Bolingbroke), Pocock has been challenged both for neglecting Machiavelli's influence among early liberals and for blurring significant differences between Machiavelli and Aristotle. See Nathan Tarcov's review of Pocock's *Machiavellian Moment, PSQ* 91 (1976): 380–82); Vickie B. Sullivan's "Machiavelli's Momentary 'Machiavellian Moment': A Reconsideration of Pocock's Treatment of the *Discourses*," *Political Theory* 20 (1992): 309–18; and Paul Rahe's *RAM*, 2: 25, 31–32, 36, 40, 67, 92–94, 139, 180–81, 200, 203, 239, 242; 3: 10, 20.

29. Rossiter, *AHC,* 142–46; and Stourzh, *AHIRG,* 44–70.

30. Paul Leicester Ford first suggested that Hamilton was the author of certain letters under the pseudonym of Caesar in the *New York Daily Advertiser* during the debates over ratifying the Constitution in New York, in his *Essays on the Constitution of the United States, Published During Its Ratification by the People, 1787–88* (Brooklyn, NY, 1892), 245, 281. Jacob Cooke discredited Ford's suggestion in "Alexander Hamilton's Authorship of the 'Caesar' Letters," *WMQ* 17, 3d ser. (1960): 78–85. Jefferson reported that during a dinner party at his home in the early years of the Washington administration, Hamilton pointed to three unidentified busts on the wall and asked who they were. Jefferson replied that they were his "trinity of the three greatest men the world had ever produced," Newton, Bacon, and Locke. Jefferson then claimed that Hamilton responded that the greatest man who ever lived was Julius Caesar. See Douglass Adair, "A Note on Certain of Hamilton's Pseudo-nyms," *WMQ* 12, 3d ser. (1955): 255. Scholars who have accepted Jefferson's tale without question include not only Adair but also Dumas Malone, *Jefferson and His Time* (Boston: Little, Brown, 1951) 2: 286; Julian P. Boyd et al., eds., *The Papers of Thomas Jefferson* (Princeton: Princeton University Press, 1971) 17: 533; and Richard Kohn, *ES,* 253. However, in "Alexander Hamilton and Julius Caesar: A Note on the Use of Historical Evidence," *WMQ* 32, 3d ser. (1975): 475–80, Thomas P. Govan re-minds us that there is no evidence for Jefferson's assertion besides the memory of an elder statesman in retirement with an ax to grind against his foremost opponent. As Stanley Elkins and Eric McKitrick suggest in the *Age of Federalism* (Oxford: Oxford University Press, 1991), 754 (hereafter *AF*), Jefferson also had a partisan ambition to "'sink federalism into an abyss from which there shall be no resurrec-tion for it.'" Govan observes that Hamilton tended to see Aaron Burr as Jefferson saw Hamilton. For Hamilton, Burr was an "embryo-Caesar." Govan also notes that Hamilton predicted the French Revolution would issue in a modern Caesar—like the Napoleon Hamilton admired for his talents but deplored for his lack of virtue. One must also consider the observation of Chancellor Kent that Bacon inspired Hamilton to consider writing a treatise on politics. Hamilton's heroes may thus have been much closer to Jefferson's trinity than the Virginian realized. Yet according to Hamilton's son, his father loved to talk about his own youth as a soldier and to read Caesar's works to his children. "When translating the commentaries of Caesar, it would seem as though Caesar were present; for as much as any man that ever lived, he had the soldier's temperament." (See John C. Hamilton, *Life of Alexander*

Hamilton [Boston, 1879], 7: 792–93, and Flaumenhaft, *ER*, 271 n.17.) Perhaps, then, the ever-suspicious Jefferson misinterpreted some indiscreet remarks of Hamilton's that a wiser man would not have made, and especially not to Jefferson. Perhaps, too, interpretation depends on what Jefferson and Hamilton meant by great. If any American of the Founding era had the capacity to be a Caesar, perhaps Hamilton was the one, but he preferred to be the American Publius, which is arguably an ambition far greater than to be a Caesar. Such an ambition, however, might well have to rely on many of Caesar's virtues (speed, decisiveness, industry, careful administration, and so on).

31. Chief Justice John Marshall, Hamilton's most successful intellectual and political heir, then showed the capacity of constitutional jurisprudence to serve the ends of state building, liberal property rights, and even liberal-republican government (by distinguishing between political questions with which the Court ought not to interfere and constitutional questions in which its review is necessary to secure vested rights). Marshall's peers on the Supreme Court, Justices Joseph Story and James Kent, were no less indebted to Hamilton. See William McDonald, "The Indebtedness of John Marshall to Alexander Hamilton," *Massachusetts Historical Society, Proceedings* 46 (1912–1913); Francis N. Thorpe, "Hamilton's Ideas in Marshall's Decisions," *Boston University Law Review* 1 (1921); Robert G. McCloskey's *The American Supreme Court* (Chicago: University of Chicago Press, 1960); Gerald Gunther, *John Marshall's Defense of McCulloch v. Maryland* (Stanford: Stanford University Press, 1969); *Marbury v. Madison* (1 Cranch 137); *Dartmouth College v. Woodward* (4 Wheat 518); Samuel J. Konefsky, *John Marshall and Alexander Hamilton: Architects of the American Constitution* (New York: Macmillan, 1964); and Rossiter, *AHC*, 240–45.

32. See Hume's "Of Commerce" and "Of Refinement in the Arts," in his *Essays, Moral, Political, and Literary* (Indianapolis: Liberty Press, 1985), 253, 265–67, and 277–78 (hereafter *Essays*). A German, Alex Bein, anticipated most of Hamilton's scholars in this century by attempting to measure the relative influence of Hume and Machiavelli in Hamilton's thought in *Die Staatsidee Alexander Hamiltons in Ihrer Entstehung und Entwicklung* (Munich and Berlin, 1927), 165–77. Useful discussions of the Scots and modern political thought are Istvan Holt and Michael Ignatieff, eds., *Wealth and Virtue: The Shaping of Political Economy in the Scottish Enlightenment* (Cambridge: Cambridge University Press, 1983), and Garry Wills, *Inventing America: Jefferson's Declaration of Independence* (Garden City, NY: Athlone Press, 1980), and *Explaining America: The Federalist* (Garden City, NY: Athlone Press, 1981). Wills has done much to popularize Hume's strong influence among the authors of *The Federalist,* but Morton White demonstrates in *Philosophy, The Federalist, and the Constitution* (New York: Oxford University Press, 1987) that its authors commonly used Locke for principles and Hume (among others) for political psychology.

33. F 9: 51; *Records of the Federal Convention of 1787,* ed. Max Farrand, 4 vols. (New Haven: Yale University Press, 1911–37), 22 June 1787, 381–82 (hereafter *Records*); Hume, "Of the Independency of Parliament," in *Essays,* 42–46, and *An*

Enquiry Concerning the Principles of Morals (Peru, IL: Open Court Publishing, 1966), 106, 114.

34. See Douglass Adair and Marvin Harvey, "Was Alexander Hamilton a Christian Statesman?" *WMQ* 3d ser., 12 (1955): 308; Rossiter, *AHC,* 123–26; Hamilton's *Statement of Impending Duel with Aaron Burr,* 28 June–10 July 1804, P 26: 280; Broadus Mitchell, *Alexander Hamilton, Youth to Maturity* (New York: Macmillan, 1957), 30; Hamilton to the *Royal Danish American Gazette,* 6 September 1772, P 1: 34–38; Hamilton to Benjamin Rush, 29 March 1802, P 24: 584; *FR,* 23 February 1775, P 1: 87; *The Cause of France,* 1794, P 17: 585–86; *The French Revolution,* 1794, P 17: 586–88; *The War in Europe,* September–December 1796, P 20: 339–40; Hamilton to Charles Cotesworth Pinckney, 15 March 1802, P 25: 562–63; Hamilton to James A. Bayard, 16–21 April 1802, P 25: 606–10; and Address to the Electors of the State of New York, 21 March 1801, P 25: 364.

35. F 1: 3; Second Draft of Washington's Farewell Address, July 1796, P 20: 280–82; *Report on the Subject of Manufactures,* 5 December 1791, P 10: 255.

36. On the mystery of the sources of national identity, see, for example, Bruce Russett and Harvey Starr, *World Politics: The Menu for Choice* (New York: W. H. Freeman and Company, 1992), 47–53 (hereafter *WP*). On the centrality of historical memory in this consciousness, see also Machiavelli, *The Prince,* trans. Harvey C. Mansfield Jr. (Chicago: University of Chicago Press, 1984), 5. 20.

37. In "Liberalism and Nationality: Grotius, Vattel and Locke," *ROP* 59 (1997): 293–322, Jeremy Rabkin explores the social bonds (religion, ancestry, language, and so on) that help form a people even before the establishment of a social contract, but he does not discuss the probably decisive impact of liberal principles (equality, rights, consent, and so on) in shaping the American national identity.

38. It is unlikely that anyone as well read as Hamilton would not have read Machiavelli and equally unlikely that he would have admitted any debts to the Florentine. Like Machiavelli, Hamilton knew Titus Livy by heart, and he cited passages from the great historian of Rome on several occasions. Thus, Hamilton often sounded like Machiavelli when the latter was being faithful to Livy (which was not always the case). Compare, for example, Machiavelli's *Discourses,* 1, 26: 253; 1, 45: 289; 1, 23: 388–92, in *Machiavelli, the Chief Works and Others,* trans. Allan Gilbert (Durham, NC: Duke University Press, 1989); *The Prince,* 8: 38; 18: 67; 20: 87; Livy, *A History of Rome,* trans. Moses Hadas and Joe P. Poe (New York: Modern Library, 1962), 8. 13; 8. 21; 9. 4; Hamilton to the New York Committee on Correspondence, 20–27 April 1777, Hamilton to William Livingston, 29 April 1777, and Hamilton's *First and Second Letters of Phocion,* 1–27 January and April, 1784, P 1: 233, 237, 243; P 3: 494–95, 553. Kramnick, "GND," 24; Pocock, *MM,* 528–33; Mansfield, *TP,* 247–78; Stourzh, *AHIRG,* 132–45; and Julius Goebel, *The Law Practice of Alexander Hamilton* (New York: Columbia University Press, 1964), 1: 211 (hereafter *LPAH*). In all probability, Hamilton's debt to Machiavelli is indirect, through the teachings of Locke, Hume, Montesquieu, and other modern theorists, who, Mansfield demonstrates, owed enormous debts to Machiavelli (*TP,* 181–248). Paradoxically, Jefferson's

political thought may have owed as much to Machiavelli as Hamilton's, with the possibility that the great feud between the Virginian and the New Yorker reflects different dimensions of the thought of the multifaceted Florentine. See, for example, Karl Walling, "Was Hamilton a Machiavellian Statesman?" and Paul Rahe, "Thomas Jefferson's Machiavellian Political Science" in *ROP* 57 (1995): 419–47, 447–81.

39. See Wood, *Creation*, 26.

40. See Bernard Bailyn's *IOAR*, 77–80, 102–3, 112–15; James Hutson's "Country, Court, and Constitution: Antifederalism and the Historians," *WMQ* 38, 3d ser. (1981): 337–68; and Lance Banning's *JP*, 24, 43, 47–69, 51–54, 69, 71, 74–90, 104, 117, 124–25, 128–40, 163–64, 177, 185–207, 249–50, 273–74, 286, 301.

2. PRINCIPLE AND PRUDENCE

1. *A Full Vindication* (hereafter *FV*), 15 December 1774, and *FR*, 23 February 1775, P 1: 46, 51, 98.

2. Pocock, *MM*, 529; Felix Gilbert, *To the Farewell Address: Ideas of Early American Foreign Policy* (Princeton: Princeton University Press, 1961), 111; Paul A. Varg, *Foreign Policies of the Founding Fathers* (East Lansing: Michigan State University Press, 1963), 72; Rossiter, *AHC*, 8; Charles A. Beard, *The Idea of the National Interest; An Analytical Study of American Foreign Policy* (New York: Macmillan, 1934), 43–49; and Hans J. Morgenthau, *The Defense of the National Interest; A Critical Examination of American Foreign Policy* (New York: Knopf, 1951), 14–18, as well as his "Mainsprings of American Foreign Policy," *APSR* 44 (1950): 833, 840.

3. McDonald, *AH*, 29, 34; Elkins and McKitrick, *AF*, 97.

4. Michael P. Zuckert, *Natural Rights and the New Republicanism* (Princeton: Princeton University Press, 1994), xix (hereafter *NRNR*); Jerome Huyler, *Locke in America: The Moral Philosophy of the Founding Era* (Lawrence: University Press of Kansas, 1995), 27–28 (hereafter *LA*); McDonald, *AH*, 29, 34; Elkins and McKitrick, *AF*, 97.

5. Hamilton, *FV*, P 1: 47–48; *FR*, P 1: 100.

6. Samuel Seabury, *A View of the Controversy Between Great Britain and Her Colonies*, in *Annals of America*, 2: 289 (Chicago: Encyclopedia Britannica, 1968) (hereafter *VC*); Hamilton, *FR*, P 1: 122.

7. Seabury, *VC*, 290; *FR*, P 1: 87.

8. Thomas Hobbes, *Leviathan*, ed. C. B. MacPherson (London: Penguin Books, 1968), 18: 228–33; John Locke, *Second Treatise of Government*, in *Two Treatises of Government*, ed. Peter J. Laslett (Cambridge: Cambridge University Press, 1991) 139: 361–62 (hereafter *ST*); Hamilton, *FR*, P 1: 86–89; and Stourzh, *AHIRG*, 22.

9. Hamilton, *FR*, P 1: 87–88; Stourzh, *AHIRG*, 9–36 passim; McDonald, *AH*, 30–31; and Locke, *ST*, 269–71: 4–7.

10. Hamilton, *FR*, P 1: 88.

11. Ibid.

12. Seabury, *VC,* 290; Hamilton, *FR,* P 1: 92–93, 99.

13. Hamilton, *FV,* P 1: 75–76; *FR,* P 1: 94, 126–27, 141; Seabury, *VC,* 292; and Locke, *ST,* 230: 417.

14. Hamilton, *FR,* P 1: 95. The quotation is from Hume's "Of the Independency of Parliament," in *Essays,* 42–43. Hume borrowed this supposition from Machiavelli (see *Discourses,* 1, 3: 201, and *The Prince,* 15: 61).

15. Machiavelli, *Discourses,* 2, 2: 333; Hamilton, *FR,* P 1: 100. The quotations from Hume are from "That Politics May Be Reduced to a Science," in *Essays,* 18–24. Hume did not italicize "provinces" in the passage; by italicizing it, Hamilton apparently wished to stress the danger of exploitation by imperialist powers even more than Hume.

16. See also Bailyn, *IOAR,* 26.

17. Hamilton, *FR,* P 1: 104–5.

18. Hamilton, *FV,* P 1: 46.

19. Little reveals the debt of early liberals like Locke and Hamilton to Machiavelli more than their shared scorn of passive resistance. Machiavelli had argued that the "current religion," or Christianity, had "made the world weak and turned it over as prey to wicked men, who can in security control it, since the generality of men, in order to go to Heaven, think more about enduring their injuries than avenging them." Thus, Christianity, when it counseled humility, had made the world "effeminate." Without saying so, Machiavelli seemed to think the recovery of liberty required the overthrow of the current religion, or perhaps more accurately (since such an overthrow was unlikely and dangerous), a radical reinterpretation of it so that it would be more compatible with preservation and freedom. Thus, he observed, perhaps disingenuously, that the problem was not with Christianity itself but with those who have "interpreted our religion according to sloth and not according to vigor. For if they would consider that it allows us," or must be interpreted to allow us, "the betterment and defense of our country, they would see that it intends that we love and honor her and prepare ourselves to be such that we can defend her" (*Discourses,* 2, 2: 238). See also Locke, *First Treatise,* in Laslett, ed., *Two Treatises,* epigraph, and 58: 182–83; *ST,* 6–7: 271; Machiavelli, *The Prince,* 26: 103, and *Florentine Histories,* 5, 8; Livy 9.1.215; Nathan Tarcov, *Locke's Education for Liberty* (Chicago: University of Chicago Press, 1984), 19–21, 63 (hereafter *LEFL*); and Thomas Pangle, *SMR,* 310 n.1.

20. Dr. Myles Cooper, *A Friendly Address,* 5, as quoted in Alexander Clarence Flick, *Loyalism in New York During the American Revolution* (New York: Arno Press, 1969), 9 (hereafter *LNY*); and *ST,* 241: 427.

21. Hamilton, *FV,* P 1: 48–51.

22. Seabury, *VC,* 293–94, and Rakove, *BNP,* 65.

23. Hamilton, *FV,* P 1: 48; *FR,* P 1: 136; and Locke, *ST,* 159: 374–75.

24. Locke, *ST,* 240: 426–27.

25. See, for example, Richard H. Cox, *Locke on War and Peace* (Oxford: Clarendon Press, 1961), 136–63 (hereafter *LWP*), and Nathan Tarcov, "PPFP."

26. Hamilton, *FV,* P 1: 51.

27. Ibid., 51–52.

28. Ibid. See also Michael Walzer, *Just and Unjust Wars: A Moral Argument with Historical Illustrations* (New York: Basic Books, 1977), 21; Russett and Star, *WP*, 363–67.

29. Hamilton, *FV*, P 1: 52–53.

30. Locke, *First Treatise*, 1: 141.

31. Hamilton, *FV*, P 1: 54–56.

32. Ibid., 56–63; *FR*, P 1: 140.

33. Hamilton, *FV*, P 1: 48; *FR*, P 1: 89–90, 99; and Seabury, *VC*, 290.

34. Seabury, *VC*, 290; Hamilton, *FR*, P 1: 88, 99.

35. Hamilton, *FV*, P 1: 77.

36. Hamilton, *FR*, P 1: 90–91, 122.

37. Seabury, *VC*, 291.

38. Hamilton, *FR*, P 1: 98–99.

39. Ibid., 91; McDonald, *AH*, 19.

40. McDonald, *AH*, 30; Pocock, *MM*, 528–31.

41. Hamilton, *FR*, P 1: 129.

3. FIT FOR WAR

1. Hamilton to James Duane (hereafter Duane), 3 September 1780, P 2: 401; Rakove, *BNP*, 288.

2. Edmund Cody Burnett, *The Continental Congress* (New York: Macmillan, 1941), 487 (hereafter *CC*); Rakove, *BNP*, 289–92, 295, 325.

3. Sue Davis, *American Political Thought: Four Hundred Years of Ideas and Ideologies* (Englewood Cliffs, NJ: Prentice Hall, 1996), 102; and Lawrence Delbert Cress, "Republican Liberty and National Security, American Military Policy as an Ideological Problem, 1783 to 1789," *WMQ* 38, 3d ser. (1981): 73–96. See also Charles Royster, *A Revolutionary People at War: The Continental Army and the American Character, 1775–1783* (Chapel Hill: University of North Carolina Press, 1979), 42–51 (hereafter *RPW*); Richard Buel Jr., "Samson Shorn: The Impact of the Revolutionary War on Estimates of the Republic's Strength," in *Arms and Independence: The Military Character of the American Revolution*, ed. Ronald Hoffman and Peter J. Albert (Charlottesville: University of Virginia Press, 1984); and Donald Higginbotham, "The Debate over National Military Institutions," in *The American Revolution: Changing Perspectives*, ed. William M. Fowler and Wallace Coyle (Boston: Northeastern University Press, 1979).

4. Carl von Clausewitz, *On War*, ed. Michael Howard and Peter Paret (Princeton: Princeton University Press, 1984), 89, and Rossiter, *AHC*, 149.

5. Duane, P 2: 417.

6. See Russett and Starr, *WP*, 134–49; John Nef, *War and Human Progress: An Essay on the Rise of Industrial Civilization* (New York: Norton, 1950), 250; and Hans

Morgenthau, *Politics Among Nations: The Struggle for Power and Peace*, brief ed., rev. Kenneth Thompson (New York: McGraw Hill, 1993), 143–54.

7. Clausewitz, *On War*, 89.

8. Duane, P 2: 401; *Continentalist* 1, 19 July 1781, P 2: 650–51.

9. Duane, P 2: 414–17, and *Continentalist* 3, 9 August 1781, P 2: 663.

10. Duane, P 2: 406; Hamilton to Col. John Laurens, 30 June and 12 September 1780, P 2: 328, 428; and Howard Peckham, *The War for Independence* (Chicago: University of Chicago Press, 1958).

11. Hamilton, *FV*, December, 1774, P 1: 54; *FR*, February 1775, P 1: 155–57; *Continentalist* 3, 9 August 1781, P 2: 662–63; Machiavelli, *Discourses*, 2, 2: 328–33; Royster, *RPW*, 25, 142, 194–95.

12. *Continentalist* 3, P 2: 663–64; Burnett, *CC*, 397, 402–3, 407, 419, 423, 427, 466, 473–74, 511; and Rakove, *BNP*, 206–14, 275.

13. Ferguson, *PP*, 9, 26, 32, 48, 52–63, 64, 110.

14. Duane, P 2: 401, 406–7.

15. Ibid., 401–2, 407–8, and Hamilton's *Unsubmitted Resolution Calling for a Constitutional Convention*, P 3: 420–21.

16. Duane, P 2: 402, 404, 406; *Continentalist* 1, 650–52; Machiavelli, *The Prince*, 1: 5–6, 24: 97, and *Discourses*, 3, 11: 458.

17. Duane, P 2: 402–3, 407–8; *Continentalist* 2–3, P 2: 654–65.

18. Duane, P 2: 403–5; Burnett, *CC*, 317, 503, 592, 605, 607; and Rakove, *BNP*, 197–205, 218.

19. Duane, P 2: 404–5; Montesquieu, *The Spirit of the Laws*, trans. Thomas Nugent (New York: Hafner, 1949), 3, 7: 25; 9, 1: 126 (hereafter *SL*).

20. Duane, P 2: 405; Hamilton's *Unsubmitted Resolution Calling for a Convention to Amend the Articles of Confederation*, July 1783, P 3: 420–21.

21. Hamilton to Robert Morris, 30 April 1781, P 2: 604–5, and Ferguson, *PP*, 118, 135.

22. Hamilton to Robert Morris, P 2: 606, and Flaumenhaft, *ER*, 19.

23. Duane, P 2: 408, 412–13; *Continentalist* 6, 4 July 1782, P 3: 105–6; and Burnett, *CC*, 493–95.

24. Duane, P 2: 414; Hamilton to Morris, 604–5, 631; Rakove, *BNP*, 302; and Ferguson, *PP*, 120.

25. See Jacques Necker, *A Treatise on the Finances of France*, trans. Thomas Mortimer, 3 vols. (London: Logographic Press, 1787), 1: ix–xiii, xxii–xxiii, xciv; Donald F. Swanson and Andrew P. Trout, "Alexander Hamilton, 'the Celebrated Mr. Necker,' and Public Credit," *WMQ*, 3d ser. 48 (July 1990): 424–30; McDonald, *AH*, 135–36, 164–71; and Robert Parks, *The European Origins of the Economic Ideas of Alexander Hamilton* (New York: Arno Press, 1977).

26. Duane, P 2: 413–15; Hamilton to Morris, P 2: 616–20, 624; and Nef, *War and Human Progress*, 293.

27. Duane, P 2: 413–16; Hamilton to Morris, P 2: 617–18; and David Hume, "Of Commerce," in *Essays*, 253–67.

28. *Continentalist* 5, 18 April 1782, P 3: 76, and David Hume, "Of the Jealousy of Trade," in *Essays*, 327–31.

29. Hamilton to John Dickenson, 25–30 September 1783, P 3: 454, and Duane, P 2: 410. See also Royster, *RPW*, 194–95, 214–15, 220–23.

30. Burnett, *CC*, 312–13, 393, 444. Hamilton also wanted to rid the army of foreign officers whose presence tended to undermine the morale of American officers, but it was difficult to cashier them without offending American allies. Pensions were ideally suited for getting rid of foreign officers without offending allies. See Duane, P 2: 402, 409–10; Hamilton to George Clinton, 13 February 1778, P 1: 149, and Hamilton to William Duer, P 1: 247.

31. Hamilton to John Jay, 14 March 1779, P 2: 17–19.

32. Burnett, *CC*, 532; Ferguson, *PP*, 143, 149, 152; and Rakove, *BNP*, 304–7, 313–16.

33. Rakove, *BNP*, 317; Hamilton to Washington, 13 February 1783, P 3: 254; and Kohn, *ES*, 18–21.

34. Hamilton to Washington, 13 February 1783, P 3: 254.

35. Burnett, *CC*, 552–55, 560; Ferguson, *PP*, 156–63; and Rakove, *BNP*, 317–18, 322.

36. See Richard Kohn, "The Inside History of the Newburgh Conspiracy: America and the Coup d'Etat," *WMQ* 27, 3d ser. (1970): 198, 201, and *ES*, 36; McDonald, *AH*, 45; Paul David Nelson, "Horatio Gates at Newburgh, 1783: A Misunderstood Role," *WMQ* 29, 3d ser. (1972): 143–51, with Kohn's rebuttal, 151–58; and C. Edward Skeen, "The Newburgh Conspiracy Reconsidered," *WMQ* 31, 3d ser. (1974): 273–91, with Kohn's rebuttal, 291–98.

37. Hamilton to John Dickenson, 25–30 September 1783, P 3: 438–58.

38. Hamilton to Washington, 25 March 1783, P 3: 306. Despite the sound and fury of Kohn's discussion of a potential coup d'etat at Newburgh, his broad conclusion that the Morrisites were willing to spark a mutiny rests on two simple premises: that General Gates and officers connected to him were willing to use force (not merely incendiary addresses) to obtain the compensation they believed they deserved, and that the Morrisites were willing to cooperate with Gates before betraying him later ("Inside History," 198, 201; *ES*, 36). Yet Nelson, "Gates," denies that Gates intended an actual mutiny. If so, it is hard to see how the Morrisites planned to betray Gates for starting one. Moreover, Skeen cites James Madison, who quoted Hamilton as saying in private company on 20 February 1783 that he had written to Washington advising him "'to be the conductor of the army in their plans for redress, in order that they might be moderated and directed to proper objects, and exclude some other leader who might foment and misguide their councils.'" According to Skeen, "Hamilton was thus conscious of the dangers in the use of the army by the nationalists and was concerned that 'some other leader,' presumably Gates, should not direct the movement" ("Newburgh," 284). If Hamilton was deliberately warning Washington of danger from Gates and if Kohn's conclusion rests on the premise that the Morrisites were willing to cooperate with Gates, then Kohn's accusations of nationalist militarism are simply without foundation, at least with respect to Hamilton. Skeen's conclusions are much more judicious than Kohn's: "There was

nothing particularly sinister" in the Morrisites' efforts to unite creditors and the army to secure an independent source of revenue; "rather it was a mark of their desperation that they would attempt to use the army as a pressure group. . . . They were quite aware of the dangers inherent in the move, but they believed that the end justified the means" ("Newburgh," 274–75).

39. Royster, *RPW*, 35–38; Kohn, *ES*, 3–7; and Higgenbotham, "Debate over National Military Institutions," 154.

40. Cress, "Republican Liberty and National Security," 77–84. See also Russell F. Weigley, *The American Way of War: A History of United States Military Strategy and Policy* (Bloomington: Indiana University Press, 1973), 3–18.

41. *Report on a Military Peace Establishment* (hereafter *RMPE*), 18 June 1783, P 3: 381–83.

42. Royster, *RPW*, 194–95.

43. Duane, P 2: 411, 413. Hamilton stuck by this conviction long after the war. At the Federal Convention of 1787, for example, he observed that one reason a "free government is to be preferred to an absolute monarchy" is the "tendency of the Free Government to interest the passions of the community in its favor" and to "beget public spirit and public confidence." See Hamilton's "Notes Taken at the Federal Convention," 1–26 June 1787, P 4: 163. On 28 June 1788 at the New York Ratifying Convention, Hamilton attributed this devotion to the public good to the hopes that parents have for their children (P 5: 125). In this respect, he was clearly following in the footsteps of Machiavelli (see *Discourses*, 2: 330–31).

44. Hamilton, *RMPE*, P 3: 382–97.

45. Ibid. Hamilton would later modify the details but retain the general principles of this plan in his draft of Washington's "Speech to Congress," 10 November 1796, P 20: 384–85, and in various proposals for reorganizing the military during the Quasi-War, P 21: 83, 342–43, 362, 486, P 22: 389–90, and P 24: 70, 310.

46. *Continentalist* 6, 4 July 1782, P 3: 102.

4. SAFE FOR LIBERTY

1. The exact number of Tories in New York is uncertain. During the war, Hamilton believed perhaps as much as one-half the population was disaffected. At war's end, he believed open or secret Tories constituted about one-third of the population. (See Hamilton to Robert Morris, 13 August 1782, P 3: 132, 141.) Flick confirms these estimates in *LNY*, 180–82.

2. See Edward Floyd De Lancey, ed., *History of New York During the Revolutionary War . . . by Thomas Jones*, 2 vols. (New York, 1879), 2: 505–6, and Morton and Penn Bordon, *The American Tory* (Englewood Cliffs, NJ: Prentice Hall, 1972), 92.

3. Flick, *LNY*, 180–82; Christopher Moore, *The Loyalists* (Toronto: MacMillan of Canada, 1984), 112.

4. Hamilton to Robert R. Livingston, 13 August 1783, P 3: 431.

5. Robert Livingston to Hamilton, 30 August 1783, P 3: 435.

6. John Jay to Alexander Hamilton, 28 September 1783, P 3: 459–60.

7. Goebel, *LPAH*, 1: 210–13; Flick, *LNY*, 163; Moore, *The Loyalists*, 111.

8. See Syrett's and Cooke's notes, P 3: 479, 483–84, and Goebel, *LPAH*, 1: 211.

9. *First Letter of Phocion*, 1–27 January 1784, P 3: 484.

10. *Second Letter of Phocion*, April 1784, P 3: 553–54. See also Nathan Tarcov, "Alexander Hamilton and the French Revolution," paper, New School for Social Research Bicentennial Conference, 24 October 1986.

11. *First Letter of Phocion*, P 3: 495.

12. Ibid., 494–95; *Second Letter of Phocion*, P 3: 553. As the editor of Hamilton's legal papers first observed, there is a Machiavellian foundation for Hamilton's position toward suspected Loyalists. Machiavelli argued that those who intend their republic to become a "great power," an empire, like Rome, should strive to increase its population. This is done in one of two ways, either through love, by keeping the ways "open and safe for foreigners" and former enemies to live in the republic, or through force, by destroying former enemies and colonizing their territory. By assimilating the vanquished, the Romans produced not only public-spirited citizens but also much larger armies than their opponents and necessarily triumphed. See Machiavelli, *Discourses*, 2, 3: 334, and Goebel, *LPAH*, 1: 221.

13. Wood, *Creation*, 404, 410–12.

14. *First Letter of Phocion*, P 3: 485–86, 494–95.

15. *Second Letter of Phocion*, P 3: 557.

16. Ibid., 534–35.

17. Ibid., 550–52.

18. Ibid., 551–52.

19. Locke, *ST*, 240: 426–27.

20. Goebel, *LPAH*, 1: 290–96.

21. Briefs no. 2 and no. 3 for *Rutgers v. Waddington*, in Goebel, *LPAH*, 1: 334, 337.

22. Goebel, *LPAH*, 1: 296–97.

23. Ibid., 311, 352.

24. Ibid., 296–97, 309–10.

25. *First Letter of Phocion*, P 3: 486, 492; and Briefs no. 2 and no. 6, in Goebel's *LPAH*, 1: 352–53, 391.

26. *Second Letter of Phocion*, P 3: 558. See also Machiavelli, *Discourses*, 1, 34: 268, and Mansfield, *TP*, 247.

27. Burnett, *CC*, 542.

28. Hamilton to George Clinton, 27 July 1783, P 3: 418.

29. Richard Harison, as quoted by Syrett, P 4: 126, 140.

30. Thucydides' *Peloponnesian War*, 1, 44: 75.

31. *Remarks on an Act Acknowledging the Independence of Vermont*, 28 March 1787, P 4: 140.

32. Ibid., 127.

33. Ibid., 126–29.

34. Ibid., 130–32.

35. Ibid., 131–32.

36. Ibid., 131–33.

37. Ibid., 132–33; Locke, *ST*, 224: 415.

38. Hamilton, *FR*, February 1775, P 1: 94.

39. *Remarks*, P 4: 133–37.

40. Ibid., 137–38.

41. Ibid., 139–40.

42. Ibid., 130; William Graham Sumner's *The Conquest of the United States by Spain* (Boston: Estes Publishers, 1899), 40, and Sumner's *Alexander Hamilton* (New York: Dodd, Mead, and Company, 1890).

43. Kohn, *ES*, 272, 285–86.

5. REPUBLICAN EMPIRE

1. The volume of literature on *The Federalist* is enormous. Martin Diamond's many essays, now collected in *As Far as Republican Principles Will Permit*, remain the essential starting point for thinking about Publius as the Founder of a modern democratic republic. In *The Philosophy of the American Constitution: A Reinterpretation of the Intentions of the Founding Fathers* (New York: Free Press, 1968), however, Paul Eidelberg makes a strong case for a much more aristocratic dimension to Publius's republicanism, which he approximates to an Aristotelian mixed regime. The best recent work on Publius is David Epstein's *Political Theory of The Federalist*. In the spirit of Diamond, Epstein treats the text as a coherent and original piece of political theory. Yet unlike Diamond, who never explained why Publius was a republican, Epstein argues that an honorable determination to vindicate the capacity of mankind for self-government is the animating passion of Publius's liberal-republicanism. Morton White's *Philosophy, The Federalist, and the Constitution,* the first account of the work by a practicing professional philosopher, says little about the republican dimension of the work. Instead, White demonstrates that Publius synthesized Lockean first principles with Humean political psychology. Following Diamond, George W. Carey, in *The Federalist, Design for a Constitutional Republic* (Urbana: University of Illinois Press, 1989), critiques the Progressives' view of Publius as an opponent of a democratic republic as this interpretation was first developed in 1913 by Charles Beard in *An Economic Interpretation of the Constitution of the United States* (New York: Free Press, 1986) and still later by Robert Dahl in *A Preface to Democratic Theory* (Chicago: University of Chicago Press, 1956). Gottfried Dietze's *The Federalist: A Classic of Federalism and Free Government* (Baltimore: Johns Hopkins University Press, 1960) was the first book to treat the work as a major contribution to the modern understanding of war and free government. In contrast, Garry Wills, in *Explaining America: The Federalist,* though he consistently reminds us of Publius's public-spiritedness, has little to say about war in the text. In *Saving*

the Revolution: The Federalist Papers and the American Founding (New York: Free Press, 1987) (hereafter *SR*), Charles R. Kesler et al. confront Beard, Wood, and other revisionists by making a strong case for understanding the work as an effort to fulfill the principles of the Revolution rather than as a repudiation of it. Within that work, Patrick J. Garrity's essay, "Foreign Policy and *The Federalist*," is one of the rare attempts by a contemporary scholar of international relations to come to terms with the strategic thought of its authors. Also helpful in that regard are Frederick W. Marks III, *Independence on Trial: Foreign Affairs and the Making of the Constitution*, and Nathan Tarcov, "War and Peace in *The Federalist Papers*," paper prepared for the Liberty Fund Symposium on *The Federalist*, Claremont, California, 12–15 January 1989. In *The Authority of Publius: A Reading of the Federalist Papers* (Ithaca, NY: Cornell University Press, 1984), Albert Furtwangler explains the enduring authority of the text in terms of its authors' candor, a quality that makes us recur to it whenever we wish to learn the truth about ourselves. Michael P. Zuckert summarizes most of this literature in "*The Federalist* at 200—What Is It to Us?" *Constitutional Commentary 7* (1990): 97–107. These accounts need to be supplemented with and tested by Thomas Engeman's *Federalist Concordance*, which allows the reader to investigate the meaning of Publius through an exhaustive index of key words and phrases in the text.

Hamilton's role at the New York Convention is much disputed. His partisans sometimes treat his speeches as a heroic effort that overcame determined opposition from George Clinton and resulted in the quasi conversion of the leading Anti-Federalist, Melancton Smith. Others explain the ratification of the Constitution in New York in light of fears that it would be isolated if it refused to ratify and the threat that New York City would secede from the state. See, for example, John Fiske, *The Critical Period in American History, 1783–1787*, 342; Andrew C. McLaughlin, *The Confederation and the Constitution* (Boston: Little, Brown, 1895), 311; Henry Cabot Lodge, *Alexander Hamilton* (Boston: Houghton Mifflin, 1895), 71–73; Frederick S. Oliver, *Alexander Hamilton, an Essay on American Union* (London: G. P. Putnam and Sons, 1912), 176–79; Louis M. Hacker, *Alexander Hamilton in the American Tradition* (New York: McGraw Hill, 1957), 124–26; Rossiter, *AHC*, 61–67; Nathan Schachner, *Alexander Hamilton* (New York: D. Appleton Century Company, 1946), 225–26; Linda Grant De Pauw, *The Eleventh Pillar: New York State and the Federal Constitution* (Ithaca, NY: Cornell University Press, 1966); John C. Miller, *Alexander Hamilton: Portrait in Paradox*, 209–15; and Robin Brooks, "Alexander Hamilton, Melancton Smith, and the Ratification of the Constitution in New York," *WMQ* 24, 3d ser. (1961): 339–58.

2. F 1: 3.

3. For Hamilton's stress on national honor during this debate, see F 15: 91–92, with his declaration that national weakness had led to the "last stage of national humiliation." In *IT*, 96–143, Frederick Marks explains the complex foreign policy issues, such as British occupation of the Northwest, which wounded American honor in 1787. For the vital role of human, national, statesmanlike, and republican honor throughout *The Federalist*, see Epstein, *PTF*, 111–25 especially.

4. Douglass Adair, "The Disputed Authorship of *The Federalist Papers*," in *Fame and the Founding Fathers*, ed. Trevour Colbourn (New York: Norton, 1974), 68 (hereafter *Fame*). As George W. Carey shows, Adair's assertion "cannot be substantiated from the text" of *The Federalist*. Adair suggested that *The Federalist* contains two alternative strategies for addressing faction, Hamilton endorsing a violent one, rooted in Montesquieu's traditional approach, in *Federalist* 9, and Madison supporting a peaceful, pluralistic solution in *Federalist* 10. One led to militarism; the other, to modern liberty. This bias was not only unfair to Hamilton, who consistently presented an energetic union as the best alternative to military enforcement of the laws, but it was also a distortion of Madison. As Carey reveals, Madison later quoted the same passage Hamilton quoted from Montesquieu to make the same point: one advantage of a federation is that its members can preserve it by uniting against members who rebel against it, or worse, seek to dominate it. Compare Hamilton's F 9: 50 with Madison's F 43: 295; and then see Carey's "Publius—A Split Personality?" *ROP* 46 (1984): 9–10.

5. F 1: 5. The danger of militarism was only one of many of the Anti-Federalists' fears about the Constitution, but it was perhaps most important in framing Hamilton's response to them. See, for example, Nathan Tarcov, "The Federalists and Anti-Federalists on Foreign Affairs," *Teaching Political Science: Politics in Perspective* 14 (1986): 38–45, and Stourzh, *AHIRG*, 126–30. Useful surveys of Anti-Federalist thought include Herbert J. Storing's *What the Anti-Federalists Were For!* (Chicago: University of Chicago Press, 1981) (hereafter *What*); Cecelia M. Kenyon's classic, "Men of Little Faith: The Anti-Federalists on the Nature of Representative Government," *WMQ* 12, 3d ser. (1955): 3–43; James H. Hutson's "Country, Court and Constitution: Antifederalism and the Historians," *WMQ* 38 (1981): 336–68; Jackson Turner Main's *The Antifederalists: Critics of the Constitution, 1781–1788* (Chapel Hill: University of North Carolina Press, 1961); Murray Dry's "Anti-Federalism in *The Federalist*," in Kesler et al., *SR*, 40–60; and Christopher M. Duncan's *The Anti-Federalists and Early American Political Thought* (DeKalb: Northern Illinois University Press, 1995).

6. See Jefferson to George Rogers Clark, 25 December 1779, as quoted by Julian P. Boyd in "Thomas Jefferson's 'Empire of Liberty,'" *Virginia Quarterly Review* 24 (1948): 549–50; Jefferson to the President and the Legislative Council, the Speaker of the House of Representatives of the Territory of Indiana, 28 December 1805, as quoted by Adrienne Koch, in *Jefferson and Madison, the Great Collaboration* (New York: Oxford University Press, 1950), 244–45; Stourzh, *AHIRG*, 191–92; Pocock, *MM*, 531–34; and Robert Tucker and David Hendrickson, *Empire of Liberty: The Statecraft of Thomas Jefferson* (New York: Oxford University Press, 1990).

7. Stourzh, *AHIRG*, 193, and F 23: 151.

8. See F 70: 471; Hamilton's *Notes Taken at the Federal Convention*, 6 June 1787, 165–66; and McDonald, *AH*, 100.

9. F 51: 350–51.

10. See Lance Banning, "The Hamiltonian Madison: A Reconsideration," *Virginia Magazine of History and Biography* 92 (1984): 3–28.

11. Some scholars have suggested Hamilton's differences with Madison were deep enough in 1787 to give Publius a split personality. Yet there is little that either Hamilton or John Jay said about war and foreign policy that Madison failed to say as well. Conversely, there is little Madison said about faction, representation, federalism, and the separation of powers that was not repeated or taken for granted by Hamilton and Jay. (Compare, for example, Jay's F 3: 15–16 with Madison's *Federalist* 10; Hamilton's F 23: 147 with Madison's F 41: 270; and Madison's F 48: 338 with Hamilton's F 73: 494.) This is not to deny differences among the authors. As Lance Banning observes in *The Sacred Fire of Liberty* (Ithaca, NY: Cornell University Press, 1995), 398–402 (hereafter *SF*), the status of federalism, judicial review, standing armies, and America's role in the world may have been latent sources of division between the two chief contributors to the text. At this stage of their careers, however, most differences seem to have been over matters of emphasis arising from the division of labor in their essay assignments. On this complicated question, see Alpheus Thomas Mason, "The Federalist—A Split Personality," *American Historical Review* 57 (1952): 625–43; Douglass Adair, "The Disputed Authorship of The Federalist Papers," *WMQ* 3d ser. (1944): 97–122, 235–64 (later reprinted in Colbourn, ed., *Fame*); and Carey, "Publius—a Split Personality?" 5–22.

12. In *AHIRG*, 193–201, Stourzh presents Hamilton as essentially emancipated from his revolutionary principles in the conduct of foreign policy. Following Adair, Stourzh suggests that Hamilton's ruling passion was the love of fame, which was best served by an aggressive foreign policy ultimately aiming at the conquest and domination of much of Latin America. For Stourzh, Hamilton belongs to Lincoln's well-known tribe of the lion and race of the eagle, that group of morally ambiguous statesmen who would win glory at any price, whether by saving a republic or overthrowing one, by setting men free or enslaving them. No one can deny Hamilton's love of fame, but Richard Loss takes both Stourzh and Adair to task for suggesting Hamilton subordinated his principles to his thirst for renown in "Alexander Hamilton and the Modern Presidency: Continuity or Discontinuity?" *Presidential Studies Quarterly* 12 (1982): 23 (hereafter "AHMP"). Loss reminds us that Hamilton believed the "'*worst* of evils'" was a "'*loss of our virtue.*'" Hamilton also warned Lafayette in France in 1789 to be "'virtuous amidst the seductions of ambition'" (23). These reminders are well taken, but Loss probably goes too far in the opposite direction. Hamilton's grand, and sometimes grandiose, sense of honor does remind us of Aristotle's great-souled man (*Nicomachean Ethics*, 1123b3–1125a20), if not even of Lincoln's confrontation with the Circe of ambition in Harry V. Jaffa's *Crisis in the House Divided: An Interpretation of the Lincoln Douglas Debates* (Garden City, NY: Doubleday, 1959). Still, it is not necessary to make Hamilton a model of almost godlike Aristotelian virtue to explain the role and problem of honor in his thought. Hamilton's reflections on fame arose not only from his classical education but also

from his reading of Hume, who was no less important for Hamilton's sense of humanity. This was not a classical virtue and was meant as a corrective to the excessively warlike spirit of the ancient republics. Besides, as McDonald observes (*AH,* 37), Hume treated the love of fame as so near to the "'love of laudable actions for their own sake'" as to be almost indistinguishable from the love of virtue itself. Hume's analysis of ambition may best describe Hamilton, whose highest objective was to deserve fame, but how? Stourzh is half right, when he argues that the answer is by establishing an American empire, but he is also half wrong, because Hamilton's ambition was truly revolutionary, to found and perpetuate the empire through the humane liberal-republican principle of consent.

13. See, for example, Benjamin F. Wright, "*The Federalist* on the Nature of Political Man," *Ethics* 59 (1949): 1–31; James P. Scanlon, "*The Federalist* and Human Nature, *ROP* 21 (1959): 657–77; Maynard Smith, "Reason, Passion, and Political Freedom in *The Federalist,*" *Journal of Politics* 22 (1960): 525–44 (hereafter *JOP*); Arthur O. Lovejoy, *Reflections on Human Nature* (Baltimore: Johns Hopkins University Press, 1961), 37–65; and Daniel W. Howe, "The Political Psychology of *The Federalist,*" *WMQ* 44, 3d ser. (1987): 485–509. Scanlon may have best expressed the focus of this line of inquiry: "How can intellectually feeble humanity understand or be moved by elaborate reasoning, and how can a morally feeble humanity safely be given political power?" ("*The Federalist,*" 658). Howe identifies the rhetorical conceit by which Publius appeals to reason among men governed by passion: "He wins us over by insisting that he will not [sic!] flatter us, that he trusts our judgment because we too understand the weaknesses of human nature" ("Political Psychology," 509).

14. Rossiter, *AHC,* 41–44; McDonald, *AH,* 94.

15. See Herbert J. Storing, "The Constitutional Convention: Toward a More Perfect Union," Works of the Mind Lecture, University of Chicago, 1961.

16. For general accounts of the Convention, see James Madison, *Notes of Debates in the Federal Convention of 1787* (Athens: Ohio State University Press, 1966); Max Farrand's *The Framing of the Constitution of the United States* (New Haven: Yale University Press, 1913) and Farrand, ed., *Records;* John P. Roche, "The Founding Fathers: A Reform Caucus in Action," *APSR* 55 (1961): 799–816; Michael Kammen, ed., *The Origins of the American Constitution* (New York: Penguin Books, 1986); Leonard W. Levy and Dennis J. Mahoney, eds., *The Framing and Ratification of the Constitution* (New York: Macmillan Publishing Company, 1987); and Edmund S. Morgan, *The Birth of the Republic, 1763–1789* (Chicago: University of Chicago Press, 1956).

17. Hamilton, *Notes for Speech on a Plan of Government,* 18 June 1787, P 4: 184, 186; Madison's version, P 4: 191–92, 195; *Plan of Government,* P 4: 207–9. Hamilton later clarified his remarks about abolishing the states. The national government required "indefinite authority" not limited by the states, which is why the nationally appointed governors could veto the legislatures in his plan. Otherwise, he feared that the largest states especially, like Virginia and Massachusetts, would be so powerful that they would "subvert" the Union (P 4: 211).

18. *Speech of 18 June 1787*, Madison's version, P 4: 193; *Plan of Government*, P 4: 207.

19. Hamilton's second *Draft of a Constitution*, 17 September 1787, P 4: 253–74.

20. *Remarks on Signing the Constitution*, 17 September 1787; *Conjectures about the New Constitution*, 17–30 September 1787, P 4: 253, 275.

21. See Farrand, ed., *Records*, 1: 402.

22. "The Essays of Brutus," in Herbert Storing's *The Anti-Federalist: Writings of the Opponents of the Constitution*, abr. Murray Dry (Chicago: University of Chicago Press, 1985).

23. Patrick Henry, speech of 5 June 1788 at the Virginia Ratifying Convention, in Storing, *The Anti-Federalist*, 300–305.

24. Storing, *What*, 31.

25. The Federal Farmer, in Storing, *The Anti-Federalist*, 2.8.23–26, 42–45. See also Richard Henry Lee, Brutus, and Demosthenes Minor, as quoted by Storing in *What*, 17, 19–20. Fearing that modern readers might find the Anti-Federalists' fears too archaic, Storing suggested we might understand their dread better by substituting "bureaucracy" for "standing army." "The Anti-Federalists," he observed, "were not so much worried about military coups or 'militarism' in the popular sense, as about the rigid rule of a large and varied republic by the force of government, of which the standing army is the ultimate expression." Storing's change in the meaning of words does not seem quite fair, however. The Anti-Federalists knew what they meant and why, when they concluded that military force would be required to uphold national laws. In 1787, it was far from clear that a republic could also be an empire. As Storing himself reveals, they believed a small republic could be free because it could realistically rely on affection to unite the community; they thought a large empire could not be free because affection decreased in empires, which traditionally based their authority more on fear. Hamilton's major contribution to this long-standing debate was to show how even a large empire could produce affection, if it were founded on consent and capable of responsible administration.

26. F 34: 212.

27. F 11: 68–69.

28. F 15: 93.

29. Ibid., 94.

30. F 17: 107–8.

31. Hamilton's pay book, 1777, P 1: 405, and *Continentalist* 2, 19 July 1781, P 2: 656.

32. *New York Ratifying Convention, Remarks of 20 June 1788*, P 5: 19–22; F 15: 95; and F 16: 101.

33. Epstein, *PTF*, 38–39, and F 16: 101–2. See also F 9: 53–54.

34. F 7: 36–43, and Dietze, *The Federalist*, 180, 193–207, 234–36.

35. F 8: 44–46.

36. Ibid., 46.

37. Marks, *IT*, 94, 103–5, 130, 197, 210, 213.

38. F 8: 46.

39. Ibid., 47–48.

40. Ibid., and F 24: 157.

41. Machiavelli, *The Prince*, 18: 65–68. See also Roger D. Masters, *Machiavelli, Leonardo, and the Science of Power* (Notre Dame, IN: Notre Dame University Press, 1996), 135–46.

42. *First Speech at the New York Ratifying Convention* (Child's version) 21 June 1788, P 5: 40, 45; McKesson's version, P 5: 49; and Melancton Smith's version, P 5: 51.

43. F 17: 107; F 27: 172; and *First Speech of 21 June 1788 at the New York Ratifying Convention*, P 5: 39, 44. See also Herbert Storing, *What*, 42.

44. F 27: 174.

45. F 16: 103.

46. Jean Jacques Rousseau, *On the Social Contract with Geneva Manuscript and Political Economy*, ed. Roger D. Masters, trans. Judith R. Masters (New York: St. Martin's Press, 1978), 1, 1: 46; 2, 4: 63; and 3, 1: 79. In "Alexander Hamilton: Rousseau of the Right," *PSQ* 73 (1958): 161, Cecelia M. Kenyon first compared Hamilton to Rousseau, by which she meant a romantic political idealist (not the tough-minded realist for which he has earned much of his reputation). As McDonald confirms (*AH*, 5), Kenyon is surely right about Hamilton's romantic streak, though she does no justice to the mixture of romantic vision and political realism that made him unique. Moreover, the differences between Hamilton and Rousseau are at least as important as the similarities. The citizen of Geneva hated commercial society, but the New Yorker is one of the Founders of American capitalism. To preserve the complete devotion of republicans to their communities, Rousseau advocated confederal unions, not the sort of empire praised by Hamilton. Most important, Hamilton treated consent as a means to secure natural rights, but the Genevan cut his ties to natural rights and made the general will the only standard of political rights.

47. F 23: 145–46.

48. F 1: 3; F 85: 594–95.

49. F 11: 72–73.

50. Stourzh, *AHIRG*, 196.

51. F 85: 594–95.

52. The former was the animating force of the Progressive critique of the Framers and is perhaps stated best by James MacGregor Burns in *The Deadlock of Democracy* (Englewood Cliffs, NJ: Prentice Hall, 1963). The latter tends to be the consensus of most American political scientists, who generally view the Constitution through the lens of Madison's *Federalist* 10 and 51. As a result, they tend to ignore the authors' many arguments for making the national government more energetic than Congress was under the Articles.

53. F 17: 105; F 34: 212; *Speeches at the New York Ratifying Convention*, 12 and 27 June 1788, P 5: 153.

54. This was no trivial argument. It had the support of such unlikely bedfellows as Immanuel Kant, who argued that perpetual peace required a constitutional pro-

hibition on the power to borrow for war, and of James Madison. Unlike the Anti-Federalists, Madison did not endorse a two-thirds majority to borrow for war. Yet during the debate over neutrality in the war between England and France in the 1790s, he did argue that peace required that all governments become republics and that republics fight only pay-as-you-go wars. When the people governed and were obliged to bear the costs of war instead of passing them to future generations, Madison hoped that their self-interest might balance their ambition, reason gain an ascendancy in the public councils, and peace become more likely. See Kant's "Perpetual Peace, a Philosophical Sketch," in *Perpetual Peace and Other Essays,* trans. David Humphrey (Indianapolis: Hackett, 1983) 109, and Madison, *Universal Peace,* in Marvin Meyers, ed., *The Mind of the Founder* (Waltham, MA: Brandeis University Press, 1981), 191–94 (hereafter *MF*).

55. *Second and Third Speeches at the New York Ratifying Convention,* 2 July 1788, P 5: 144–45, and Montesquieu, *SL,* 11: 6: 154–55.

56. F 23: 146–48; *New York Ratifying Convention, Remarks of 27 June 1788,* P 5: 98; F 23: 147; F 34: 211; and F 36: 230.

57. F 25: 162–63. See also Machiavelli, *Discourses,* 1, 34: 268.

58. F 23: 150; *Remarks at the New York Ratifying Convention,* 27 June 1788, P 5: 95.

59. *Third Speech at the New York Ratifying Convention,* 21 June 1788, P 5: 54.

60. See Epstein, *PTF,* 179–85, and Flaumenhaft, *ER,* 94–95, 192, 286.

61. *Speech at the New York Ratifying Convention,* 24 June 1788, P 5: 68–69.

62. Ibid., 68–69, 73–74.

63. Ibid., and *First Speech at the New York Ratifying Convention,* 25 June 1788, P 5: 73–74, 85.

6. EXECUTIVE ENERGY AND REPUBLICAN SAFETY

1. For Hamilton's limited role in framing Article 2 of the Constitution, see William B. Michaelson, *Creating the American Presidency, 1775–1789* (Lanham, MD: University Press of America, 1987), 130, and Charles E. Thach, *The Creation of the American Presidency, 1775–1789* (Baltimore: Johns Hopkins University Press, 1923).

2. See Edward S. Corwin, ed., *The Constitution of the United States of America: Analysis and Interpretation,* S. Doc. 170, 82d Cong., 2d sess., 381 (Washington, DC: GPO, 1955), and *The President, Office and Powers, 1787–1984,* 5th rev. ed., ed. Randall W. Bland et al. (New York: New York University Press, 1984), 209–10; Rossiter, *AHC,* 248; and Jeffrey K. Tullis, The Rhetorical Presidency (Princeton: Princeton University Press, 1987), 7.

3. Forrest McDonald, *The American Presidency: An Intellectual History* (Lawrence: University Press of Kansas, 1994), 6, 334–45 (hereafter *AP*). For McDonald's accounts of Hamilton's contribution to the presidency, see also his *AH* and *The Presidency of George Washington* (Lawrence: University Press of Kansas, 1974) (hereafter *PGW*).

4. Theodore Roosevelt, *An Autobiography* (New York: Macmillan, 1913), 83.

5. Woodrow Wilson, *Constitutional Government in the United States* (New York: Columbia University Press, 1921), 56.

6. Richard Loss, "AHMP" 6–7, 18–19. Loss goes on to demonstrate that Roosevelt considered himself a disciple of the "'Jackson-Lincoln theory of the Presidency,'" not a Hamiltonian one. Though Loss shows no sympathy for Lincoln's situation during the Civil War, which would have challenged anyone who meant to preserve both the Union and the Constitution, he does reveal that Corwin knew Hamilton's works well enough to see the differences between his theory of energy and the claims to limitless powers that Loss attributes to Roosevelt and Wilson. Corwin, he suggests, developed a "Platonic noble lie" in order to make "constitutional interpretation and presidential action more responsible by anchoring the modern theory of the presidency in Hamilton's thought" (7, 21). Loss elaborates this thesis in *The Modern Theory of Presidential Power: Alexander Hamilton and the Corwin Thesis* (Westport, CT: Greenwood Press, 1990).

7. Pocock, *MM*, viii, 507–10, 529–33; Stourzh, *AHIRG*, 132–45 passim; Mansfield, *TP*, 247–78; Machiavelli, *Discourses*, 1, 6: 209–10; 1, 20: 246; 2, 19: 378–79; 3, 9: 452–53.

8. This appears to be the implied thesis of Mansfield's *TP*.

9. Machiavelli, *Discourses*, 1, 33: 264; 1, 34: 267–69.

10. In "AHMP," 8, 22–23, Loss suggests Hamilton had nothing but contempt for the acquisitive individualism he associates with Locke. In *LA*, 279–91, Jerome Huyler focuses almost exclusively on domestic policy issues in Hamilton's disputes with the Jeffersonians. He therefore fails to take into account the significant role of Locke's federative power in Hamilton's discussions of foreign policy. The best corrective to these views is Nathan Tarcov's "War and Peace in *The Federalist Papers*," paper prepared for the Liberty Fund Symposium on *The Federalist*, Claremont, California, 12–15 January 1989. See also his "Principle, Prudence, and the Constitutional Division of Foreign Policy," in *Foreign Policy and the Constitution*, ed. Robert A. Goldwin and Robert A. Licht (Washington, DC: American Enterprise Institute, 1990), 20–40.

11. Hamilton never spoke of prerogative in his *Pacificus* essays. According to Engeman et al., *The Federalist Concordance* (420), Hamilton and Madison used the term in *The Federalist* on thirty occasions (fifteen each). They almost always used it in the loose, non-Lockean sense of a traditional privilege of sovereignty or the British Crown. Hamilton used the term most often (six times) in *Federalist* 69, with prerogative covering matters from shielding political cronies from legal prosecution to declaring war and forming alliances (Locke's federative power). His fundamental point, however, was the same as Madison's: the American president was not a king and did not possess these prerogatives. When Hamilton defended energy, he therefore meant something quite different from prerogative.

12. For Locke, prerogative also included the right to reapportion the legislature when it became unrepresentative. See *ST*, 364–66: 143–48; 374–80: 159–68; Montesquieu, *SL*, 11, 6: 151; McDonald, *AP*, 50–52; and Cox, *LWP*, 123–29.

13. Morton J. Frisch, "Executive Power and Republican Government," *PSQ* 17 (1987): 281–90, and J. C. Vile, *Constitutionalism and the Separation of Powers* (Oxford: Clarendon Press, 1967) (hereafter *CSP*).

14. F 70: 472. For an exhaustive account of unity and duration in Hamilton's thought on administration and the Constitution, see Flaumenhaft, *ER*, 82–157.

15. F 70: 471. For the Anti-Federalists' fears of executive energy, see Storing, *What*, 49.

16. F 70: 471–72.

17. Ibid., 475–76; F 74: 500.

18. F 70: 472, 475–76.

19. Ibid., 473–74.

20. F 47: 324; F 70: 474, 477; and Locke, *ST*, 143: 364.

21. F 71: 481.

22. F 71: 485. See also Epstein's *PTF*, 182.

23. F 72: 486. See also Flaumenhaft's *ER*, 86.

24. *The Defense* 2, 25 July 1795, P 18: 498–519.

25. F 72: 487.

26. Ibid., 488.

27. Ibid., 487.

28. F 25: 163.

29. F 72: 491–92; Machiavelli, *Discourses,* 1, 34: 267.

30. See Arthur M. Schlesinger Jr., *The Imperial Presidency* (Boston: Houghton Mifflin, 1973), 235, and Frisch, "Executive Power and Republican Government, 1787," 283.

31. F 71: 483–84.

32. *Speech at the New York Ratifying Convention,* 21 June 1788, P 5: 38; F 71: 483. See also Epstein, *PTF,* 130–33.

33. F 71: 483.

34. See Hume's "Idea for a Perfect Commonwealth," in *Essays,* 519, 521.

35. F 74: 501–2.

36. Machiavelli, *Discourses,* 3, 12: 459–62; F 74: 501–2.

37. See McDonald's *AH,* 298, and Thomas P. Slaughter, *The Whiskey Rebellion* (New York: Oxford University Press, 1986), 175–89.

38. Kohn insists on "Hamilton's eagerness to use force" during this crisis; indeed, he claims that "Hamilton provoked the Whiskey Rebellion by unnecessarily prosecuting delinquent distillers in federal courts in order to brandish the government's military power and chill opposition" (*ES,* 157–70, 278). Forrest McDonald originally accepted this conventional view of Hamilton's intentions as it was first developed by Leland D. Baldwin in *Whiskey Rebels: The Story of a Frontier Uprising* (Pittsburgh: University of Pittsburgh Press, 1939) 110–12. McDonald too suggested that Hamilton called for federal subpoenas to "provoke resistance so that he could crush it with force" in *PGW,* 145–46. Yet following Jacob Cooke, in "The Whiskey Insurrection: A Reevaluation," *Pennsylvania History* 30 (July 1963): 326–28, McDonald later

changed his mind in *AH,* 431, nn 27–28; he observes that the source of the charge, which bears a remarkable resemblance to Kohn's claim that Hamilton incited a mutiny in order to crush it at Newburgh, was William Findley, one of Hamilton's inveterate political enemies. There is absolutely no evidence to confirm it. In the absence of such evidence, one must presume that the subpoenas that helped spark the rebellion were issued not on Hamilton's instigation, but as the law provided, by the federal district judge on application of the federal district attorney. McDonald suggests that Kohn's claim that Hamilton was "eager" to use force is "based mainly on a distortion of Hamilton's language in his letter to Washington of September 1, 1792." Kohn "overlooks the fact that one of Hamilton's expressed reasons for advocating a proclamation (to Washington, September 9, 1792, in Syrett, ed., *Papers,* 12: 345)" warning distillers to comply with the law was that it might "'prevent the necessity of ulterior coercion.' Curiously Kohn . . . interprets Washington as having a moderating influence on a trigger-happy Hamilton because the president said that force should be used only as a 'dernier resort'; and yet he fails to mention that in the letter in which Hamilton allegedly expressed his eagerness to employ force, Hamilton himself said that force was to be used only as a 'last resort.'" To be sure, different members of Washington's cabinet had different views on when this last resort would be necessary. By 1794 Hamilton probably believed sooner was more likely than later, but fairness requires acknowledging that he too meant to avoid the last resort, so far as that was possible. One must also consider that Hamilton argued throughout the crisis (and his career) that government must rest either on force or on law. Kohn quotes Hamilton to this effect but then distorts his meaning again, as if the former were as equally acceptable to Hamilton as the latter, if not even more so. In truth, Hamilton did not support suppressing the rebellion as an alternative to the rule of law but as an unfortunate means required to uphold it when the normal procedures of the courts were no longer capable of doing so. On this issue, see also Kohn's "The Washington Administration's Decision to Crush the Whiskey Rebellion," *JAH* 59 (December 1972): 570.

39. Hamilton to Thomas Mifflin, 10 October 1794, and Hamilton to Angelica Church, 23 October 1794, P 17: 317–38, 340. See also Machiavelli, *The Prince,* 17: 67.

40. *Tully* 1–4, 2 September 1794, P 17: 132–33, 149, 159–60, 179.

41. See Aaron Wildavsky, "The Two Presidencies," *Transaction* 4 (1966): 13–20.

42. See Madison to George Washington, 16 April 1787, in *The Letters and Other Writings of James Madison,* ed. William C. Rives and Philip R. Fendall, 4 vols. (Philadelphia: J. P. Lippincott, 1865), 2: 348–49 (hereafter *LWJM*).

43. F 75: 503.

44. See *Helvidius* 1, in Meyers, ed., *MF,* 209.

45. F 75: 504–5.

46. F 64: 432–38; F 75: 505.

47. F 75: 505–6.

48. *The Defense* 36, P 20: 6–7. See also Locke's *ST*, 135–41: 357–63. The Supreme Court went far beyond both Locke and Hamilton by ruling that a treaty can override the Constitution in *Missouri v. Holland*, 252 U.S. 416 (1920).

49. *The Defense* 36, 2 January 1796, P 20: 7.

50. Ibid., 8.

51. Ibid., 37, 6 January 1796, P 19–20.

52. Ibid., 2–6 January 1796, P 20: 9–10, 16, 20.

53. Banning, *JP*, 216.

54. See Douglass Adair, in Colbourn, ed., *Fame*, 73.

55. *Pacificus* 1, 29 June 1793, P 15: 37–38.

56. Montesquieu, *SL*, 11, 6: 151.

57. *Pacificus* 1, P 15: 39–40. See also Mansfield's *TP*, 276–77, and Locke, *ST*, 129: 352. In F 77: 515, Hamilton made an often-noted mistake in his discussion of the removal power, which he suggested would require the consent of the Senate. Ironically, it was Madison in the House who helped save the executive from the embarrassments that would have followed from Hamilton's clearly ill-considered early views of this power.

58. *Pacificus* 1, P 15: 40–41.

59. Ibid., 41–42.

60. Ibid.

61. See Ralph Ketcham, *James Madison* (New York: Macmillan, 1971), 346.

62. *Helvidius* 1 and 4, in Meyers, ed., *MF*, 200–212. Madison made several errors while transcribing from *Pacificus*. He wrote, "In support of this conclusion [that Hamilton was supporting prerogative] it would be enough to echo, 'that the prerogative, in this active sense, is connected with the executive in various capacities—as the organ of intercourse between the nation and foreign nations—as the interpreter of treaties . . . as the power which is charged with the execution of the laws, of which treaties make a part—as that power which is charged *with the command and execution of the public force*'" (*Helvidius* 4: 210). Hamilton's actual words were that the power to declare neutrality "appears to be connected with the executive in various capacities, as the *organ* of intercourse the nation and foreign nations—as the interpreter of treaties when the judiciary is not competent, that is the cases between Government and Government—as that Power which is charged with the Execution of the Laws, of which treaties form a part,—as that power which is charged with the command and application of the Public Force" (*Pacificus* 1, P 15: 38). Although Hamilton did not use the word "prerogative" in this passage or anywhere else in *Pacificus*, Madison used it three times in the paragraph preceding his misquotation, thus creating the illusion that Hamilton's own words supported his conclusion. Madison also left out Hamilton's qualifying phrase, "where the judiciary is not competent, that is the cases between Government and Government." Last of all, he added italics to Hamilton's phrase, "command and application of the public force." Scholars' failure to compare what Madison said about Hamilton with what

Hamilton actually said goes far to explain why we assume what we have no right to conclude, that Hamilton was advocating prerogative, when in fact he was seeking energetic ways to avoid it.

63. Ibid.

64. F 41: 270.

65. F 6: 33.

66. F 41: 270.

67. *New York Assembly, First Speech on the Address of the Legislature to Governor Clinton's Message,* 19 January 1787, P 4: 11. See also Hamilton's *Third Speech at the New York Ratifying Convention,* 21 June 1788, P 5: 57; and *Remarks at the New York Ratifying Convention,* 27 June 1788, P 5: 94–95.

68. Banning, *JP,* 217.

69. F 8: 46; F 25: 163. One might add an important Tocquevillian observation to Hamilton's fear that prerogative would undermine the rule of law. It might even threaten the spirit of liberty, for "it is not the exercise of power or habits of obedience which depraves men, but the exercise of a power which they consider illegitimate and obedience to a power which they think usurped and oppressive" (*DA,* author's introduction, 14.)

70. In defending this purchase, Jefferson spoke about himself in the third person: "The executive in seizing the fugitive occurrence which so much advances the good of their country, have done an act beyond the Constitution." He did not advocate a Lockean appeal to the people to judge his conduct but left the responsibility for invoking prerogative to Congress. "The legislature in casting behind them metaphysical subtleties [strict construction?], and risking themselves like faithful servants, must ratify and pay for it, and throw themselves upon their country for doing for them unauthorized, what we know they would have done for themselves had they been in a situation to do it" (Jefferson to John Breckenridge, 12 August 1803, in Peterson, ed., *PJ,* 497.)

7. NATIONAL SECURITY, POPULAR SOVEREIGNTY, AND A LIMITED CONSTITUTION

1. F 78: 524–25.

2. Ibid., 523–25, 528.

3. Ibid., 523–35.

4. F 22: 143–44. At the beginning of the Washington administration, Hamilton spoke with England's confidential agent in America, Maj. George Beckwith, about making a commercial agreement to allow Americans more or less the same access to British markets that they had enjoyed before the Revolution. Beckwith, however, insisted that nothing could be done unless Americans lived up to their treaty obligations to pay compensation for property confiscated during the Revolution and to enforce the collection of prewar debts to British creditors. In response,

Hamilton reminded Beckwith of the passage of the first Judiciary Act establishing the federal courts and the Supreme Court. It would take time for cases to work their way through the judicial process, but he assured Beckwith that the judiciary gave teeth to the treaty power and that the Judiciary Act would make the courts effective in asserting that power against the states. Therefore, England could trust the United States to honor its treaty commitments and make other agreements beneficial to both nations. See *Conversation with George Beckwith*, October 1789, P 5: 486–87.

5. F 3: 14.

6. Marks, *IT*, 11.

7. F 3: 14–17.

8. Ibid., 15.

9. Ibid., 15–16. See also Nathan Tarcov's "War and Peace in *The Federalist Papers.*"

10. F 4: 17–18, and Tarcov, "War and Peace."

11. F 3–4: 17–23.

12. F 80: 535–37. Initially at least, Madison seemed to agree with Hamilton about the necessity of establishing some substitute for the royal veto, which helped to sustain the British Empire before the Revolution. Shortly before the Federal Convention, Madison observed that the royal negative was essential to preserve the "harmony of [the British] empire." He then suggested that a "negative *in all cases whatsoever* on the legislative acts of the States, as heretofore exercised by the Kingly prerogative, appears to be absolutely necessary" to preserve the American Union (Madison to Washington, 16 April 1787, in Meyers, ed., *MF*, 65–69). According to Lance Banning (*SF*, 400), Madison later changed his mind about the veto (and perhaps even judicial review?), which he presumably came to see as more dangerous to a compound republic than useful or necessary to a durable union.

13. F 22: 143–44; F 80: 535; and *The Examination* 5, 29 December 1801, P 25: 477–78.

14. F 80: 835, and *Remarks on the Repeal of the Judiciary Act* (First and Third Versions), 11 February 1802, P 25: 523, 526.

15. F 80: 535–38.

16. See, for example, Donald M. Snow's *National Security: Defense Policy for a New International Order* (New York: St. Martin's Press, 1995); David A. Deese, ed., *The New Politics of American Foreign Policy* (New York: St. Martin's Press, 1994); and Charles W. Kegley Jr. and Eugene R. Wittkopf, *American Foreign Policy*, 5th ed. (New York: St. Martin's Press, 1996). Because the influence of Hamilton's imperial chamber is indirect, none of these standard texts has anything to say about the judiciary as an instrument of American national security policy.

17. Rossiter, *AHC*, 93–95.

18. F 78: 524.

19. *Opinion on the Constitutionality of an Act to Establish a Bank*, 23 February 1791, P 8: 98, 102–3, 107.

20. For Hamilton as a Hobbesian see, among many others, Banning, *SF*, 310. The common tendency to reduce Hamilton to Hobbes results from confusion about

Locke's relation to Hobbes. Locke certainly agreed with Hobbes that without a common judge, or sovereign, the state of nature tends toward a state of war. He also made enormous room for Hamiltonian responsibility in his discussion of the federative power. This pushed both Locke and Hamilton in the direction of an unlimited sovereign, at least with respect to foreign affairs. Yet in common with Hamilton, Locke insisted that even war is governed by the law of nature. In sum, they generally agreed with Hobbes's (and Machiavelli's) descriptions of political behavior, and the necessities that may arise from it, especially in relations between sovereign states. Yet fear of arbitrary power led them to the non-Hobbesian conclusion that revolution is justified when the absolute power sometimes required for the ends of civil society is used arbitrarily. This view led Locke to preach vigilance as well as responsibility and even induced Hamilton to practice vigilance when it seemed appropriate, such as at the beginning of the American Revolution. Also consider Hamilton's almost Jeffersonian remark that the security of liberty in the kind of constitution he advocated "must altogether depend on public opinion, and on the general spirit of the people and the government." See Locke, *ST*, 135–39: 357–62, and F 84: 580.

21. *Opinion on the Constitutionality of an Act to Establish a Bank,* 23 February 1791, P 8: 98, 102–3, 107.

22. Ibid., P 8: 103, 107, 109.

23. See F 23: 150–51; F 27: 172; and F 31: 197–98.

24. F 78: 527.

25. Ibid., 529.

26. Federal Farmer 16, in Herbert J. Storing's *The Complete Anti-Federalist* (Chicago: University of Chicago Press, 1984), 2.8.96.

27. Jefferson to Madison, 15 March 1789, in Peterson, ed., *PJ,* 489.

28. Brutus, 15, in Storing's *Complete Anti-Federalist,* 2.9.186, 193, and Storing's *What,* 50.

29. Banning, *SF,* 325–33; Madison's speech in the House of Representatives, 2 February 1791, in *The Papers of James Madison,* ed. Robert A. Rutland et al. (Chicago and Charlottesville: University Press of Chicago and University Press of Virginia, 1962–), 13: 376–78 (hereafter *PJM*); and Jefferson's *Opinion on the Constitutionality of a National Bank,* 15 February 1791, in Peterson, ed., *PJ,* 261–68.

30. Jean Yarbrough, "Republicanism Reconsidered: Some Thoughts on the Foundation and Preservation of the American Republic," *ROP* 41 (1979): 61–95; Banning, *SF,* 332–33, 340–65; and Rahe, *RAM,* xx–xxi, 60, 237–39.

31. Tocqueville, *DA,* 1, 5: 88.

32. Hamilton to Duane, 3 September 1780, P 2: 407–8; F 17: 105. See also Storing, *What,* 50. Think, for example, about the Department of Defense today, which is a virtual state within the American State. Did any of the Founders contemplate establishing housing subdivisions, schools, and recreation areas, including golf courses and scuba diving clubs, for military personnel and their dependents? None of these frills is strictly necessary to an effective military establishment, but the general morale

and welfare of officers and enlisted ranks benefit greatly from close contact with their families. The need to keep the troops happy (or more pessimistically, less miserable) by making their families less miserable then leads to a seemingly exponential proliferation of benefits. Madison was right: there was no end to the powers that Hamilton's broad construction might imply, but his willingness to follow a chain of implications to its end was neither absurd nor dishonest. Even in 1787, he argued that the powers to raise troops and money for war ought to be unlimited. If appropriating money to pay for scuba diving clubs helps to make troops more willing to serve their country, such appropriations serve a legitimate national purpose, and from this point of view, are clearly constitutional.

33. Tocqueville, *DA*, 1, 2: 57.

34. Consider, for example, the internment of Japanese Americans during World War II, and then see again F 8: 45–48.

35. F 37: 234–37, and Epstein, *PTF*, 114–18.

36. F 28: 179.

37. Locke, *ST*, 240: 426–27.

8. COMMERCIAL REPUBLICANISM

1. On Hamilton's synthesis, see Syrett's discussion of the diverse sources of Hamilton's political economy in his notes to Hamilton's *Report on the Subject of Manufactures*, 5 December 1791, P 10: 1–15, as well as Elkins and McKitrick, *AF*, 261, and Donald F. Swanson and Andrew P. Trout, "Alexander Hamilton's Invisible Hand," *Policy Review* (winter 1992), 86–87. For Hamilton as a critic of the theory of commercial republican peace, see Ralph Lerner, "Commerce and Character," in *TR*, 195–221; Pocock, *MM*, 531; and Stourzh, *AHIRG*, 145–53.

2. Banning, *SF*, 323; Elkins and McKitrick, *AF*, 138–39; John S. Bassett, *The Federalist System* (New York: John M. Cooper Publishers, 1906), 31 (hereafter *FS*); John C. Miller, *The Federalist Era, 1789–1801* (New York: Harper, 1960), 56, 76 (hereafter *FE*); and Drew R. McCoy, "Republicanism and American Foreign Policy: James Madison and the Political Economy of Commercial Discrimination, 1780–1794" (hereafter "RAFP") *WMQ* 3d ser. (1974): 642.

3. Madison, *Vices of the Political System of the United States*, April 1787, in Meyers, ed., *MF*, 58, and McCoy, "RAFP," 634–35.

4. See, for example, Francis Fukuyama, "The End of History," and Michael Doyle, "Liberalism and World Politics," in *The New Shape of World Politics*, ed. Fareed Zakaria (New York: Norton, 1997), 1–25, 39–66.

5. For the specific Anti-Federalists Publius sought to refute, see Murray Dry, "Anti-Federalism in *The Federalist*," in Kessler et al., *SR*, 40–60.

6. "First Letter of Agrippa," 23 November 1787, in Dry's *Anti-Federalist*, 230.

7. "Seventh Letter of Agrippa," 25 December 1787, in ibid., 243.

8. Montesquieu, *SL*, 9, 2: 127–28; 11, 3: 150–51; 20, 1–2: 316–17; 21, 14: 358–59; and 20: 366. See also Stephen J. Rosow, "Commerce, Power, and Justice: Montesquieu and International Politics," *ROP* (1984): 366–96.

9. F 6: 28–29; Hamilton to Duane, 3 September 1780, P 2: 403; Thucydides, *Peloponnesian War*, 1. 88. 50–51. For the levels-of-analysis approach to understanding international conflict, see James N. Rosenau, "Pre-Theories and Theories of Foreign Policy," in *Approaches to Comparative and International Politics*, ed. R. Barry Farrell (Evanston, IL: Northwestern University Press, 1966), 27–93, and Schuyler Foerster and Edward N. Wright, "The Twin Faces of American Defense Policy, International and Domestic," in *American Defense Policy*, ed. Schuyler Foerster and Edward N. Wright (Baltimore: Johns Hopkins University Press, 1990).

10. Hamilton to George Clinton, 3 October 1783, P 3: 468, and F 7: 39–40.

11. F 7: 40.

12. F 6: 29; F 9: 51.

13. F 6: 32–33.

14. *Continentalist* 5, 18 April 1782, P 3: 76–77. See also Hume's "Of the Jealousy of Trade," "Of Commerce," and "Of Refinement in the Arts," in *Essays*, 253–80, 321–27.

15. F 8: 47; F 24: 156.

16. Huntington, *SS*, 290.

17. Tocqueville, *DA*, 2, part 2, 22–23: 645–54. Tocqueville's observations also suggest why democratic statesmen sometimes feel compelled to overstate threats to their nations: that is perhaps the best way to overcome their instinctive pacifism.

18. *The Defense* 10, 26 August 1795, P 19: 174; F 6: 35.

19. F 22: 135–37.

20. See Syrett's notes to Hamilton's *Conversation with Beckwith*, October 1789, P 5: 482; Elkins and McKitrick, *AF*, 124, 137–38; and Miller, *FE*, 38, 41, 53.

21. *Defense of the Funding System*, July 1795, P 19: 8. Hamilton did not make the seventh point after the fact. In his *Report Relative to a Provision for the Support of Public Credit*, P 6: 106, he did not say that a public debt was a blessing but that "the proper funding of the present debt will render it a national blessing." He was "so far from acceding to the position, in the latitude in which it is sometimes laid down, that 'public debts are public benefits,' a position inviting to prodigality, and liable to a dangerous abuse,—that he ardently" hoped to see "it incorporated, as a fundamental maxim, that the creation of debt should always be accompanied by the means of extinguishment." Hamilton regarded this approach as the "true secret of rendering public credit immortal." See also Donald F. Swanson and Andrew P. Trout, "Alexander Hamilton's Economic Policies After Two Centuries," in *New York History* (July 1971): 297.

22. *Defense*, P 19: 2–3.

23. Ibid., 4.

24. Ibid., 5–7.

25. Ibid., 20. Funding was not simply equitable, however. The states that had paid off most of their debts, such as Virginia, were being asked to pay the debts of other

states. This is a common though insufficient explanation of their opposition to assumption. In the case of Madison, opposition to assumption and support for discrimination also arose from a deep-seated hostility to the speculation that goes hand-in-hand with a credit economy. In Madison's view, Lance Banning observes, Hamilton's system was "immoral, inconsistent with the spirit of a federal republic, and part of a disturbing trend toward unjust and dangerous domination of the Union by New England" (*SF,* 298). To help Virginia and other states overcome their fear of being taxed to pay off the debts of various states, Roger Sherman apparently proposed a compromise, an outright grant to them, and Virginia received $3.5 million. As the story goes, Hamilton threw in a capital on the Potomac, near Virginia, to sweeten the deal. Not surprisingly, the final settlement of accounts revealed that many states, including Virginia, had been overpaid. See Bassett, *FS,* 34, and Miller, *FE,* 46–48, 53.

26. *Defense,* P 19: 22–26, 30.

27. Ibid., 37–38, and Elkins and McKitrick, *AF,* 120.

28. *Defense,* P 19: 37–38, 42–43.

29. Ibid., 37–38, 42–47. Hamilton's list of priorities is of some importance for evaluating his overall success as a statesman. If one assumes his ultimate goal was one national government without states, he obviously failed, but he denied this was the objective of his system (P 19: 42). By the time he retired from the Treasury, his funding system was so firmly rooted that he certainly succeeded in linking creditors to the survival (not triumph) of the national government. Civil war was a recurring threat in the United States from 1787 to 1861. Despite the controversy it created, assumption may well have eliminated one of the most likely sources for quarrels within the Union. Funding also increased the borrowing capacity of the government for war; so on balance, Hamilton succeeded in what he set out to do. For accounts giving higher priority to political integration by fiscal means in Hamilton's political thought than Hamilton did himself, see Elkins and McKitrick, *AF,* 118, and Bassett, *FS,* 28.

30. *Defense,* P 19: 60–62.

31. McDonald, *AH,* 166–67.

32. *Report Relative to the Provision of the Public Debt* (First Report on Public Credit), 9 January 1790, P 6: 67; Bassett, *FS,* 30.

33. *First Report,* P 6: 84–85, 106. As Donald F. Swanson and Andrew P. Trout suggest in "Alexander Hamilton's Hidden Sinking Fund," *WMQ* 49, 3d ser. (1992): 111, in 1795 Hamilton believed all the debt could be paid, if other circumstances did not get in the way. Though the War of 1812 slowed this process down, the debt from the Revolutionary War was retired in 1829. In "Money, Credit, and Federalist Political Economy," in Beeman et al., *Beyond Confederation,* Janet A. Rieseman notes another hidden sinking fund in Hamilton's system. Interest on the government's 20 percent share in the stock of the Bank of the United States could be used to retire the debt, too. In this regard, see also Hamilton's *Second Report,* P 7: 337–42; Donald F. Swanson, *The Origins of Hamilton's Fiscal Policies* (Gainesville: University of Florida Press, 1963), 77; and McDonald, *AH,* 164, 171.

34. *First Report,* P 6: 96–97; *Defense,* P 19: 39, 96–97.

35. *Defense,* P 19: 56, and Madison, "Universal Peace," in Rives and Fendall, eds., *LWJM,* 4: 470–72.

36. *Defense,* P 19: 52.

37. Ibid., 52–53. See also the *First Report,* P 6: 96.

38. Ferguson, *PP,* 9, 26, 32, 48, 52–63, 61, 110; Kramnick, "GND," 26.

39. *Defense,* P 19: 59–60. See also Elkins and McKitrick, who correctly suggest Hamilton derived this understanding of statesmanship from David Hume's essay, "Of Commerce" (*AF,* 109).

40. *Defense,* P 19: 59–60. See also Hume's "Of Refinement in the Arts," in *Essays,* 280, and F 34: 210–11.

41. *Defense,* P 19: 62. As Miller observes (*FE,* 50), speculation actually drove securities toward par, so it was ultimately more stabilizing than often acknowledged. Hamilton also considered it more than a little hypocritical for individuals who speculated in land, as anyone with even a little money apparently did, to criticize speculation in government securities. A far more serious problem, perhaps, was that before the funding system was established, the debt was concentrated in very few hands. Continental securities, worth at least $12.3 million, were owned by 3,300 individuals, 100 of whom owned $5 million of them. It is hard to know how much more was bought up by monied men before Hamilton proposed funding and assumption. It was probably a significant amount, however, and helps explain Madison's increasing opposition to Hamilton (see Banning, *SF,* 294). Speculation thus resulted in a substantial transfer of wealth from the many to the few (and probably, from the South to the North); the question is whether it could be justified. Though Hamilton did not emphasize it in his *Defense,* he generally followed Hume in thinking that investment capital was more productive and useful to society as a whole when it was concentrated in a few hands rather than in many. His trickle-down theory anticipates contemporary debates over tax breaks and capital gains deductions—should fiscal policy favor investors, the middle class, or the poor? There are no absolutely certain answers to this question. They depend on whether the circumstances demand greater emphasis on the development or on the distribution of wealth. In 1790 Hamilton saw a need for a stable and expanding money supply to spur investments that would ultimately help all Americans; but obviously, the incentives could lead to maldistribution of wealth and power, as Madison believed it had (see Elkins and McKitrick, *AF,* 111, 140).

42. *Defense,* P 19: 69–71.

43. Approximately $11 million of the continental debt consisted of loan certificates from monied men; $17 million consisted of final settlement certificates issued to both soldiers and civilian suppliers at the end of the war; another $13 million consisted of indents (certificates of accrued interest). See Elkins and McKitrick, *AF,* 137–38; Miller, *FE,* 42; and Banning, *SF,* 314.

44. Bassett, *FS,* 32.

45. Banning, *SF*, 315.

46. Hamilton to Lt. Col. Anthony Walton White, P 1: 334, and Hamilton to Col. Clement Biddle, P 2: 380.

47. *Defense*, P 6: 75–78, and Elkins and McKitrick, *AF*, 114.

48. *Final Version of the Second Report on the Further Provision Necessary for Establishing Public Credit (Report on a National Bank)*, 13 December 1790, P 7: 309–10, 329–30, and Bassett, *FS*, 39–40.

49. On the politically utopian dimension of the *Report,* see again Cecelia M. Kenyon, "Alexander Hamilton: Rousseau of the Right," 161–78, and John R. Nelson's insightful "Alexander Hamilton and American Manufacturing: A Reexamination," *JAH* 65 (1979): 974. According to Nelson, Hamilton failed to give sufficient attention to the artisans in New York City and elsewhere who worked in American manufacturing. They generally wanted much more protection from foreign competition than he suggested in his *Third Report.* Thus, his plan lacked sufficient carrots not only to attract the agrarian but also to keep the manufacturing vote. According to Nelson, Hamilton's party paid dearly for this, and other problems, in the New York elections in 1800. Had Hamilton been more of a protectionist, he might therefore have been more successful as a democratic politician. For Elkins and McKitrick, not only Hamilton but Jefferson and Madison as well were utopians of different kinds: Madison because his country lacked the power to carry out his trade policy; Jefferson because, in practice, agrarianism did not lead to a community of virtuous farmers but to the spread of slavery and brawling frontiersmen who were generally dominated by rich planters; and Hamilton because of his well-known impatience (the vice that sometimes accompanied his virtue of energy) (see *AF,* 101, 198).

50. See Madison's speeches of 8 and 25 April 1789, his speeches of 13, 14, 25 May 1790, and his letter to Thomas Jefferson, 30 June 1789, in *PJM,* 12: 66, 109, 119, 125–30; 13: 213, 256; Banning, *SF,* 300–301; and McCoy, "RAFP," 636.

51. Bassett, *FS*, 120–21, 130–31.

52. See Elkins and McKitrick, *AF,* 88–90, 113, 123–24, and Merrill D. Peterson, "Thomas Jefferson's Commercial Policy, 1783–1793," *WMQ* 22 (1965): 600.

53. *Conversation with Beckwith,* P 5: 483–89.

54. Hamilton to Jefferson, 11 January 1791, P 7: 423.

55. Ibid., 13 January 1791, P 7: 425–26; *The Defense,* 10, 26 August 1795, P 19: 174–76.

56. *Report on the Subject of Manufactures,* P 10: 262–65, and Peterson, "Thomas Jefferson and Commercial Policy, 1783–1793," 609.

57. *Report on the Subject of Manufactures,* 5 December 1791, P 10: 230, and Elkins and McKitrick, *AF,* 130–31, 258.

58. *Report on the Subject of Manufactures,* P 10: 231–35, 261–63, 266, and Adam Smith, *The Wealth of Nations,* ed. R. H. Campbell et al., 2 vols. (Indianapolis: Liberty Press, 1981) 1: 463–64, 2: 708.

59. See Huyler, *LA*, 282, and Nelson, "Alexander Hamilton and American Manufacturing," 975.

60. *Report on the Subject of Manufactures*, P 10: 291, 299–301, 313–17, 334.

61. Ibid., P 10: 255. Elkins and McKitrick note that Hume was among the first moderns to recognize the expansion of opportunity made possible by a commercial society (*AF*, 110).

62. Jefferson's *Notes on the State of Virginia* (Query 19), in Peterson, ed., *PJ*, 216–17, and McCoy, "RAFP," 640–45.

63. Pocock, *MM*, 423, 495; then compare Machiavelli's *Discourses*, 1, 55: 306–10, and his *Art of War*, 7: 205.

64. See Machiavelli, *The Prince*, 21: 91; Locke's *ST*, 42: 297–98; Hume's "Of Refinement in the Arts," in *Essays*, 277–78; Smith's *WN*, 1: 401–2; and Hamilton's *Remarks of 27 June 1788 at the New York Ratifying Convention*, P 5: 101.

65. See Drew R. McCoy, *The Elusive Republic*, 10. In "Commercial Farming and the 'Agrarian Myth' in the Early Republic," *JAH* 68 (1982): 833–49, among other writings, Joyce Appleby also objects to characterizing the quarrel between Hamilton and Jefferson as the struggle between classical and liberal ideas of political economy. She sees the struggle arising from a dispute over which form of capitalism would be best, a Hamiltonian one emphasizing limited state support of manufacturing or a more laissez-faire Jeffersonian one stressing commercial farming. The great advantage of Appleby's view of the conflict is that it can fit Jefferson's agrarianism within the larger context of his faith in progress and other modern ideas. She may therefore be right about the character of the struggle, but even so, fairness requires acknowledging a quality vaguely Aristotelian about Jefferson's agrarianism. For Aristotle, the great danger of commerce and maritime power was the introduction of foreign ways inconsistent with the habits of character a Founder sought to establish in a regime. Jefferson's hostility to educating Americans abroad clearly reveals his effort to prevent corruption in this sense. Yet Aristotle was not the only republican of antiquity. Pericles, the leader of the greatest maritime commercial republic of Greece, praised Athens for many of the dynamic qualities admired by Hamilton and Hume in their discussions of commerce. Our word "energy" comes from the Greek *energeia,* the term Aristotle used to describe the actualization of potential, including human potential. Hamilton may not have known the etymology of the energetic side of his character, and he may not have cared, but he did make a strong case that a commercial republic supplied greater opportunities for self-actualization than an agrarian one. See Jefferson to John Bannister, 15 October 1785, and Jefferson to Samuel Kercheval, 12 July 1816, in Peterson, ed., *PJ*, 392–95, 552–64; Jacob Klein, "Aristotle: An Introduction," lecture at St. John's College, Annapolis, Maryland, 20 April 1962, 13; Aristotle, *Nicomachean Ethics*, 1106a17–28, and *Politics*, 1327a15; and Thucydides, *Peloponnesian War*, 2. 37–41: 109–12.

66. Jefferson to Benjamin Austin, 9 January 1816, in Peterson, ed., *PJ*, 547–52; and Miller, *FE*, 74.

9. THE GATHERING STORM

1. Miller, *FE*, 219; Elkins and McKitrick, *AF*, 731.

2. Kohn, *ES*, 194–95, 225, 227, 229, 231, 236, 248–49, 252–54, 266, 272, 278, 285–86.

3. McDonald, *AH*, 265.

4. Hamilton, *Americanus* 2, 7 February 1794, P 16: 14. See also McDonald, *AH*, 264–65; Gilbert Lycan, *AHAFP*, 175; Banning, *JP*, 213–14; and Elkins and McKitrick, *AF*, 341.

5. See Gouverneur Morris to Hamilton, 24 December 1793, P 13: 376; Elkins and McKitrick, *AF*, 309, 337–38; Lycan, *AHAFP*, 132–37, 152; and McDonald, *AH*, 272.

6. See Hamilton's conversation with George Hammond, March–April 1793, P 14: 193–94; Hamilton to John Jay, 9 April 1793, P 14: 297–98; John Jay to Hamilton, 11 April 1793, P 14: 308–10; Alexander Hamilton and Henry Knox to George Washington, 2 May 1793, P 14: 372–84; Jefferson's Opinion on the French Treaty, 28 April 1793, P 14: 368–76; Hamilton to Washington, 2 May 1793, P 14: 398–400; *Pacificus* 2, 3 July 1793, P 15: 56; *Pacificus* 3, 6 July 1793, P 15: 66–67; McDonald, *AH*, 271–75; Lycan, *AHAFP*, 129, 139; Miller, *FE*, 129–31; Elkins and McKitrick, *AF*, 337–40; and Banning, *JP*, 215.

7. Hamilton to Washington, 2 May 1793; *Pacificus* 2, 3, 5, and 6, July 1793, P 14: 401–7; P 15: 56–62, 85–86, 92–95, 101, 131–33, 671–72; McDonald, *AH*, 278; and Locke, *ST*, 6: 270–71.

8. Elkins and McKitrick, *AF*, 338; McDonald, *AH*, 265, 272–73; Banning, *JP*, 211–12; Lycan, *AHAFP*, 149; and Madison, *Helvidius* 1, Meyers, ed., *MF*, 200, 208.

9. Banning, *JP*, 210–11; McDonald, *AH*, 280; and Thomas Jefferson to William Short, 3 January 1794, in Peterson, ed., *PJ*, 464–65.

10. Hamilton and Henry Knox to Washington, 2 May 1793, P 14: 368–75, 389–92; Hamilton to Washington, 2 May 1793, P 14: 401–7; Hamilton's Letter to ———, 18 May 1793, P 14: 473–76; *Pacificus* 2 and 3, July 1793, P 15: 59–61, 67–72; *Americanus* 1 and 2, January–February 1794, P 15: 670–72, P 16: 14–19; Lycan, *AHAFP*, 141–45, 151, 172; McDonald, *AH*, 271, 280; Miller, *FE*, 127; and Elkins and McKitrick, *AF*, 331–33, 359–60.

11. Elkins and McKitrick, *AF*, 334.

12. Hamilton to Washington, 15 September 1790, P 7: 38–41; Hamilton's *The Case of the Little Sarah*, 8 July 1793, P 15: 70–73; *The Stand* 4, 16 April 1798, P 21: 420; Elkins and McKitrick, *AF*, 333, 342–49; McDonald, *AH*, 267–81; Lycan, *AHAFP*, 146–48, 167, 170; Miller, *FE*, 134–37, 374; Bassett, *FS*, 88, 92–93, 95.

13. McDonald, *AH*, 289; Banning, *JP*, 378; Lycan, *AHAFP*, 162–63; Elkins and McKitrick, *AF*, 140–41; Bassett, *FS*, 118.

14. Hamilton to Washington, 8 March 1794, P 16: 130–36; Hamilton to Washington, 14 April 1794, P 16: 272–74; *The Defense* 5, 5 August 1795, P 19: 95–96; and McDonald, *AH*, 265–70.

15. See Hamilton to Washington, 14 April 1794, P 16: 130–36; Hamilton to Washington, March–May 1794, P 16: 224; Hamilton to Washington, 14 April 1794, P 16: 269–76; *The Defense* 2, 25 July 1795, P 18: 494–96; McDonald, *AH*, 267, 291–94; Lycan, *AHAFP*, vii; Banning, *JP*, 223–25; and Bassett, *FS*, 123.

16. Hamilton to Washington, 14 April 1794, P 16: 278; Hamilton to Washington, 23 April 1794, P 16: 319; McDonald, *AH*, 293, 308; Banning, *JP*, 233–34; Miller, *FE*, 126.

17. Remarks on the Jay Treaty, 9–11 July 1795, P 18: 451–52; *Horatius* 2, July 1795, P 19: 74–76; *The Defense* 3, 9 September 1795, P 19: 245–50; *The Answer*, 8 December 1796, P 20: 434; *The Defense* 2 and 5, 25 July–7 August 1795, P 18: 494, 498–99; P 19: 90–92, 99; Banning, *JP*, 234–35; McDonald, *AH*, 316–17.

18. See Washington to Hamilton, 2 November 1796, P 20: 362–65; Hamilton to Washington, 4–5 November 1796, P 20: 372–74; *The Answer*, 8 December 1796, P 20: 422; Hamilton to Washington, 25–31 January 1797, P 20: 480–81; *The Warning* 1, 27 January 1797, P 20: 493–94; Lycan, *AHAFP*, 144, 176, 278–79; Elkins and McKitrick, *AF*, 538, 565; Bassett, *FS*, 228; and McDonald, *AH*, 323–33.

19. Rufus King to Hamilton, February 1797, P 20: 507; Hamilton to Timothy Pickering, 29 March 1797, P 20: 556–57; Hamilton to Oliver Wolcott, 30 March 1797, P 20: 567–68; Hamilton to James McHenry, March 1797, P 20: 574–75; Hamilton to Oliver Wolcott, 5 April 1797, P 21: 23; Hamilton to William Loughton Smith, April 1797, P 21: 21, 33–36 and 37–39; Hamilton to Pickering, 11 May 1797; P 21: 81–82; Elkins and McKitrick, *AF*, 539, 545; McDonald, *AH*, 328, 334; and Lycan, *AHAFP*, 304–7.

20. See McDonald, *AH*, 331, 338–39; Miller, *FE*, 203, 206–7; Bassett, *FS*, 223–24, 234–35; Lycan, *AHAFP*, 261, 312, 332–35; Elkins and McKitrick, *AF*, 544, 583–84; Banning, *JP*, 252.

21. McDonald, *AH*, 327, 331, 337; Elkins and McKitrick, *AF*, 583–84; Bassett, *FS*, 235.

22. See Lycan, *AHAFP*, 335–36, 344–57; McDonald, *AH*, 327, 335–43; Elkins and McKitrick, *AF*, 545; Miller, *FE*, 218.

23. For a good survey of eighteenth-century fears of standing armies, see Kohn, *ES*, 305.

24. Ibid., 231; McDonald, *AH*, 331; Elkins and McKitrick, *AF*, 640.

25. See Elkins and McKitrick, *AF*, 589, 596, 634, 643, 647, 653, 659; Bassett, *FS*, 238; Miller, *FE*, 217; Lycan, *AHAFP*, 349, 356; Kohn, *ES*, 230–31, 243.

26. Hamilton to McHenry, 17 May 1798, P 21: 462; McDonald, *AH*, 330–31, 338. On the revolution in war introduced by the political revolution in France, see Theodore Ropp, *War in the Modern World* (New York: Macmillan, 1962), 98–142, and Michael Howard, *War in European History* (Oxford: Oxford University Press, 1976).

27. Miller, *FE*, 198–99; Banning, *JP*, 245, 263; Lycan, *AHAFP*, 276, 355.

28. Lycan, *AHAFP*, 368–69, and Miller, *FE*, 192.

29. *The Warning*, 27 January 1797, P 20: 494–95; Hamilton to Rufus King, 8 April 1797, P 21: 26–67; *The Stand* 1, 30 March 1798, P 21: 382–87; *The Stand* 2, 4 April 1798,

P 21: 396–97; Hamilton to McHenry, January–February 1798, P 21: 345; *The Stand* 3, 7 April 1798, P 21: 402–8; *The Cause of France*, 1794, P 17: 585–88; *The French Revolution*, 1794, P 17: 586–88; and *The War in Europe*, September–December 1796, P 20: 339–40.

30. Hamilton to Timothy Pickering, 22 March 1797, P 20: 543–46; Hamilton to Oliver Wolcott, 30 March 1797, *The Stand* 6, 19 April 1798, P 21: 434–36; Rufus King to Hamilton, 9 March 1799, P 22: 525; General Wilkinson to Hamilton, April 1799, P 23: 47–48; Lycan, *AHAFP*, 339–40; Machiavelli, *The Prince*, 1: 6.

31. Lycan, *AHAFP*, 340; *The Warning* 6, 13 March 1797, P 20: 542; Hamilton to Timothy Pickering, 22 March 1797, P 20: 545–46; *The Stand* 6, 19 April 1798, P 21: 437–40; and a letter Hamilton drafted for Washington to send to James McHenry, 13 December 1798, P 22: 341–52.

32. Hamilton to William Loughton Smith, 10 April 1797, P 21: 29–34; Hamilton to James McHenry, 29 April 1797, P 21: 63–67; Hamilton to Timothy Pickering, 11 May 1797, P 21: 81–83; *The Stand* 6, 19 April 1798, P 21: 434–35; and James Wilkinson to Alexander Hamilton, 15 April 1799, P 23: 47–48.

33. Hamilton to William Loughton Smith, 10 April 1797, P 21: 35.

34. Lycan, *AHAFP*, 373–80; *The Warning* 2, 7 February 1797, P 20: 509–12; *The Warning* 3, 21 February 1797, P 20: 520; *The Stand* 1, 30 March 1798, P 21: 382–87; Hamilton to Rufus King, 6 June 1798, P 21: 490. See also Sir Winston Churchill, "The Tragedy at Munich," in *The Gathering Storm* (Boston: Houghton Mifflin Company, 1948), 319–21.

35. For Republican invocations of national honor, see Banning, *JP*, 220–21.

36. See Karl Walling, "Alexander Hamilton on Honor and American Foreign Policy," in *Honor Among Nations: Intangible Interests and Foreign Policy*, ed. Elliott Abrams (Washington, DC: Ethics and Public Policy Center, 1998), 57–98.

37. *The Stand* 1, 30 March 1798, P 21: 382–87.

38. Russett and Starr, *WP*, 94–95, 134.

39. Hamilton to William Loughton Smith, 10 April 1797, P 21: 37–39; Hamilton to James McHenry, April 1797, P 21: 73–74; and Hamilton to Oliver Wolcott, 5 June 1798, P 21: 485.

40. Hamilton's first draft of the Farewell Address, P 20: 85; Miller, *FE*, 221; Lycan, *AHAFP*, 292.

41. Lycan, *AHAFP*, 386–87; Hamilton to William Loughton Smith, 10 April 1797, P 21: 36–39; Hamilton to McHenry, April 1797, P 21: 73–74; and Hamilton to Wolcott, 5 June 1798, P 21: 485.

42. See Lycan, *AHAFP*, 357; Elkins and McKitrick, *AF*, 595; McDonald, *AH*, 338, 342; Miller, *FE*, 207; Kohn, *ES*, P 21: 243, 485; Hamilton to William Loughton Smith, 10 April 1797, P 21: 38–41; Hamilton to James McHenry, 27 January–11 February 1798, P 21: 341–45; *The Stand* 3, 7 April 1798, P 21: 403–8; Hamilton to Washington, 2 June 1798, P 21: 479; Rufus King to Hamilton, 21 January 1799, P 22: 425; Hamilton to McHenry, 6 February 1799, P 22: 467; Hamilton to McHenry, 19 January 1800, P 24: 202; and F 16: 101–2; F 26: 169–72; F 28: 179–80.

43. Hamilton to Oliver Wolcott, 5 June 1798, P 21: 485; Hamilton to McHenry, 19 August 1799, P 23: 325–27; Hamilton to Jonathan Dayton, October–November 1799, P 23: 599–604.

44. Hamilton to Rufus King, 2 October 1798, P 22: 192; Hamilton to McHenry, 27 June 1799, P 23: 227; Bassett, *FS*, 242.

45. See Hamilton to McHenry, 17 May 1798, P 21: 345; Pickering to Hamilton, 25 March 1798, P 21: 370–76; Hamilton to McHenry, 17 May 1798, P 21: 462; Hamilton to McHenry, 13 December 1798, P 22: 342–52; Hamilton to McHenry, 27 June 1799, P 23: 227; Hamilton to Washington, 9 September 1799, P 23: 407; Washington to Hamilton, 15 September 1799, P 23: 417–28; James McHenry to Hamilton, 16 October 1799, P 23: 536; Hamilton to James McHenry, 12 October 1799; P 23: 518; Hamilton to James Wilkinson, 31 October 1799, P 23: 592–98; Lycan, *AHAFP*, 330–31, 360–61, 371–78; McDonald, *AH*, 338, 346; Miller, *FE*, 220; and Elkins and McKitrick, *AF*, 616.

46. Hamilton to Washington, 15 June 1799, P 23: 192; General Wilkinson to Hamilton, 6 September 1799, P 23: 383–84; Hamilton to John Adams, 7 September 1799, P 23: 394; McHenry to Hamilton, 16 October 1799, P 23: 536; Lycan, *AHAFP*, 377, 387–88; and Elkins and McKitrick, *AF*, 715.

47. Hamilton to Harrison Gray Otis, 26 January 1799, P 22: 441; Hamilton to McHenry, 27 June 1799, P 23: 227.

48. McDonald, *AH*, 338; Lycan, *AHAFP*, 377, 383; Hamilton to McHenry 27 January–11 February 1798, P 21: 345; Francisco Miranda to Hamilton, 7 February 1798, P 21: 348–50; Miranda to Hamilton, April–June 1798, P 21: 399–402; Hamilton to Wolcott, 5 June 1798, P 21: 485–86; Hamilton to Rufus King, 22 August 1798, P 22: 154–56; Hamilton to McHenry, 27 June 1799, P 23: 227.

49. Hamilton to Pickering, 21 February 1799, P 22: 492–93.

50. *Design for a Seal for the United States,* May 1796, P 20: 208–9.

51. Hamilton to Timothy Pickering, 8 June 1798, P 21: 501; Hamilton to McHenry, 27 June 1799, P 23: 227; Lycan, *AHAFP*, 362.

10. SHIPWRECK

1. Aristotle, *Politics,* 1341bl20–1242bl20.

2. Wood, *Creation,* 113n, 118, 119n, 418; Hamilton, F 9: 50; Madison, F 10: 61–62; Aristotle, *Politics,* 1183al18–1184al50.

3. Aristotle, *Poetics,* in *An Introduction to Aristotle,* ed. Richard McKeon, 2d ed. (Chicago: University of Chicago Press, 1973), 1448–51.

4. For a helpful discussion of this dimension of Shakespeare's trilogy, see Allan Bloom's "The Morality of a Pagan Hero," in *Shakespeare's Politics,* ed. Allan Bloom and Harry V. Jaffa (Chicago: University of Chicago Press, 1963), 75–112.

5. Plutarch, "Life of Coriolanus," in *Lives of the Noble Greeks and Romans,* trans. John Dryden (New York: Modern Library, 1949), 262–89.

6. See Lycan, *AHAFP*, 388; John Adams, Letter 13 in *The Boston Patriot*, 1809, in *The Works of John Adams*, ed. Charles Francis Adams (Boston, 1850–1856); Henry Adams, *The Life of John Adams* (Philadelphia, 1897), 170; Manning Dauer, *The Adams Federalists* (Baltimore: Johns Hopkins University Press, 1953), 47; and Kohn, *ES*, 252, 272–73, 284–86.

7. John Adams, *Reply to the New Jersey Militia*, 31 May 1798, and Hamilton to Oliver Wolcott Jr., 5 June 1798, P 21: 485–88.

8. For the charge that Hamilton supported both the Alien and Sedition Acts, see James Morton Smith, *Freedom's Fetters: The Alien and Sedition Acts and American Civil Liberties* (Ithaca, NY: Cornell University Press, 1956), 153–56 (hereafter *FF*). For dissenting opinions, see Elkins and McKitrick, *AF*, 490; and Miller, *FE*, 229–35.

9. Hamilton to Timothy Pickering, 7 June 1798, P 21: 494–95. For the final versions of these acts, see *Statutes at Large of the United States* (Boston, 1845–1873) 25 June 1798 and 6 July 1798, 1: 570–72, 577–78; and Smith, *FF*, 438–41.

10. *Second Letter from Phocion*, April 1784, P 3: 534; Hamilton to Oliver Wolcott Jr., 29 June 1798, P 21: 522–23; and Article 3, section 3 of the Constitution. See also Machiavelli, *The Prince*, 17: 65–68, 19: 73; Jefferson to Madison, 20 December 1787, in *The Papers of Thomas Jefferson*, ed. Julian P. Boyd (Princeton: Princeton University Press, 1950), 12: 442, and Smith *FF*, 109.

11. See Banning, *JP*, 255–57; Miller, *FE*, 229–36; Elkins and McKitrick, *AF*, 590–91.

12. See Jefferson's *Kentucky Resolutions of 1798* in *The Debates of the Several State Conventions . . . and Other Illustrations of the Constitution*, ed. Jonathan Elliot, 5 vols., 2d ed. (New York: Burt Franklin, 1888), 5: 540–41; and Banning, *JP*, 256.

13. Banning, *JP*, 264; Elkins and McKitrick, *AF*, 723–24; Miller, *FE*, 242; Bassett, *FS*, 265.

14. Hamilton to Rufus King, 5 January 1800, P 24: 168, and Jefferson's *Kentucky Resolutions*, 540–41.

15. Madison's *Report on the Virginia Resolutions*, 7 January 1800, in Rutland et al., *PJM*, 17: 310; Banning, *SF*, 288–89, 390–92; and Bassett, *FS*, 269, 274.

16. Hamilton to Washington, 18 August 1792, P 12: 253.

17. See, for example, Rahe, *RAM*, 3: 146–54, 226, 237.

18. Jefferson Davis, Inaugural Address of the President of the Provisional Government, 18 February 1861, in *The Messages and Addresses of Jefferson Davis and the Confederacy*, 9 vols. (New York: Little, Brown, 1966), 1: 32–33; Miller, *FE*, 239; Banning, *SF*, 393; Bassett, *FS*, 275.

19. See Hamilton to Theodore Sedgwick, 2 February 1799, P 22: 452–53; Miller, *FE*, 240; Elkins and McKitrick, *AF*, 720. See also Madison on foreign influence in F 18: 115–16, and Hamilton's draft of Washington's Farewell Address, 10 August 1796, P 20: 298–301.

20. Hamilton to Theodore Sedgwick, 2 February 1799, P 22: 452–53.

21. See Hamilton to Theodore Sedgwick, 2 February 1799, P 22: 452–53; Kohn, *ES*, 251; Elkins and McKitrick, *AF*, 715–16.

22. See William Heth to Alexander Hamilton, 18 January 1799, P 22: 422–24, and n.6; Hamilton to McHenry, 18 March 1799, P 22: 552; Hamilton to Jonathan Dayton, October–November 1799, P 23: 599–604; McDonald, *AH*, 241; Lycan, *AHAFP*, 389; Miller, *FE*, 241.

23. Hamilton's first draft of Washington's Farewell Address, 10 August 1796, P 20: 275; F 1: 3; speech of 18 June 1787 (Madison's version), P 4: 194; and F 1: 3.

24. Hamilton to McHenry, 29 July 1799, P 23: 293–94.

25. Hamilton to Jonathan Dayton, October–November 1799, P 23: 601–2. See also Machiavelli, *The Prince*, 25: 99–100.

26. Hamilton to Jonathan Dayton, October–November 1799, P 23: 603.

27. See Hamilton to Jonathan Dayton, October–November 1799, P 23: 603–4. See also Madison's speech at the Federal Convention, 28 June 1787, in *Notes of Debates of the Federal Convention of 1787*, 208; and Jefferson to John Adams, 28 October 1813, in Ford, ed., *WTJ*, 6: 226.

28. Hamilton to Jonathan Dayton, 31 October 1799, P 23: 604; Banning, *JP*, 208–46. For Jefferson's claim that Hamilton headed the conspiracy, see Jefferson to Washington, 9 September 1792, in Boyd, ed., *Papers*, 24: 351–60. For Hamilton's defense against this charge, see Hamilton to Edward Carrington, 26 May 1792, P 11: 443.

29. Smith, *FF*, 154–55.

30. *Address to the Electors of the State of New York*, 21 March 1801, P 25: 364.

31. Hamilton to William Hamilton, 2 May 1797, P 21: 77–78; Hamilton to Washington, 5 November 1795, P 19: 395–97; Thucydides, *Peloponnesian War*, 3.42–43. 80–81; Machiavelli, *Discourses*, 1, 8: 214–17; McDonald, *AH*, 319.

32. Miller, *FE*, 233–34, 264–66.

33. To trace Hamilton's protests against these sorts of slanders, see (as the tip of a huge iceberg of resentment) his Speech of 18 June 1787 (Madison's version), P 4: 193, *The Vindication* 1, May–August 1792, P 11: 463–64; Hamilton to Edward Carrington, 26 May 1792, P 11: 443–44; Hamilton to Washington, 18 August 1792, P 12: 228–37; Hamilton to Washington, 18 August 1792, P 12: 248–52; *Amicus*, 11 September 1792, P 12: 354–56; *Catullus* 3, 29 September 1792, P 12: 498–505; *Catullus* 6, 22 December 1792, P 13: 355; Hamilton to Timothy Pickering, 16 September 1803, P 26: 147–49; and McDonald, *AH*, 25, 291–92, 336.

34. John C. Miller, *Crisis in Freedom: The Alien and Sedition Acts* (Boston: Little, Brown, 1951), 58. For the original, see also Hamilton's *Reynolds Pamphlet*, 1797, P 21: 242–43.

35. Hamilton's *Time Piece*, 22 May 1798, P 21: 468.

36. For the first view, see, for example, Kohn, *ES*, 272; for the latter, see Theodore Sedgwick to Hamilton, P 22: 471; McDonald, *AH*, 331. Elkins and McKitrick try to weigh these views in *AF*, 612, 716–17.

37. Hamilton's pay book, 1777, P 1: 390. For highly similar praise of the initiative, see Machiavelli's *Art of War*, 7: 202–4, and Clausewitz, *On War*, 6: 259.

38. See Sedgwick to Hamilton, 22 February 1799, P 22: 495; Hamilton to Washington, 21 October 1799, P 23: 545–56; Washington to Hamilton, 27 October 1799, P 23: 574; Hamilton to King, 5 January 1800, P 24: 168; McHenry to Hamilton, 20 May 1800, P 24: 508; Elkins and McKitrick, *AF*, 555, 606–36; Lycan, *AHAFP*, 367, 390, 396; McDonald, *AH*, 343–47; Banning, *JP*, 267; Bassett, *FS*, 247, 283; and Miller, *FE*, 243.

39. Hamilton to John Marshall, 2 October 1800, P 25: 133–39; McDonald, *AH*, 346–47; Lycan, *AHAFP*, 391, 401; Miller, *FE*, 243; Kohn *ES*, 262–63.

40. Miller, *FE*, 261; McDonald, *AH*, 343–44, 349; Bassett, *FS*, 205.

41. McHenry to Hamilton, 31 May 1800, P 24: 555–62; Sedgwick to Hamilton, 13 May 1800, P 24: 482.

42. See Joanne B. Freeman, "Dueling as Politics: Reinterpreting the Burr-Hamilton Duel," *WMQ* 3d ser. (1996): 289–318.

43. McDonald, *AH*, 249.

44. Ibid., 350; Miller, *FE*, 262; Hamilton to John Adams, 1 August 1800, P 25: 51; Hamilton to Oliver Wolcott Jr., 3 August 1800, P 25: 54–55; George Cabot to Alexander Hamilton, 10 August 1800, P 25: 62–64; Hamilton to James McHenry, 27 August 1800, P 25: 97; Edward Carrington to Alexander Hamilton, 30 August 1800, P 25: 98–101; Oliver Wolcott Jr. to Alexander Hamilton, 3 September 1800, P 25: 104–10; Hamilton to Wolcott, 26 September 1800, P 25: 122; Hamilton to Adams, 10 October 1800, P 25: 126; Letter from Alexander Hamilton, Concerning the Public Conduct and Character of John Adams, 24 October 1800, P 25: 169–234.

45. Hamilton to Theodore Sedgwick, 10 May 1800, P 25: 475.

46. Hamilton to John Jay, 7 May 1800, P 24: 464–65.

47. Hamilton's conversation with Arthur Fenner, 25–26 June 1800, P 24: 595–96; McDonald, *AH*, 351–52.

48. Hamilton to James A. Bayard, 16 January 1801, P 25: 319–27; Syrett's notes, P 25: 178–85.

49. Fisher Ames to Alexander Hamilton, December 1800, P 25: 284. See also Alexander Pope, *An Essay on Man, Epistles to a Friend,* 3 vols. (London: Printed for J. Wilford, 1733–1734), 1: 123–29.

50. George Cabot to Alexander Hamilton, 29 November 1800, P 25: 247–50; Pope's *Essay on Man,* 4: 265–66. The quotation actually reads "All fear, none aid you, and few understand."

51. McDonald, *AH*, 348.

52. F 27: 489; Hamilton's General Orders, 18 May 1800, P 24: 500; Hamilton to Wilkinson, 20 May 1800; P 24: 514; Hamilton to McHenry, 31 May 1800, P 24: 544; Kohn, *ES*, 253, 263, 267.

53. Syrett's notes, P 25: 435–36; Rahe, *RAM*, 3: 111–12. Alexander Hamilton to James A. Hamilton, June 1804, P 26: 281.

54. Hamilton's letter to ——, 26 September 1792, P 12: 480; Hamilton to Jay, 18 December 1792, P 13: 338; Hamilton to James Bayard, P 25: 56–58; Hamilton to

Wolcott, 6 August 1800, P 25: 287; Hamilton to Bayard, 16 January 1801, P 25: 319–25; Lycan, *AHAFP*, 411, 419.

55. McDonald, *AH*, 360–61; Hamilton to ——, 21 September 1792, P 12: 408; Hamilton to Oliver Wolcott Jr., 16 December 1800, P 25: 257–58; Hamilton to John Rutledge Jr., 4 January 1801, P 25: 293–98; Speech at a Meeting of Federalists in Albany, 10 February 1804, P 26: 187–90; Aaron Burr to Alexander Hamilton, 18 June 1804, P 26: 242–46; Hamilton to Aaron Burr, 20 June 1804, P 26: 247–49; disclaimer of Alexander Hamilton, 25 June 1804, P 26: 265–66; William P. Van Ness to Nathaniel Pendleton, 27 June 1804, P 26: 272–73; Hamilton's statement on impending duel with Aaron Burr, 28 June–10 July 1804, P 26: 278–80; Alexander Hamilton to Elizabeth Hamilton, 10 July 1804, P 26: 307–8; and joint statement by William P. Van Ness and Nathaniel Pendleton on the duel between Alexander Hamilton and Aaron Burr, 17 July 1804, P 26: 334.

56. Hamilton to James A. Hamilton, June 1804, P 26: 281.

EPILOGUE: VIGILANCE AND RESPONSIBILITY RECONSIDERED

1. Thucydides, *Peloponnesian War*, 1.22.14; 6.33–41.396–402; 8.53.533; 8.90. 555–56.

2. Bassett, *FS*, 204–5, 251; Elkins and McKitrick, *AF*, 529–33, 603; Miller, *FE*, 246, 267; Kohn, *ES*, 273.

3. See McDonald, *AH*, 347–48, 357; Forrest McDonald, *The Presidency of Thomas Jefferson* (Lawrence: University Press of Kansas, 1976), 60–68 (hereafter *PTJ*); Elkins and McKitrick, *AF*, 663–65; Lycan, *AHAFP*, 412, 418; Kohn, *ES*, 263, Henry Adams, *History of the United States of America During the Administrations of Jefferson and Madison*, 2 vols. (New York: Modern Library, 1986), 1: 238–54; Jacob E. Cooke, "Country Above Party: John Adams and the 1799 Mission to France," in *Fame and the Founding Fathers*, ed. Edmund Willis (Bethlehem, PA: Moravian College, 1967), 72ff.; Hamilton, *An Address to the Electors of the State of New York*, 21 March 1801, P 25: 353; Hamilton to Charles Cotesworth Pinckney, 29 December 1802, P 26: 71–72; and Hamilton's Purchase of Louisiana, 5 July 1803, P 26: 129–30.

4. McDonald, *AH*, 318–19.

5. Banning, *JP*, 273–74.

6. F 6: 32.

7. Rahe, *RAM*, 2: 51–60, 67, 97–98, 137–38, 144, 153–54. See also Immanuel Kant, "An Answer to the Question: What Is Enlightenment?" in *Perpetual Peace and Other Essays*, 33.

8. McDonald, *PTJ*, 62, 64, 110, and *AH*, 358–61; Banning, *JP*, 275, 280, 299; Lycan, *AHAFP*, 415; Kohn, *ES*, 303; Thomas A. Bailey, *A Diplomatic History of the American People* (New York: Prentice Hall, 1980), 164; Madison's Seventh Annual Message to Congress, 5 December 1815, in Meyers, ed., *MF*, 297–306; and Jefferson to Benjamin Austin, 9 January 1816, in Ford, ed., *WTJ*, 387–93.

9. See *An Address to the Electors of the State of New York,* 21 March 1801, P 25: 349–71; Hamilton to Gouverneur Morris, 29 February 1802, P 25: 544–55; Hamilton to Richard Peters, 29 December 1802, P 26: 69–70; Hamilton to James A. Bayard, 16–21 April 1802, P 25: 605–6; Hamilton to Charles Cotesworth Pinckney, 29 December 1802, P 26: 71; and Lycan, *AHAFP,* 413.

10. Speech in the Case of Harry Croswell (Waite's version), in Goebel, *LPAH,* 1: 809, 813, 820, 831. For the impact of the Croswell case on free speech in America, see Goebel's remarks, ibid., 1: 796, 844–48.

Index